Decision Support Systems in Urban Planning

Decision Support Systems in Urban Planning

Edited by

Harry Timmermans

Department of Architecture,
University of Eindhoven, The Netherlands

Spon Press
Taylor & Francis Group

LONDON AND NEW YORK

First published in 1997 by
Spon Press,
2 Park Square, Milton Park, Abingdon, Oxon OX14 4RN

Simultaneously published in the USA and Canada by
Spon Press,
711 Third Avenue, New York, NY 10017

Spon Press is an imprint of the Taylor & Francis Group, an informa business

First issued in paperback 2011

Typeset in 10/12pt Palatino by Saxon Graphics Ltd, Derby

A catalogue record for this book is available from the British Library

ISBN 13: 978-0-419-21050-4 (hbk)
ISBN 13: 978-0-415-51441-5 (pbk)

Contents

Contributors

Yoshitsugu Aoki
Department of Architecture
Faculty of Engineering
Tokyo Institute of
Technology
Tokyo 152
Japan

Theo Arentze
Department of Architecture and
Urban Planning
Eindhoven University of
Technology
PO Box 513
5600 MB Eindhoven
The Netherlands

Bola Ayeni
Department of Geography
University of Ibadan
Ibadan
Nigeria

Aloys Borgers
Faculty of Architecture and Urban
Planning
Eindhoven University of
Technology
PO Box 513
Eindhoven
The Netherlands

Elise Bright
School of Urban and Public
Affairs

University of Texas at Arlington
Box 19588
Arlington TX 76019
USA

Noel Campbell
University of Greenwich
Geography Division
Humanities School
Woolwich
London SE18 6PF
UK

Nor Azina Dahlan
Department of Urban and
Regional Planning
Universiti Teknologi Malaysia
Skudai, 80990
Johor Bahru
Malaysia

Guy Engelen
Research Institute of Knowledge
Systems b.v.
PO Box 463
6200 AL Maastricht
The Netherlands

Josep Maria Fargas
Dtec Consulting S.L.
08037 Barcelona
Spain

Thomas Gordon
GMD FIT
Artificial Intelligence Research
Division
German National Research Centre
for Information Technology
D-53754 Sankt Augustin
Germany

Paul Hendriks
Katholieke Universiteit Nijmegen
Faculteit der
Beleidswetenschappen
PO Box 9108
6500 HK Nijmegen
The Netherlands

Ashraf Ismail
18 Arundel Court
18/19 South Parade
Southsea PO5 2JE
UK

Foziah Johar
Department of Urban and
Regional Planning
Universiti Teknologi Malaysia
Skudai, 80990
Johor Bahru
Malaysia

Nikos Karacapilidis
GMD FIT
Artificial Intelligence Research
Division
German National Research Centre
for Information Technology
D-53754 Sankt Augustin
Germany

Romulo Krafta
Department of Urbanism
Faculty of Architecture
Federal University of Rio Grande
do Sul

Av. Oswaldo Aranha
Porto Alegre
RS 90050
Brazil

Kevin McCartney
School of Architecture
University of Portsmouth
Portsmouth PO1 2DY
UK

Naoto Muraoka
Department of Architecture
Faculty of Engineering
Tokyo Institute of Technology
Tokyo 152
Japan

Thomas O'Reilly
University of Greenwich
School of Land and Construction
Management
Oakfield Lane
Dartford
Kent DA1 2SZ
UK

Robert Peckham
Joint Research Centre
Institute for Systems
Engineering and Informatics
I-21020 Ispra (VA)
Italy

Wolf Reuter
Department of Architecture and
Cityplanning
University of Stuttgart
Keplerstraße II
70174 Stuttgart
Germany

Jos Smeets
Faculty of Architecture and Urban
Planning
Eindhoven University of
Technology
PO Box 513
5600 MB Eindhoven
The Netherlands

Joan Antoni Solans
Town Planning Department of
Catalonia, Spain

Jan Teklenburg
Faculty of Architecture and Urban
Planning
Eindhoven University of
Technology
PO Box 513
5600 MB Eindhoven
The Netherlands

Harry Timmermans
Faculty of Architecture and Urban
Planning
Eindhoven University of
Technology
PO Box 513
5600 MB Eindhoven
The Netherlands

Inge Uljee
Research Institute for Knowledge
Systems b.v.
PO Box 463
6200 AL Maastricht
The Netherlands

Peter van der Waerden
Faculty of Architecture and Urban
Planning
Eindhoven University of
Technology
PO Box 513
5600 MB Eindhoven
The Netherlands

Hans Voss
GMD FIT
Artificial Intelligence Research
Division
German National Research Centre
for Information Technology
D-53754 Sankt Augustin
Germany

Dirk Vriens
Katholieke Universiteit Nijmegen
Faculteit der
Beleidswetenschappen
PO Box 9108
6500 HK Nijmegen
The Netherlands

Roger White
Department of Geography
Memorial University of
Newfoundland
St John's
Newfoundland
Canada

Frank Witlox
Department of Economic and
Social Sciences
University of Antwerp
Rodestraat 14, R 204
B-2000 Antwerp
Belgium

Ray Wyatt
Department of Geography and
Environmental Studies
University of Melbourne
Parkville 3052
Australia

Ahris Yaakup
Department of Urban and
Regional Planning
Universiti Teknologi Malaysia
Skudai, 80990
Johor Bahru
Malaysia

Andreas Zauke
GMD FIT
Artificial Intelligence Research
Division
German National Research Centre
for Information Technology
D-53754 Sankt Augustin
Germany

Introduction

Geographical information systems (GIS) have been introduced in urban planning with high expectations. It was felt that these systems would improve the quality of the planning process, as these systems would allow the use of advanced analysis and modelling tools. The current state of the art certainly indicates that geographical information systems are increasingly used in both the public and private sectors. There is some doubt, however, that they are used to their full potential. The systems seem to be used primarily for data storage and graphic output, and there does not seem that much beyond mapping.

There may be different reasons for this situation. The field is in need of better models and tools of analysis. Commercial systems do not incorporate available modelling tools, and hence these are difficult to use unless users have access to additional software that allows them to use these tools, although even in that case the integration of the modules with geographical information systems into a full decision support system (DSS) is still problematic. It has also been argued that current systems do not truly support the users' needs or support only part of a plan development process. Finally, the inherent relevance of many of the existing tools might be limited. To improve the situation, active research along each of these lines can be identified.

The current volume includes part of this research. It consists of edited chapters that were originally presented as papers at Design and Decision Support Systems Conferences, organized by the Urban Planning Group of the Eindhoven University of Technology. Ongoing research can be divided into theoretical research that discusses the nature and role of decision support systems in decision-making processes, development work that tries to improve or build new models and tools of analysis, and applications. The chapters included in this volume are organized along the same lines: theoretical papers, papers on developments in tools, and applications of geographical information and decision support systems in urban planning. Of course, some chapters cover two or more of these aspects.

Part One on theory contains six chapters with different perspectives on the role and future directions of decision support systems in urban planning. *Ayeni* argues that planning methodology over the years has shifted from situations whereby planners think, plan and design for the people to one whereby both people and planners have become important components of the planning process. Consequently, the important urban planning methodology of the last two decades that utilized mathematical models in the planning process is fast becoming obsolete. He continues to argue that model-building should move to the creation of decision support systems for the planning process through the development of expert system shells that interface existing planning models with the knowledge content of planning and planners. The expert system shells as the set of decision rules for determining how existing supply-and-demand relationships are applied for modelling, for instance, land use and transportation would be responsible for guiding the development of appropriate geographical information systems, supporting land use and other models in a coordinated manner, for communicating with these other systems components and for guiding interactions between them and the user. Furthermore, decision support systems should be designed to bring the whole of the knowledge base to bear on a problem through a flexible and adaptive solution system that makes explicit use of both the analysts' models and the decision-makers' expert knowledge. It is argued that this understanding leads to the development of three crucial issues for the design of decision support systems in urban and regional planning; namely the development of user-friendly integrated urban land use–transportation models, the development of expert geographical information systems and the development of expert system shells for many of the routine tasks with which planners deal.

In their chapter, *Vriens and Hendriks* take this argument one step further by considering the nature of the implied decision-making process. They argue that research into decision-making seems to suffer from two related weaknesses. The first is lack of attention for the dynamic nature of the decision process and environment. Research attempts to encompass dynamic features are sparse. The second weakness is the allegation that decision alternatives can be discerned on an *a priori* basis, thus facilitating the use of a choice rule to pick the 'optimal' or 'satisficing' alternative (this is the basic assumption of the prevailing rationalistic approach of decision modelling). However, the assumption of an *a priori* conception of alternatives is not realistic, since it ignores the fact that the exploration and elaboration of alternatives forms an integral part of the decision process. Although several attempts have been made to overcome these problems, a coherent theory seems to be lacking. They, therefore, explore the possibilities of systems theory as an offset for new decision modelling. A system (in the cybernetic sense) is, roughly speaking, a collection of elements related in such a manner that emergent properties (i.e. properties that consist at the level of the whole, not at the level of its parts) come about. There are many different approaches to systems theory and not all of these are equally useful for decision research. Systems that have 'adaptive' properties are worthwhile because they may encompass dynamic features. Furthermore, the use of adaptive, dynamic systems leads to a solution for the problem of the 'disembodied' conception and choice of alternatives, since the choice options automatically follow from the defined system and may change because of its dynamic nature. The important question is how a system can be defined in order to capture the dynamic nature of decision-making. The authors argue that dynamics can be captured by defining them 'functionally', i.e. in terms of the goals that enter the decision process.

Reuter also argues that, in all stages of the design and planning process, alternatives or alternative ways of action are generated. Hence, the process is dynamic: participants communicate about questions of feasibility, advantages and disadvantages of particular alternatives, expected consequences, and other possibilities. They exchange positions and arguments, upon which finally they base their weighting of aspects and their personal judgement. He then argues that this process of argumentation and evaluation can be formalized and supported by formal methods. It should be realized, however, that decisions about alternatives by different people are not only based on explicit argumentation and/or formal evaluation procedures, but also on the use of power. Reuter distinguishes different means of power and several decision-making procedures which control the misuse of power are discussed.

These three chapters thus differ in terms of the importance that can be attached to decision support systems. Positions in the field differ from important technical contributions to an embedding of decision support systems in a more general theory of decision-making. *Campbell and O'Reilly's* chapter represents an attempt to locate GIS, as a particular example of a decision support system, in the context of the built-environment professions, rather than in the context of computer science, recognizing the integrated but limiting approach of viewing GIS from a strictly computer/spatial science perspective. The chapter reviews the conflicts and tensions appearing in the GIS debate, seeing them as reflecting the differences between the perceptions and interests of software developers and those of the professions. The 'spatial science versus professional tool' dilemma is therefore critically assessed. Science is identified as the dominant paradigm within which GIS development has taken place. This encompasses the emphasis on GIS as spatial science; the interest in particular forms of spatial analysis; and a narrow approach to the idea of information. They argue that the interests and activities of the professions cannot be encompassed within the pre-existing science paradigm. Their chapter identifies the interest the professions have had in broad geographical issues, as distinct from narrow spatial issues. It recognizes the different conventions and procedures used in recording and using geographical information, not all of them objective or scientific. It views the computer, not as a 'scientific engine', but as a modern medium for representing and analysing information. This approach suggests a framework for research of a nature more sympathetic to the needs of the built-environment professions in particular.

The feeling that decision support systems have to be developed to reflect the needs of their user is also key in *Peckham*'s contribution. He first argues that there is a clear need for advanced spatial decision support systems due to the increasing complexity of modern human activities, the increase in awareness of the negative consequences of mankind's technological development on the environment, and the need to respect new regulations and legislation regarding environmental impacts. Such spatial decision support systems need to manipulate and analyse a wide variety of spatially referenced information, frequently in large quantities. He argues that geographical information systems are now the chosen means for storing such information, but that further work is required to develop and link analysis modules and decision aids and make the system more useful for their users. Examples of applications of these ideas to real management problems, including waste management, river management and site management, are given to show how spatial information can now be manipulated to aid decisions, and to arrive at some of the design requirements for more flexible and applicable decision support systems. The merits and disadvantages of several different approaches to design and implementation of decision support systems, especially from the users' point of view, are discussed.

Analysis, however, is only one aspect of the planning process. The development of a strategic plan is another critical aspect. The chapter written by *Wyatt* focuses on a mechanism by which planners and designers are thought to reduce complexity. The mechanism involves choosing a potentially profitable direction of search, or choosing a potentially profitable set of aims to pursue, within which a detailed solution might be found, while rejecting all potentially unprofitable directions of search. Wyatt argues that designers base such initial choice of direction on the relative scores of their candidate aims for eight key parameters: probability, returns for effort, delay, robustness, difficulty, effectiveness, present satisfaction and dependence. He then describes a piece of decision support software which, by eliciting any user's scores for their candidate aims on the eight key parameters, is able to order such aims into a strategic plan. Such software also incorporates a simulated neural network which attempts to 'learn', from users' recorded responses to the software-suggested strategies, how users actually weight the relative importances of the eight key parameters. The neural network is hoped to discover some prototypical pattern(s) of weightings.

Part Two on methodology consists of four chapters. *Krafta* suggests a new model that combines the best of spatial interaction modelling and space syntax. Spatial interaction models conceptualize flows in cities in terms of a concentration of activities and distance between them. Spatial interaction models have been criticized for their poor theoretical under-pinnings and lack of concern for specific spatial situations. In general, planners and large-scale urban scientists have been more comfortable with them than designers and urban morphologists, whose questions about space configuration are dealt with awkwardly in such a frame-work. Recently, space syntax has been suggested as an alternative to describe possible roles of space in the urban system. Its theory looks very complex – a deep cultural, anthropological connection between man and space, an atavistic impulse driving the shaping of space – but in fact it is very simple and not far from the rude assumptions of spatial interaction models: a matter of distance and orientation. Axial lines are used to describe connectivity; they describe space more efficiently than the tradi-tional zones or links used in spatial interaction models. Spatial interaction says little about configuration, space syntax says little about interaction between spaces and activities, and both say nothing about morphology, or the configurational development of urban systems. Krafta therefore suggests an alternative approach. Grid axiality is taken as a measure of connectivity and orientation, as in space syntax, while the built form is taken as a measure of attraction, as in spatial interaction modelling. Furthermore, it is assumed that the locations of activities and flows strongly condition change of the urban spatial configuration in the long run. Location and flow patterns create an increasing conflict between ris-ing land values and declining building values. As a result, configuration is taken as a particular state of a morphology whose transformation rules are an economic expression of spatiality. Flows are cause and effect in the lagged process of mutual transformation which shapes the urban space.

The dynamic relationship between land use and interaction is also the core of the contribution by *Engelen, White and Uljee*. They present a deci-sion support system developed to assist urban designers, planners and policy-makers to explore and evaluate possible urban layouts and their growth patterns. The core of the system consists of a modelling shell allowing the user to specify cellular automata-based models of urban and regional systems. These models capture the effect of local spatial processes in which the use, or desired use, of each parcel or cell of land is determined partly by institutional and environmental factors, and partly by the activities present in its neighbourhood. Since each cell affects every other cell within its neighbourhood, a complex dynamic emerges. Unlike conventional cellular automata, the models are defined with a large neighbourhood – over a hundred cells – and a relatively large number of states – more than a dozen in some applications – representing socioeconomic and natural land uses. The approach permits the straightforward integration of detailed physical, environmental and institutional constraints, as well as including the effects of the transportation and communication infrastructure. These models thus permit a very detailed representation of evolving spatial systems. Consequently, they are well suited to form the core of a DSS, which provides the user with a number of tools for exploration, analysis and evaluation of alternative futures of the system as they result from policy interventions that are imposed by means of 'What-if?' experiments and scenario analysis. For example, the DSS is able to identify areas in which pressure for change in land use restrictions may become critical under particular development strategies.

The previous two chapters are concerned with analysis or forecasting tools. Another methodologically relevant line of research is concerned with incorporating expert knowledge in decision support systems. *Witlox, Arentze and Timmermans* investigate a methodological issue associated with the use of decision tables. In particular, a predominant problem in this field concerns the categorization of the condition and action states in a decision table. This categorization is assumed to exhibit a discrete (or crisp) character. Although sharply defined discrete categorizations imply an accurate and precise decision-making process, in many real-world problems it proves to be a too stringent and severe assumption to impose on the decision-maker. In order to solve this problem, they enhance the decision table formalism to incorporate elements from the theory of fuzzy sets. The construction of a fuzzy decision table is explained in a step-by-step manner and illustrated by means of a brief example in the field of location theory.

Aoki and Muraoka's chapter is also concerned with location theory. They propose an optimization method using a genetic algorithm to find optimal location patterns. Potential locations are expressed by a chromosome. Each chromosome consists of genes, and each gene expresses a located facility. Alternative location patterns are generated by using genetic procedures; crossing-over, mutation and selection. For each alternative, the behaviours of users is estimated by a spatial interaction model. The effectiveness of the location pattern is measured by a total sum of distances between the facility and the user. The chapter considers both a hypothetical example and a successful application to an actual problem in a Japanese town.

Part Three consists of eight applications of decision support systems in urban planning. First, *Solans and Fargas* construct a theory of decision support system design, based on the three independent concepts of reliability, power and speed borrowed from epistemology. They argue that a system is reliable if a large part of its performance is useful or correct, that it is powerful if it performs in a useful way in a variety of situations of interest, and that it is fast if its behaviour is consistently dynamic. They then use this framework to argue that a successful deployment of decision support technology must take into account the balance between reliability, power and speed. This approach is illustrated with the case of a hybrid system for studying urban transportation issues in the Greater Barcelona Region, contrasting it with more conventional tools such as traditional geographic information systems or traffic analysis software. The hybrid system is shown to sacrifice the reliability and speed characteristic of commercially available software for a powerful set of computational tools developed specifically for the problem at hand. This trade-off process is formalized using an analysis based on second-order reliability, power and speed concepts. They show that micro-level sacrifices of one of these properties are often inversely correlated with the same characteristics at the macro-level. Finally, they extend their design theory to a methodology for characterizing decision support systems in general, and argue that the hybrid technologies approach is more likely to result in systems reflecting the user's domain knowledge and skills.

The second application concerns the use of a geographical information system for local government. *Yaakup, Johar and Dahlan* discuss a system which is under development to monitor the surveillance of compliance with planning regulations and serves as an early-warning system with regard to sources of shortfalls in the process of urban planning. To optimize the use of the system, they first examine the functions of a local authority particularly in the context of planning and urban management. This analysis and the types of data that are available to support their planning decisions provide the fundamental framework upon which a model of geographic data and their relationships is developed. Further, a customized menu-driven user interface is developed to allow planners and decision-makers to view and analyse the planning scenarios interactively before deciding on the final plan. Ultimately, the system should provide a complete local authority coverage of up-to-date and accurate information at the parcel base. It can then assist planning decisions, taking into account, among other things, the current scenario of the proposed development, physical constraints and future impacts.

Bright reports on the development and application of ALLOT, a user-friendly, flexible computer model which has been designed to help governmental jurisdictions and private landowners to achieve more economically efficient and environmentally sound land use and development patterns in a short period of time. ALLOT has the capability to allow the incorporation of a wide variety of previously ignored environmental characteristics and up-to-date land use patterns. The system contains two major parts. The first part employs a GIS database to conduct land suitability analyses for the area. It then produces maps showing the most suitable areas for various land use types. The second part, which is different from most other computerized land use planning models, combines the results of the suitability analysis with forecast demand for various land use types to produce 'optimum' future land use patterns. The model is capable of quickly analyzing a wide variety of forecasts, allowing easy comparison of different growth scenarios; and it can also be modified to reflect community goals and objectives, such as protection of wildlife habitat or attraction of industry. Two applications are described. First, three alternative future land use patterns were developed for a rural lakeside area. The area had rural characteristics and was lacking infrastructure, but a large influx of people was expected as the lake was filled. The success of this effort led to the decision to test its use as a method for facility siting (using landfill siting as an example). The siting was also done without sacrificing optimum utilization of the land. This was achieved by involving future demand for all land use types in the calculations.

Another application is described by *Smeets*. In particular, he describes a system that is meant to support performance evaluation in housing management, using two housing corporations in the Netherlands as an example. The performance measurement is an element of a broader methodology of intervention planning and market positioning of housing estates. The system requires information about market characteristics and price, in addition to technical and functional performances and consumer evaluation. The system/methodology provides insights into the market position of the estate, the performances of the dwelling and residential environment, and the relative position of the estates. Various aspects of performance and performance levels are distinguished. Performance is measured from the perspective of the dwelling and residential environment, and from the perspective of the target group. These measurements are the basis of various management decisions, such as quality policy, rent policy, target groups policy and policies concerning neighbourhood management.

As we have indicated earlier, spatial interaction models and space syntax methods have received a different acceptance between urban planners and urban designers. *Teklenburg, Timmermans and Borgers* argue that at the intra-urban scale level the cooperation between urban designers and urban planners can be facilitated by shared planning and design tools in an integrated task environment. They therefore first propose extended space syntax models as such a common tool. The goal of these space syntax models is to relate the description of urban morphology to actual behaviour. The chapter describes the principles of standard, morphological space syntax models, and explains why there is a need to include the distribution of functions across an area in order to improve their predictive quality. The combination of morphological and extended models (including functions) increases the applicability of space syntax in the urban planning/design process: morphological models may be used in the first, global phases, while the extended models are suited to prune location decisions in more final, detailed phases. Morphological models are of primary use to designers, but are of interest to planners because of the possibility to extend them with aspects of the functional layout. In this way space syntax models can become a communication tool between the parties involved in the urban planning process. Next, they describe the integration of CAD and GIS environments. In particular, they suggest the implementation of planning and design tools in dedicated geographical information systems, called engines, that are dynamic and at the same time make use of and update databases of traditional geographical information systems. A particular implementation of extended space syntax models in a CAD environment is discussed.

Ismail and McCartney present another such application, but this time at the edge of architectural design and urban planning. In particular, they developed a computer-based decision support tool to use during the conceptual stages of architectural design. Its main functions are being designed in order to check design compliance with the requirements of local planning authorities, with regards to building size, height, plot ratios, circulation and accessibility, and the preservation of natural features on site. The measures to determine proper evaluation are based upon site development briefs, and design guides produced by the local planning authorities. This tool is being developed to operate under the AutoCAD environment, the construction industry standard computer-aided design software, following standard layering convention, integrated command lines and pull-down menus. It also provides many functions for editing two- and three-dimensional drawings specifically for the environmental analysis tasks. In addition to the common graphical output of AutoCAD, i.e. plans, elevations and three-dimensional models, the tool will generate textual analysis of the design in report format to use as part of the environmental impact statement of proposed development.

The notion of integration is also central to the chapter written by *Gordon, Karacapilidis, Voss and Zauke*. In particular, they address the problem of the integration of recent advancements on geographical information systems with a framework that supports fair, rational and efficient decision-making procedures to assist government and businesses with the retrieval, use and re-use of information in cooperative, distributed planning procedures requiring access to spatial data. They provide an overview of a computer-mediated group decision support system for the World-Wide Web, namely ZENO. The target is to provide intelligent assistance to human mediators and other kinds of 'trusted third parties' during the above procedures. The role of the system is to remain neutral and help assure that the interests and goals of all members of a group, regardless of their status, are respected and appreciated. In this chapter, the system's features are illustrated with a retrospective model of a real urban planning example, concerning the allocation of a new technology park in the area of the city of Bonn, where more than 80 communities, local and federal authorities, and other organizations have been requested to submit their suggestions, objections and comments on a spatial planning problem.

Another example of integrating a geographical information system with a model is described in the final chapter of this volume. *Van der Waerden and Timmermans* use a geographical information system to manipulate, analyse and present data of various databases, and link these databases to a simulation model of parking behaviour. A hypothetical case is presented to show how a parking simulation modelling approach can be integrated with GIS technology.

Harry J.P. Timmermans

Urban Planning Group
Eindhoven University of Technology

PART ONE

Theory

The design of spatial decision support systems in urban and regional planning

1

Bola Ayeni

INTRODUCTION

Planning methodology has changed over the years as emphasis has shifted from situations in which planners think, plan and design for the people, to one in which both people and planners have become important actors in the planning process. The arguments have been that planners do not necessarily have all the knowledge and the ability to perform planning tasks alone, and consequently should interact more with the people for whom the plan is being made. Indeed, the people consist of two groups: the decision-makers who eventually consider and approve plans, and the common people for whom the plans are being made. It is probably true to say that, for a long time, both groups of people have looked upon the planner as a technocrat whose main interest lies in imposing rules, laws and regulations without much consideration for the views of the people. The need to involve not only planners but also policy-makers in the planning process calls for the introduction of new planning approaches that integrate these three groups of people.

One way to integrate the actors in the planning process is through the use of spatial decision support systems, which in turn depends to a considerable extent on the development of user-friendly mathematical models through the use of expert systems. A major aim of this chapter is to outline the need for, and the incorporation and institutionalization of, decision support systems into an integrated spatial planning framework.

Decision Support Systems in Urban Planning. Edited by Harry Timmermans. Published in 1997 by E & F N Spon. ISBN 0 419 21050 4

Consequently, we shall discuss the roles of geographical information systems (GIS) and the use of expert systems in facilitating these processes in urban and regional planning. In particular, we shall emphasize the fact that GIS needs many more improvements and innovations to be really useful to solve the sort of problems that planning urban development poses. We shall also show that the capability of GIS to communicate graphically and by visualization is not only an asset but could constitute the basis for the development of decision support systems. We shall also describe a prototype decision support system within the framework of mathematical modelling and spatial analysis.

SPATIAL DECISION SUPPORT SYSTEMS

Spatial decision support systems (SDSS) are off-shoots of decision support systems whose origins may be traced to the frustration with the use of management information systems in the cognate discipline of management science. However, decision support systems (DSS) are decision aids and occur in all areas of scientific analysis and investigation. As computer-based systems, decision support systems assist decision-makers in semi-structured tasks, support rather than replace judgement, and improve the effectiveness of decision-makers rather than its efficiency. A DSS assumes that there is no single solution or answer to a problem, but allows users to bring their expertise to the solution of the problem. In this way users are able to use intuition and expert judgement about 'unmodellable' aspects of the problem. Furthermore, since only one formulation of the problem is evaluated at any stage, the process allows groups to evaluate solutions and revise specifications of the problem. Decision support systems are designed to solve ill- or semi-structured problems, i.e. where objectives cannot be fully or precisely defined. They must have an interface that is both easy and powerful to use; enable the user to combine models and data in a flexible manner; and make full use of all the data and models that are available. Furthermore, they must help the user to explore the solution space (the options available to them) by using the models in the system to generate a series of feasible alternatives. Decision support systems support a variety of decision-making styles, and are easily adapted to provide new capabilities as the needs of the user evolve (Geoffrion, 1983).

Spatial decision support systems are decision support systems developed for use with a domain database that has a spatial dimension, or for situations where the solution space of a problem has a spatial dimension (Wright and Buehler, 1993, p. 123). Spatial decision support systems integrate a geographical information system with a computer-based spatial analysis module and map analysis and display modules. Such systems typically employ a personal computer in such a way that planning scenarios can be determined, analysed and adopted according to the planning standards that are being set up by planners and decision-makers. The use of these support systems is highly desirable when professional planners, politicians and decision-makers must act jointly to effect certain decisions.

Spatial decision support systems are computer programs designed to bring the whole of the knowledge base to bear on a problem through a flexible and adaptive solution system that makes explicit use of both the analysts' models and the expert knowledge of decision-makers. Definitions of spatial decision support systems (SDSS) often focus on their characteristics. Thus, an SDSS will provide database management, model base management, and graphical and tabular reporting capabilities under a unified and possibly intelligent user interface. Densham (1994) posits that, in general, a spatial decision support system will possess all of the following attributes:

1. Support for the capture of spatial and non-spatial data
2. Ability to represent complex spatial relations among spatial data that are needed for spatial query, spatial modelling and cartographic display
3. A flexible architecture, enabling the user to combine models and data in a variety of ways
4. Methods peculiar to spatial and geographical analysis, including spatial statistics
5. Ability to generate a variety of outputs, including maps and other more specialized forms
6. A single, integrated, user interface that supports a variety of decision-making styles
7. An architecture that supports the addition of new capabilities as user needs evolve

A decision support system comprises three components: a *knowledge subsystem*, containing data and data manipulation procedures; a *language subsystem*, which is the user interface; and a *problem processing subsystem*, which links and coordinates models and data (Turban and Watkins, 1986). Spatial decision support systems are geared to solving specific problems and are designed to generate alternative solutions and incorporate performance criteria that are of interest to planners. They have an edge over conventional geographical information systems in that they incorporate a greater level of analytic and statistical modelling than is required to assist the process of decision-making. Furthermore, they are better than conventional modelling techniques because models are just part of the problem processing subsystem of a fully developed decision support system (Armstrong, 1993; Armstrong *et al.*, 1993).

GEOGRAPHICAL INFORMATION SYSTEMS AND URBAN PLANNING

The 1960s and 1970s were periods of soul-searching for the planning profession in general and for urban and regional planning in particular. It was a time when serious attempts were made to evaluate the theoretical basis of planning as well as when computation became accepted as part of the *sine qua non* for rational decision-making. Nonetheless, the use of computations was fraught with numerous problems, some conceptual and others technical (Batty, 1993). The conceptual problems arise from notions not unrelated to issues of optimality in decision-making and the extent to which predictive models may be used as planning tools. On the other hand, the technical issues deal with the inadequacy of available data and the inability of computational methods to display and show results in forms easily amenable to the appreciation of decision-makers. As noted by Batty (1993), GIS shows promise in removing many of these problems because of its emphasis on visualization and communication.

The rational decision-making model of planning is based on the simple notion that the planning process embodies an analytical phase in which the problem is explored, followed by a synthetic base in which the solution is devised or generated. Problems are informed by data and survey relating to the issue in question, and progress towards the solution is cast in terms of general goals and more detailed objectives. The analysis involved is oriented towards generating a requisite understanding of the problem, thus enabling some prediction of immediate states of the system. In the synthetic phase, solution of the problems involves some intuition that generates a range of alternative scenarios, which are then evaluated simultaneously. Decisions are made to adopt and implement a particular plan based on these results. The iterative process involved in the solution phase allows the initial problem to be better defined and solutions better refined.

Urban models were thus seen as props around which such a rational planning process may be developed. For instance, urban models were informed by the nature of the problems at hand, and the goals and objectives of the planning process, which in turn inform the sort of models used to optimize alternative planning scenarios. Evaluation, choice and implementation were in turn informed by a variety of urban models (Fig. 1.1). Inevitably, this mode of planning depended and will continue to depend on a number of information systems that include management information systems, land information systems, and a variation of what we describe today as geographical information systems. This latter was made up of socioeconomic and physical information about various locations in the city as well as the transport system that linked them together

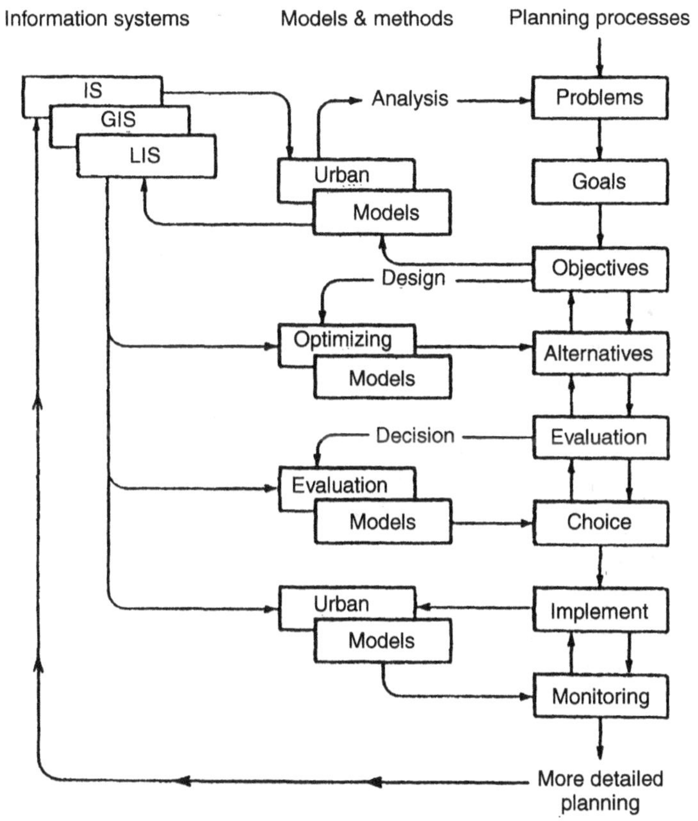

Fig. 1.1   Planning support systems incorporating models and information systems. (After Batty, 1993.)

and the cost of traversing space. Figure 1.1 provides a good description of this conception of the planning process.

Existing GIS contain only the most rudimentary of functions relevant to the sort of analytical, simulation and prediction and design tasks that dominate strategic planning. For instance, a typical urban planning problem will require the presence of a broad range of databases developed as information systems and at varying spatial scales and levels of variable aggregation. For example, at the urban planning level, we will be dealing with data and models whose basic unit would be either the street or network or a set of relevant attributes associated with some geometric area such as the block or the census tract. Various aggregations of zones will be required while different types of networks are needed. The set of information in a typical strategic planning situation will include demographic and economic data, land use data, transportation data and data concerning urban economic structure, all cast in the form of employment, population by age–sex group, and interactions of people, goods and information flows. Physical data pertaining to the quality of the landscape, topography, soils, geology, land use type and housing structures would also form part of the assembly (Batty, 1993). Only very few GIS can at present embrace this type of data and map it successfully, let alone develop this data for the various models and forecasting purposes required in urban and regional planning.

Nonetheless, the process of planning within cities constitutes one of the best examples of dealing with loosely structured problems for a number of reasons. First, in any planning situation, there is considerable unmodelled information and knowledge on the part of the planners and decision-makers. Secondly, the urban planning process shows such variability and complexity to require judgement and experimentation with available tools. Furthermore, the decision-maker's definition of the problem and identification of key factors are continually being revised during investigation. Moreover, the problem is sufficiently ill-defined for a decision-maker to treat development of its solution as part of the problem-solving process. Requirements for modelling these types of situations must be treated as open-ended. Attempts in the past to see models as providing solutions to problems were therefore misplaced, as models can only be a decision aid. This is the essence of developing decision support systems.

Many GIS have emerged in areas of concern to planning, e.g. land use zoning, transportation planning, natural resource management, utility companies, etc. These are applications of GIS to subsets of the problems as in the case of the use of TransCAD for transport development issues or ARC/INFO, SPANS, etc., for numerous other applications. These functions, though useful in planning, are partial attempts, and so tend to be less important than those based on models, methods and design protocols. Consequently, they are not the ones to provide the lifeblood for urban and regional planning. As noted by Batty (1993), 'the sort of functions which are required in urban planning and spatial policy analysis are usually absent from the archetypal GIS whose functionality embodying spatial analysis and modelling is weak'.

Nonetheless, there are important developments that cannot but change the way planning will be done in the future. Some of these pertain to the development of expert systems in various areas, the integration of which constitutes urban and regional planning. For instance, as far back as 1990, Kim *et al.* (1990) published a text that explored the use of expert systems technology in urban planning. In the last few years, there have been important and path-breaking studies in the development of expert systems for land use control (Leary, 1993), the checking of compliance with building codes (Heikkila *et al.*, 1990), and local government planning (Davis and Gant, 1987). Indeed, expert systems are being developed in various areas of environmental planning (Wright *et al.*, 1993). Added to these is the increasing application of the use of knowledge-based systems (Wright *et al.*, 1993) to various aspects of the planning process, including transport systems and the review of environmental impact assessments. There is no doubt that planning is at a threshold of some developments, the impacts of which could be much longer-lasting than what happened with the quantitative revolution.

SPATIAL DECISION SUPPORT SYSTEMS FOR URBAN PLANNING

Decision support systems in the area of the location of urban land use and infrastructure pose some serious challenges. First, this is an area where the process of planning is dynamic and where mathematical modelling has suffered serious criticisms, ranging from total outright rejection (Lee, 1973) to one of scepticism. Secondly, urban land use and infrastructure location is very unlike public facilities whose analysis can be easily subsumed under a theory like the theory of public goods or a service development theory (Rushton, 1988). For instance, urban infrastructure such as buildings, roads, water and sewage systems exist as props around which urban activities are organized. Consequently, their effects are often not easily measured as the demand for them is derived rather than direct. For example, a measure of the adequacy of urban infrastructure such as buildings in an urban system may be described in terms of over-crowding, which in turn may be defined as a function of the population per unit area, or in terms of activities that the urban centre is supposed to provide. Furthermore, there is a wide range of activities that can be tied to a particular infrastructure. For instance, a building may be used for residing as well as for commercial activities. These infrastructures are thus unlike those for educational services, where it is known and accepted that educational infrastructures are used solely for educational purposes. It is clear therefore that there is a need to possess some understanding of the location behaviour of different activities in an urban system in order to understand and evaluate the location and distribution of urban infrastructure.

We shall define urban infrastructure to include the stock of buildings, commercial and industrial buildings, etc., the transport system comprising the route network and the movement patterns on them. The development of a spatial decision support system for urban planning will depend on coupling together a number of subsystems, such as a database subsystem, a monitoring subsystem, a modelling subsystem, etc. We shall see that each of these subsystems is better developed as a spatial decision system in order to fully address the issues faced by urban planning. We shall describe these as an urban development information system (UDIS), urban development monitoring system (UDMS) and urban modelling system (UMS) respectively. Figure 1.2 shows an approximate representation of the subsystems and the interactions between them.

The urban development information system (UDIS) is a support system for the other components and subsystems of the decision support system such as case processing and urban services impact systems. Generally speaking, it is a specialized database that will contain certain information on land development projects. The database subsystem has been equipped with a number of expert systems that facilitate the processes of data query, data search and data analysis that constitute a geographical information system. The expert geographical information system (EGIS) will be a GIS that has been equipped with some elements of expert systems; in other words, it will be a decision support system. For instance, it would consist of 'intelligent' databases while retaining the basic characteristics of a geographical information system, namely the ability to couple powerful database management systems with cartographic and other methods of displaying data and information.

The urban modelling system (UMS) consists of a variety of models that are being used to study, understand, predict and plan urban development. The framework for model development ranges from optimization methods to models of spatial interaction using the methods of entropy maximization. The Penn–Jersey regional growth model developed in

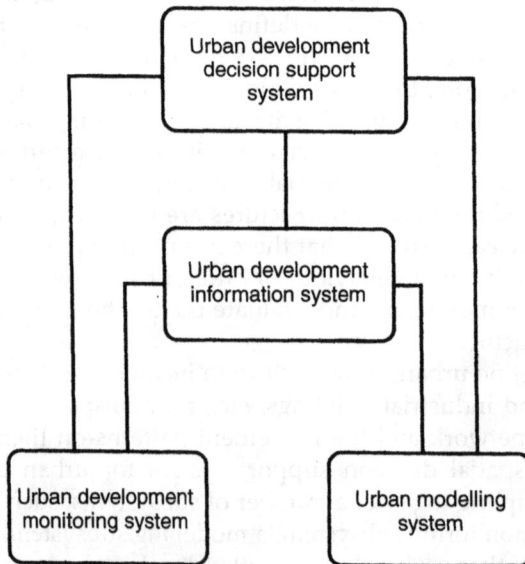

Fig. 1.2   The development of an urban infrastructure decision support system.

1962 provides the most well known optimization land use modelling framework. It simulates market conditions for residential location operating according to microeconomic theory. TOPAZ (Technique for the Optimal Placement of Activities in Zones), developed by Brotchie and Sharpe at CSIRO in Australia, is another optimization model that combines elements of spatial interaction modelling (Brotchie *et al.*, 1980). For a region divided into n zones and considering the allocation of m types of land use activities, the objective function of the model determines the allocation of activities that minimizes the overall combined cost of new development. Lowry's framework for urban modelling (Lowry, 1967), combining spatial interaction models with economic base principles, remains the most comprehensive approach for urban development modelling (see the next section below).

An urban development monitoring system (UDMS) is a basis for documenting and monitoring current levels of local development activity in order to assess the ability of a community to provide new development with needed infrastructure. The urban development monitoring system, in addition to tracking the permitting status of development projects, can be used for short-term planning and forecasting and for projecting small-area population, employment, construction and land use changes. It therefore will consist of at least three components: a case processing system, an urban services impact system, and an urban information system.

The urban services impact system, on the other hand, is an analytic tool for assessing a local government's ability to provide infrastructure to proposed development that is yet to be constructed. In essence, it provides an excess capacity analysis of each local infrastructure component during the development review process to determine if adequate facilities will be available for the new development in question. The system should have the capability to provide an adequate facilities analysis for all individual land use and development project decisions (e.g. for a rezoning decision, a subdivision plan analysis, building permit issuance, etc.) and should also be able to provide an aggregate estimate of short-term infrastructure demand resulting from build-out of all development projects at various stages of regulatory approval (e.g. all development for which building permits have been issued, all approved subdivisions for which building permits have yet to be requested, etc.).

The urban services impact system will need to access project-related information from the information system as well as other information from land parcel records and the geographical information system files contained elsewhere. A case processing system is mainly an accounting system that tracks the status of all land development activity in process at any given time in a local regulatory system. A case processing system is a local regulatory activity tracking system designed to keep track of the status of all current development, including re-zonings, site plan reviews and the issuance of building permits.

A case processing system is conceptually capable of tracking all status information from each major step in the local planning and regulatory process that affects the development potential of a parcel. This includes: its authorized use under a comprehensive plan; all plan amendments affecting the parcel; re-zoning information; subdivision approval information; special permits information, including data on permits issued under local landscaping and environmental protection ordinances; and building permit status (including information on inspections and certificates of occupancy). Information derived from the case processing system can also serve other useful functions, such as monitoring local supplies of developable land and for permit management purposes.

Furthermore, case processing systems can be programmed with 'smart' functions, such as the ability to prevent permit issuance over inter-agency objections serious enough to put a project on hold, and can also be set to track development approval conditions automatically to ensure compliance. More powerful case processing systems are linked with comprehensive land databases that allow many parcel attributes, such as ownership, street address, tax status, land use, infrastructure access and other information, to be cross-referenced with the development project under review. Furthermore, the case processing system will rely on the information system for all information regarding project location, ownership, existing and proposed land use, public facility needs, regulatory status and other details associated with any development project.

Given the numerous issues attending the development of a spatial decision support system for urban planning, it is clear that researchers and planners must continue to perfect their tools in the areas of developing spatial decision support systems for subsystems of the urban planning process. Such subsystems could include any of the categories described above or even systems developed from particular subsystems. For instance, in the area of the urban modelling system, one can decide to look critically at the issue of the urban transport modelling system because such an investigation is the bedrock of developing a sound urban planning system. We shall in the next section take another look at the urban land use–transport system and the requirements for making a spatial decision support system.

URBAN LAND USE–TRANSPORT DECISION SUPPORT SYSTEM

In the area of urban planning and policy analysis, it is clear that a spatial decision support system that will be of interest to planning must be capable of addressing those issues that have been encountered under the general title of urban land use–transport system. Such a decision support system will involve the integration of models of urban land use into the spatial analysis and planning framework. An urban land use–transport decision support system is well posed to integrate the development in urban systems modelling of the 1960s and 1970s into concepts of decision support and geographical information systems of the 1980s and 1990s.

An urban land use–transport decision support system will consist of a number of components, as shown in Fig. 1.3. The more important of these are the expert geographical information system (EGIS), the urban transportation planning and modelling system, and a control system consisting of the set of options that are available to planning (Fig. 1.3). The expert geographical information system could include information on existing land uses, the structure of the transport network and other data

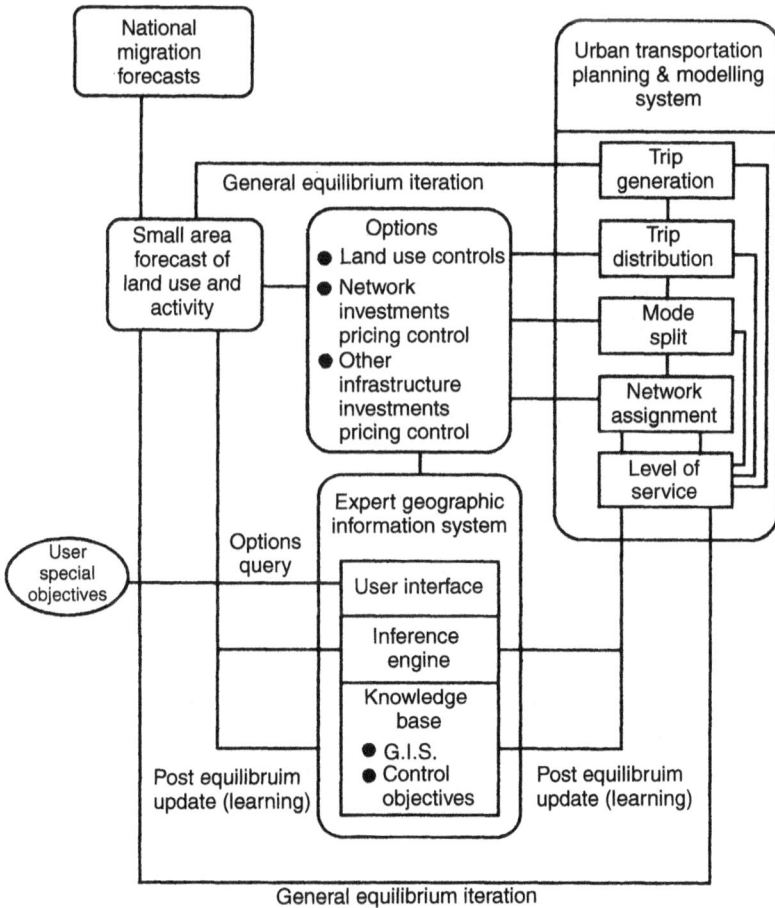

Fig. 1.3 An urban land use–transport planning decision support system.

regularly used by planning agencies. There would be a set of decision rules that would be used in deciding how some considerations should be applied in the search for feasible alternatives. However, the database management programme is a key component of the decision support system, as it serves as a kind of data switching yard that provides data to the analysis, display and report-generation modules of the decision support system. Decision rules that are used for determining how existing supply-and-demand relationships should be applied in the area of urban and regional planning are elements of the knowledge base that must be assembled for modelling the impact of land use changes on infrastructure. For instance, there would be a need to assemble the knowledge base of planners for the development of expert system shells for each set of activities like building approval, land use planning and control, traffic forecasting, design, control and monitoring, etc.

Expert systems will be responsible for guiding the geographical information system and for supporting land use and other models in an iterative planning process to explore alternatives by using a feedback mechanism. The expert systems will also be used to interface the database with the chosen models by retrieving and structuring the data as necessary, and to communicate with other components of the decision support system. Expert systems will thus be responsible for guiding interactions between the user and the decision support system, on the one hand, and for interacting with the analyst in alternative modelling strategies, on the other. In other words, expert systems will assist users in selecting models, provide judgemental elements in models, simplify model-building, enable friendlier user interfaces and provide explanation capacity (Turban and Watkins, 1986; Heikkila *et al.*, 1990).

URBAN LAND USE MODELLING

Large-scale computer models of urban spatial structure and processes first appeared in the USA during the early 1960s. These models were both experimental and operational and varied tremendously because each was developed for a specific purpose. Accordingly, several model developers relied on different theories of the urban activity system and used various techniques of urban spatial analysis. Transportation was the first component of the urban system to motivate early developments in urban modelling in the USA. The rapid growth in automobile ownership during the 1940s and early 1950s led to dissatisfaction with traditional physical land use planning based on existing urban forms. In other words, the traffic congestion that resulted from a dramatic increase in automobile ownership rates forced planners and researchers to find ways to understand how the trip-making behaviour of urban residents imposes requirements for new transportation facilities.

Nonetheless, by the late 1950s, the rudiments of model structure for transportation planning had been established. The models dealt with trip generation, trip distribution and the assignment of trips to the transportation network. Trip generation was modelled by using some approaches that include categorical analysis and linear regression methods. The academic success in developing transportation planning models spurred efforts to develop similar models of urban land use. Research activity on urban and location economics emerged during the 1960s with several attempts to formulate operational models of urban land use. In particular, two theoretical models of urban structure were proposed at this time by Wingo, and Alonso established for urban systems an economic theory that constituted the basis for further development in urban modelling (Batty, 1978).

Large-scale integrated land use and transportation models were developed to generate and test land use plans for a number of metropolitan areas such as Boston, Baltimore, Connecticut, Penn–Jersey, Pittsburgh and San Francisco. The models were extremely large and expensive to develop. They were large because they incorporated such dimensions of urban spatial structure relating to population forecasting, employment forecasting, transportation analysis and the forecasting of other infrastructure like sewers, solid waste, recreation and housing. While several of them became operational, others were abandoned before they could be fully developed. In Great Britain, during the late 1960s and early 1970s, relatively modest, small-scale and low-cost urban models were developed, largely based on an extension of the Lowry model. Even though urban modelling was rapidly spreading to many other countries during the 1970s, the USA witnessed a general decrease in modelling as a form of urban analysis. In the late 1970s and early 1980s, however, renewed interest in urban modelling resurfaced.

The development of large-scale, theoretical and empirical urban models was an area of intense activity. On the theoretical plane, researchers attempted to improve the framework of the Lowry model along two major directions. The first involved the model's allocation mechanisms, while the second involved the integration of the economic base concept into the modelling framework. Thus, in the first case, models based on entropy maximization replaced the simplistic potential models used by Lowry. In the second case, the economic base was improved through both disaggregation and a recognition that the coefficient of the economic base mechanism could be generated from a system of difference equations within an econometric framework. The use of entropy maximization as the basis for the development of allocation models within Lowry's modelling framework also implied that the coefficients or parameters of these models could be more satisfactorily estimated. Consequently, parameter estimation has become a major activity of urban moddelling (Batty, 1976). Indeed, it has become possible to test the significance of these parameters in fairly satisfactory ways.

The greater use of urban models in metropolitan planning circles became a major development in urban modelling activities and, in turn, tremendously influenced the approach and activity of urban model-builders. For instance, increasing use of these models has meant greater attention to the consequences of model disaggregation and parameter estimation, leading to better prediction and a greater use of the models. Nonetheless, urban models have not produced all the answers that planners require when it comes to issues of location and infrastructure development. Although the models were generally satisfactory in the way they handle issues of location and distribution of people and employment, they tend to neglect the link to infrastructure development. Indeed, infrastructure was considered an exogenous input into most of the models.

THE INTEGRATED TRANSPORTATION–URBAN LAND USE MODEL

The integrated urban land use–transportation model developed in the 1970s (Wilson, 1974; Batty, 1976; Ayeni, 1979) is a general model for urban infrastructure modelling and can be used to illustrate how the model component of an infrastructure decision support system might be developed. The model (described extensively elsewhere) is a coupling together of a number of spatial interaction models around economic base assumptions to predict different types of urban activities, attributes of the urban transportation, and the land uses associated with them.

Generally speaking, the urban land use–transport model consists of location and transportation network models. A typical version contains four principal models and a number of minor sub-models and utility programs. The principal models are a small-area forecasting model of land use and activity, a residential location model and a service location model. A trip distribution model is generally used for the simultaneous location of residential and service activities and the distribution of trips. When possible, this trip distribution model may also be equipped with modal split and network assignment functions. Wilson's formulation of trip distribution models (Wilson, 1974) allows these to be done within a single modelling framework.

The general configuration of an integrated land use–transport location model is shown in Fig. 1.3. The minor sub-models handle such tasks as calculating intra-zonal travel times and various transportation network congestion measures as well as land consumption. The sequence of operations of the principal models is straightforward. Following system initialization, the model begins with the small-area forecasting for time t using input variables such as employment of type k in all zones at time t, population of all types in all zones at time t, total area per zone for all zones, and zone-to-zone travel cost (or time) between zone j and all other zones at time t. The forecast of employment for time $t + 1$ is the most important data requirement for this exercise.

After the location of employment has been determined, the small-area forecast models produce a set of residence location predictions. The input variables consist of residents of all h types in zone i at time t, land used for residential purposes in zone i at time t, and the percentage of the developable land in zone i that has already been developed at time t. Other variables are the vacant developable land in zone i at time t, inter-zonal travel cost (or time) and employment figures.

Once the residence location forecast has been made, it is necessary to split trips by mode and to assign vehicle trips to the transportation network(s). The origin–destination work trip matrix is produced simultaneously with residence location. In addition, the model produces matrices of work-to-shop and home-to-shop trips. These three trip matrices must be expanded to represent total trips and converted from trip probabilities (the actual form in which they are calculated) to actual person and/or vehicle trips. These trips are then split into trips by mode, yielding transit person trips plus automobile vehicle trips. The automobile trips are then assigned to the highway network. One of the outputs is a set of inter-zonal highway travel times (costs), which are then combined with the transit times to yield a composite time (cost) matrix.

Potential models of interaction were initially used as location models by Lowry (1967). However, the projected land use model (PLUM) of Goldner replaced the potential models by gravity models. Even then, the spatial interaction model of residential location embedded in the Lowry model framework is simplistic and highly unrealistic. Nonetheless, Wilson's (1974) development of more theoretically sound models of spatial interaction that disaggregated persons by types (especially incomes) and houses by categories, with price varying by type and location, has become the foundation of the location models. The interaction models may be states as

$$T_{ij}^{kw} = A_i^k B_j^w H_i^k E_j^w e^{-\beta^w c_{ij}} e^{-\mu^w \left[p_i - q^w (W - c_{ij}') \right]} \tag{1.1}$$

where

$$A_i^k = \left[\sum_j B_j^w E_j^w e^{-\beta^w c_{ij}} e^{-\mu^w \left[p_i - q^w (W - c_{ij}') \right]} \right]^{-1} \tag{1.2}$$

and

$$B_j^w = \left[\sum_i A_i^k H_i^k e^{-\beta^w c_{ij}} e^{-\mu^w \left[p_i - q^w (W - c_{ij}') \right]} \right]^{-1} \tag{1.3}$$

A_i^k and B_j^w must be calculated to ensure that

$$\sum_j T_{ij}^{kw} = H_i^k \tag{1.4}$$

and

$$\sum_i T_{ij}^{kw} = E_j^w \tag{1.5}$$

where w and k indicate income and house types, respectively. T_{ij}^{kw} is the interaction variable, the number of w-income people living in a type-k house in zone i, working in zone j. The model assumes that H_i^k, the number of type-k houses in each zone i, E_j^w, the number of income-w jobs in zone j, and p_i^k, the price of a type-k house in zone i, are given (i.e. exogenously determined). The average amount that a w-income household spends on housing after journey-to-work costs have been deducted is denoted as q^w; c_{ij}' is the money or out-of-pocket part of the travel cost; and $q^w (w - c_{ij})$ is the average amount available for housing for a w-income household living in zone i and working in zone j.

The prop of the location models is the employment generation model. The earliest models were based on the economic base concept and the use of the basic:non-basic ratio. The economic base concept posits that the levels of employment and population in an urban system are determined by basic activities. Basic activities are defined either as those activities whose locations are independent of the distribution of population or as activities that export products to outside sources and hence attract revenue to the urban area (Ayeni, 1979, pp. 66–69; Massey, 1973). In its simplest formulation, the relationship between the basic employment E_t^B at time period t, the service employment E_t^S, the total employment E_t^T and the population P is as follows:

$$E_t^T = E_t^B + E_t^S \tag{1.6}$$

$$P = \alpha E_i^T \quad \alpha \geq 1 \tag{1.7}$$

and

$$E^S = \beta P \quad 0 < \beta < 1 \tag{1.8}$$

where α is the inverse of the activity rate and β the population:service ratio. From equations (1.6) to (1.8), we can derive the relationship

$$E_t^T = \frac{E_t^B}{(1 - \tau)} \tag{1.9}$$

where the quantity $\tau = \alpha\beta$ is shown to possess the characteristics of the basic:non-basic ratio (Ayeni, 1979, pp. 66–69). Furthermore, Ayeni (1979, pp. 314–315) has shown that, by introducing simple lags into equation (1.9), one can derive a basic employment stock generation model, which, properly calibrated, can be used to trace the trajectory of an urban system. This model is of the form

$$E_t^T = E_0^T + \sum_{t=1}^{n} \delta_t \Delta E_0^B + \sum_{t=1}^{n-1} \delta_t \Delta E_1^B + \dots + \sum_{t=1}^{2} \delta_t \Delta E_{n-2}^B + \delta_t \Delta E_{n-2}^B \quad (1.10)$$

where $\delta_t \Delta E_t^T$ is the increase in employment generated from an increase in basic employment at time period t and

$$\Delta E_t^T = E_{t+1}^T - E_t^T \quad (1.11)$$

The economic base concept remains the most criticized in the literature. It is difficult to operationalize and may not provide unique values for the basic:non-basic ratio. However, Massey (1973) not only provided a review and critique but also gave clear and explicit guidelines on operationally defining the basic:non-basic ratio as well as how to use it in urban and regional planning.

It is clear from the above that the economic base formulations around which models are developed are essentially accounting models. Accounting models are generally statistical models and it is essential that these be put into a dynamic or quasi-dynamic framework. Both Batty (1976) and Ayeni (1979) have described approaches for doing this. Furthermore, approaches outlined by Rees and Wilson (1977) for developing accounting frameworks for populations may also be explored for performing these tasks.

Urban models should make significant improvements in the next few years, not only because geographical information systems promise a wealth of databases for model calibration and testing but also because cognate developments will lead to the development of models that are user-friendly and that are more versatile than the models of the 1980s. The user-friendliness will be the key issue in whether the models survive in spatial decision support systems. Urban models and urban modelling should become less mechanistic in both development and use as part of this user-friendliness.

CONCLUSION

Geographical information systems and the computer are making data much more easily available to planners in larger quantities than hitherto. Furthermore, the ability to use such information has also kept on the increase with such developments as expert systems and the use of knowledge-based systems. For some of the more well defined areas of planning, prototype expert systems are being developed and tested. Indeed, there are aspects of urban and regional planning where the development of decision support systems has attained important dimensions.

Consequently, the development of operational decision support systems for the urban planning process may not be too far away. It is nonetheless a multidisciplinary task for which planners need to be very much mentally prepared as these are developments that will revolutionize the methods of planning as well as the planning profession.

The use of expert systems will improve the development of urban infrastructure models. Therefore, how to do this should constitute an important area of research. Crucial to this undertaking will be the conceptualization of planning and our ability to construct expert systems given the high level of certainty required and the fact that, in the best of situations, the repertory of human expertise is imprecise and uncertain. Since expert systems depend on the quantity and quality of knowledge acquired, an expert system will provide advice that is as good as the knowledge base. Consequently, the role of the human designer comes into focus and also his or her ability to resolve conflicting knowledge and validate expert systems.

Furthermore, the development of spatial decision support systems must explicitly address the problem of scale, which manifests itself in many ways. This problem could be particularly serious in urban and regional planning because of the need to focus on intra-urban variations at various spatial scales such as blocks, tracts, counties, urbanized regions, states, etc. For instance, when maps are aggregated, disaggregated or generalized to different scales, we introduce the problem of changing and presenting information. Besides the need to communicate these effectively, there is also the need to describe them efficiently through the computation of appropriate statistics. The procedure for aggregating and disaggregating spatial data within GIS environments remains not very well defined or understood at the present moment.

ACKNOWLEDGEMENTS

I acknowledge the financial support of the Council for International Exchange of Scholars, Washington DC, USA, for the award during the 1994/95 session of a Senior Fulbright Fellowship, which enabled me to develop the ideas contained in this chapter. I am however solely responsible for all errors and omissions.

BIBLIOGRAPHY

Armstrong M.P. (1993) Perspectives on the Development of Group Decision Support Systems for Locational Problem-Solving Geographical Systems. *Geographical Systems*, Vol. 1, pp. 69–81

Armstrong M.P., Lolonis P. and Honey R. (1993) A Spatial Decision Support System for School Redistricting. *Journal of the Urban and Regional Information Systems Association*, Vol. 5(1), pp. 40–52.

Ayeni B. (1979) *Concepts and Techniques in Urban Analysis*, London, Croom Helm; New York, St Martins Press.

Batty M. (1976) *Urban Modelling*, Cambridge, Cambridge University Press.

Batty M. (1978) Urban Models in the Planning Process. In Herbert J.D. and Johnston R.J. (eds), *Geography and the Urban Environment*, Vol. 1, *Progress in Research and Applications*, Chichester, John Wiley.

Batty M. (1979) Progress, Success and Failure in Urban Modelling. *Environment and Planning A*, Vol. 11, pp. 863–878.

Batty M. (1993) Using Geographic Information Systems in Urban Planning and Policy-Making. In Fischer M.M. and Nijkamp P. (eds), *Geographic Information Systems, Spatial Modelling and Policy Evaluation*, Berlin, Springer-Verlag.

Brotchie J.F., Dickey J.W. and Sharpe R. (1980) *TOPAZ – General Planning Techniques and its Applications at the Regional, Urban and Facility Planning Levels*, Berlin, Springer-Verlag.

Davis J.R. and Gant I.W. (1987) ADAPT: A Knowledge-Based Decision Support System for Producing Zoning Schemes. *Environment and Planning B: Planning and Design*, Vol. 14, pp. 53–66.

Densham P. (1994) Integrating GIS and Spatial Modelling: Visual Interactive Modelling and Location Selection. *Geographic Systems*, Vol. 1, pp. 204–213.

Fischer M.M. (1994) Expert Systems and Artificial Neural Networks for Spatial Analysis and Modelling: Essential Components for Knowledge-Based Geographical Information Systems. *Geographical Systems*, Vol. 1, pp. 221–235.

Fischer M.M. and Nijkamp P. (1992) Geographical Information Systems and Spatial Analysis. *The Annals of Regional Science*, Vol. 26, pp. 3–17.

Fischer M.M. and Nijkamp P. (eds) (1992) *Geographic Information Systems, Spatial Modelling and Policy Evaluation*, Berlin, Springer-Verlag.

Geoffrion A.M. (1983) Can OR/Ms Evolve Fast Enough? *Interfaces*, Vol. 13, p. 10.

Heikkila E.J. and Blewett E.J. (1992) Using Expert Systems to Check Compliance with Municipal Building Codes. *Journal of the American Planning Association*, pp. 72–80.

Heikkila E.J., Moore J.E. and Kim T.J. (1990) Future Directions for EGIS: Applications to Land Use and Transportation Planning. In Kim T.J. *et al.* (eds), *Expert Systems: Applications to Urban Planning*, New York, Springer-Verlag.

Hewitson B.C. and Crane R.G. (eds) (1994) *Neural Nets: Applications in Geography*, Dordrecht, Kluwer Academic.

Kim T.J., Wiggins L.L. and Wright J.R. (eds) (1990) *Expert Systems: Applications to Urban Planning*, New York, Springer-Verlag, pp. 191–201.

Kim T.J., Han S. and Adiguzel I. (1993) Machine Learning, Expert Systems, and an Integer Programming Model: Application to Facility Management and Planning. In Wright J.R. *et al.* (eds), *Expert Systems in Environmental Planning*, New York, Springer-Verlag.

Leary M.E. (1993) Expert Systems in British Land Use Planning. In Wright J.R. *et al.* (eds), *Expert Systems in Environmental Planning*, New York, Springer-Verlag.

Lee D.B. (1973) Requiem for Large Scale Models. *Journal of the American Institute of Planners*, Vol. 39, pp. 161–178.

Lowry I.S. (1967) *A Model of Metropolis*, Santa Monica, California, Rand Corporation.

Massey D.B. (1973) The Basic:Service Categorization in Planning. *Regional Studies*, Vol. 2, pp. 1–15.

Ortolano L. and Penham C.D. (1990) Applications to Urban Planning: An Overview. In Kim T.J. *et al.* (eds), *Expert Systems: Applications to Urban Planning*, New York, Springer-Verlag, pp. 191–201.

Rees P. and Wilson A.G. (1977) *Spatial Population Analysis*, London, Edward Arnold.

Rushton G. (1988) Location Theory, Location Allocation Models and Service Development Planning in the Third World. *Economic Geography*, Vol. 64, pp. 97–120.

Turban E. and Watkins P.R. (1986) Integrating Expert Systems and Decision Support Systems. *MIS Quarterly*, June.

Wilson A.G. (1974) *Urban and Regional Planning Models in Geography and Planning*, London, Pion.

Wilson A.G. (1990) A Spatial Interaction Dynamic Approach. In Bertuglia C.S. *et al.* (eds), *Urban Dynamics*, London, Routledge.

Wright J.R. and Buehler K.A. (1993) Probabilistic Inferencing and Decision Support Systems. In Wright J.R. *et al.* (eds), *Expert Systems in Environmental Planning*, New York, Springer-Verlag.

Wright J.R., Wiggins L.L., Jain R.K. and Kim T.J. (eds) (1993) *Expert Systems in Environmental Planning*, New York, Springer-Verlag.

How to define problems: a systemic approach

2

Dirk Vriens and Paul Hendriks

INTRODUCTION

Research into decision-making seems to suffer from two related weaknesses. The first is the lack of attention to the dynamic nature of the decision process and environment. Research attempts to encompass dynamic features are sparse. The second weakness is the allegation that decision alternatives can be discerned on an *a priori* basis, thus facilitating the use of a choice rule to pick the 'optimal' or 'satisficing' alternative (this is the basic assumption of the prevailing rationalistic approach of decision modelling). However, the assumption of an *a priori* conception of alternatives is not realistic, since it ignores the fact that the exploration and elaboration of alternatives forms an integral part of the decision process. Although several attempts have been made to overcome these problems, a coherent theory seems to be lacking. This chapter explores the possibilities of systems theory as an offset for new decision modelling. Among the many different approaches to systems theory, those that allow systems to have 'adaptive' properties are worthwhile because they can handle dynamics. Furthermore, the use of adaptive, dynamic systems leads to a solution for the problem of the 'disembodied' conception and choice of alternatives, since the choice options automatically follow from the defined system and may change because of its dynamic nature. The important question is how a system can be defined in order to capture the dynamic nature of decision-making. In order to answer this question, the chapter starts with a short overview of problems with traditional modelling in decision-making and systems theory. Next, it will be argued that the crux of defining

Decision Support Systems in Urban Planning. Edited by Harry Timmermans. Published in 1997 by E & F N Spon. ISBN 0 419 21050 4

systems that are capable of dealing with complex problems is to define them with regard to the goals that enter the decision process. An outline of a method to do this will be given. In the last part the consequences for computerized decision support will be stated.

DECISION SUPPORT: SUPPORT WHAT?

Traditionally decision support theory focuses on how to find a solution for the problem or problems the decision-maker faces. Problem-solving is conceived as taking some sort of inventory of possible ways out of the problem and deciding which line of action is most likely to be successful. That is, the focus is on comparing alternatives, and making a decision is seen as the choice of one of the alternatives. Differences between competing theories along these lines occur when comparison functions, choice criteria and methods for establishing these come into play.

Although the basic train of thought sketched above has its appeal, our starting point here is that for most problems the approach is unsatisfactory. A requisite assumption of the approach is that the problem to be solved is of a basically static nature, i.e. the problem is, so to speak, there to be solved. Even from a cursory consideration of decision situations, one learns that getting more insight into the nature of the problem forms an integral part of problem-solving. Conceiving a problem and solving it are (usually) indiscernible aspects of the decision process. Our starting point therefore is that this mainstream approach to decision support addresses the issue of problem-solving and decision support at the wrong end. The implicit assumption of traditional decision theory – that decision problems and their alternative solutions can be fixed on an *a priori* basis – cannot be substantiated. Their complexity implies that they are open for alternative conceptions, which makes them too mouldable to be caught in the relatively rigid framework sketched before. The main problem therefore is not to find the solution but to conceive the problem. Instead of concentrating on alternative solutions for a given problem, we propose to explore ways to envision the decision problem itself. By doing this we may find, as will be indicated below, that the problem put before the decision-maker actually hides underlying problems that may be left unaddressed if the decision-maker considers the apparent problem in isolation. To put it somewhat bluntly: traditional decision support in a great number of situations simply supports the solutions of the wrong problems. Or, in the words of von Winterfeldt and Edwards (1986, p. 29): 'The most common pitfall in decision analysis is to produce a sophisticated solution to the wrong problem.' This chapter will elaborate this thesis.

The shift in attention indicated above implies more eye for the earlier phases of decision-making: the 'intelligence' or identification phase becomes the main focus for our modelling efforts. What we aim to do in this chapter is to explore ways for a formal representation of the problem identification phase. The reason for aiming at formalization is our underlying goal to investigate possibilities for support of the decision process, possibly by means of automated tools. Without a formal representation, any attempt to conceive decision support tools will be futile.

MODELLING PROBLEMS RATHER THAN SOLUTIONS

Once we have decided to focus on modelling the problem instead of the alternative solutions, we have to ask ourselves what the distinctive features in this modelling process will be. What are the characteristic obstacles we are bound to run into that will have to be dealt with? It should be stressed beforehand that these obstacles are the same as the reasons why a conventional solution-geared approach is to be deemed unsatisfactory. From a careful consideration of the decision process, one learns that the process of conceiving the problem and looking for a solution are not two separate processes but are in fact highly integrated activities. The basic challenge when dealing with problem-solving is how to achieve this integration. There are two sides to it: even a partial reconceptualization of the problem may lead to a different perspective on the solution space, whereas variations in the set of perceived solutions (new insights, changing circumstances, etc.) may lead to a new conception of the problem. Put another way, avoiding an *a priori* definition of solution paths and finding a way to deal with the fundamentally dynamic nature are the two (dependent) key issues.

A simple example may help to clarify this. Suppose we want to take a vacation and try to make up our mind about destination, means of transport and type of lodging. This may seem to be a relatively trivial matter: make a list of alternatives, find the appropriate choice criteria, and evaluate the alternatives given these criteria. A number of factors may, however, confuse the situation. The first is that a conflict may arise when various objectives have to be met simultaneously. This may be the case when various players in a decision process have different interests in mind (for instance, children and their parents planning a joint vacation). It may also be the case when no such conflict of interests is at stake, but when limiting conditions (e.g. time, money) prevent all goals from being fully reached at the same time. Clearly, these conflicts cannot be solved by finding a measure (cf. utility) that will allow alternatives to be compared. What is important here is not finding a solution with maximum or 'satisficing' utility for all parties involved. Rather, what is important is exploring as many alternative ways as possible out of the problem. In the given example, if parents have different goals in mind when considering how to spend their vacation than their children, they should not compare the relative utilities of their solutions. They should instead try to explore alternatives that will eventually result in a win–win combination. Of course, another standard way out of these kinds of problems is not by means of negotiations, but through a decree of the most powerful party. But this is certainly not by definition the most fruitful way out.

A further complication is the fact that goals and objectives are not stable entities, but may be subject to change. Part of the decision process should be to try to anticipate these changes and find ways to deal with the turbulence in order to survive. In the vacation example, if persons have to be accessible for their employers even during their vacation, their planning should be such that they can be reached at all times while at the same time the continuation of their vacation will not be unnecessarily frustrated (for instance, aim at combining destinations where fax machines are present).

Next we have to be aware that in some cases the problem put before the decision-maker is not the 'actual' problem, but masks an underlying problem for which the given problem may be seen as a solution. In terms of the example, it is conceivable that going on vacation is not the actual goal for all the parties involved. For instance, for some 'recovering from too much work' for others 'being away from home' are goals that going on vacation should help to meet. If this is the case, there is a twofold risk. The first is that solving the problem at hand ('going on vacation') may not be effective in solving the underlying problem (for instance, if the decision process on where to go generates more stress than the vacation will help to dissolve). Or, to put it differently, the higher-order problem will provide the reasons why and when the lower-order problem is effectively solved. If these reasons are not considered in the decision process, it becomes unavoidable for the solution to get the character of casualness. The second risk of not asking for underlying goals given a problem is that perfectly valid solution areas may remain undiscovered, simply because thinking of the problem as one specific solution with alternatives available will help to open new horizons for problem-solving.

A last point to be mentioned is that our insight into the relation between problem and solution will very often be imperfect. Furthermore, our degree of insight may vary for different solution areas. This introduces the risk of biasing our judgement towards those solutions that are better understood.

Of course, this criticism of decision theory and decision support centring on the comparison of alternatives is not new; it may be heard in a number of forms by e.g. Ackoff (1978), Checkland (1981), Vriens (1993) and Winograd and Flores (1986). All these authors share our concern with the early intelligence stages of problem-solving. What they seem to lack, however, is a coherent theory that will provide the sufficiently solid founding called for when we aim to provide support tools. We direct our attention to providing exactly such a firm ground in the remainder of this chapter.

Wrapping it up, we may establish that what we want to be able to catch in our formal address of problem support is flexibility and dynamics in a variety of ways:

- More than one goal may enter the decision process, possibly obstructing the realization of other goals or conflicting with these.
- Goals are not stable entities. They may change in the process, they may become more clearly visible, or they may disappear out of sight. Reification of goals should therefore be avoided at any stage.
- Goals may effectively hide higher-order goals, therefore blurring out 'what we really want to achieve', and introducing the risk of solving the problems we do not actually want to solve. This also stresses that what we see as a (generic) goal may be a (specific) solution if we establish that the given goal has an underlying justification.
- Our insight into the relationship between goals and solutions may be imperfect, as well as subject to change. In combination with the awareness that goals on one level of abstraction may be solutions on another, this also indicates that a bias may be introduced in our problem conception. We may tend to have more eye for given goal–solution pairs, while overlooking others.

ADAPTIVE SYSTEMS AND DECISION-MAKING

Given the fundamentally dynamic features of decision problems as sketched in the previous section, what we are looking for is an offset for a new formal framework to represent the elements of the decision situation. Systems theory seems to offer this offset. A system (in the cybernetic sense) is, roughly speaking, a collection of elements, related in such a manner that emergent properties (i.e. properties that exist at the level of the whole, not at the level of its parts) come about. There are many different approaches to systems theory and not all of these are equally useful for decision research. For our purposes, systems that have 'adaptive' properties are worthwhile because they can deal with dynamics.

The hallmark of an adaptive system is that it can show behaviour aiming at 'maintaining the essential variables within [...] limits' (Ashby, 1960, p. 58). Adaptivity is closely related to stability: it has to do with 'stabilizing' the system in reaction to environmental disturbances. To survive in a dynamic situation, a system constantly changes in order to reach a new state of equilibrium. An adaptive system, therefore, combines changing – the system adapts – with remaining the same – what adapts is one system. What, one may then ask, remains stable in systems showing behaviour that allows them to change? This question is answered by Maturana and Varela (1988) in introducing the concepts of 'organization' and 'structure'. The 'organization' of a system abstracts from material properties, in describing a system in terms of its constituting 'network of relations among components'. It concerns 'all relations that have to exist among the components of a system to remain a member of a certain class' (Maturana and Varela, 1988, p. 37). The 'structure' on the other hand refers to the actual components and relations regarding a particular system at a particular time. When one would try to pin down the 'organization' of a car as a system, one states that 'a motor', 'coachwork', 'wheels', etc., should be related in some way. The structure describes a specific spatial realization: a real car having a specific motor, specific coachwork, etc., that are related in the way that is indicated by its organization. It follows that a structure realizes an organization in time and space and that different structures may realize the same organization.

An adaptive system can now be described as a system that strives to maintain its organization by allowing its structure to change. Such a system constantly changes to maintain its class identity in a dynamic environment. This change in structure is bound to certain limits. When it gets warmer, a human 'system' changes its structure by perspiring. When it gets too hot, however, human systems can no longer generate structures that allow it to survive. In systemic terms, when a system cannot generate a structure that realizes its organization, it disintegrates (dies). Because an adaptive system can only change the structure it consists of, it is said to be 'structure-determined'. Each generated structure is determined by the previous one. Within the limits posed by this determination, a system should aim at being able to generate as many different structures as possible. For the wider the range of possible structures, the greater the chance of finding one that can suit the needs of the system in a changing environment. This is a translation of Ashby's law of requisite variety (Ashby, 1959): to deal with environmental variety, a system should itself generate variety.

A change in structure can be brought about in a reflected or non-reflected way. The change in skin cells, due to rising temperature, is best seen as a non-reflective systemic change in structure. We speak of a reflected change in structures when a system somehow consciously deliberates on this change. This is where decision-making comes in: decision-making could be described as 'a reflective mechanism for maintaining viability'. When described in this fashion, decision-making should encompass the following:

1. Defining the 'current structure': what is the starting point for reflection?
2. Analysing the range of possible new structures (which may lead to a redefinition of the 'current structure').
3. Selecting a new structure.

In this 'decision-making' process the system first has to translate its current structure (the offset for reflection) into something that can be reflected upon. We suggest that the product of this translation takes the form of a map or network of interrelated (systemic) goals plus the current (or planned) realizations of these goals (see also next section). Because the need for translation is usually triggered by some 'problematic' situation, the translation will be biased towards this problem. That is, a system will select only those goals and realizations that it perceives to be relevant for some problem. When 'spending a vacation' is considered as a problematic situation, i.e. as a situation that must be reflected upon, a decision-maker immediately selects goals and realizations that are related to this 'problem', like 'where to go' (with a preferred destination as its 'realization', or no realization at all) and 'how to get there' (realized by e.g. 'car'). When an initial 'network of goals and realizations' is constructed, the system must analyse the possible new networks that can be generated from this initial network. Extending Rapoport (1975), this generation can be captured by the function: $F(N, E, R, CoA)$. In this function, N stands for the initial network (as defined above), E for relevant environmental factors (possible disturbances), R for the return for the system ('gain' in viability) and CoA for possible courses of action that can alter the network. The function describes a reflective process, where one considers changes in the initial network. Altering the network can take the form of adding/removing goals and/or realizations. In the example described before, a decision-maker may, for instance, add the goal 'availability', thereby excluding several vacation options where one is hard to reach. The first two steps are highly integrated: during reflection it may appear that other 'translations' of the structure are possible and should be investigated. The generation function F yields a class of possible structures (which again take the form of networks of goals and realizations) from which one is selected, eventually. To sum up: decision-making is defined as a process that reflectively transforms the translation of the structure of a system.

When decision-making is explicitly described as a viability-maintaining mechanism, it may be possible to circumnavigate the pitfalls of traditional theorizing (see earlier sections). This description emphasizes the importance of 'translating' (in traditional terms, the importance of the intelligence phase) and it yields an important decision-making 'maxim', related to the law of requisite variety: generating as many structures as possible. Translation and generation are two sides of one coin: the translation gives the offset for generation, while in reflecting upon generated networks, it may seem that the translation should be altered. When altered, it may lead to the generation of different networks, which, in turn, may lead to altering the translation, etc.

FORMALIZING FOR SUPPORT

The proposed concept of decision-making implies new demands for decision support. In line with recent criticism of traditional support (see e.g. Forgionne, 1991), it is proposed to focus on the earlier phases of decision-making. In the 'adaptive-system' context this would mean: focus on the steps of 'translating' and 'generating' and their mutual dependence. The question is how these steps could be supported. To this aim, we will discuss a formalization in this section. The starting point for reflection is some 'decision object' (the original problem), around which the 'translation' is built up, and new networks are generated. We propose a formalization that can be helpful in 'supporting' both steps concurrently. The simple example of deciding how to spend one's vacation may be helpful again. The objective 'spend vacation', when seen as a problem, implies an exploration of the various elements to solve the problem involved. It may be noted that finding a way to meet the given objective is similar to defining the object class 'vacation' in this given instance. Suppose, as we did before, that three solution elements are recognized: destination, transportation, and type of lodging. These three solution elements are represented by the three vertical boxes linked to the 'Object' box (Fig. 2.1). What the decision-maker will have to ask is whether or not the combination of these three will indeed lead to reaching the objective. Put another way, is the solution set complete? Next, the alternative solutions for every element will be filled in. These alternative realizations are represented with the 'A's in the vertical boxes, with subscripts indicating the subgoal to which they belong, as well as their identification within the set

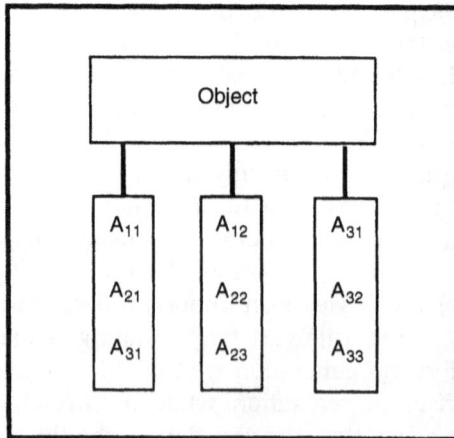

Fig. 2.1   Translation of problem definition into decision objects.

for this subgoal. For instance: if the first box represents the transportation problem, A_{11} may stand for 'car', A_{21} for 'train', and A_{31} for 'plane'. Similarly, A_{13} through A_{33} may represent 'hotel', 'tent' and 'bungalow'. It is vital for the introduction of flexibility to explore as many alternative ways as possible (see the decision-making maxim, mentioned above). The result (Fig. 2.1) is a starting point for further reflection: it covers a simple 'network' of three goals (the vertical boxes) and several realizations of these goals (the alternatives). As such, it covers the translation of the current structure as well as some alternative realizations.

Next, if we want to combine the knowledge gathered at a given point to inspect the solution space, what we do is we create a number of horizontal intersections, as visualized in Fig. 2.2. The shaded box indicates a possible solution to the problem of spending one's vacation. It may be noted that the status of every individual alternative is highlighted in its being what Mackie calls an INUS condition, or an 'Insufficient but Non-redundant part of an Unnecessary but Sufficient' condition (cf. Hendriks, 1986). The INUS-conditionality of the various alternatives underlines once again the fact that functional relations between problems and solutions are quite different from causal relations, and that a wide exploration of the solution space is possible without actually pinpointing predefined solution paths or decision trees.

An attractive feature of the representation is that it allows the same basic structure to be used for modelling the problem at various levels of abstraction. As has been indicated before, a problem may be seen as one of the alternative solutions of a higher-order goal or problem. In the given problem, 'going on vacation' may actually hide the goal 'recover

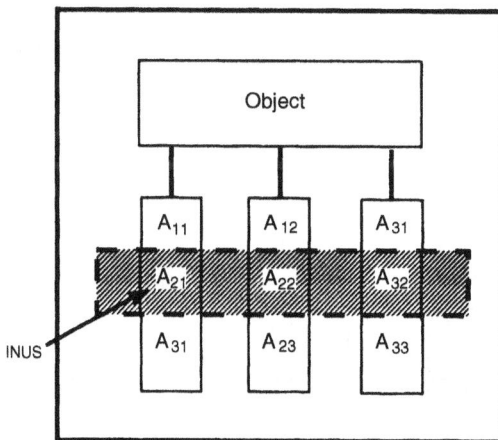

Fig. 2.2 Alternative decision object realizations and INUS conditions.

from too much work'. A similar relation may also be introduced at a lower level of abstraction: every solution element, 'transportation', 'destination' and 'type of lodging', may also be conceived as a goal in itself at a lower level of abstraction. If we try to conceive the relation between our original problem and its underlying higher-order goal in the same terms as the alternative ways to solve our original problem, we find that this introduces an element of recursiveness (Fig. 2.3). When trying to combine the relevant pieces of the puzzle, the decision-makers may decide that certain pieces are worth some further consideration. So they may want to 'zoom in' on some of the pieces. When doing so they will find that these pieces in themselves are new puzzles, with their own problems and alternative solutions. This element of recursiveness when working at different levels of abstraction further illustrates the flexibility of the framework we represented. Remember that this flexibility was introduced by defining a problem as a set of goals and relating these to alternative ways of reaching the goals. The further need for flexibility that may be introduced when trying to reach objectives simultaneously at different levels of abstraction is handled in a straightforward way. The recursiveness also covers the idea of 'redefining' the original network: it may appear that a decision object at a level other than the original object level should be the offset for reflection. The features of decision-making, such as building an initial network and 'transforming it' (generating new networks), can now be seen to be captured by means of the proposed formalization.

OUTLOOK

Problem-solving is not just a matter of coming up with alternatives and finding the most suitable of these. An integral part of the task that deci-

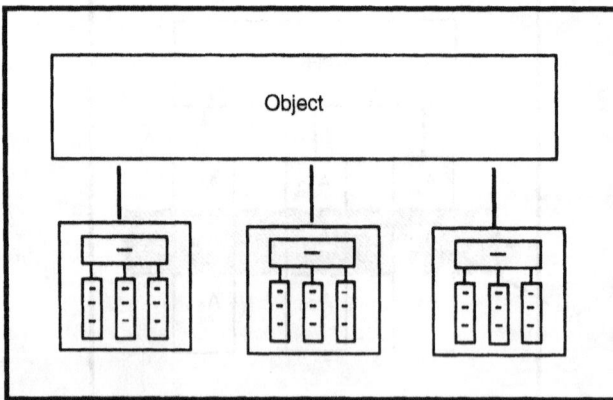

Fig. 2.3   Recursive relations introduced by decision object levels.

sion-makers face is trying to discover what the problem itself 'really' is about, and trying to find as many alternative solutions for problems at various levels of abstraction as may be necessary to find a way out of the problems. What this chapter has stressed is the need for creative problem-solving, not just based on looking for and comparing alternatives, but also based on a more fundamental rethinking of the decision problem itself. For decision-makers, creativity is core business. This implies that rigid models that apply arithmetic calculus to identify the best choice are of limited use here. This does not exclude the possibility of a formal representation of the decision problem and its elements. True, the traditional formal decision models do not have much to offer here since they start only when creativity stops, so an exploration of alternative formalizations is called for. It is exactly this formal basis for the support of the early phases of the decision process that this chapter has explored. It has been indicated that the aim is not to model the ultimate decision but to provide a frame of reference to organize the relevant insights. The main objective for such a framework is to guarantee an appropriate amount of flexibility in combination with a solid formal base. The introduction of decision elements into systems theory, and more specifically the theory of adaptive systems, was presented as the hallmark of the approach.

REFERENCES

Ackoff, R.L. (1978) *The art of problem solving*, Wiley, New York.
Ashby, W.R. (1959) *An introduction to cybernetics*, Chapman and Hall, London.
Ashby, W.R. (1960) *Design for a brain*, Chapman and Hall, London.
Checkland, P.B. (1981) *Systems thinking, Systems practice*, Wiley, Chichester.
Forgionne, G.A. (1991) Decision technology systems, *Information Systems Management*, 6, pp. 34–43.
Hendriks, P.H.J. (1986) *De relationele definitie van begrippen; Een relationeel realistische visie op het operationaliseren en representeren van begrippen*, Nederlandse Geografische Studies, No. 24; KNAG, Amsterdam.
Maturana, H.R. and Varela, F. (1988) *The tree of knowledge: the biological roots of human understanding*, New Science Library, Boston.
Rapoport, A. (1975) Research paradigms for the study of dynamic decision behaviour. In: Wendt, D. and Vlek, C. (eds), *Utility, probability and human decision making*, Riedel, Dordrecht, pp. 349–369.
Von Winterfeldt, D. and Edwards, E. (1986) *Decision analysis and behavioral research*, Cambridge, Cambridge University Press.
Vriens, D. (1993) Problem-setting support. In: Bots, P.W.G., Sol, H.G. and Traunmüller, R. (eds), *Decision support in public administration*, IFIP Transactions A-26; North Holland, Amsterdam, pp. 29–41.
Winograd, T. and Flores, F.L. (1986) *Understanding computers and cognition*, Ablex, Norwood.

Planning as argumentation and power-acting: theory and methods

3

Wolf Reuter

INTRODUCTION

The more we know in detail about the problem-solving of planners, the better we can support this planning process by computer. A short characterization of planning problems is given in this chapter. The final plan is seen as the output of a process where different parties and persons (including the planner) attempt to push through their interests. It is differentiated mainly between two kinds of action, both labelled as *pragmatic acts*: argumentation and power-acting. Both are characterized as models of planning. Owing to a special need for methodological and informational support for *discoursive planning*, IBIS (Issue-Based Information Systems) was developed. It is a knowledge-based system with special strength in the early planning phases. It is shown in detail, including a computer application. IBIS also functions as a network connecting different *support systems* under the focus of a planning problem. Some aspects of a model of *planning as power-acting* are shown: decision procedures as regulations for distribution of power, means of power, the logic of power, and some support systems against the misuse of power in design and planning.

Those who would like to invent support systems for design and planning need to know what planning is and how it works. We need a theory of planning which is sufficiently operational in such a way that the steps, operations and procedures of design are accessible for artificial systems. Therefore we strive for a more precise knowledge about these processes.

Decision Support Systems in Urban Planning. Edited by Harry Timmermans. Published in 1997 by E & F N Spon. ISBN 0 419 21050 4

With that aim in mind we exclude a large amount of mental, neuronal activities of the designer. Joy, pleasure, stress, rage, emotional overflows or piling-ups as trigger devices of creative ideas, anarchically associating, to indulge in fantasies – until now these were not to be represented by a model and dubious to support, unless we extend the term *support systems* to manipulations of the physical and social environment, electrical manipulations (diodes positioned in the neurosystem), genetic manipulations or chemical interventions like cocaine or wine.

The overlap between thinking and feeling is not even known. What is neurologically/biologically the difference? Already here our project could fail principally, but we have some good reasons to proceed.

1. Planning is oriented to a purpose and to that extent it is bound to the calculus of instrumental thinking.
2. Many procedures of planning are communicable by speech and thus they are bounded to its rationality.
3. Observing the planners' activity one can find some typical characteristics of their way of thinking when they solve problems. This is due to the kind of problems they deal with.

Therefore we will first have a look at these problems.

CHARACTER OF PLANNING PROBLEMS

Planners produce plans for objects, states or processes in the future. They start because somebody declares the *status quo* as insufficient, as a problem, and develops a plan according to a new idea of what ought to be. Different people try to influence the final plan because the plan regulates the distribution of advantages and disadvantages. Interests arise. So planning problems are societal problems with a profile of special properties. Rittel and Webber (1973) called them 'wicked' problems in contrast to the so-called 'tamed' problems of scientists.

A first characteristic of planning problems is that what somebody indicates as insufficient *status quo*, implicates the solution. In addition, ideas about what ought to be are normally different. So already the definition of the planning problem – as the difference between what is and what ought to be – seems to be impossible.

Every planning problem can be seen as a symptom of another one; the level of solution is not a given.

Prognoses about consequences of measures differ just as explanations of a bad state of affairs do. Every solution is 'a one-shot operation' and is irreversible. Every solution is 'unique', which means it is not transportable to another problem; some feature will always be different.

A test about the rightness of a solution (like in science) is impossible since the consequences of planned measures lead to infinite causal chains. The categories right/wrong are not adequate. A solution at best can be judged as good or bad; depending on which advantages or disadvantages somebody expects from a solution, the judgement differs.

This property deserves special attention. Owing to this property of planning problems we have to realize that there are no logical rules nor reasons based on data which lead inevitably and definitely to a solution. Ultimately, judgements determine the result of the planning process. The notorious lack of sufficient reason throws the planner back to his or her ability to judge.

If ought-to-be statements on the basis of judgements determine the process of planning, the outcome will always be uncertain. Facts, data and forecasts may give helpful orientation. But the so-called *Sachzwang* does not exist by logical reason: it is not allowed to deduce ought-to-be statements from empirical data, facts.

If understanding, level, explanation and solution of a problem are principally controversial, what should a planner do now? Similarly, what should be done if there are no universally valid norms from which single judgements could be deduced; if in the opposite norms, aims and interests, rather than converge, in Western and now also Eastern social systems, become more and more divergent, heterogeneous, pluralistic; if scientific findings do not allow conclusions on what ought to be done?

MODELLING THE PLANNING PROCESS – PRAGMATIC ACTS

If there are no external authorities who can guarantee the rightness of a planning step, the persons involved have to help themselves. The professional planners as well as all other persons and groups who are interested in or concerned by the planning output are participants in the planning system. They bring in their interests and try to put them through. In order to do it successfully they act. For example, they exchange arguments; they establish irreversible facts; they make use of experts; they take all different kinds of actions, immaterial ones like communication as well as physical ones like using barricades or occupying houses, but all related to an intended change of reality. With a generic term they can be called *pragmatic acts*. They are postulated as the smallest units of the planning process. There might be many possibilities to classify pragmatic acts in planning. The focus here is set mainly on two different kinds: argumentation and power-acting. Two models represent the two kinds of pragmatic acting: the discourse or argumentative model, and the model of planning as power-acting.

PLANNING AS ARGUMENTATION

Within the framework of a general theory of society Habermas (1973) develops a model of discourse. It says that ethical norms generally and particularly are valid only if their legitimation can be made reasonable in a discourse for all participants. Legitimation can be achieved by a discourse only, if it is free of repressions, without restriction in participation, if all motives except that of the cooperative search for truth are excluded.

Similarly well-founded and formulated for planning as a special case of societal action Rittel develops his argumentative model (Kunz and Rittel, 1970). On the one hand he reacts on the realization that the opinions of people involved in planning about factual and desired states, about measures and their consequences, are principally and ever controversial. On the other hand he bases his ideas on the observation that the reasoning of designers in fact, whether in a single head or distributed on many participants, is argumentative.

Both models are non-technocratic. In both models it is evident that planning is far away from concepts where solutions can be derived.

Even if, as is often the case, a planner plans alone, he argues with himself. It is an argument that causes an architect to tear up a piece of transparent paper and on the new piece of paper draw a new answer to a design problem, which maybe he rejects because of another argument, and so on.

PLANNING AS POWER-ACTING

Discourse and argumentative models of planning have the disadvantage that some phenomena of the planning reality are not represented. Planning is not only the pure search for truth; it is more than just the disciplined exchange of arguments with the altruistic aim that the better one may win, leading to the victory of the better argument.

During the planning process the parties involved try to influence the outcome. They have interests, which they try to put through, even against resistance. This is definitely power-acting. The argument turns out to be only one of many available means of getting through. Already when uttering arguments, other additional factors are set in motion; e.g. the authority of the person who presents the argument can be calculated; also effective are the propagation of arguments by the media, their steady repetition or their packaging. We have already crossed the border to power-acting.

The argument of a town-planner, who wants more measures of environmental control, convinces an entrepreneur not by pure argument, but by the power of the state to impose sanctions against him. And the entrepreneur threatens with an alternative location outside the town, which means a loss of taxes. Or he just does it. There are several means to constitute a situation of power and several ways to behave in that situation, for the holder of power as well as for the subject.

RELATION OF THE TWO MODELS

Argumentation and power-acting interfere. Therefore some remarks on the relationship of discourse and power are given here.

The discourse situation intended by Habermas has ideal character. One may approximate but never reach it. However, it is necessary to exclude power in order to protect the freedom of decision. The hope is to differentiate norms (here plans) which can be legitimated from those which stabilize relations of power (Habermas, 1973).

In the face of the ideal character of the discourse situation, we have to drop the concept to use that kind of discourse in real planning situations as a quasi-mechanical means that guarantees a solution free of power. More realistic is the concept of giving the discourse a dialectic role in a model of planning, such that against the use of power a postulate is opposed of the form, for example, 'act in such a way that on demand you can legitimate (justify) your action to the demander, such that he accepts it'. The argumentative discourse generates a subversive power against power-acting. If a model of planning should not only represent factual reality but also claims normative validity, the model of argumentative discourse is the favourite one.

As a model of representation of planning as societal role-playing the model of power-acting is more comprehensive. Both models relate to each other complementarily in a dialectic way. Drawing a synthesis, those who bet on the power of arguments, the protagonists of the ratio-nalistic discourse, in the tradition of the Enlightenment, become one of many participants in the power game of planning. Arguments are a sub-set of pragmatic acts, which altogether are thought to influence the out-come of the design decision process.

We are interested in every form of a planner's action, the argumenta-tion as well as the power-oriented action. We now see planning as a process where different views of the *status quo*, options about the desired status and about the instruments by which it is to be reached, are attempted to be put through with different kinds of pragmatic acts (like argumentation or acts of power), in order to influence the final plan.

Therefore, we shall deal with argumentative methods as well as with methods of power, in order to support planning procedurally.

IMPACTS FOR INFORMATION SUPPORT SYSTEMS

The character of planning problems and the models representing the planning process induce certain characteristics of a support system.

- If there are many participants whose contributions are crucial for the output of the planning process, an information support system should be open for their contributions.

- If the view of the problem changes during a planning process, an information support system should have the ability to change its content and to grow.
- If controversy is expected, a support system should be able to represent controversial knowledge, and offer the communication structure to exchange it.
- If planning is an exchange of arguments, a support system should be able to enhance or to represent argumentation.
- If the view of a problem changes and new aspects emerge, if new details become interesting, it should support the tracing and finding of new sources of knowledge, which are unknown at the beginning.
- If the needed knowledge does not fit within the limits of scientific disciplines or political resorts, it should be organized independently of limits.

AN ARGUMENTATIVE METHOD – A PROCEDURE AND AN INFORMATION SYSTEM (IBIS)

Rittel developed a system which reacts to such special demands. It is an instrumental version of the argumentative model. He connects the essential elements of a discourse – issues, positions and arguments – in a knowledge-based information system, which is able to represent and support the discourse of planners. He called it Issue-Based Information Systems (IBIS) (Kunz and Rittel, 1970). Therefore some features of the instrument, which already exists in some computerized versions, are demonstrated.

Argumentation of planners grows around certain issues which mark the missing knowledge. Kunz and Rittel distinguish five kinds of knowledge that occur in the discussions of planners. These kinds of knowledge correspond to kinds of questions or issues, which formulate the respective need for information.

1. *Factual issues* ask for the status of the world. They may have the form 'What is the case?' (was the case, will be the case).
2. *Deontic issues* ask for the desired situation, how the world (an object, a building, a town, a traffic system) should be. ('Should X be the case?')
3. *Instrumental issues* ask for means, measures, techniques, by which a desired status could be reached. ('How, by which means can a situation be reached?')
4. *Explanatory issues* ask for reasons in the past and for chains of consequences of a considered action in the future. ('What are the causes/consequences of a state/measure?')
5. *Conceptual issues* or issues of definition ask for what somebody understands or wants to understand by a term. ('What is this or that?')

The answers to these issues are normally controversial. They have the quality of positions, e.g. 'yes' or 'no' to deontic issues. Different participants with different world-views or interests take different positions. The experience teaches that, not only to deontic issues, but also to instrumental issues, explanatory and even factual issues, the answers are controversial.

Positions can be supported or challenged according to real discourse. This is the category of arguments.

Various issues can be subsumed under a problem area. The choice of a problem area depends on the dominant interest. It could be a resort, a scientific discipline or a kind of measure. Figure 3.1 shows the elements of the system.

Relations connect the issues to networks, thereby representing the interdependence of planning aspects across the classification borders of disciplines or resorts. To operate the system, a strong operative nucleus seems to be necessary in order to stimulate permanent communication and to regulate the procedure.

A procedural part has to be designed for every special case in order to regulate steps, accessibility, sequences and, if desired, decision-making.

Using the IBIS method sequences of steps can be identified which follow the logic of the planner's thinking. For example, it is one of the permanent iterations that a planner creates a lot of possibilities and then chooses one with which he will proceed. According to Rittel it is the sequence of generation of variety and its reduction by judgement. This corresponds to the sequence of an instrumental issue (Which possibilities exist?) and some deontic issues (Should the possibility A (B, C,...) be chosen?).

Rittel worked out in detail such an iterative routine (Rittel, 1988), which a conscious planner would follow each time he considers a measure (see Fig. 3.2)

Some pictures demonstrate a recent computer application concerning the planning controversy about the location of a rapid train system in south Germany. On the basis of Hypertext, a special HYPERIBIS was developed (Isenmann *et al.*, 1992). Its nodes are the different kinds of issues, positions, answers, arguments and sources. Topics are problem areas to which different issues may belong. Links relations are possible between all nodes. If a node is created, input of textual information is possible. Figure 3.3 shows which possibilities of further action at an actual treated node are given by a menu.

Figure 3.4 shows under the topic (new location for railway Stuttgart–Ulm) a deontic issue (should a new location be planned?), a list of positions and arguments and the text of two arguments.

Figure 3.5 shows the structure of the network created by systematic questioning and argumentation around that one issue (whether the H-location should be planned).

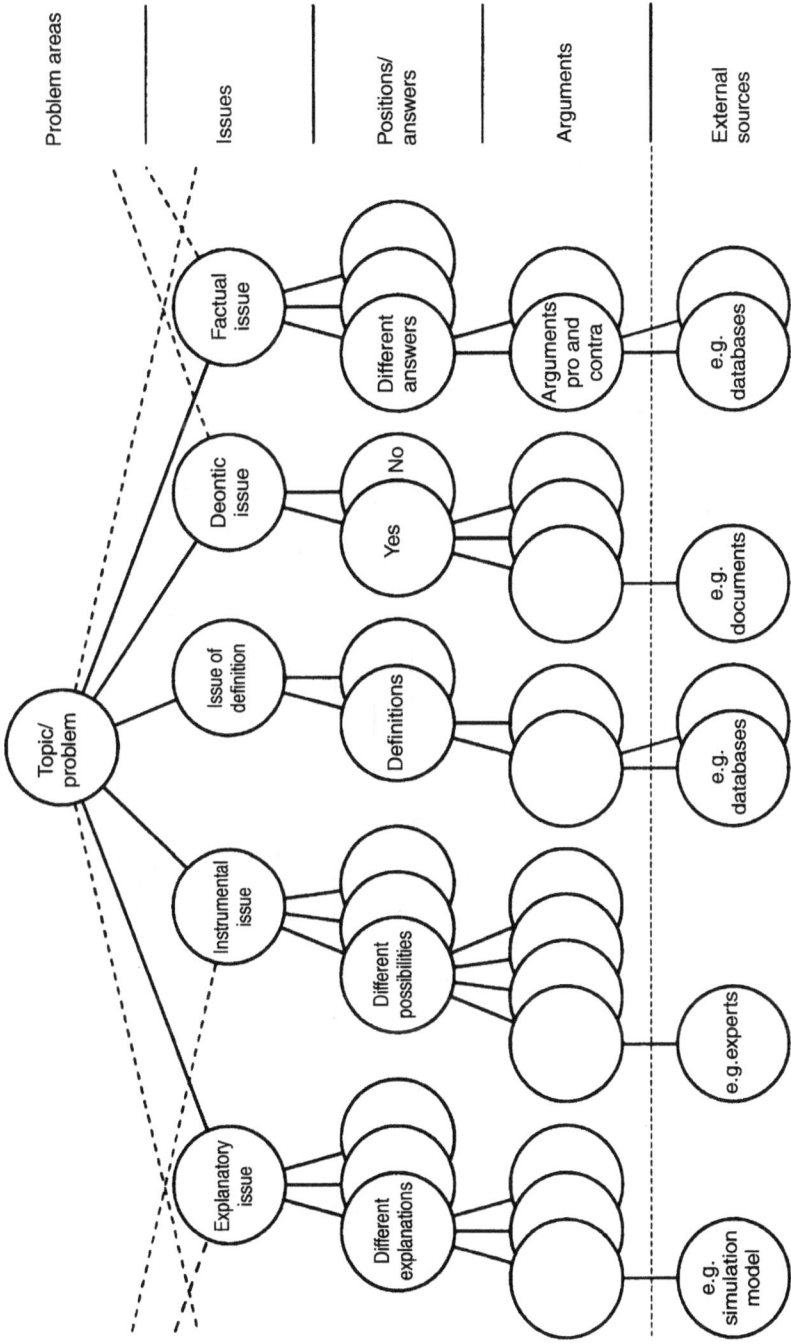

Fig. 3.1 Elements of IBIS. (After Kunz et al., 1980.)

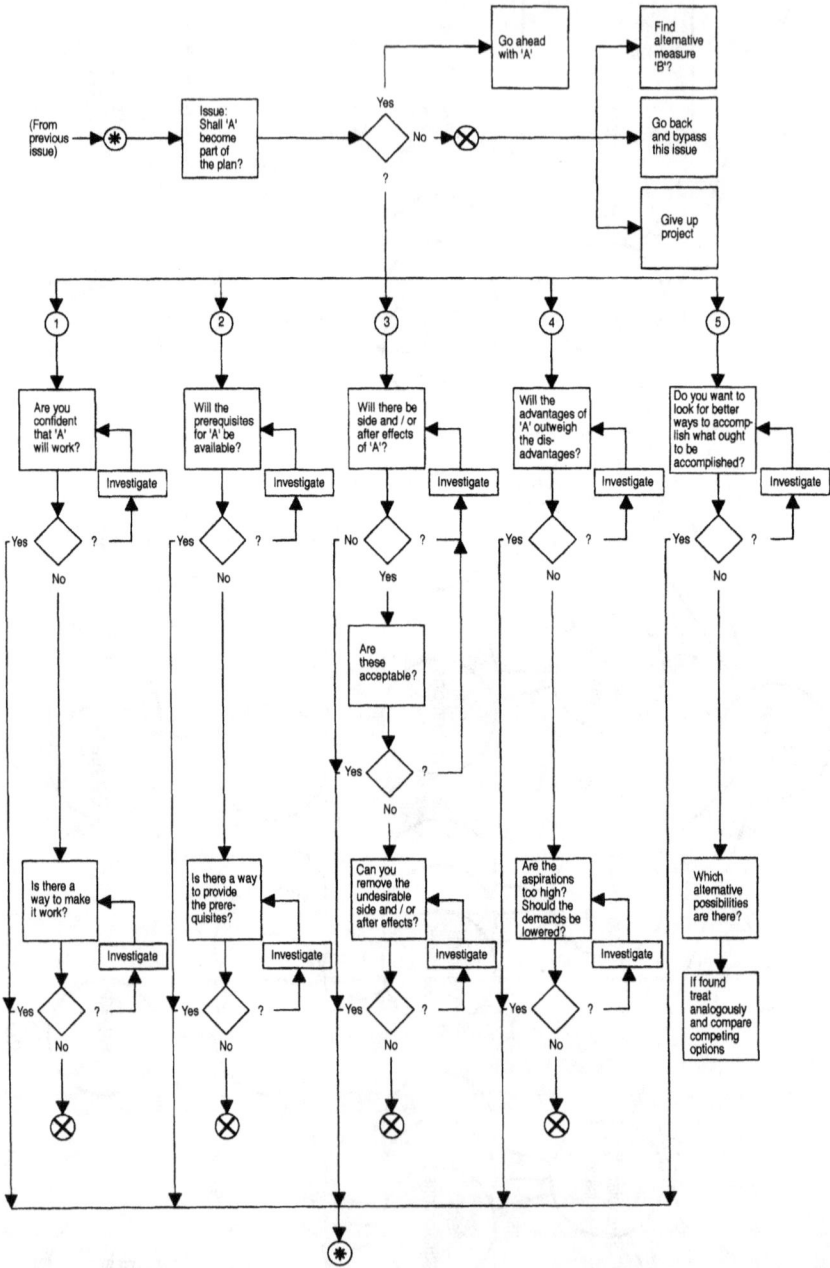

Fig. 3.2   Pattern of reasoning. (After Rittel, 1988.)

```
┌─────────────────────────────────────────────────────┐
│  Topic  new railway route Stuttgart - Ulm   quit  prnt  ↕│
│  The existing railway from Stuttgart to Ulm through the│
│  Filsvalley is a bottleneck in quality and capacity.  │
│  What could be done?                                   │
└─────────────────────────────────────────────────────┘
```

```
        ┌─────────────────────────────────────────────┐
        │  Arg  Computer Integrated Railroading   quit  prnt  ↕│
        │  The capacity of the existing routes can be increased up│
        │  to 30 % by Computer Integrated Railroading. Then new│
        │  routes would be unnecessary.                 │
        └──────────────────────┬──────────────────────┘
                               │  ──── Arg - Menu ────  │
                               │  • generation of argument 'to'│
                               │  • generation of argument 'against'│
┌──────────────────────────┐  │  • generation of argument 'for'│
│  Arg          quit  prnt  ↕│  ├──────────────────────┤
│  no shortening on travel time│  │                      │
│  Computer Integrated Railroading does│  │  • generation of issue │
│  not bring higher velocity and│  ├──────────────────────┤
│  therefore no shortening of traveltime.│  • integration of graph │
└──────────────────────────┘  ├──────────────────────┤
                               │  • treatment of unit  │
                               ├──────────────────────┤
                               │  • cancel references  │
                               ├──────────────────────┤
                               │  • graphical browser  │
                               └──────────────────────┘
```

Fig. 3.3 Menu at an argument node in HYPERIBIS. (After Isenmann *et al.*, 1992.)

If according to the theory the system represents the totality of planning, all support systems should have their place in the system. On the one hand it focuses all knowledge, which is relevant for a planning case, on the point of the acute planning issue. So all databases, documentation systems, literature and expert opinions are made accessible and included by references, interfaces or direct connection.

Material for the answers is also recruited from simulation models in the case of explanatory questions. Such a question could be, for example: 'What is the effect on one's perception if one places the staircase at a distance of x and a triangle of y opposite the entrance?'

The simulation model, which helps to produce an answer, may be a hand-drawn perspective, or produced by CAD. Every walk through a virtual reality is a test of the effects of planned measures, and so an answer to the question for consequences. Another simulation model could support the position that air pollution and less attractiveness for economic investment in consequence of cross-border traffic can only be hindered by road pricing.

One can imagine that all planning support systems have their places at the ends of a network of issues, positions/answers and arguments. An argumentative planning system like IBIS functions as a network, connecting the support systems under the focus of a planning problem.

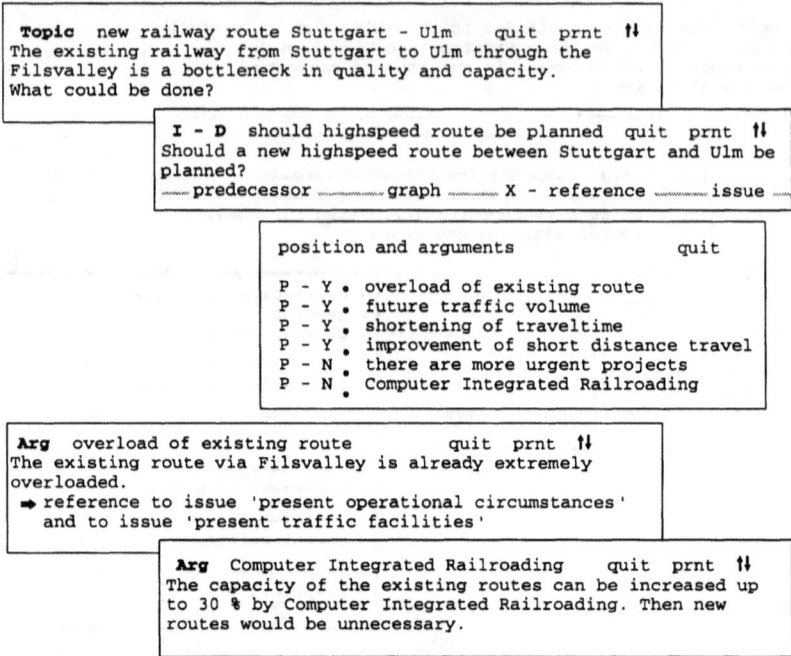

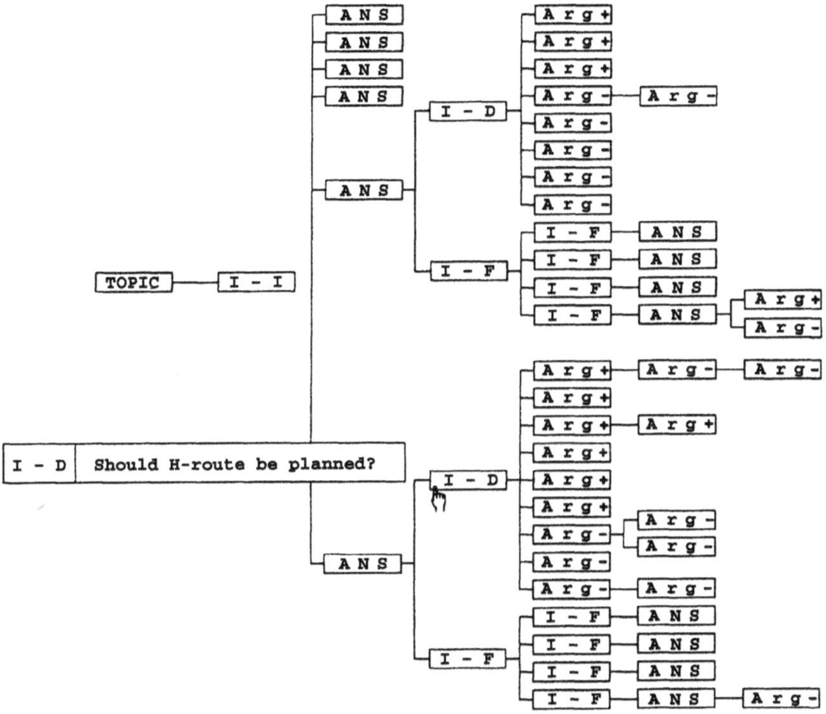

Fig. 3.5   Network in HYPERIBIS. (After Isenmann *et al.*, 1992.)

METHODS OF POWER-ACTING

Working with such a system that helps to activate and to communicate knowledge aids in preparing design decisions. They will not be easier. The more opponents, the more aspects and the more positions, the more difficult the decisions will be. They will, however, be based on a better foundation.

The decision itself belongs to the area of power relations. Here we proceed from the finding that the better argument does not necessarily win. (Who says which one it is?) Representatives of interests with much more power and bad arguments often influence decisions more. Decisions are made according to rules regulating the distribution of power. Classic distributions are:

1. The leader decides
2. The majority decides
3. A qualified majority decides (e.g. two-thirds)
4. As 2 or 3, but the leader has the right of veto

Recent research in political science doubts the best of all bad rules, the majority rule. They discuss other decision procedures (Guggenberger and Offe, 1984):

Table 3.1   Designer's/planner's knowledge and support systems

Type of issues or knowledge	Support systems
Factual knowledge (Is X the case? What is the case?)	Databases (documentations of objects, persons, literature, techniques, environmental pollution, locations, layout of transportation systems,...)
Deontic knowledge (Should X be the case?)	Evaluation procedures Discourse procedures Decision procedures Cost–benefit analysis Expert systems
Instrumental knowledge (What means, measures, techniques are there?)	Models of associations Morphologies Configuration graphs, dual graphs Systematic doubt Databases (e.g. constructions, building materials, active solar techniques, steel roofs, etc.)
Explanatory knowledge (what are the reasons for a status, what are the effects or consequences of a measure?)	Models – symbolic/mathematic – verbal – iconic – draft – cardboard models – 2D, 3D in computers – virtual realities Semantic differential
Definition knowledge (What is...?)	Lexicons, concepts

5. Only concerned people decide
6. Bargaining until consent or compromise is reached
7. Proportional consideration of interests
8. Arrangements similar to contracts with regard to minorities
9. Decentralization of decisions/principal of subsidiary
10. Self-help/self-administration/autonomy of client systems
11. Formal evaluation procedure with aggregation of partial judgements

Once cannot replace artificially judging which is inherent to every decision procedure. However, one can support the procedure by representing the form of the procedure in an algorithm.

Often the decision is preceded by an extensive power game with the means of power. There exists an abundant repertoire (Reuter, 1989). Means of power can be personal attributes like charm or charisma, display behaviour, rhetoric brilliance; material means such as money or weapons are common. Mental means such as expertise, patent holdership, advantages of information, being ahead in knowledge, use of media, become more and more effective. To have a function gives power.

Additional techniques of power include: to give information in well-measured doses; to establish irreversible facts; to divide large projects into pieces; to satisfy the need or desire for influence on decisions by offering symbolic decision-making; to pretend *Sachzwänge*; to make use of experts; to launch arguments via persons of public authority; to bring into play persons with special skills in argumentation; to divide opposing groups; to intimidate them; to spread a well-calculated rumour; to defame opponents; wrong citation; wrong information; to keep things secret; to mislead; to criminalize; to provoke; to infiltrate; to use institutional authority; to use newspapers or television.

Still other means of power, especially for those on the other side, are mobilization of concerned people, their solidarity, all forms of participation aiming at real influence on the decision process, counterplanning, recall, referendum, initiative, symbolic acts, civil disobedience, mobilization of public opinion, etc.

This quasi-Machiavellian neutral list of means and techniques of power does not implicate their acceptance. Those who want to work against the misuse of power effectively need an intimate knowledge about its phenomena and about the way they are used instrumentally.

At any time in a planning process there is a special constellation of the involved persons concerning their influence on a decision. However, any distribution of power does not determine the exit of a power game. The outcome cannot really be forecast. Distribution of power has always been unstable; it depends on changes in the base of power, the means of power, the amount of power, or the scope of power that someone has. One of the reasons for change can be found in the logic of power.

LOGIC OF POWER

We use a concept where power is a three-figure relation (Reuter, 1989). It is the relation between a holder of power, a subject of power, and the amount of directives the holder of power can or could get through against the subject. The following has to be valid in order to constitute a situation of power:

1. Holder A and subject B communicate (or could do so).
2. The holder A decides to give directives to the subject B (or could do so). (The term *directives* is used here to demarcate it from all other possible kinds of content of communication such as *statements* or *explanations*. The form of directives may range from command, via request,

wish, up to gestures, miming or an expectation of the subject based on conventions.)
3. The subject B judges (or would do so); the consequences of refusing to follow the directive are more detrimental for the subject than the consequences of observing it.
4. The subject B follows the directives of the holder A (or would do so in case of given directives).

If these conditions are given, there exists a situation of power. In the normal case, the holder A creates the situation by threatening the subject B with a measure. The subject B has to believe that the holder can execute the threatened measure.

Where is the room to move the margin? It lies in the possibility of A to decide to give no directives and of B to decide against a directive in spite of a threat. There is a calculation of B about a choice. Both results, to follow and to refuse, are possible. In the case of refusal, B risks the threatened measure or maybe he has a strategy of counter-power up his sleeve. The logical openness of the power game explains and stimulates the use of the means and strategies.

Normally the participating actors try to hold down their risk. Their weighting follows a calculus which we can represent. It is a calculus of mutual images: B thinks about how to react on a threat of A. A develops an image of the consideration of B and thinks about possible reactions. From this image of A, about the thinking of B, B for his part develops a new image and so on.

Figure 3.6 shows the scheme of the mutual estimation about the calculus of the respective other party. Figure 3.7 shows the first step, the image of B about A as well as considered reactions. Figure 3.8 shows the calculus of B, if A answers B's threat with a counter-threat.

One of the results of the analysis was that there is a limited number of possible behaviours, which come up again and again in the images of oneself and the others acting. And secondly that there are only a few possibilities in order to end the escalation of power-acting. One is that the threatening party makes concessions to the threatened one by him- or herself. Another one is that the parties bargain, which may end in a compromise that is satisfactory for both. So even power-acting seems to end up in argumentation.

Following the assumption that the unjustifiable use of power is not to be hindered by abstract ethical norms or by protagonists of a discursive ethic, it is better to rely on procedures that by their construction are directed against misuse of power. Such methods are (Reuter, 1989):

- Self-determination, self-organization, self-help in planning, financing, building.

```
                    ┌──────────────────────┐
                    │   A threatens B      │        Legend:
                    │     (D_A(B))         │         I   image of
                    └──────────────────────┘         R   reaction
                              │                      A,B parties
                              ▼                       D  threat
                    ┌─────────────────┬──────┐      D_A(B)  threat of A against B
                    │  I_B(D_A(B))    │ +R_B1│
                    └─────────────────┴──────┘
┌──────┬────────────────────────────┐      │
│ +R_A1│ I_A(I_B(D_A(B)) +R_B1)      │ ◄────┘
└──────┴────────────────────────────┘
        │                                    ┌──────────────────────────────┬──────┐
        └───────────────────────────────────│ I_B(I_A(I_B(D_A(B))+R_B1)+R_A1)│ +R_B2│
                                             └──────────────────────────────┴──────┘
┌──────┬────────────────────────────┐                    │
│ +R_A2│ I_A(I_B(I_A(..........)+R_A1)+R_B2)│ ◄───────────┘
└──────┴────────────────────────────┘
        │                                    ┌──────────────────────┬──────┐
        └───────────────────────────────────│   .................  │ +R_B3│
                                             └──────────────────────┴──────┘
┌──────┬────────────────────────────┐                    │
│      │                            │ ◄ ─ ─ ─ ─ ─ ─ ─ ─ ─ ┘
└──────┴────────────────────────────┘
```

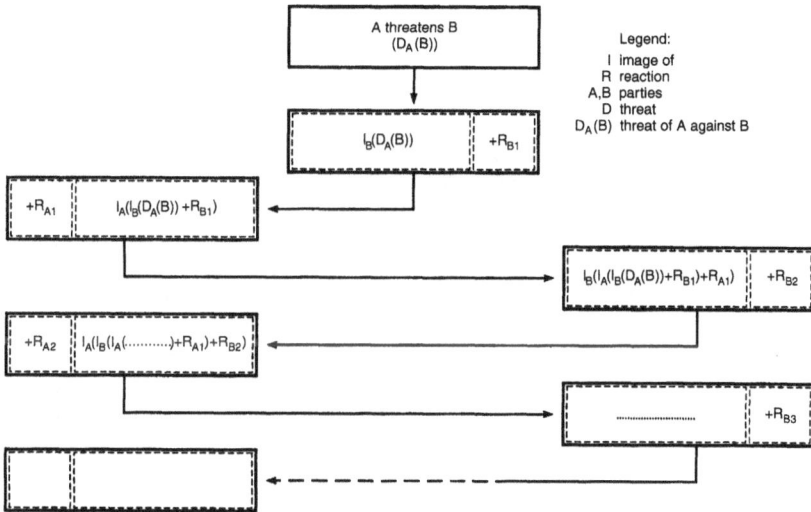

Fig. 3.6 Mutual images. (After Reuter, 1989.)

- Minimal planning (e.g. only a few definitive measures by the planner, the others are in the hand of the user).
- Reduction of the amount of power by formal installation of the right of participation or even the right of resistance, for those who did not participate in the planning decision.
- Reduction of range of power (only decisions with little effects in space and time on less people), reversibility of measures.
- Piecemeal engineering, strategy of small steps.
- More rights to minorities.
- Majority rule only for public not for private areas.
- Corporative agreements instead of voting.
- Proportional consideration of interest groups (see list above concerning decision procedures).
- Strengthening of legislation against executive.
- Strengthening of media as control power.
- Consumers' associations controlling the products of design and planning.

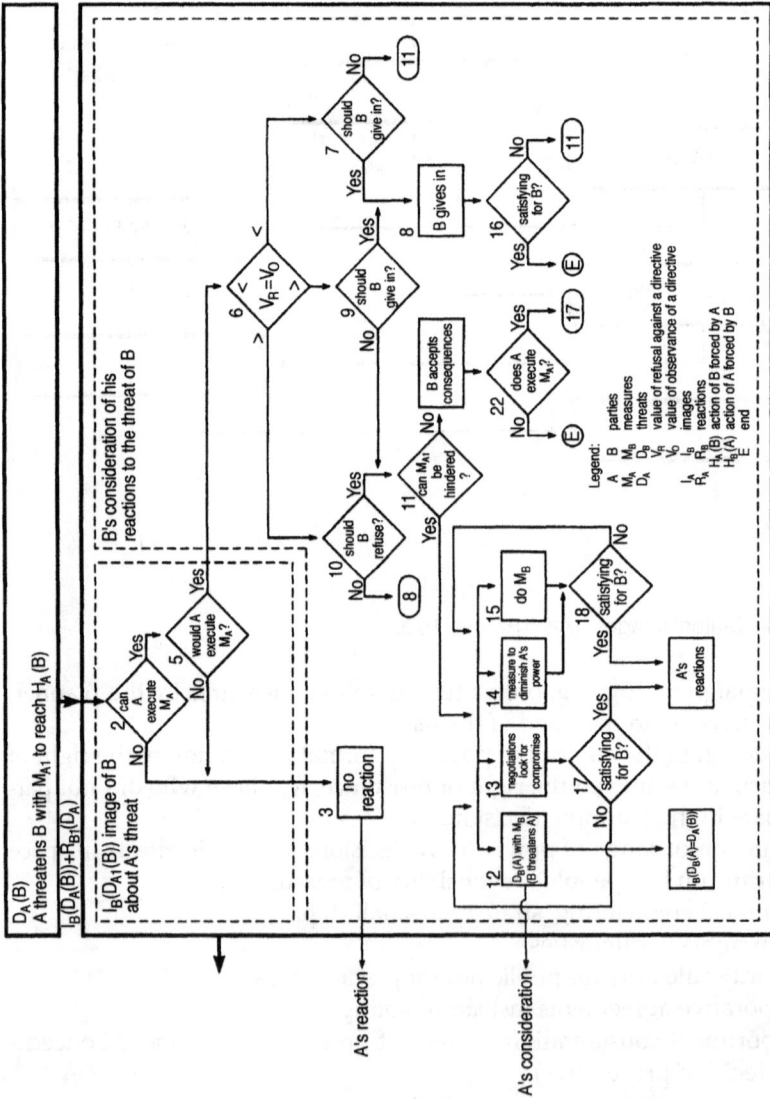

Fig. 3.7 Image of B about A and its own reactions. (After Reuter, 1989.)

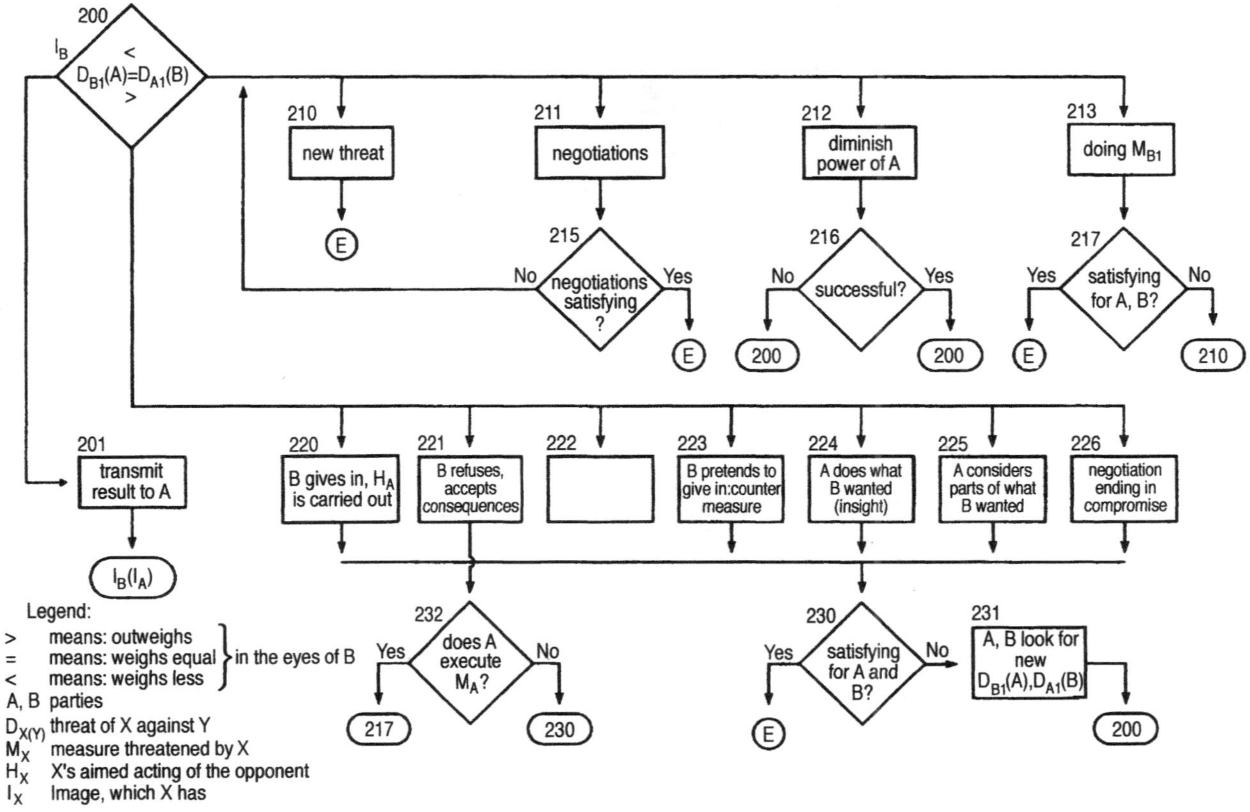

200 I_B

$D_{B1}(A) = D_{A1}(B)$ $\begin{array}{c}> \\ = \\ <\end{array}$

210 new threat → E

211 negotiations

215 negotiations satisfying? — Yes → E / No

212 diminish power of A

216 successful? — Yes → 200 / No → 200

213 doing M_{B1}

217 satisfying for A, B? — No → 210 / Yes → E

201 transmit result to A → $I_B(I_A)$

220 B gives in, H_A is carried out

221 B refuses, accepts consequences

222

223 B pretends to give in: counter measure

224 A does what B wanted (insight)

225 A considers parts of what B wanted

226 negotiation ending in compromise

230 satisfying for A and B? — Yes → E / No

231 A, B look for new $D_{B1}(A), D_{A1}(B)$ → 200

232 does A execute M_A? — Yes → 217 / No → 230

Legend:

> means: outweighs
= means: weighs equal } in the eyes of B
< means: weighs less

A, B parties

$D_{X(Y)}$ threat of X against Y
M_X measure threatened by X
H_X X's aimed acting of the opponent
I_X Image, which X has

Fig. 3.8 Calculus of B after counter-threat of A. (After Reuter, 1989.)

- To detect anonymity of planning for each measure, each plan, each design; there is always somebody who is responsible (there is no way out).

But this is a field of another generation of support systems.

REFERENCES

Guggenberger, B. and Offe, C. (1984) *An den Grenzen der Mehrheitsdemokratie*, Westdeutscher Verlag, Opladen.

Habermas, J. (1973) *Legitimationsprobleme im Spätkapitalismus*, Suhrkamp, Frankfurt.

Isenmann, S., Lehmann-Waffenschmidt, M., Reuter, W. and Schulz, K.P. (1992) Diskursive Umweltplanung: Computergestützte Behandlung 'bösartiger' Umweltprobleme, *Zeitschrift für angewandte Umweltforschung*, Jg. 5, A. 4, pp. 466–485.

Kunz, W. and Rittel, H. (1970) *Issues as Elements of Information Systems*, Working Paper No. 131, University of California, Institute of Urban and Regional Development, Berkeley.

Kunz, W., Reuter, W. and Rittel, H. (1980) *UMPLIS – Entwicklung eines Umweltplanungs-Informationssystems*, Saur, München.

Reuter, W. (1989) *Die Macht der Planer und Architekten*, Kohlhammer, Stuttgart.

Reuter, W. and Werner, H. (1983) *Thesen und Empfehlungen zur Anwendung von Argumentativen Informationssystemen*, Institut für Grundlagen der Planung, University of Stuttgart, Stuttgart.

Rittel, H. (1988) *The Reasoning of Designers*, Institut für Grundlagen der Planung, University of Stuttgart, Stuttgart.

Rittel, H. and Webber, M. (1973) Dilemmas in a General Theory of Planning, *Policy Sciences*, Vol. 4, No. 4, pp. 155–169.

Establishing the design professions' perspective on GIS

4

Noel Campbell and Thomas O'Reilly

INTRODUCTION

The growing use of the digital computer in business and the professions is often related to the reducing hardware costs, the increasing power of the software, the greater speed and the increasingly sophisticated interfaces that make it easier to use.

The importance of the digital computer to business and the professions is not only related to the computer itself but also to the wide range of associated new digital information technologies being developed (Megarry, 1985; *Scientific American*, 1991). They now include a variety of information-capturing tools, keyboards, the digital measuring instruments and scanners; of communication tools, transmitters, receivers, cables and switches; of output devices, televisions, videos, printers; and of stored library materials in bulletin boards and archives. All of these, it is argued, are changing the context within which business and the professions operate and require a positive response (Horrocks, 1992).

Information technology (IT) has developed in parallel with computer science. However, it is evident that a full understanding of the impact and use of IT in and for the built-environment professions involves just as much consideration of the practices employed in the professions as it does the systematic knowledge employed in computer science. This point is made about the development of technology in general, that it is as much related to craft, to the practice and skills used in 'doing and making', as it is to systematic, scientific knowledge (Fores and Rey, 1986; Archer, 1986). The development, application and refinement of IT involves a two-way process (Heath, 1972; Burns, 1984, p. 21). The devel-

Decision Support Systems in Urban Planning. Edited by Harry Timmermans. Published in 1997 by E & F N Spon. ISBN 0 419 21050 4

opment of the first spreadsheet, VisiCalc, for example, was based on the computer science knowledge of Bob Frankston linked to the needs of the business student Dan Bricklin (Saunders, 1988, p. 374). For computer-aided design (CAD) the link is with design, and CAD software houses are continuously responding to agents' comments about the needs of their users. Image processing, music synthesizing and hypermedia software are all developing in conjunction with varied practices and tasks.

This chapter is concerned only with those built-environment professions concerned with design. In this chapter they will be referred to as the design professions. In the UK context they include architecture, landscape architecture, aspects of civil engineering and planning. For the professions the impact of IT and its further development will depend not only on cost, speed, power, ease of use, etc., but also on the outcome of the interaction between the systematic knowledge of computer science on the one hand and professional practice on the other (fig. 4.1).

Geographical information systems (GIS) technology developed out of work and research in sections of geography, cartography and other spatially oriented disciplines. In part it grew out of the progressive development of computer science and the new methods developed for the capture, storage and analysis of digital information. The development is also related to new themes and issues being addressed by researchers in universities and in central and local government and by the development and use of new sources of information (Tomlinson, 1990, p. 18; Maguire, 1989, p. 173).

THE DOMINANT NARRATIVE

This chapter argues that from within the above context a dominant narrative has developed in GIS discussion and debate centred on what will be called here 'classical science', that is, on an emphasis on empiricism and logical positivism. The dominant narrative grows out of the intellectual common ground shared notably by geography on the one hand and computer science on the other (Johnston, 1991, p. 110). It is based on a well-defined set of principles and concepts and a discrete set of proprietary GIS technology products.

One strand in the development of GIS was in those departments of geography (and cartography) which in the 1960s and 1970s were inter-

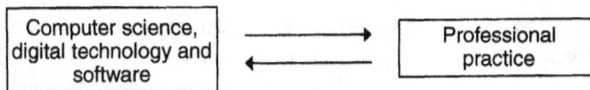

Fig. 4.1   Interaction between knowledge and practice.

ested in the use of mathematics, statistics and quantitative methods. They were early users of the new computer technology and the methods of computer science. These departments were interested in the science of the geographical or environmental subject matter. This included not only the subject matter of ecology, geology, botany, hydrology, etc., but also the interests of the human and social sciences in housing, hospitals, supermarkets, etc. Classical science provided an integrating perspective for this work (Holt-Jensen, 1988, p. 86ff.).

The second related strand developed out of computer science and the logical and systematic procedures which inform the software and hardware products, how they function, what they can do, and, by extension, how and where they should be applied. Computer science was and still is central to the development of GIS technology (Marble *et al.*, 1984; Burrough, 1986). Knowledge of computer science is necessary for an understanding of the wide range of associated products and instruments. Classical science provides an integrating perspective on knowledge about computer hardware and software, the principles and properties of GIS, and the science of its application.

Within the dominant narrative, within classical science, there is an easy and relatively unproblematic combination of the science of geography and the environment and the science of computing. In the narrative classical science, computer science and the functions of the GIS technology have primacy. The subject matter of geography or the professions become areas of applied classical science, applied computer science and applied GIS (Fig. 4.2).

The design professions use a variety of systems for handling geographical or spatial information. They regularly deal with issues and problems involving cross-referenced spatial and non-spatial information, but they are relative newcomers to the GIS debate and to the use of GIS technology. There is a strong sense that GIS technology will have a growing impact on professional practice and that the professions need to be involved in its development (Department of the Environment, 1987). This chapter argues that the involvement will need to challenge the dominant narrative and change the direction of GIS discussion away from the narrow focus on the concerns of classical science and spatial analysis towards a broader view, a cultural or professional view, which sees GIS as a tool for the spatial representation of objects and features.

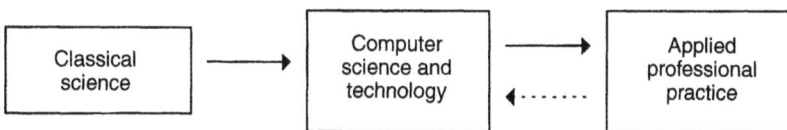

Fig. 4.2   The dominant narrative.

This chapter argues that the association of GIS principles and concepts with science and especially classical science results in a narrow view of 'geography', 'information' and 'system', and a misdirected sense of how the technology can and should be used in the design professional's practice.

CLASSICAL SCIENCE AND THE 'GEOGRAPHY' OF GIS

The adoption of the term 'geographical' in GIS reflects on its origin and is a pointer to the potential scope of its subject matter and also to the varied scales, perspectives and methodologies used in information gathering.

With the maturing of interest in GIS there have been attempts to refine the definition of the field. The UK surveying profession has shown an interest in the term 'land' in place of 'geographical' to produce 'land information systems' (Dale and McLoughlin, 1985). This narrows the scope of the subject matter of GIS and the scales of enquiry. It addresses land, property and development but it retains an interest in scientific survey and measurement and an interest in classifying and recording on an absolute, abstract, universal grid.

There are key players within mainstream GIS who seem happy to retain the term GIS but are proposing a view that effectively reduces the broad 'geographical' to the narrower 'spatial'. The term 'spatial' is arguably an appropriate substitution for the architect or the civil engineer, but the change in this case is towards seeing the old GIS become a new spatial science (Goodchild, 1990). This narrowing around science reduces the range of perspectives and methodologies involved in information gathering and interpretation.

This chapter argues that GIS viewed as a new spatial science is separated from the design professions by being more squarely located in computer science, mathematics and geometry. Geographical and/or design knowledge covers a wide range of subject matter, at different scales, using a variety of perspectives and methodologies including, but not limited to, those of classical science. The design professions are not solely concerned with scientific analysis and explanation.

Criticisms of the idea of a spatial science were already being raised during the 1960s and 1970s (May, 1970, p. 251). It was applied to a branch of geography – the new geography based on classical science. This was the very branch from which GIS grew (Johnston, 1991). The criticisms that applied to the new geography then apply to the spatial science view of GIS today. It is that, outside of the abstractions of mathematics, physics and geometry, there can be no independent science of space (Sack, 1980, pp. 84–85).

The idea that geography is a science of space is based on a Kantian view of space as a container (May, 1970). Space in this view had an independent existence and is capable of being described using an abstract, universal grid based on Eucliden geometry. This perspective clearly supports the use of the grid, the layer and the plane to locate spatial objects. These are primary elements in CAD and GIS technologies.

This Kantian view is controversial and was criticized for separating objects (substance or things) from space (Sack, 1980, p. 26). The counter-argument is that objects cannot be separated from space, that space is a property of objects. Space is not a container. Objects are primary not space. This supports Burrough's view that the database (of objects) is the primary element in a GIS with space as a property of a database object (Burrough, 1986, p. 7).

This criticism is developed further with the argument that there can be no science of space, only a science of objects, e.g. a science of geology or of botany.

These criticisms do not require a break in the association of geography and GIS with science. Geography and GIS are defined not by their objects (subject matter), but by knowledge that derives from their spatial perspective. Objects and space can combine in a synthesizing science which borrows its substance laws from the other object-oriented sciences but contributes understanding of the spatial outcomes (Holt-Jensen, 1988, p. 125ff.). Even outside of the generalizations and laws of science, each can act as a synthesizing discipline with a concern for the (unique) inter-play of objects and their spatial relations which gives rise to the particular qualities of places, localities and regions. This wider perspective on geography and GIS begins to incorporate questions and issues related to culture and the arts and also, arguably, the concerns of the design professions.

This chapter argues, then, that there are problems with geography, and by extension GIS, viewed as spatial science. The dominant narrative which adopts this view is in danger of moving the field in the direction of the abstractions of physics, geometry and mathematics and away from the practical concerns of the design professions.

CLASSICAL SCIENCE AND THE 'INFORMATION' OF GIS

In the GIS literature 'information' tends not to be problematized. The dominant view is that information is given and is independent of its context, already ordered and classified, that it is about 'facts' or 'things', rather than a part of a 'process' of being informed by science or some other perspective. Information is, however, a part of a search for order. It is embedded in a context which includes other objects, events or relationships, some of which may have been ignored. It is independent of the purposes of the person/author creating the information. Information technology can so easily decontextualize information, particularly as it is electronically stored and communicated.

The problem of information has not received enough attention in the GIS literature even though it is at the heart of the subject. It is beginning to be addressed in some critical discussions about IT (Liebenau and Backhouse, 1990; Poster, 1990; Roszak, 1986) and in critical discussions of the media including advertising (Morgan and Welton, 1986) and photography (Tagg, 1988).

The loosely ordered list of definitions outlined below shows the easy relationship between classical science and computer science through the common language of mathematics, algebra and geometry. Each is concerned with order and formal rules for organization and analysis. Only the last two definitions in the list come close to indicating the way information might relate to the design professions and to professional practice.

> Information is only the difficulty in transmitting the sequences (i.e. messages) produced from one information source.
> The distillation of data through its being processed results in the creation of information.
> The meaning of information is precisely the reduction in uncertainty.
> Information is a pattern or design that rearranges data for instrumental purposes.
> Information is knowledge communicated concerning some particular fact, subject or event.
> Information is data recorded, classified, organised, related or interpreted within context to convey meaning.
> > (Selected from Liebenau and Backhouse, 1990, p. 2)

Information for professional practice involves knowledge and understanding which are additional to those of classical science. It involves forms of recording and analysis that grow out of the different purposes of the professional, the different way they view places and environments, and the different significance they give to their observations and records and importantly their need to act and to intervene. Consider Heim's more professionally or culturally oriented treatment of information:

> Information is a unit of knowledge which by itself has only a trace of significance. Information presupposes a significance context but does not deliver or generate one. Because context does not come built in, information can be handled and manipulated, stored and transmitted at computer speeds. For us significant language always depends on the felt context of our limited experience. Infomania erodes our capacity for significance.
> > (Heim, 1992)

While the professions may borrow and use the methods and techniques of classical science, professional knowledge relates more directly to the complexity of construction, development, finance, the market, design or planning. Their purposes are to understand so as to act and make decisions and to intervene in particular situations or contexts. Their purpose is not simply scientific coding, analysis and explanation.

The dominant classical science perspective makes some aspects of the information-gathering process into peripheral themes and topics, e.g. privacy, ownership, copyright, freedom of information, tradable information, data protection, etc. The design professions arguably would wish to place these more centrally when considering IT and GIS. They relate to authorship, to context and to the way information is processed.

SCIENCE AND THE 'SYSTEM' IN GIS

We need to be cautious about the way computer-based systems relate to professional systems and the decision-making process.

Classical science and its formal language has the capacity to model systems which include not only the objects or elements of the system but the rules that define their interrelationship within both science and computer science. Systems in professional practice are less easy to characterize (Frank and Mack, 1991; Nijkamp and Scholten, 1993).

Professional systems are much more complex and varied: they may involve different languages; different conventions and codes; different procedures and rules; they are as likely to be informal as to be formal; to involve human language terms, conventions and procedures as well as machine language terms, conventions and procedures; to be intuitive and to be instrumental; etc. They are affected by personal, social or political factors, which affect not only information gathering, but also the management and use of the system and its outputs (Elkins, 1991; Medyckyj-Scott, 1989).

Some aspects of professional systems may be made internal to a formal computer-based system, but not all. Professional systems depend upon a complex dialogue between professionals themselves, between professionals and their context, and between the professionals and their various IT tools.

These more open, interactive systems can be thought of as pseudo-GIS. They allow a number of contributing elements in different arrangements. Word-processed files can contribute to systems at defined times during a transaction process. Standard tables in spreadsheets or databases can contribute as parts of systems of formal coding or interaction between professionals or professionals and their clients (Poster, 1990). Some aspects of professional systems of practice may be expressed in computer software, some may be external and more personally defined, residing in those personal, social and political contexts which also influence professional decision-making. The GIS literature tends to see 'system' as one which is, or should be, integrated and internalized in the computer. This chapter suggests that this overstated view of the technology's potential again grows out of the dominant classical science perspective on GIS.

This chapter is critical of the view that GIS is limited to classical science or that it is a new spatial science. This view, if it doesn't confuse the distinction between GIS principles and concepts and GIS technology, then it combines them within the framework of the language of mathematics, algebra and geometry. GIS drawn in this direction may contribute to abstract theoretical knowledge but this chapter argues that it will fail to address professional knowledge, understanding and practice.

GIS EDUCATION AND GIS IN LOCAL GOVERNMENT PRACTICE

The dominant narrative has also informed the way GIS has entered higher education and local government. Local government was one of the earliest and is one of the most important users of the technology.

GIS EDUCATION

The approach taken to GIS in higher education is that it should involve education and not training. It is argued that a GIS syllabus should focus on the knowledge about GIS principles and concepts, not just the operation of a software package – certainly not one software package, which would be GIS training. The classical science approach which dominates the published syllabus statements on *education about* GIS introduces knowledge about coordinate systems, raster and vector data structures, databases, etc. (Goodchild and Kemp, 1990; Unwin, 1990; Burrough, 1986). The GIS educated student is being drawn into a body of abstract knowledge in the disciplines at the heart of computer science, i.e. mathematics, algebra, geometry and physics. Mainstream GIS is not presented as *instruction and training in how to use* GIS tools to assist the existing practices of the disciplines and professions, as is the case with cartography or quantitative methods and statistics. Instead, it is professional knowledge and practice which is secondary, an 'application', just as data protection, copyright and privacy are 'issues'.

GIS IN LOCAL GOVERNMENT PRACTICE

Outside the universities the departments of central and local government showed early interest in GIS technology. They contain large quantities of spatially referenced information (Campbell and Masser, 1992).

Topographic mapping provides a base and the national grid a geographical reference system for additional record-keeping, inventory and archiving. It was perceived that the use of GIS technology would prevent unnecessary duplication, would increase speed, would increase efficiency, would reduce costs and would support strategic decision-making. Recent UK survey results indicate a different outcome (Campbell, 1991). There is evidence that these expectations were too ambitious. Despite the use of an absolute grid and careful classification and measurement, it has become clear that information gathered for one purpose is not necessarily suitable for another. There have been problems of data conversion, data classification, measurement, error checking and the integration of data. The costs tended to be underestimated and there were often no cost savings. The technology has influenced inventory and routine record-keeping but it does not contribute to strategic decision-making in the way some expected. There are reports of its under-use, of lack of 'ownership' of the systems by staff and the separation of the technical gurus from those directly involved in planning and providing the services (Allinson, 1993).

Many of these recent, critical observations are also made about the application of IT in general (Roszak, 1986; Weisenbaum, 1980; Lyons, 1988) including, for example, the use of management information systems (Keen *et al.*, 1991). In part they are a reaction to an overstatement of the promise of the technology by those who developed and sold the software. In the case of proprietary GIS, this chapter argues that the problems reflect the poverty of a classical science-based narrative and the lack of understanding of areas of local government or professional practice. While the technology may assist with routine inventory and organization, it is clear that neither it nor social science theory has reached a level of development which can support strategic decision-making.

THE SHORTCOMINGS OF THE DOMINANT NARRATIVE

The dominant classical science-based narrative has a number of shortcomings when viewed from the perspective of the professions in general. These are:

1. Professional practice uses not only classical science knowledge, concepts and methodologies but others as well. It is concerned not only with (scientific) explanation but with other forms of understanding.
2. Professional practice is concerned not only with interpretation and analysis but also with defining standards and norms; with decision-making; with action and control; and with planning and design.
3. Professionals use formal codes and rules, formal languages, other than those associated with mathematics, algebra, geometry and physics.

4. Professional practice incorporates into judgements, decisions and actions informal aspects of understanding based on experience, precedent and intuition.
5. Professional practice involves the use of systems which are defined more in terms of human factors than technology.

A PARADIGM SHIFT

This chapter develops a cultural or professional perspective on GIS which has the following characteristics:

1. It begins by seeing GIS principles, concepts and practices as already a part of professional practice (as they are of geography) but capable of being extended and refined by the use of information technology tools. Almost all professional practices use word-processing software to store, edit and reproduce text; use spreadsheets and databases for coding and arranging numbers and text in tables; and use graphical packages for digitizing drawing, plotting, etc.
2. It sees GIS skills acquisition and training as a part of professional education (like statistics and drafting) and not as a separate discipline.
3. It encourages critical judgement about the level of technology penetration into existing practices. The technology might involve the use of: proprietary GIS (e.g. ArcInfo); pseudo-GIS (e.g. spreadsheets, databases and a linked mapping package); or no GIS technology as possible outcomes.
4. It encourages a critical appraisal of the advantages and disadvantages of GIS technology in the professions.
5. It encourages professional participation and research in GIS.

A CULTURAL AND PROFESSIONAL PERSPECTIVE

The use of the new information technologies is not confined to science nor to the computer as a numerical engine. The critical analysis of the new IT receives attention in the social sciences (Siefert *et al.*, 1989), in fine art (Jenkins, 1992), in law (Kapor, 1991) and in media studies (McQuail, 1987). From the cultural perspective the new information technologies are described as a part of a sequence of developments from speech, to writing, to print, to the electronic media (Compaine, 1988; Ong, 1982), which challenge old disciplines and practices and offer new possibilities of expression and communication.

The professions in general are involved in a wide range of uses of IT for organization, management, control, design, planning, or communication with clients, etc. This chapter proposes an approach to IT and GIS which is centred on the needs of the design professions. The technology

is treated as a medium within which ideas can be represented. It can deal with words and the written language of the humanities, with numbers and tables and the algebraic symbols of science, with graphical forms and shapes and with the world of design.

This approach encompasses a distinction which some would wish to make between observations that originate in the 'real' world, the surveyed, topographic map and remotely sensed image, and those which originate in the 'world of the mind', the design, the architectural drawing and the plan. These very different representations both belong in a GIS (Van Der Schans, 1990). A GIS is potentially as much a tool for design or planning, organization and control as it is for scientific or spatial analysis. It is as much a tool for 'true' statements as for advertisements, propaganda and falsehood (Tagg, 1988; Pickles, 1992).

It is as valid to locate professional practice within a cultural as within a classical science perspective. A cultural perspective on the professions not only references analysis and explanation in the sciences, but also understanding in the humanities and doing and making in design (Archer, 1986). These different perspectives involve different languages and terms. Objects and spaces are represented in different ways. All of them have an influence on the use of the computer and the new electronic media.

This approach is holistic, but unlike the classical science perspective it begins by uniting the objects and spaces; the author and subject; the professional enquiry and the wider context. The approach focuses on those things which can be treated systematically, on the codes, practices and procedures which define and give direction to professional life. Technology is then treated as a tool which people use, to change, and maybe challenge, existing codes, practices and procedures including their own work or the work of other people. The approach helps to give insight into the tensions surrounding the introduction of GIS technology and its value for the built-environment professions.

PURPOSE, DISCOURSE, CONVENTIONS AND REPRESENTATIONS

Foucault's work gives insight into the way the use and influence of IT on social and cultural life can be assessed (Poster, 1990, pp. 69–98). Applied here to the professions the argument is that the purposes of the professions give rise to a discourse; a set of conventions and procedures; specialized codes, terms and forms of representation which bring order and serve to structure professional life.

In the professional context, and as the essence of professional activity, interpretation, analysis and design are guided by code, convention, procedure and protocol. These are established and given authority by the history of decisions made by the profession. The professions not only use the codes, conventions, etc., to control, act in, design, change and understand their world, but also to maintain the importance, power and status of the profession. They are united in a common systematic education, rules of membership. They use specialized languages, including sets of terms, defined by conventions and protocols which regulate the events for which they take responsibility. The agreed practices and procedures grow out of the internally organized debates. Externally they engage with politics and the state, and are influenced by new laws, statutes, circulars and guides. Central and local level interact with the design professions and exercise control over land title; ownership and registration; taxation and other fiscal controls; enumeration of the population; topographic survey for defence; resources management; etc. These activities give rise to national conventions for the representation of property boundaries (Larsson, 1991, pp. 29–56), topography, demography (Dewdney, 1983, pp. 1–15), etc., all of which are relevant to the use of GIS technology. Different national histories and different views about the role of the state, ownership, wealth, etc., result in different conventions and cause problems for comparisons between European Community countries and for European Community policy-making. These are already being confronted as the influence of the European Union grows (Arnaud *et al.*, 1993; Lievesley and Masser, 1993).

The members of the design professions also engage in social worlds and with the structures and bureaucracies of other organizations. Tagg outlines, for example, the way the new technology of the photograph in the late nineteenth century became authoritative evidence in the debate about public health and slum clearance in Leeds, England. That new technology was used by the professionals to support their case in the courts against the wishes of some of the local residents (Tagg, 1988, pp. 117–152). The actions of the professions may also be challenged by wider social reactions and movements which in a longer timescale may produce changes in professional practice.

PURPOSE, DISCOURSE AND THE PROFESSIONS

Foucault's work helps to draw a connection between the purposes of the professions, the discourses they engage in and the tools which are used. The built-environment professions are differentiated in different ways in the nations of Western Europe and design is linked to a range of professional practices. In the UK the purpose of the architect and civil engineer is broadly to design and complete a structure at an agreed quality and cost by an agreed time. They have a narrower focus on a specific site, the materials of construction, the construction process and cost in the market. The landscape architect's purposes are similar but the interest relates to the processes in the natural environment where design and construction have different meaning. Cost remains significant and geographical scope is likely to be greater. The purpose of the planner in the public sector is broadly to exercise control over development and to plan the environment for the future on behalf of the public or the State. They address the natural and artificial environments and processes.

Different purposes and discourses point to different codes, conventions and procedures which are formally and systematically developed and used in the different professions. These in turn indicate where the traditional system and practice may be supported, changed or improved by the new GIS technology. All of the design professions are involved in different objects of study to be coded and treated in different ways, but they have a common interest in database technology to organize, manage and control their different types of information. All are also involved in some form of spatial representation, for management and control, or for planning or for design. From this starting point the value of GIS technology for the design professions can receive critical consideration.

THE DESIGN PROFESSIONS AND THE TREATMENT OF OBJECTS

In developing a critical approach to GIS for the design professions, two points from the debate in geography need to be made. The first is the primacy of the objects of the professions. Geography and the professions need to be object-oriented. Space is directly related but secondary in the sense that there is no place for an independent science of space and no use for GIS as a tool of spatial science. The primacy of objects underlines the importance of the database as a tool even for the design professions. The second point from the debate is that there is a place for GIS technology as a synthesizing tool, where the rules or laws are borrowed from other substance sciences and the GIS is used to evaluate the spatial outcomes. The design professions' interest extends to other purposes involving organization, management and control, design and intervention, and forms of evaluation and understanding in addition to explanation and scientific synthesis (Fig. 4.3).

The different professions' purposes mean that objects are systematically described using different codes and measures, etc., for example 'The Standard Method of Measurement' agreed by the Royal Institute of Chartered Surveyors and the Building Employers Federation (RICS, 1987) and 'The Code of Measuring Practice' agreed between the RICS and the Incorporated Society of Valuers and Auctioneers (RICS, 1988). The need for different kinds of knowledge about objects can require different descriptions of space.

Classical science

Purpose

Substance rules → Explanation → Spatial outcome

Professions:

Purpose

Substance rules, codes, conventions, procedures → Organisation, management, control, design, planning → Spatial outcome

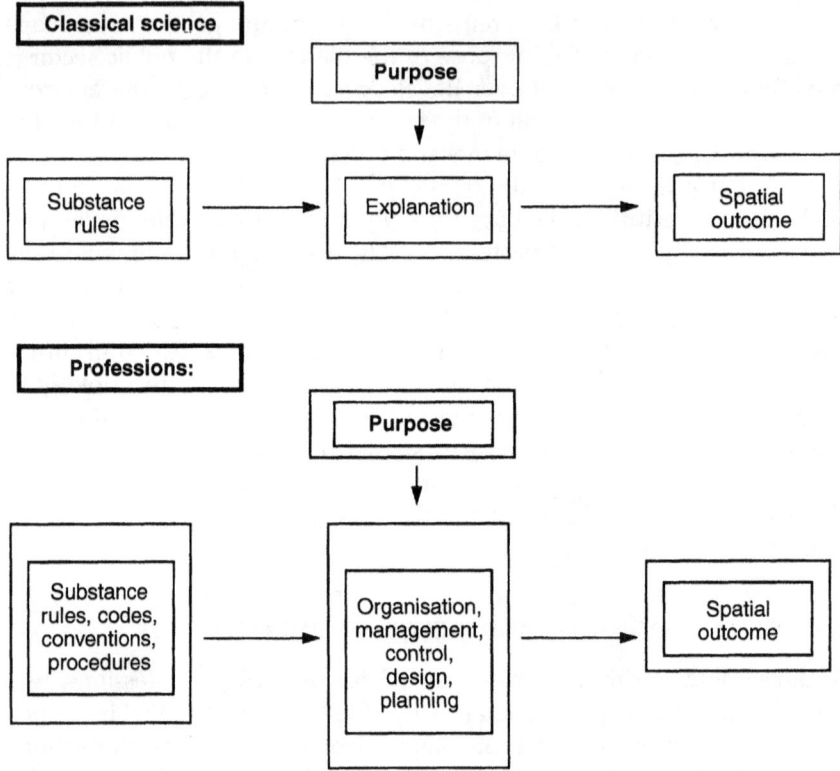

Fig. 4.3 Comparison of the treatment of objects by classical science and the design professions.

THE DESIGN PROFESSIONS AND THE TREATMENT OF SPACE

If the design professions are to use current proprietary GIS systems, then they are committed to coordinates and a continuous Euclidean grid. This next section questions the necessity of the coordinates and grid and looks at alternative conventions used for describing spatial form and relative locations.

The continuous Euclidean grid

Only in some cases is there a need for a continuous space and therefore for proprietary GIS technology. This description of space is useful where the purpose is to organize, manage and maintain a continuous spatial record system, describing spatial objects by their coordinates. GIS is used in central and local government for this purpose and spatial analysis is used. However, the process of planning involves other forms of evaluation, analysis leading to decision-making, and is less directly affected by GIS. The demand for local government GIS seems to derive from its responsibility for borough-wide understanding of demography, employment, transport, housing, environment, etc.

The discontinuous space

Some of the design professions' purposes do not require a continuous grid. Space may be treated as discontinuous for the purposes of a particular study or project. In a study of disrepair in a local authority's housing estates, a map may be required for each estate to show objects such as buildings, roads and open spaces, etc., but a name may be used to show the relative locations of estates across the whole local authority area. This again points to the importance of the database for the analysis of disrepair, but a separate CAD system may be adequate to show the spatial associations within the separate estates and the proposed improvements. The functions of proprietary GIS technology may be unnecessary or under-used.

'Visualization'

Visualization is concerned with the final representation and display of spatially arranged objects and not with the processes connected with management, control, design, etc., which relate object to object and object to space.

The photograph as visualization

The shape, form and relative location of objects can be illustrated using photographs. They can serve different discourses and purposes, cultural and professional as well as scientific. Photographs involve conventions related to, for example, perspective, positioning, lighting and colour. Conventions are carefully applied where a photographic image enters a discourse as formal evidence (Tagg, 1988, pp. 60–65).

In a discourse design professions may be happy with, and may even prefer, certain highly conventionalized images such as those produced by GIS technology. Scanned, digital images ('photographs') may be added or substituted when reference is being made to a wider public. While these 'photographs' are subject to certain conventions, they are often more accepted, more easily read, more 'realistic', more holistic, less formal, less geometric, less obviously modelled and rules-bound than the products of GIS technology. These, of course, involve quite different representations of objects and their relative locations. The oblique photograph does not have a formal grid and it does not allow for changes in the arrangement of objects or of perspective. Some modern databases can store a scanned digital image as an attribute of an object. Hypermedia technology allows a walk through a raster representation of a building or other space. For some purposes these treatments of space may be more appropriate than objects defined strictly by coordinates on a Euclidean grid.

The artist's impression as visualization

Computer-generated images can be used as a base for drawing and painting. Alternatively images can be 'improved' by texturing (the use of stochastic or other mathematical processes might claim to be scientific); masking, draping, rendering; lighting or by touching up using fine art techniques and skills. These add extra detail, texture, colour, etc., to produce greater 'realism'. These practices reflect on the effect of the conventions and rules on the general public which the design professions are otherwise happy to use.

Techniques related to visualization are independent of the principles which govern the way objects and spaces are treated in a GIS.

The zone or region

Where relative locations are described in broad zones and regions which are frequently referenced in the profession, then a simpler mapping package rather than a GIS may be more appropriate.

The symbol or icon

There are many other conventions for dealing with the shape and form of an object besides the use of a name. Symbols and icons can be used for frequently used shapes and forms. CAD packages have libraries of symbols which relate to the needs of different design professions, e.g. types of trees or different motor vehicles. The design professions are involved in creating and setting standards for the development of these libraries just as they have been in the past in relation to traditional media and practices.

The name

An extreme, yet simple, alternative to the grid is a name. Where the shape or form of an object or the relative location of objects need only a name to describe them, then there is no need for spatial representation, nor for a proprietary GIS. Names may be strictly related to the conventions and procedures used in the professions. Other names such as 'sash window' or a 'spiral staircase' immediately create a mental image of their shape and form. Relative locations can be evoked by names as in 'London', 'Birmingham' and 'Manchester'. In certain design contexts the naming is a perfectly adequate way to describe space. It may evoke whole sets of spatial and non-spatial associations and references which may be internal to a design profession discourse and centred on discrete codes and conventions. For example, in local government planning much spatial information is in the form of named streets or postal districts (Hardie, 1993) which may usefully and adequately be combined with information about age, tenure, land use, etc. Names can be associated with other information in a spreadsheet or database. It may be less systematic, less formal and less rigorously defined than in classical science but it can still contribute to geographical or spatial knowledge. The interpretation of this type of information relates to discourses in the humanities and social sciences.

PLANNING DESIGN AND FLEXIBLE SPACE

Electronic sketchpads and paintboxes allow the design professional to create graphical images on a raster grid, but these do not differentiate objects nor can their attributes be stored. There are interesting 'Windows', hypermedia and even spreadsheet developments which allow objects (buttons or icons) in one graphical plane to reference information elsewhere. The entry of object-oriented thinking and programming into these worlds, and GIS (e.g. Rojas-Vega and Kemp, 1993), may provide even more appropriate tools to match the needs of the design professions.

GIS was designed to allow empirical detail to be inserted in an absolute gridded space. For planning, particularly for organization, management and control, GIS has proven to be a useful tool despite the constraints in its design. It may even be possible to automate some planning controls by building rules into the GIS governing acceptable development, e.g. related to density, height, access or use. In contrast, where planning involves thinking about the future, GIS technology has not provided the benefit it at first promised (Allinson, 1993). It seems that these activities, and also design, are organized on the basis of different principles to those used in current GIS and may require different tools (Fig. 4.4).

Strategic planning and design are never completely free from constraints and they do need to work within certain rules, conventions, codes. However, planning for the future and design also involve challenging some rules, conventions and codes to consider new objects, with new forms, involving new geometries and new sets of spatial relationships. A high-speed train may change the whole geometry and pattern of movement in a region, or grants to farmers may alter aspects of the rural

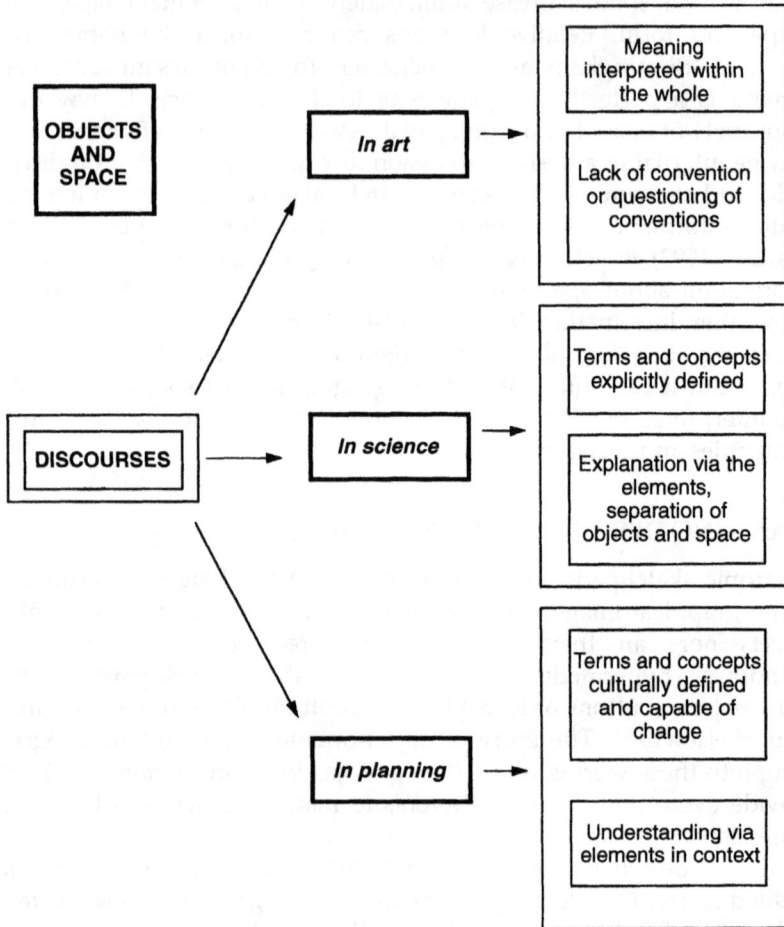

Fig. 4.4   Comparison of the treatment of objects and space in art, science and planning.

landscape. The Euclidean container does not allow for flexible thinking about new objects, new spaces, new designs. This is not a question of computer speed but of the ability to define and change objects and their relationships quickly. It involves thinking through the type of space occupied by an object and the need to consider the interaction between different types of spaces. It involves moving between abstract and conceptual thoughts and closely observed existing landscapes.

Although GIS has become associated with Euclidean geometry and the grid, it may be possible to provide the tools for future planning and design. Strategic planning and design require flexibility to describe objects and their spatial arrangements in ways which mirror the creative mind. The systems would need to move between names, abstract shapes and icons to detailed forms and precise spatial relationships. GIS at this stage in its development cannot provide this high level of sophistication, flexibility and interaction between user and system and between objects and spaces, and while it is based on the Euclidean grid it never will.

CONCLUSION

Professions are continually responding to and acting in new situations and will respond to GIS, to the new electronic media. The design professions will wish to 'own' and use GIS technology when it directly engages with codes and conventions they already employ. They will respond to threatening changes happening elsewhere and will want to retain ownership or exercise control over their traditional territory.

Policy-making at the European level is creating a demand for comparable information and in time is likely to influence professional practice. Similarly the creation of the single European market is also likely to challenge differences in the national design conventions and procedures.

This chapter is addressed to built-environment professionals. The chapter develops and outlines a professional perspective on GIS, that is, one where the emphasis is deliberately centred on professional knowledge and practice. The aim is to change the focus of discussion on GIS so that it is centred on the needs of the professions. The aim is to arrive at a better understanding of where the professions' needs can be met by the use of GIS tools and where the professions' interests lie in the further development of GIS.

Built-environment professions already use systems for handling geographical information. The chapter has attempted to outline a perspective on professional conduct and practice which helps to form an assessment of the value of GIS technology. The chapter is aimed at stimulating discussion and research but some critical points emerge. There can be no doubt about the value of the database even for the design professions. The Euclidean grid serves the purposes of some aspects of government planning. For other design profession purposes CAD, mapping or visualization packages, or routines attached to a database, may be more appropriate and cost-effective. Object-oriented techniques may be developed to relate more closely to the nature of the design process but flexibility in dealing with objects will need to be matched with flexibility in dealing with space, certainly for design and strategic planning. Finally this perspective makes it seem unlikely that it will be possible to make internal to a closed computer system the range and variety of codes, conventions and procedures which define professional discourse. It seems most likely that professionals will be interacting with an electronic medium using an increasingly sophisticated range of tools.

REFERENCES

Allinson, J. (1993) Breaking the Third Wave: The Demise of GIS. *Planning Practice and Research*, 8 (2), 30–33.

Archer, B. (1986) The Three R's. In Cross, A. and McCormick, R. (eds), *Technology in Schools, A Reader*. Open University Press, Milton Keynes, pp. 49–56.

Arnaud, A.M., Craglia, M., Masser, I., Salge, F. and Scholten, H. (1993) The Research Agenda for the European Science Foundation's GISDATA Scientific Programme. *Int. J. Geographical Information Systems*, 7 (5), 463–470.

Burns, A. (1984) *New Information Technology*. Ellis Horwood, Chichester.

Burrough, F.A. (1986) *Principles of Geographical Information Systems for Land Resources Assessment*. Clarendon Press, Oxford.

Campbell, H. (1991) *Organisational Issues and the Utilization of Geographical Information Systems*. Regional Research Laboratory Initiative, Discussion Paper No. 9, University of Sheffield.

Campbell, H. and Masser, I. (1992) *GIS in Local Government: An Overview of Take-up and Implementation*. Dept of Town and Regional Planning, University of Sheffield.

Compaine, B.M. (1988) Information Technology and Cultural Change: Toward a New Literacy. In Compaine, B.M. (ed.), *Issues in New Information Technology*. Ablex, New Jersey, pp. 145–178.

Dale, P.F. and McLoughlin, J.D. (1985) *Land Information Management – An Introduction with Special Reference to Cadastral Problems in Third World Countries*. Clarendon Press, Oxford.

Department of the Environment (1987) *Handling Geographical Information*. Report of the Committee of Enquiry, Chaired by Lord Chorley. HMSO, London.

Dewdney, J.C. (1983) Censuses Past and Present. In Rhind, D. (ed.), *A Census Users Handbook*. Methuen, London, pp. 1–15.

Elkins, P. (1991) Getting the 'Mix' Right – Reflections on GIS Project Management. *Mapping Awareness*, 5 (9), 14–17.

Fores, M.J. and Rey, L. (1986) Technick: the Relevance of a Missing Concept. In Cross, A. and McCormick, R. (eds), *Technology in Schools, A Reader*. Open University Press, Milton Keynes.

Frank, A.U. and Mack, D.M. (1991) In Maguire, D.J., Goodchild, M.F. and Rhind, D.W. (eds), Language Issues for GIS. *Geographical Information Systems*, Vol. 1. Longmans, New York.

Goodchild, M.F. (1990) Keynote Address: Spatial Information Science. *Proceedings, Fourth International Symposium on Spatial Data Handling*, Zurich, Vol. 1, pp. 13–14.

Goodchild, M.F. and Kemp, K. (1990) *The NCGIA Core Curriculum*. National Centre for Geographical Information and Analysis, University of Santa Barbara, California.

Hardie, P. (1993) Using a Gazetteer and Spatial Analysis to Integrate Local Authority Records. *Mapping Awareness*, 7 (10), 28–30.

Heath, F.G. (1972) Origins of the Binary Code. *Scientific American*, August, pp. 76–83.

Heim, M. (1992) The Dark Side of Information. *The Independent* newspaper, 30 December.

Holt-Jensen, A. (1988) *Geography, History and Concepts*. Paul Chapman, London.

Horrocks, S. (1992) Networks and Communications. In Feenan, R. and Dixon, T.J. (eds), *Information and Technology Applications in Commercial Property*. Macmillan, London.

Jenkins, J. (1992) And Then What? *The Independent* newspaper, 29 February.

Johnston, R.J. (1991) *Geography and Geographers*. Edward Arnold, London.

Kapor, M. (1991) Civil Liberties in Cyberspace. *Scientific American*, September, pp. 116–120.

Keen, J., Buxton, M. and Packwood, T. (1991) Complexity and Contradiction in NHS Computing. *Public Money and Management*, Autumn, pp. 23–29.

Larsson, G. (1991) *Land Registration and Cadastral Systems: Tools for Land Information Management*. Longman, Harlow, Essex.

Liebenau, J. and Backhouse, J. (1990) *Understanding Information: An Introduction*. Macmillan, London.

Lievesley, D. and Masser, I. (1993) An Overview of Geographic Information in Europe. *Mapping Awareness*, 7 (10), 9–12.

Lyons, D. (1988) *Information Society: Issues and Illusions*. Blackwell, Oxford.

Maguire D.J. (1989) *Computers in Geography*. Longmans, Harlow, Essex.

Marble, D.F., Calkins, H.W. and Peuquet, D.J. (1984) *Basic Readings in Geographical Information Systems*. SPAD Systems Ltd, Williamsville, New York.

May, J.A. (1970) *Kant's Concept of Geography – and its relation to recent geographical thought*. University of Toronto Press, Toronto.

McQuail, D. (1987) *Mass Communications Theory: An Introduction*. Sage, London.

Medyckyj-Scott, D. (1989) *The Problems of User and Organisational Acceptance of Geographical Information Systems*. Midlands Regional Research Laboratory, Research Report No. 4, University of Leicester.

Megarry, J. (1985) *Inside Information: Computers, Communication and People*. BBC Publications, London.

Morgan, J. and Welton, P. (1986) *See What I Mean: An Introduction to Visual Communications*. Edward Arnold, London.

Nijkamp, P. and Scholten, H.J. (1993) Spatial Information Systems: Design, Modelling and Use in Planning. *Int. J. Geographical Information Systems*, 7 (1), 85–96.

Ong, W. (1982) *Orality and Literacy: The Technologizing of the Word*. Methuen, London.

Pickles, J. (1992) Text, Hermeneutics and Propaganda Maps. In Barnes, T.J. and Duncan, J.S. (eds), *Writing Worlds: Discourse Text and Metaphor in the Representation of Landscape*. Routledge, London, pp. 193–230.

Poster, M. (1990) *The Mode of Information: Poststructuralism and Social Context*. Blackwell, Oxford.

Rojas-Vega, E. and Kemp, Z. (1993) Object-Orientation and the SDTS Data Structure Model. *GIS Research UK 1993*, Conference at Keele University.

Roszak, T. (1986) *The Cult of Information*. Lutterworth Press, Cambridge.

RICS (1987) *Standard Method of Measurement (SMM7)* (7th edn), Royal Institute of Chartered Surveyors and Building Employers Federation, London.

RICS (1988) *Code of Measuring Practice: A Guide for Surveyors and Valuers*. Royal Institute of Chartered Surveyors and The Incorporated Society of Valuers and Auctioneers, London.

Sack, R.D. (1980) *Concepts of Space in Social Thought*. Macmillan, London.

Saunders, D.H. (1988) *Computers Today*. McGraw-Hill, New York.

Scientific American (1991) Communications, Computers and Networks: How to Work, Play and Thrive in Cyberspace. *Scientific American* Special Issue, September.

Siefert, M., Gerbner, G. and Fisher, J. (eds) (1989) *The Information Gap*. Oxford University Press, Oxford.

Tagg, J. (1988) *The Burden of Representation: Essays on Photographies and Histories*. Macmillan, London.

Tomlinson, R.F. (1990) Geographic Information Systems – A New Frontier. In Peuquet, D.J. and Marble, D.F. (eds), *Introductory Readings in GIS*. Taylor and Francis, London, pp. 18–29.

Unwin, D. (1990) A Syllabus for Teaching Geographical Information Systems. *Int. J. Geographical Information Systems*, **4** (4), 457–465.

Van Der Schans, R. (1990) The WDGM Model, a Formal Systems View on GIS. *Int. J. Geographical Information Systems*, **4** (3), 225–239.

Weisenbaum, J. (1980) Once More the Computer Revolution. In Forester, T. (ed.), *The Micro-electronics Revolution*. Blackwell, Oxford.

Geographical information systems and decision support for environmental management

5

Robert Peckham

INTRODUCTION

During the last decade there has been a sharp increase in awareness of the adverse impacts of mankind's technological development on the environment. This has led to many new initiatives aimed at researching and understanding the mechanisms involved, and to new legislation aimed at minimizing or ameliorating the negative effects of development. These actions are generating growing amounts of information on the phenomena and problems concerned and this is leading, in some areas of activity, to information management problems. At the same time there has been a remarkable increase in the power and diffusion of information technology which can be applied to support and analyse the information generated, and one of the key elements in the new armoury is the geographical information system (GIS).

The problems concerned can be broadly described as 'environmental management problems'. Examples of environmental management problems range from those of global scale (climate change, ozone depletion), through international scale (atmospheric transportation of radiation and pollutants), to regional and local scales (river pollution, siting of potentially hazardous facilities). What they have in common is that they are all concerned with spatially distributed phenomena. This means that the infor-

Decision Support Systems in Urban Planning. Edited by Harry Timmermans. Published in 1997 by E & F N Spon. ISBN 0 419 21050 4

mation relating to the phenomena can be spatially referenced and an appropriately chosen GIS is now the natural means to support and analyse such information. In addition to information management and analysis there is also frequently a requirement for assistance in making decisions which are effectively choices between alternative possible future courses of action, and hence the need for decision support systems (DSS). The need for such decision support systems is now growing, particularly in urban and regional planning, where environmental impacts must now be taken into account and new regulations and directives respected. In the context of urban planning, the environmental management approach is particularly required with respect to atmospheric and acoustic pollution, protection of parks and green areas, and layout and siting decisions which have a bearing on risks to the population and solar exposure. All these aspects can now be addressed to some extent by the use of GIS.

GIS AS AN INSTRUMENT FOR DECISION SUPPORT

GIS can be seen as providing three essential types of facility: database, graphical display and spatial analysis. The first two, database and linked graphical display, can already provide a powerful instrument for decision support in many contexts, particularly in facilities management. The possibility to interrogate appropriate spatially referenced information through a map-based graphical interface can frequently provide the decision-makers with the information needed to address and manage their problems.

Spatial analysis provides a way of enriching the information available to the decision-makers by generating new parameters from the spatially referenced data. In environmental management such parameters are typically indicators of the environmental impacts of proposed developments, or the number of people or other living species exposed to risk, noise and pollution. Existing GIS now provide a range of spatial analysis facilities, such as Boolean and numerical operations on different thematic layers, area analysis and network analysis, but it is frequently necessary to link the spatial analysis to other external calculations or simulation models in order to arrive at the required parameters on which to base a decision. One of the interesting challenges posed by currently available GIS technology is to devise ways of using the available spatial analysis facilities to generate parameters that are of most relevance to the required decisions. Another challenge is to develop new types of spatial analysis which are appropriate for a given decision context.

An important aspect of GIS that is relevant to any planning situation is the capacity to integrate spatially referenced information coming from different sources. For example, in the context of urban planning the different sources could typically include cadastral maps, population census data, maps of technical networks such as water and electricity lines, aerial photographs and even satellite remote sensing data. Once the data from different sources are structured in an integrated system, with possibilities for analysis and combination, the whole becomes more useful than the sum of the separate parts. An overview of applications and progress in the use of GIS in urban and regional planning is given in Scholten and Stillwell (1990).

THE NEED FOR LINKS WITH MULTI-CRITERIA DECISION AID

A feature that many environmental management problems have in common, in addition to being spatially distributed, is that they are multi-criteria problems. Environmental management problems are normally concerned with complex, interrelated phenomena, and the criteria on which decisions must be based are usually multiple. To take the example of reduction of river pollution, the indicators of pollution are frequently multiple (several biological and several chemical) and, even if the problem is restricted to the reduction of only one pollutant, the criteria involved in the reduction strategies would remain multiple (cost, employment, other social factors, other impacts of clean-up technology). Furthermore the multiple criteria are frequently conflicting. Cost is typically in conflict with other criteria which the decision-makers are trying to satisfy, but there can also be conflicts between criteria other than cost. For example, reducing impact on one class of land use, by altering a siting decision, would normally imply increasing the impact on some other class.

Now it has already been amply demonstrated that GIS can support the required spatially referenced data and provide further insights into the decision problem through spatial analysis, but there remains the problem of arriving at the final decision, in the face of multiple and conflicting criteria. This problem seems destined to become more severe as the quantity of information supported, and the number of criteria that can and should be considered, increases. This is therefore where linking multi-criteria decision aid (MCDA) to GIS can be of great assistance.

It is also a characteristic of many environmental management problems that the decisions involve not one individual or organization, but many. This leads to conflicts not only between criteria, but also between different interpretations of the criteria and different sets of preferences among the different actors. As will be shown in the next section, MCDA has already gone some way towards providing methods for handling these conflicts.

MULTI-CRITERIA DECISION AID

MCDA is a well established field within the general area of operations research, and in which a substantial body of theoretical and practical knowledge has been built up over several decades. The aim is to provide techniques and algorithms to aid the making of decisions in situations of multiple and conflicting criteria.

Techniques have been developed for both discrete and continuous decision problems. In discrete situations a decision has to be made between a well determined set of alternatives, such as alternative sites or transportation routes. All discrete problems require the creation of the *decision matrix* (sometimes called the *evaluation matrix*), which is a two-dimensional table listing the alternatives in one direction and the criteria under consideration in the other. In continuous cases there is a spectrum of alternatives, which can, in principle, be infinite in number, such as target values for physical indicators or costs.

The generation of the decision matrix, complete with values for all criteria, can be seen as a significant step towards the solution of a decision problem. It is a well structured, and fair, description of the problem in the sense that all alternatives have been given similar consideration. It contains a condensed description of the available problem information in a form which apparently requires only a statement of the decision-makers' preferences, and a suitable algorithm for its solution. In continuous problems the extreme values of the criteria define the bounds of the decision space within which the solution should be found.

For the solution of discrete problems, outranking algorithms are normally used; while for continuous problems which can involve unlimited numbers of alternatives in the decision space, multi-objective programming techniques (Keeny and Raiffa, 1976) are usually used. The formulation of the required statement of preferences can present problems, especially in cases where there is more than one decision-maker; for example, the weights are probably different for the separate actors, and the actors frequently wish to modify their preferences when they see their impact on the solution. One approach used in discrete problems is to express the preferences in terms of binary relations stating the relative importance of pairs of criteria, and to allow the preferences to be restated, to generate new solutions, and thus provide more information on how they affect the whole problem. In continuous problems, interactive modelling of aspiration levels can be used.

Experience with MCDA has shown that finding a solution (arriving at a decision) does not imply one run of the chosen algorithm to identify the best alternative, but rather a process of generating solutions together with information on why certain solutions are better, restatement of preferences and generation of new solutions, until the decision-makers have obtained sufficient insights into the problem under consideration, and into their own statements of preferences, to be confident that the final decision is the correct one. In this way MCDA provides structured, documented information on the problem, a focus for discussion, and a means for resolving conflicts by revealing how different preferences lead to different solutions. The information generated can also provide a basis for negotiation between the different actors.

The spatial analysis functions of GIS can provide ready-made facilities for generating values of criteria to go into the decision matrix. Looked at the other way round, the decision matrix and MCDA provide a way of using the results of spatial analysis to arrive at decisions. This is illustrated in the next section by means of several examples of typical environmental management problems.

Some further examples of the linking of GIS and MCDA can be found in Fedra (1986), Janssen (1992) and Carver (1991).

EXAMPLE APPLICATIONS RELEVANT TO URBAN PLANNING

STRATEGIES FOR TREATMENT AND DISPOSAL OF INDUSTRIAL WASTE

We will consider the case of decision support for strategies for industrial waste management. A prototype of such a system has been developed at the Joint Research Centre for the Lombardy Region under contract to the Italian Ministry of the Environment (Paruccini *et al.*, 1993; Peckham, 1993). While this prototype in fact refers to the management of the wastes on a regional scale, most of the waste is produced in urban areas. It is also clear that similar methods could be applied for urban waste management and similar techniques applied to other aspects of urban planning. In this case the GIS should support information on the quantities of the different classes of toxic wastes being produced in different sub-regions, and on the locations, types and capacities of facilities for waste treatment and disposal. Spatially referenced information on population, land use, geology, rivers and water bodies, and the location of natural parks and sites of special interest for nature conservation, are required in order to assess the impacts of different strategies on these features. A description of the transportation network should also be included in order to estimate costs, risks and environmental impacts associated with the transportation of the wastes from the sites of production to the disposal sites.

Once this information is set up in the GIS the spatial analysis facilities can be applied in the following ways:

1. In the assessment of the environmental impact of waste disposal facilities on the different classes of land use, for example by calculating the percentage areas of the different classes of land use in the sub-regions containing the facilities, or within a given radius of the facilities.
2. In the assessment of impact of waste disposal facilities on natural parks or biotopes, for example by finding the distance from each facility to the nearest biotope. Using this distance as a criterion, strategies can be devised giving preference to use of sites located further from biotopes.

3. In the assessment of risks to population, by calculating population densities in the areas surrounding facilities.
4. In the assessment of transportation risk, by calculating population densities near to transportation routes; if a path generator is included, alternative transportation routes and their corresponding risk criteria can be analysed automatically.
5. In the assessment of impacts on underground water by relating locations of facilities to maps of geology and depth of water table.

In 1–4 above the spatial analysis provided by GIS can generate parameters which, after normalization to become indices (on a scale 0–1), can be usefully inserted directly into the decision matrix. In 5, however, the spatial analysis may in some cases need to be linked to a ground-water simulation model (not a standard feature of GIS) for detailed analysis before useful parameters can be derived. This case shows that the integration of GIS and MCDA must in some cases provide for both direct transfer of the results of spatial analysis to the decision matrix, and for more complex information transfers via simulation models or other evaluation modules.

URBAN ATMOSPHERIC POLLUTION

The principal sources of urban atmospheric pollution are typically domestic heating plants, plants for generation of industrial and process heat, other industrial processes, and traffic.

Heating plants can be represented in the GIS as point sources of emission, the spatially referenced information being for example plant size, theoretical efficiency, type of fuel, frequency of maintenance, date of last maintenance and measured efficiency (if available). If detailed survey data is not available, residential areas can be represented as polygonal sources characterized by area averages of sampled data. Emissions from traffic can be represented as line sources, where data for each stretch of road is obtained from measurements of the traffic flow and recordings of vehicle types. A GIS set up with such information can be used to evaluate different scenarios for emission reductions, such as improved heating plant maintenance, plant substitution, alterations to traffic patterns and changes of vehicle fuel. Spatial analysis can be used to identify areas with a high risk of heavy pollution by summing point, line and area sources (of the same pollutant) to create new maps of total emissions per unit area. In areas where terrain geometry has a strong influence on atmospheric concentrations, the spatially referenced information may need to be linked to an atmospheric simulation model for detailed evaluations.

Again we see in this example that spatial analysis can generate criteria which can be used in the decision matrix (after appropriate scaling or normalization), but it may also be necessary to include the use of simulation models not normally found in GIS.

An example of the use of GIS for air pollution monitoring and mapping is given in Galetto *et al.* (1993) and for pollution emissions inventory in Trozzi and Vaccaro (1993). Another traffic-related example, where the objective is the reduction of urban noise rather than air pollution, is given by Bilanzone *et al.* (1993).

SITE MANAGEMENT

An example of the use of GIS for site management, which is closely related to urban planning, has arisen in the Ispra Ecocentre Project. This is a project to move towards a more environmental approach to the management of a research centre site that is 1.8 by 1.8 kilometres in size, incorporates several hundred buildings and employs almost 2000 people. In addition to the office and laboratory buildings, the site contains several large experimental facilities as well as substantial wooded areas and several lakes. The intention is to develop an approach to the management of the site which will preserve and protect natural habitats and concentrate building development so as to reduce travelling within the site. This together with installation of energy conservation measures should also reduce overall carbon dioxide emissions.

A GIS is being set up to assist with the planning and analysis of the interventions proposed in the Ecocentre project. In the GIS a number of thematic maps of the site, covering structural and ecological aspects, are assembled and registered to the same coordinate system. In some cases graphical features on the maps are linked to attribute information stored in a database; for example buildings are linked to information on their construction characteristics, dimensions, energy use and occupancy. This can be used for planning and evaluation of proposed changes, preparation of new maps and monitoring of changes over time. The spatial analysis facilities provided by GIS software will also be used to make scientific studies of various aspects of interest, such as risk to people, animals and plants, the results of which can also be presented to the decision-makers by means of maps.

The system developed so far includes two-dimensional information on roads, car parks, buildings, planning zones, lakes and wooded areas. A three-dimensional model of the terrain and buildings has also been developed for use in visualizing the site and the impact of new construction.

The system has already proved useful in the definition and measurement of areas of the different planning zones, estimation of the areas of lakes and woods, and in the interpretation of the aerial infra-red survey of the site. As more information is included, the possibilities for further useful analysis will increase.

THE INTEGRATION OF DIFFERENT SYSTEM MODULES

The above examples have served to illustrate that the spatial analysis facilities of GIS can be used to derive information of direct relevance to decisions in urban and environmental management, but while such information may be necessary it is not always sufficient. Frequently other parameters are required to be estimated or calculated and this requires additional modules such as simulation models to be included in the DSS. To avoid bias in the selection or creation of alternatives, some method for alternative generation may also be required to be included. It seems that the design of the complete DSS needs to be tailored specifically to suit each problem case, and it is difficult to derive a general-purpose scheme suitable for design and implementation of all systems of this type (linking GIS, simulation models, MCDA and possibly other modules). Nevertheless some attempt at defining and analysing different possible approaches to design and schemes for implementation does seem to be worthwhile as it could lead to a clearer picture of the requirements for such systems and eventually to better-structured and more rigorous implementations. Currently the integration of the various modules is usually done on an *ad hoc* basis, with the system being tailored to fit the designers' view of the problem. In this way particularities of the system design could clearly influence eventual decisions, for example by focusing on one particular aspect of the problem to the detriment of others.

The integration of the different modules of a DSS is essentially a software engineering task, which follows from the specification of the modules to be included and the required information flows. This can now be eased by using object-oriented approaches and tools, by making use of development facilities provided with some GIS, or by adopting the 'federated approach' (see later subsection). Nevertheless implementation choices are clearly crucial to the functioning of the system, its appropriateness, its acceptability to the foreseen users, and the outcome of exercises made with it. Since there is no established formal methodology for design, the implementation choices must be made very carefully. We first consider some of the prerequisites and choices to be made in the early design phase.

PREREQUISITES FOR DESIGN

Initially it is necessary to consider which type of DSS is required. Haastrup (1994) has provided a brief taxonomy or classification of these systems as:

- Single user or group DSS
- Single or multiple criteria

- Decision aid or decision-making
- Operational or strategic

In urban planning, with an environmental management approach, the DSS is likely to be for group use, with multiple criteria, strategic, and for decision aid rather than decision-making.

To this list can be added further classifications regarding the type of multi-criteria techniques used:

- Discrete or continuous problem
- Quantitative or qualitative information
- Method for preference modelling (weights/interactive procedures)

A careful consideration of the decision context where the DSS will be used should lead to answers to the following questions:

- Who are the users?
- What decisions will be aided?
- What will be the alternatives?
- What will be the decision criteria?

The latter two are essentially describing the form the decision matrix should take. If this can be defined, many other aspects of the system design follow, in particular what themes should be covered by the GIS and what type of analyses are required in order to derive values to fill the decision matrix. It should then be possible to define which additional modules need to be included to satisfy requirements not fulfilled by the GIS, e.g. linked database, alternative/scenario generation, simulation model(s).

The prospective users should certainly be involved in these choices and the design and implementation process should be iterative, including at least one stage of prototype development with trials by and feedback from the users.

THREE APPROACHES TO IMPLEMENTATION OF DSS

WHOLLY CUSTOM PROGRAMMING

In principle this approach involves designing and programming the whole system from scratch using an appropriate language and development tools. In practice libraries of subroutines, for example for graphics, interface components, or mathematical functions, are usually available or will have been built up during the course of development of previous systems so that total programming from scratch is rarely necessary. Nevertheless an important advantage is that the system developer has complete access to all source code of all system modules. Using this approach the designer has complete control over the functionality and 'look and feel' of every aspect of the whole system, and graphical aspects of the interface design can be tailored to suit the user's view of the problem. The system can be designed to 'guide' the user through the required steps, for example generation of alternatives, evaluation, statement of preferences and ranking.

Some of the most advanced examples of this approach can be found in the work of Fedra (e.g. Fedra *et al.*, 1987) including applications to air pollution modelling, ground-water pollution and risk assessment. During the course of various developments a modular GIS, XENVIS, has been built up and is customized for each case.

USE OF COMMERCIAL GIS AND ITS DEVELOPMENT LANGUAGE

Most well established commercial GIS are provided with a macro language or a development language which allows the system to be customized for specific applications. It is usually also possible to link to external simulation or analysis modules. This approach has the advantage that existing GIS capabilities, such as those for linking to external databases, graphical display and spatial analysis, can be used as they are, and any additional functionalities required for the specific implementation can be added using the development language and integrated with the same kind of user interface. Other advantages will stem from the increasing diffusion of commercial GIS in local and regional authorities, and the building up of databases on many themes appropriate to planning decisions.

An example of this approach in which GIS and spatial analysis are used to provide values for multi-criteria analysis in the selection of sites for nuclear facilities is described by Carver (1991). Another example where routines to facilitate multi-objective decision-making in land allocation have been developed within the GIS IDRISI is given by Eastman *et al.* (1993).

THE FEDERATED APPROACH

In this approach, described in Hershey and Whitehead (1991), several cooperative packages or applications are used, all operating in the same windowing environment and having interfaces with similar look and feel. Each application provides typically only a few of the functionalities required for the whole system and a high degree of data transferability between different applications is required. While Hershey and Whitehead describe the concept applied to GIS, with different applications providing different functionalities, the concept can clearly be extended to DSS by incorporating appropriate modules, for example for alternative generation, simulation modelling and MCDA. The approach is now feasible on different personal computer and workstation platforms.

This approach avoids the difficulties of building all the foreseeable functionalities into the GIS system, and the possible confusions of having them available in the one application. Specialist modules can be developed or supplied by the appropriate specialists and a high degree of flexibility is introduced. It allows the use of existing applications, for example for word processing (report generation), database and spreadsheet. Familiarity with these simpler applications which are already in widespread use could ease the learning process and transition to use of the DSS modules by some users who may otherwise not contemplate the use of techniques such as MCDA.

A present difficulty with this federated approach is that few of the MCDA and other specialist modules are currently available for use in this way. Also as stated a high degree of data transferability must be built in to all modules, and, perhaps more importantly, the required types of data transfers must be foreseen. This could be eased by the use of object-oriented techniques (e.g. dynamic data exchange and object linking and embedding (Microsoft, 1991)) and the definition of standards, for example for certain types of graphical, geographical and numerical objects which can be transferred between applications.

CONCLUSIONS

Geographical information systems are being increasingly used as components of decision support systems for urban and environmental management. Since these kinds of management problems involve multiple criteria there is a strong case for including MCDA techniques within the DSS. Additional modules for generation of alternative scenarios and their simulation may also be required. There is no established formal methodology for design and implementation of such systems, but design and implementation choices can have a strong bearing on eventual conclusions and decisions made with such systems. An attempt has been made to derive some of the prerequisites for the design of useful DSS incorporating GIS, MCDA and other modules, and the advantages and disadvantages of three different implementation approaches have been described. The choice of approach should depend on the specific problem, and on the availability of existing systems, modules and data, but in the longer term the federated approach, making use of advances in object-oriented techniques for software development and information transfer, appears to offer a means for arriving at a consistent and reliable approach to design and implementation and for overcoming some of the barriers to use of these techniques in urban planning practice.

ACKNOWLEDGEMENTS

Thanks are due to several colleagues for making useful comments, in particular to Palle Haastrup, Giusseppe Munda, Massimo Paruccini and Jeremy Ravetz.

86   Robert Peckham

REFERENCES

Bilanzone C., Chini P. and Salis A. (1993) A Case Study for a Noise Reduction Planning System for the City of Ancona. *Proceedings of the 4th European Conference on Geographical Information Systems*, Genoa, Italy, March 29–April 1, 1993, pp. 96–105.

Carver S.J. (1991) Integrating Multi-criteria Evaluation with Geographical Information Systems. *International Journal of Geographical Information Systems*, 5, pp. 321–339.

Eastman J.R., Kyem P.A.K. and Toledano J. (1993) A Procedure for Multi-Objective Decision Making in GIS Under Conditions of Conflicting Objectives. *Proceedings of the 4th European Conference on Geographical Information Systems*, Genoa, Italy, March 29–April 1, 1993, pp. 438–447.

Fedra K. (1986) *Advanced Decision-oriented Software for the Management of Hazardous Substances. Part II: A Prototype Demonstration System*, CP-86-10, International Institute for Applied Systems Analysis, Laxenburg, Austria.

Fedra K., Li Z., Wang Z. and Zhao C. (1987) *Expert Systems for Integrated Development: A Case Study for the Shanxi Province, the People's Republic of China*, SR-87-1, International Institute for Applied Systems Analysis, Laxenburg, Austria.

Galetto R., Rinaldi S. and Velona F. (1993) Realization of a GIS Prototype for Air Pollution Monitoring and Mapping. *Proceedings of the 4th European Conference on Geographical Information Systems*, Genoa, Italy, March 29–April 1, 1993, pp. 30–37.

Haastrup P. (1994) Designing Risk and Environmental Management Support Systems. In Beroggi G.E.G. and Wallace W.A. (eds), *Computer Supported Risk Management*, Kluwer Academic, Dordrecht, pp. 49–59.

Hershey R. and Whitehead D. (1991) The Federated GIS – A Macintosh Approach. *Proceedings of the 2nd European Conference on Geographical Information Systems*, Brussels, Belgium, April 2–5, 1991, pp. 449–458.

Janssen R. (1992) *Multiobjective Decision Support for Environmental Management*. Kluwer, Dordrecht.

Keeny R. and Raiffa H. (1976) *Decision with Multiple Objectives: Preferences and Value Tradeoff*. John Wiley, New York.

Microsoft (1991) *Microsoft Windows User's Guide (Version 3.1)*. Microsoft Corporation, Redmond, USA.

Paruccini M., Mendes I. and Peckham R.J. (1993) *A Computer-Based Decision Aid for Industrial Waste Management on Regional Scale*, EUR Report No. EUR 15272 EN, Joint Research Centre, Ispra, Italy.

Peckham R.J. (1993) Linking GIS and MCDA to Manage Lombardy's Industrial Waste. *Geo Info Systems*, 3 (3), pp. 46–50.

Scholten H.J. and Stillwell J.C.H. (1990) *Geographical Information Systems for Urban and Regional Planning*. Kluwer, Dordrecht.

Trozzi C. and Vaccaro R. (1993) Air Pollutants Emissions Inventory and Geographic Information System. *Proceedings of the 4th European Conference on Geographical Information Systems*, Genoa, Italy, March 29–April 1, pp. 47–56.

Reversing decision support systems to reveal differences in human strategizing behaviour

6

Ray Wyatt

INTRODUCTION

This chapter assumes that all planning consists of three stages:

1. Deciding what sorts of plans to formulate
2. Plan-formulation
3. Deciding which plans to adopt

Although most decision support systems concentrate on the middle phase, plan-formulation, this chapter will focus on the other two decision-making phases, which we will refer to as 'strategizing'.

Strategizing has always been left for humans to perform rather than entrusting it to computers. This is because of its key importance and because computers cannot do it as well as humans can. But it is theoretically possible to attach a self-improvement mechanism to most decision support systems. Such a mechanism enables the system to learn how to make better and better recommendations the more it is used. Such a system will therefore get closer and closer to becoming a valid strategizer.

Before readers become alarmed about the development of computer systems to tell humans what to do, remember that this is a very old idea which was actually achieved a long time ago. Samuel (1963) wrote a computer program that would not only play draughts/checkers but would also self-improve. After much training, this program learned how to play better

Decision Support Systems in Urban Planning. Edited by Harry Timmermans. Published in 1997 by E & F N Spon. ISBN 0 419 21050 4

draughts/checkers than Samuel, its creator. Its strategic advice about what plans to investigate, and about what move was best to make next, was usually better than Samuel's and most other people's opinions. A match was therefore arranged between this program and the world champion draughts/checkers player of that time. It ended in an honourable draw.

Yet such successes pertain only to be contrived, simplified games that have been set up to simulate human strategizing. No program has achieved comparable success in any real-world, complicated discipline like urban planning. However, some degree of progress in this direction would still be useful.

Accordingly, the author has developed a self-improving decision support system for strategizing. It learns to get better, as did Samuel's draughts/checkers program, by taking advice from humans. That is, it uses neural network technology to 'learn' how to mimic the way its past users decided between strategies. Whether or not this system will lead to better real-world strategizing will be a subject for future research. Here we would rather report on one of the system's unexpected 'spin-off' benefits.

Since the system learns how to mimic past users' strategizing behaviour, it follows that when it is used by one group of users and then by another group it will learn first how to mimic the first group and then how to mimic the second group. Hence by studying the groups' respective converged networks we can gain insight into differences between the two groups' strategizing styles. The two groups studied here were architects and urban planners.

This chapter will therefore begin by describing our system's rationale through an examination of what constitutes good strategizing and by identifying eight key, strategy-evaluation criteria. It will then describe how our system can extract, from different groups of past users, relative 'importances' which they assign to these strategy-evaluation criteria. The final section will outline differences in such importances between the architects and the urban planners. A tentative conclusion will be that the architects place more importance on criteria which encourage them to adopt high-risk strategies, whereas urban planners are more cautious.

GOOD STRATEGIZING

Although strategizing is both an essential prerequisite and an essential post-requisite of all planning, it has always been regarded as difficult to analyse because it is powered by mechanisms deep within people's psyches. For example, Aristotle divided human activity into two types: thinking and doing. Thinking is concerned with contemplating one's place in the cosmos, whereas doing is concerned with practical things, like plan-formulation. Deciding what to do – 'hypothesizing' – is part of thinking, not doing.

Such attitudes persisted into the Renaissance and so they posed a dilemma for philosophers of the day. If the 'scientific method' consists of observing, hypothesizing and verifying, how can the middle one, hypothesizing, be mechanized into standard procedures like observing and verifying can? Clearly, hypothesizing is resistant to standardization.

More recently, Popper has maintained that hypothesizing is beyond the realms of rational analysis. Moreover, the German philosopher Habermas believes that all human activity stems from three types of human attitude: the philosophical, the political and the dramaturgical. That is, people's planning stems not only from their self-perception and from their ideals, but also from their dramaturgical attitudes – their deepest beliefs and desires. It is the latter which drive hypothesizing, and it is they which are so resistant to investigation and mechanization.

BRAINSTORMING

Yet some people have remained undaunted by this. For example, developers of brainstorming techniques believe they can help people hypothesize better (Fabian, 1990). They assume that if strategizers can be helped to generate more ideas, the chances of them eventually choosing a high-quality strategy will be increased. That is, any boost in quantity of hypothetical strategies will increase quality of the eventual strategy adopted.

There are at least two things wrong with this assumption. First, to the author's knowledge it has never been tested and so it could simply be untrue. Secondly, when we think of a brilliant idea we have not necessarily finished strategizing, as illustrated by the following example.

A municipal council's brainstorming group once agonized over the problem of one-hour parking signs, parking meters, parking inspectors, parking fines and unhappy parkers. A brilliant idea was duly generated to solve such problems: pass a local bye-law to prevent all drivers from switching off their headlights after parking. Since most car batteries run flat within an hour, most motorists will return to their vehicles by that time and drive away. There would thereafter be no need for one-hour parking signs, parking meters, parking inspectors, parking fines or ill-feeling. The parking problem would be eradicated at a stroke.

Yet when this idea went to the strategy-formulation group for fashioning into a workable plan of action, it failed. People became concerned about possible wear and tear on car batteries, the need for tow-trucks, unemployed parking inspectors and the loss of municipal revenue. Clearly, a brilliant, hypothetical strategy is not the end of the strategizing process. Good strategizing requires some resistance to being sold glib 'quick fixes' by brainstormers. It is necessary for brainstormers and strategy-formulators to work in mutually supportive symbiosis, as shown in Fig. 6.1.

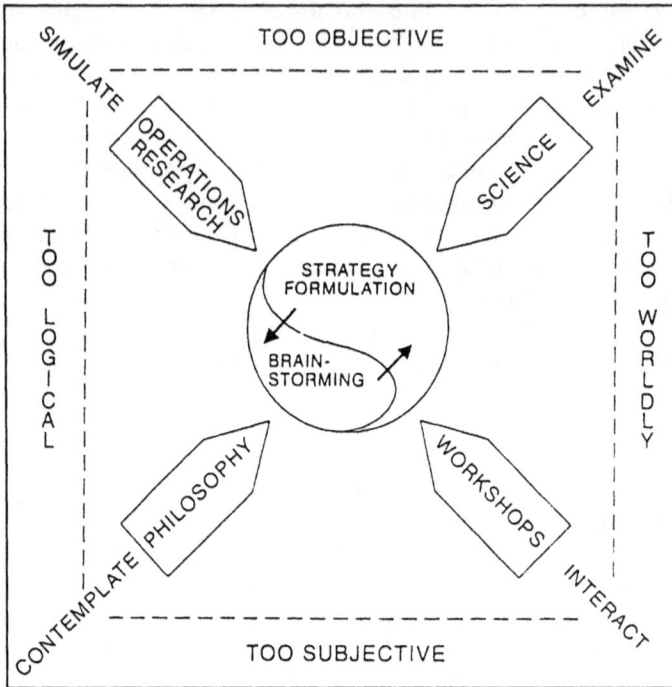

Fig. 6.1 Good strategizing.

BALANCE

Also shown in Fig. 6.1 is the need for good strategizing to be balanced. It should be neither too esoterically logical nor too pragmatically worldly. Moreover, it should neither be too coldly objective nor too whimsically subjective. Yet far too few strategic planners occupy this middle ground. They, and their decision support systems, spend most of their careers working within the security of the corners in Fig. 6.1. It is far more reassuring to work close to a corner because procedures there are conventional and so there is little ambiguity about what one should do.

Hence many 'planners' can be characterized by the corner in which they work. For example, 'examiners' work within in the objective and worldly realm of empirical science, and 'simulators' work within the equally empirical but abstract corner of the 'operations research' tradition. Thirdly, working in the abstract but subjective corner we find 'contemplators' who prefer to philosophize about the world; and in the subjective and worldly corner we find those who 'interact' with the world by arranging events like planning workshops.

Note that the northwest–southeast axis of Fig. 6.1 represents 'town' because most practitioners either simulate or interact with reality. By contrast, the northeast–southwest axis represents 'gown' because most academics spend a lot of time contemplating or examining. Good strategizing is at the intersection of these two axes. Indeed, it needs to borrow concepts from all four corners if it is to be performed properly. For this reason there are arrows, pointing inwards towards the middle, in Fig. 6.1.

STRATEGY-EVALUATION CRITERIA

We will therefore visit each corner in turn to search for suitable strategy-evaluation criteria.

SCIENTIFIC CRITERIA

Beginning with the scientists on the top right, many psychologists believe that planning is an attempt to satisfy humans' underlying needs. But they seldom focus on the act of actually deciding between such needs – strategizing – as they are more interested in 'The "concrete" behavioural form of the need itself' (Nuttin, 1984, p. 140). That is, most behavioural scientists focus on the process of concretizing needs into 'behavioural projects' – plans. They fail to consider the initial act of deciding what needs should be satisfied or the final act of deciding what plans should be adopted.

This is possibly because many psychologists see human planning as a simple process which resembles a thermostat. Thermostats operate on the 'TOTE' model. That is, behaviour is assumed to begin with testing to see if the current state approximates the desired (temperature) state. If it does not, the thermostat operates, followed by another test to see whether the gap between present state and goal state is now satisfactorily small. If it is, the process exits. Thus planning is a process of Test, Operate, Test and Exit – TOTE.

However, if planning takes place within a complex, socially oriented and politically delicate domain, it can never be so automatic. It will not begin with a test of the gap between present and goal states. Something else needs to occur before testing can even start – the actual choosing of the strategic aims. Moreover, 'operating' will not occur automatically. One needs to choose consciously and carefully between many possible alternative strategies.

The TOTE model is therefore not very useful for complex, real-world planning. It ought to be converted to something like the STSOTE model – Strategize, Test, Strategize, Operate, Test and Exit. However, some psychologists do look at how humans choose between underlying needs, which they refer to as 'motivations'. They assert that choice is made on the basis of the different motivations' intensity, or 'valance'. Nuttin (1984) has even suggested some criteria for calculating motivations' valances.

These include 'temporal distance', 'perceived instrumentality', 'reality character' and 'difficulty'.

Note that the first three of these have been adopted by plan-formulators (Wyatt, 1989). For instance, temporal distance actually means 'lead time', or the extent of delay before the motivation will be satisfied. This concept is well known to planners who use critical path and scheduling algorithms – a good plan is one whose longest delay sequence, or critical path, is short.

Moreover, perceived instrumentality actually means effectiveness at satisfying a motivation, whilst reality character is a quaint way of saying probability. Both effectiveness and probability are concepts used by plan-formulators who use decision trees – a good plan is one whose expected utility (or whose 'effectiveness times probability product') is high.

Logically, such concepts can also be used to score strategies. That is, the *delay, effectiveness, probability* and *difficulty* of each strategy are likely to be an indication of its overall desirability. Accordingly, these four concepts will be adopted as our first four strategy-evaluation criteria.

OPERATIONS RESEARCH CRITERIA

Moving to the 'modellers' on the top left of Fig. 6.1, some of them see plan-formulation as a simulation process whereas others see plan-formulation as an optimization exercise. The simulators believe that artificially simulating the situation at hand, along with how this situation might alter if it is tampered with, is all that needs to be done for successful plan-formulation.

In the social sciences such simulation models usually take a mathematical form, and those building them soon become aware of the concept of dependence. That is, some plans are dependent on the achievement of many other plans for their own attainment, whereas other plans are more independent.

For instance, a plan like 'less inflation' is probably dependent on the achievement of other plans, like less imports, more exports, high unemployment and low interest rates, for its own attainment. By contrast, a plan like 'higher taxes' is more independent. One simply increases taxation rates and there is usually little need to achieve related plans.

Again, we will assume that the dependence concept is relevant to strategizing. If some strategy is overly dependent on a large number of other strategies, it is probably less desirable than a more independent one. Hence *dependence* is here adopted as our fifth strategy-evaluation criterion.

The optimizer conceives of plan-formulation as an 'objective function' that has to be maximized or minimized (von Winterfeldt and Edwards, 1986). This involves searching across many alternative combinations of variables to test which one is optimal. For example, if one is planning factory production, one might test a number of combinations of different products to see which of them maximizes company profit.

But there are an infinite number of such product mixes within the 'domain of feasible solutions'. Hence the essence of optimization algorithms is to jump from feasible solution to feasible solution in such a way that each one is better than the last one, until the ultimate, optimal solution is found.

In order to ensure that the search proceeds in this continuously improving manner, any optimizer has to be aware of each product's marginal return. That is, he or she has to be conscious of how much payoff, in terms of improving the objective function, is associated with each extra unit of each variable. Yet again, this concept is probably relevant to strategizing – each strategy's return for effort will influence how attractive it is. Hence *marginal return* is adopted here as our sixth strategy-evaluation criterion.

A PHILOSOPHICAL CRITERION

Until now we have only considered plan-formulation methods for when the problem involves just one goal, or a few goals, such as increased profit. But when planning involves many simultaneous goals it is difficult to assess all of them. Yet planning still gets done, somehow, in such circumstances.

Simon (1983) has suggested that it is achieved because of 'satisficing'. That is, desperate and confused planners will simply accept any plan that yields a satisfactory, as distinct from a best possible, solution (Cherniak, 1986). Put another way, in complicated problem domains plan-formulators do not necessarily optimize. Satisfactory achievement of goals is enough.

Satisfactory achievement is often simply that level which is an improvement over the current level of satisfaction. Hence in order to identify a 'satisficing' plan, any planner needs to have some idea of how well each goal is being satisfied at the moment. This is because plan-formulators look more favourably towards those plans where there is scope for progress to be made, as distinct from those plans which have already been largely achieved.

Again therefore, (present) satisfaction is likely to be a pertinent consideration when strategizing. One is more likely to favour a strategy whose record of achievement has so far been abysmal rather than one which, for one reason or another, has already been largely attained. Accordingly, *satisfaction* is here retained as our seventh strategy-evaluation criterion.

A WORKSHOP CRITERION

Our first six strategy-evaluation criteria were derived from operations research methods like scheduling, decision trees, simulation and optimization. It was only when we got to 'satisficing' that we escaped from these rather mechanistic approaches to planning.

Some plan-formulators have taken this further. They have declared all operations research techniques to be far too mechanical for mirroring the incredible richness of human plan-formulation (Rosenhead, 1989). Such 'interactors', at the bottom right of Fig. 6.1, believe that operations research generates plans which are inapplicable to the real world. They therefore plan by immersing themselves within the real world (Friend, 1992).

More specifically, such plan-formulators conduct events like planning workshops (Bowers and Benford, 1991; Eden, 1992) which are discussion groups where all participants have some insight into the problem at hand. Such workshops are predicated on a belief that an amicable agreement will eventually be reached about a satisfactory plan of action.

Such an approach, whilst seemingly better able to reflect the complexities of real-world plan-formulation, frequently cannot. This is because workshops can become confused and inconsistent (Russo and Schoemaker, 1989) as well as plagued by over-subjectivity, 'group think', dominance by overbearing individuals and other saboteurs of good plan-formulation (Janis and Mann, 1977).

Nevertheless, there is one concept that is frequently discussed at planning workshops which should be useful when trying to strategize rigorously. This is robustness – the propensity of a plan not to inhibit the achievement of other plans. It refers to how benign a plan is. Such a concept in fact has a strong pedigree, being known as 'resilience' in ecological planning, as 'flexibility' in budgetary planning and as 'hedging' in financial planning. Accordingly, *robustness* will be here adopted as our eighth and final strategy-evaluation criterion.

EXTRACTING IMPORTANCES OF STRATEGY-EVALUATION CRITERIA

Our system's assumption is that these eight strategy-evaluation criteria – *delay, probability, effectiveness, difficulty, dependence, marginal return, satisfaction* and *robustness* – are generic parameters which will be useful within many strategizing domains. If so, it should be possible to test what importances are placed on each of the criteria, by different groups, when they strategize. Our system for operationalizing this is called, of course, 'STRATEGIZER'.

THE STRATEGIZER SYSTEM

At the time of this experiment, STRATEGIZER was written in 'Oxford Systematics Professional Plus 2 PROLOG' and it ran on any PC computer of 286 capacity or above. Although each user can enter their own particular problem, for this experiment STRATEGIZER was fed two contrived strategizing problems, one for the architects shown in Fig. 6.2, and another for the urban planners shown in Fig. 6.3. These figures are in fact representations of screen dumps of STRATEGIZER in action. In Fig. 6.2 it is asking the user a question about strategies' *effectiveness*, and in Fig. 6.3 the question is about *probability*.

The architects' problem was to design an acclaimed city square for Melbourne, Australia, and the three alternative strategies for achieving this aim were the seeking of an aesthetic city square, seeking a workable city square and seeking a low-cost city square. Moreover, the urban planners' problem was to achieve cleaner air for Melbourne by reducing car pollution. The three candidate strategies for achieving this aim were smaller cars, consolidation of the city into a higher-density form so as to decrease the need for suburban car travel, and more expensive fuel.

Scores are elicited, from the user, for each strategy's performance on various strategy-evaluation criteria, using Saaty's (1994) paired comparisons method. After this had been done for one, some or all of the criteria, STRATEGIZER was able to recommend a strategy, as shown in Fig. 6.4. The latter shows STRATEGIZER suggesting, based on strategies' scores on strategy-evaluation criteria and on criteria's relative importances, that

```
                            STRATEGIZER

 (Dialogue)                              (Aims)
 e 5                                     acclaim  ────────┐      (for city square)
                                         <advisable>      │   aesthetics
 * is - aesthetics                       <advisable>      ├   workability
 9)  hugely more      effective          <advisable>      └   low cost
  8)  greatly more      effective
   7)  clearly more      effective
    6)  slightly more      effective
     5)  minutely more      effective
      4)  minutely less      effective
     3)  slightly less      effective
    2)  clearly less      effective
   1)  greatly less      effective
  0)  hugely less      effective
 * than - low cost
 (input a number)


 (Explanation)                            (Interrupt Menu)
 Effective aims greatly influence         (e)xplain (w)hy? (u)gh     (m)ove (c)hang
 achievement of the parent aim            (s)trategy                 (q)uit  (r. )e-start
```

Fig. 6.2 STRATEGIZER asking a question during the 'city square' experiment.

```
┌─────────────────────────────────────────────────────────────────┐
│                          STRATEGIZER                              │
└─────────────────────────────────────────────────────────────────┘

┌─ (Dialogue) ──────────────────────┐  ┌─ (Aims) ───────────────────────┐
│                                   │  │ Clean air ──────┐  (for Melbourne)│
│  * is - small cars                │  │   <advisable>   │  small cars     │
│  9)  hugely more     probable     │  │   <advisable>   │  consolidation  │
│   8)  greatly more    probable    │  │   <advisable>  ─┘  expensive petrol│
│    7)  clearly more     probable  │  │                                 │
│     6)  slightly more     probable│  │                                 │
│      5)  minutely more   probable │  │                                 │
│      4)  minutely less   probable │  │                                 │
│     3)  slightly less    probable │  │                                 │
│    2)  clearly less    probable   │  │                                 │
│   1)  greatly less    probable    │  │                                 │
│  0)  hugely less    probable      │  │                                 │
│  *  than - consolidation          │  │                                 │
│  (input a number)                 │  │                                 │
└───────────────────────────────────┘  └─────────────────────────────────┘

┌─ (Explanation) ────────────────┐  ┌─ (Interrupt Menu) ──────────────────┐
│                                │  │ (e)xplain  (w)hy?  (u)gh   (m)ove (c)hang│
│                                │  │ (s)trategy              (q)uit  (r. )e-start│
└────────────────────────────────┘  └─────────────────────────────────────┘
```

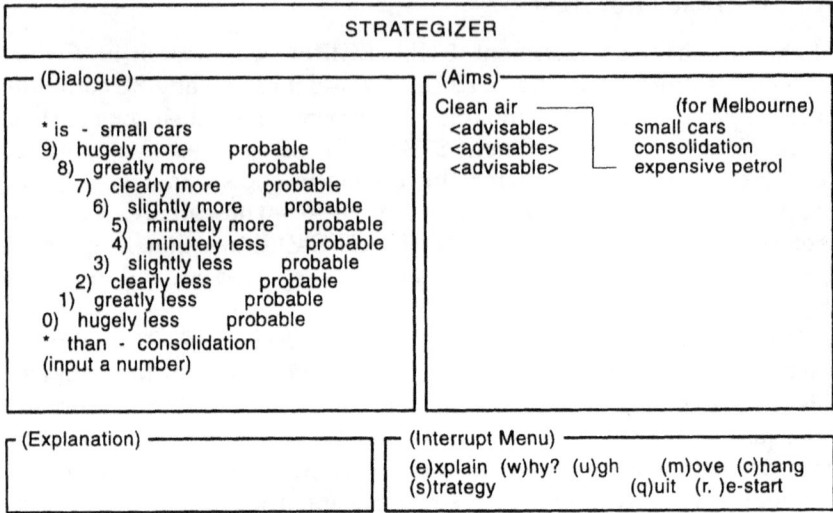

Fig. 6.3   STRATEGIZER asking a question during the 'clean air' experiment.

it is best to adopt the small cars strategy, that the expensive petrol strategy is the next wisest, and that the urban consolidation strategy is the worst one.

But the system's stored criterion importances might be wrong. It therefore attempts to learn from the user what the correct importances should be. This is shown in Fig. 6.5 where the user is telling the system that the expensive petrol strategy should have scored as highly as the small cars strategy, given strategy-evaluation criterion scores that have been fed in.

This is a signal to the system to massage its criterion importance weightings so that, given the criterion scores that have just been input,

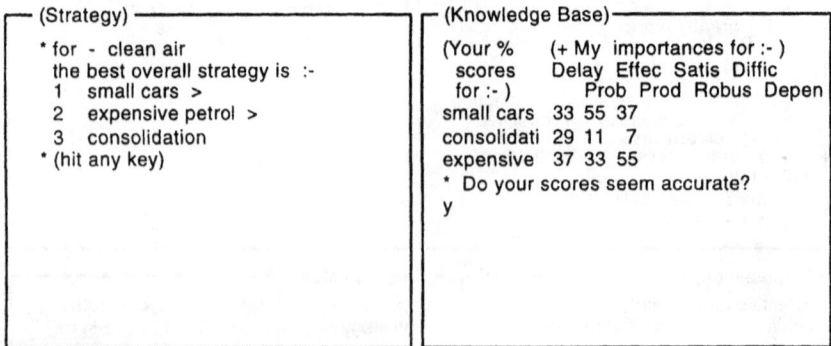

```
┌─ (Strategy) ───────────────────────┐  ┌─ (Knowledge Base) ──────────────────┐
│  * for - clean air                 │  │ (Your %     (+ My  importances for :- )│
│  the best overall strategy is :-   │  │  scores    Delay  Effec  Satis  Diffic│
│  1   small cars  >                 │  │  for :- )        Prob Prod Robus Depen │
│  2   expensive petrol  >           │  │ small cars  33 55 37                  │
│  3   consolidation                 │  │ consolidati 29 11  7                  │
│  * (hit any key)                   │  │ expensive   37 33 55                  │
│                                    │  │ *  Do your scores seem accurate?      │
│                                    │  │ y                                     │
│                                    │  │                                       │
│                                    │  │                                       │
│                                    │  │                                       │
│                                    │  │                                       │
└─────────────────────────────────────┘  └─────────────────────────────────────┘
```

Fig. 6.4   STRATEGIZER suggesting a strategy.

```
┌─ (Strategy) ──────────────────┐  ┌─ (Aims)────────────────────────────┐
│                                │  │                                     │
│  Based on scores for :         │  │ Clean air ─────┐      (for Melbourne)│
│    probability effectiveness   │  │  <advisable>   │      small cars     │
│    delay  ;                    │  │  <advisable>   │      consolidation  │
│  I believe that to get - clean air│ │  <advisable>   └─     expensive petrol│
│    the best overall strategy is :-│ │                                     │
│    1   small cars >            │  │                                     │
│    2   expensive petrol >      │  │                                     │
│    3   consolidation           │  │                                     │
│  *  Should I have ranked some aim│ │                                     │
│     HIGHER                      │  │                                     │
│  y                             │  │                                     │
│  Which aim ?   (input a number)│  │                                     │
│  2                             │  │                                     │
│                                │  │                                     │
└────────────────────────────────┘  └─────────────────────────────────────┘
```

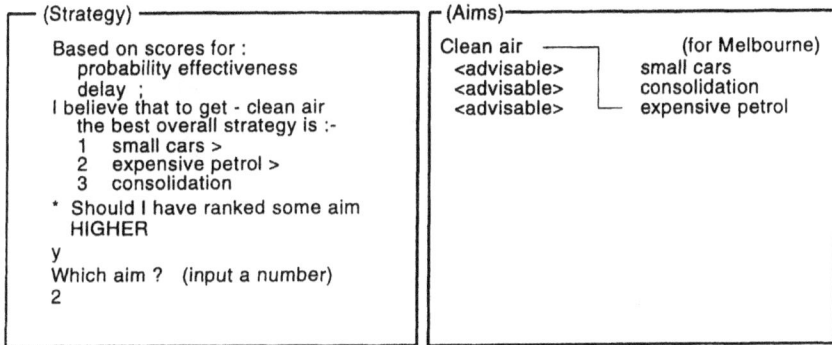

Fig. 6.5   STRATEGIZER recording a user's reaction(s).

the expensive petrol strategy will hereafter tend to score at least as highly as the small cars strategy. Hence across a complete group of users the system will gradually learn to mimic that group's strategizing behaviour.

NEURAL NETWORK-BASED LEARNING

The method used for doing this was, at the time of the experiment, a simulated neural network. More specifically, public domain neural network software was taken from the back-jacket of McClelland and Rumelhardt (1988), and an indication of how it works is given in Fig. 6.6. This figure shows the weights that the software has learned to assign to arcs in order to make the network mimic the attitudes of some past user.

Hence any strategy's score for the *delay* criterion should be multiplied by 0.4; to this answer should be added its score for probability times 0.0, and so on, in order to calculate the activation level of that first hidden node which is situated near the bottom left of Fig. 6.6.

Similarly, the strategy's score for *delay* times 0.3, plus score for probability times –1.0, and so on, should be amalgamated to calculate the activation level of the second hidden node, and likewise for the rest of the hidden nodes. If these hidden nodes' activation levels exceed their designated 'sigmoid function' threshold, they will fire, and so the network will multiply their activation levels by –3.7, 4.9, –7.7 and –10.7 respectively to generate an output, overall desirability score for that strategy.

If this score is said by a user to be wrong, as in Fig. 6.5, the true output score for that strategy will then be stored on the hard disk, along with its previously input criterion scores. Such data is later fed to the neural network training software. The latter will make adjustments to the arc weightings in Fig. 6.6 so that the network thereafter generates an output closer to the user-suggested one.

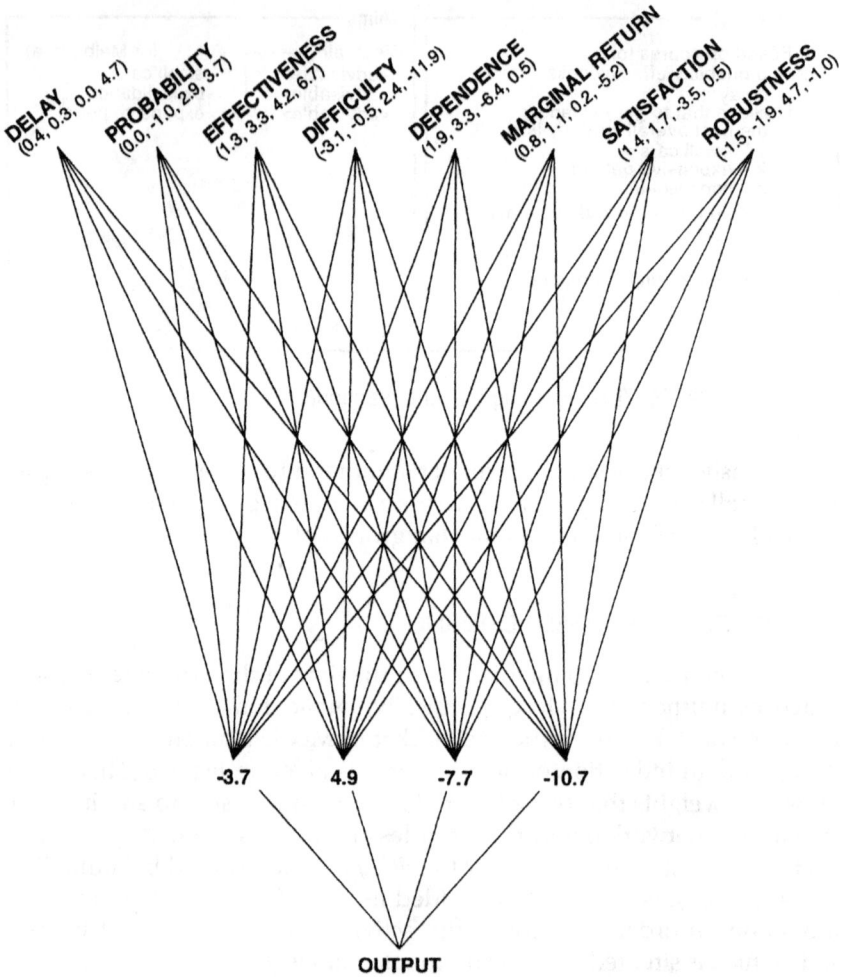

Fig. 6.6 An example of a converged neural network.

It should be remembered that deducing criterion importances in this manner is different to using techniques like linear multiple regression analysis. Therefore, on no account should the arc weightings in Fig. 6.6 be thought of as surrogate regression coefficients. Unlike regression coefficients, network weights can simulate how different criterion scores sometimes act in various simultaneous combinations, as quantified by the hidden nodes. Moreover, the hidden nodes' sigmoid functions simulate the real-world tendency for some combinations of criterion scores to influence output only after they have reached a certain threshold.

NETWORK CONVERGENCE

The neural network approach is actually regarded as a superior model for machine learning of strategy-evaluation criterion importances (Wyatt, 1995). So long as there is a coherent relationship between strategies' criterion scores and their overall desirability scores, a network which contains one or more layers of hidden nodes, as in Fig. 6.6, should 'learn' how to mimic it. For this experiment involving six architects and ten urban planners, in all but one case a neural network was able to learn individuals' criterion importances.

However, when training data was amalgamated into one training file for all respondents, the neural network did not converge either for the architects or for the urban planners. This suggested that there was a large amount of contradictory training information implicit within different respondents' replies to STRATEGIZER – so much that the neural network could not learn any coherent, group-wide priorities from it.

But it was then realized that much of this training information actually contained different combinations of criterion scores because the system had not yet asked the user to score some of the criteria, and such varying inputs would have inhibited the neural network's ability to learn. Accordingly, training files were constructed which contained only data generated by respondents who had scored all the strategy-evaluation criteria – full-criterion responses. All neural networks based on such files, including amalgamated, group-wide files, converged.

Nevertheless, full-criterion responses still might not be as accurate as was first thought. This is because subjects were supposed to nominate strategy desirabilities based on their eight-dimensional criterion scores and such a complex task was possibly avoided by simply rating strategies in a general way rather than on the basis of criterion scores.

For this reason it was decided also to assemble training files which contained nominated strategy desirabilities based on just one criterion – one-criterion responses; the other criterion scores would all be zeros. Such files would at least reflect situations so simple that correspondence between criterion score and overall strategy desirability would be accurate, although only some rather than all criteria were covered by such files.

DEDUCING DIFFERENT CRITERION IMPORTANCES

Note that it is very difficult to ascertain, by looking at converged neural networks such as Fig. 6.6, the importances of the different criteria. Since neural networks predict things by 'soaking up' information in a human, brain-like way rather than in an obviously logical way, they are difficult to interpret logically. That is, it is easy to see whether a neural network works, but it is difficult to see *how* it works. As such, we never really know whether or not a trained network is likely to continue working under changed circumstances in the future. This is why many analysts dislike neural networks.

This chapter certainly cannot resolve the pro- versus anti-neural network debate, which reflects the science versus 'mere engineering' controversy that has dogged Western civilization for several hundred years. Suffice to say that STRATEGIZER was originally conceived as 'mere engineering'. It was a humble attempt to improve strategic planning within socially sensitive domains. Whether or not humanity will be advantaged by attaching to it some sort of neural network software is here left for the philosophers of science to argue about.

MEASURING CRITERIA'S DIRECTIONS OF INFLUENCE

Meanwhile, we may be able to glean some information about how people view importances of strategy-evaluation criteria. More specifically, by looking at converged networks we may be able to hazard guesses about each criterion's overall directional effect on output score.

For example in Fig. 6.6, the sum of the multiples which represent the *delay* criterion's influence on output score is 0.4 times –3.7, plus 0.3 times 4.9, plus 0.0 times –7.7, plus 4.7 times 10.7, which comes to –50.3, which is negative. That is, scores for *delay* seem to have a negative effect on strategy desirability – as a strategy's rating for *delay* increases, its overall desirability decreases.

It cannot be over-emphasized that such simple directional multiples are a very crude attempt to quantify criterion influences on strategy desirability. Any criterion's effect is always filtered by whether or not the hidden node's activation reaches threshold level, and whether or not it does so will depend on the unpredictable impact of many other criteria on that same hidden node. Put differently, the second number within all the simple multiples is unreliable.

The best we can therefore hope for, somewhat forlornly, is that such unreliability will tend to balance itself out across the total network. But we have no way to confirm or to confound whether it will. Despite this, simple multiples were actually calculated for every criterion in every subject's converged network and the most common directional sign, for each criterion, is shown under 'method 1' in Figs 6.7 and 6.8.

Figure 6.7 actually shows criteria's directional influences according to the architects, and Fig. 6.8 shows such directional influences according to the urban planners. Also shown are method 1 type results deduced from the one-criterion training files and from the full-criterion training files, both across all individuals and for those amalgamated files which

IDENTIFIED POSITIVE AND NEGATIVE INFLUENCES OF :-

MEASURED BY :-	DELAY	PROBABILITY	EFFECTIVENESS	DIFFICULTY	DEPENDENCE	MARGINAL RETURN	SATISFACTION	ROBUSTNESS
Method 1								
Mode of individual responses	+	+	–	+	+	–	+	–
Mode of individual one-criterion responses				+				
Mode of individual full-criteria responses	+		–	–		–		
Amalgamated one-criterion responses		–					+	
Amalgamated full-criteria responses	+	–	–	–		–		–
Method 2								
Mode of individual responses		+	+	+	+	+	–	+
Mode of individual one-criterion responses		+						
Mode of individual full-criteria responses		+	+	+	–	+	+	+
Amalgamated one-criterion responses		+		+			+	
Amalgamated full-criteria responses	+	+	–	–			+	–
Method 3								
Mode of individual responses	+	–	–	+	+	–	+	–
Mode of individual one-criterion responses				+			+	
Mode of individual full-criteria responses	+		–	–	–	–	–	
Amalgamated one-criterion responses		–					+	
Amalgamated full-criteria responses	+	–	–		+	–	+	–
VERDICT	+	+	–	+	+	–	+	–

Fig. 6.7   Criteria's directional influences found in the 'city square' experiment.

converged. Remember that amalgamated files of raw responses did not converge.

Figures 6.7 and 6.8 also show criteria's directional effects when they are measured in two other ways. Method 2 involves calculating a more complicated 'composite multiple' for each criterion. For example, the composite multiple for the *delay* criterion in Fig. 6.6 is 0.4 times the activation level of hidden node 1, plus 0.3 times the activation level of hidden node 2, plus 0.0 times the activation level of hidden node 3, plus 4.7 times

IDENTIFIED POSITIVE AND NEGATIVE INFLUENCES OF :-

MEASURED BY :-	DELAY	PROBABILITY	EFFECTIVENESS	DIFFICULTY	DEPENDENCE	MARGINAL RETURN	SATISFACTION	ROBUSTNESS
Method 1								
Mode of individual responses	+	+	–		+		+	
Mode of individual one-criterion responses								
Mode of individual full-criteria responses	+	–	–	+	+	–	+	
Amalgamated one-criterion responses	+	–	+		+		+	
Amalgamated full-criteria responses	–	–	–		+	+		–
Method 2								
Mode of individual responses	+	+	–	–	+	+	+	+
Mode of individual one-criterion responses								
Mode of individual full-criteria responses	–	+	–	+	–	+		+
Amalgamated one-criterion responses	–	+			–		–	
Amalgamated full-criteria responses	+	+		+			+	
Method 3								
Mode of individual responses	+		–		+	–	+	–
Mode of individual one-criterion responses	+	+	–				+	
Mode of individual full-criteria responses	–	–	–		+		+	
Amalgamated one-criterion responses	+	–			+		+	
Amalgamated full-criteria responses		–	–		+		+	
VERDICT	+	?	–	+	+	+	+	?

Fig. 6.8   Criteria's directional influences found in the 'clean air' experiment.

the activation level of hidden node 4. Moreover, any hidden node's activation level is calculated by summing all other criteria's effects on that node. For example, the activation of hidden node 1 is 0.0 times the strategy's *probability* score, plus 1.3 times its *effectiveness*, and so on across all criteria except *delay*.

Yet composite multiples are likely to be inaccurate also, because activation of a hidden node is affected not only by the number by which a criterion score is multiplied, but also by the absolute magnitude of that criterion score. Such unknown magnitudes are therefore problematic except in the unlikely event that they will balance each other out across all criteria and/or users.

Accordingly, the most reliable measure of a criterion's directional influence is perhaps just a simple count of its positive and negative influences – method 3. For example, in Fig. 6.6 the method 3 count of influences for *delay* will be plus one if 0.4 times –3.7 is positive, zero if it is zero or minus one if it is negative; plus one, zero or minus one depending on whether 0.3 times 4.9 is positive, zero or negative; zero because 0.0 times –7.7 is zero; and minus one because 4.7 times –10.7 is negative. That is, the overall directional influence of *delay* on output score is –1 + 1 + 0 – 1 which equals –1, which is negative.

Such a method could be inaccurate because of unknown size effects. For example, only one large instance of a sign might actually overcompensate for the effect of many more, but much smaller instances of the opposite sign, and this would not be identified using method 3. However, the odds seem high that such perturbations will balance one another out across the whole network, and so method 3 is probably our most accurate method.

Turning therefore to, say, Fig. 6.8, remember that when a result was inconclusive the relevant cell was left blank. Look down the cells in each criterion's column. The *delay* criterion column's most frequent result is positive; in fact all the signs in that column are positive. That is, *delay* seems to have a positive effect on overall strategy desirability.

This seems plausible since most respondents interpreted the three alternatives as strategies which all had to be achieved eventually. Hence if there was likely to be a long delay between achieving a strategy and the eventual attainment of the overall goal, then such a strategy would have relatively high priority in view of the need to start working on it sooner rather than later.

ARCHITECTS COMPARED TO URBAN PLANNERS

Figure 6.9 accumulates the results of Figs 6.7 and 6.8. It can be seen that both architects and urban planners believe that *difficulty, dependence, delay* and *satisfaction* affect strategy desirability in a positive direction. This suggests that they prefer to start working first on those strategies which are difficult, dependent, delayed and satisfactory.

This seems reasonable. Both groups prefer to tackle first those strategies which are problematic. Although strategies which have largely been satisfied already can hardly be described as problematic, post-survey interviews with respondents suggested that they misinterpreted the meaning of the word 'satisfactory'. They saw it as meaning legitimacy, or validity of a strategy in terms of being suitable to pursue the parent goal.

ARCHITECTS Believe a strategy deserves :-	URBAN PLANNERS Believe a strategy deserves :-
POSITIVE emphasis if it is :- Difficult ⟷ Dependent ⟷ Delayed ⟷ Satisfactory ⟷ Probable	**POSITIVE** emphasis if it is :- Difficult Dependent Delayed Satisfactory (Productive)
NEGATIVE emphasis if it is :- Effective ⟷ Robust (Productive)	**NEGATIVE** emphasis if it is :- Effective

Fig. 6.9   Summary of findings.

If so, it is quite logical that both groups would give more initial emphasis to legitimate strategies.

Also, both groups singled out *effectiveness* as a negative influent on strategy desirability. That is, both groups want initially to avoid strategies that are effective. They prefer to begin work on less effective strategies in order to start making some headway against them. Similar comments apply, at least for the architects, when it comes to *robustness*. The architects saw no pressing need to work straight away on robust strategies because they are less problematic. The urban planners had no dominant view on this.

Moreover, in terms of the *probability* criterion, the architects regarded it as a positive influent on strategy desirability and again the urban planners had no strong views about it. To both groups *probability* possibly meant something analogous to credibility, in the sense of 'probability of being accepted' by the community. If so, the architects were keen to begin work on problematic strategies so long as they have community acceptance, but the urban planners were less interested in community acceptance.

This leaves only one real difference between the architects and urban planners. Urban planners saw *productivity* as a positive influence on strategy desirability whereas architects saw it as a negative influence. This means that urban planners saw productive strategies, the ones which have high marginal return for effort, as being of immediate priority. By contrast, the architects preferred to postpone working on such 'safe-bet' strategies until later.

Hence we have found that the architects and the urban planners are similar in their strategizing behaviour except for a slight hint of a more cavalier postponing of productive strategies amongst the architects and a more conscientious, 'sleeves rolled up' approach from the urban planners. Both are keen to start work early on problematic strategies but the planners are keener to make early progress by focusing more on high-return goals.

CONCLUSIONS

This chapter has gone to some lengths to focus on the neglected art of strategizing. It has argued that strategizing can be assisted by a generalist decision support system if it incorporates a self-improvement mechanism. It was then shown how such a decision support system can be used in reverse by deducing, from its trained neural networks, what sorts of priorities different groups of past users place upon various strategy-evaluation criteria.

In an extremely tentative and preliminary experiment, one whose results should never be accepted until further studies have been completed, a small difference between the strategic planning styles of two groups was found. Architects seemed to be more relaxed about making early progress towards solving the overall problem, whereas planners were keener to make significant initial progress.

However, this could have been a result of the two groups addressing different problems. Designing a city square is easier in the sense that mistakes can be more easily corrected. By contrast, planners who implement strategies like smaller vehicles or higher-density living will be acutely aware that it takes a long time to rectify any mistakes they might make. Hence while the architects could afford to be more casual, the planners needed to be more conscientious and intent upon making valid progress as soon as possible.

Hence this chapter's conclusions should never be used to comment on the different planning styles of architects and urban planners. Such comments await more definitive research which at least involves both groups addressing the same problem. This chapter's contribution has been different. It has demonstrated the user-exploration potential of self-improving decision support systems.

REFERENCES

Bowers, J.M. and S.D. Benford (eds) (1991) *Studies in Computer Supported Cooperative Work*. Amsterdam, North Holland.

Cherniak, C. (1986) *Minimal Rationality*. Cambridge, Mass, Bradford/MIT Press.

Eden, C. (1992) Strategy Development as a Social Process. *Journal of Management Science*, 29: 6, 799–811.

Fabian, J. (1990) *Creative Thinking and Problem Solving*. Chelsea, Mich Lewis.

Friend, J. (1992) New Directions in Software for Strategic Choice. *European Journal of Operational Research*, 61, 154–164.

Janis, I.L. and L. Mann (1977) *Decision Making: A Psychological Analysis of Conflict, Choice and Commitment*. New York, Macmillan.

McClelland, J.L. and D.E. Rumelhardt (1988) *Explorations in Parallel Distributed Processing*. Cambridge, Mass, MIT Press.

Nuttin, J. (1984) *Motivation, Planning and Action*. Hillsdale, New Jersey, Lawrence Erlbaum/Leuven University Press.

Rosenhead, J. (ed.) (1989) *Rational Analysis for a Problematic World: Problem Structuring Methods for Complexity, Uncertainty and Conflict*. Chichester, John Wiley.

Russo, J.E. and J.H. Schoemaker (1989) *Decision Traps: Ten Barriers to Brilliant Decision Making and How to Overcome Them*. New York, Doubleday.

Saaty, T. (1994) *Fundamentals of Decision Making and Priority Theory with the Analytic Hierarchy Process*. Pittsburgh, RWS Publications.

Samuel, A.L. (1963) Some studies in machine learning using the game of checkers. In E.A. Feigenbaum and J. Feldman (eds), *Computers and Thought*. New York, McGraw-Hill.

Simon, H.A. (1983) *Reason in Human Affairs*. Stanford, Stanford University Press.

von Winterfeldt, D. and W. Edwards (1986) *Decision Analysis and Behavioural Research*. Cambridge, Cambridge University Press.

Wyatt, R. (1989) *Intelligent Planning*. London, Unwin Hyman.

Wyatt, R. (1995) *Evaluation of Strategies*. Unpublished MSc Minor Thesis, Psychology Department, University of Melbourne, Melbourne.

PART TWO

Methodology

Urban convergence: morphology and attraction

7

Romulo Krafta

INTRODUCTION

In previous papers (Krafta, 1993, 1994) the problem of spatial differentiation has been examined in terms of inner configurational issues and their possible role within the urban spatial structure. Their fundamental proposition was a set of synthetic measures of urban morphology, named the *potential/centrality model*, which may provide the urban designer or policy-maker with instruments to assess the performance of intra-urban spatial systems. The model's potential module simulates the distribution of built-form increments across the system of urban spaces, for which the first module, centrality, evaluates locational conditions for each built-form type. In this sense, centrality is a measure of morphological state, whereas potential acts as a morphological simulator. This chapter takes the centrality model one stage further, by introducing specificities which are expected to produce finer insights into the mechanics of urban space structuring.

Several modes of capturing and describing urban spatial differentiation have been suggested, the various forms of accessibility measuring being better known. Arentze *et al.* (1994) quote three groups of accessibility measures, ranging from the simplest ones, based on travel costs faced by consumers in the process of satisfying their demands, up to more complex measures which express accessibility in terms of the surplus value, benefit or utility consumers gain from facilities. In the same paper, Arentze *et al.* propose a new, 'multi-stop travel model' to explore the particularities of chain trips usually performed by consumers during their shopping. Another simple form of using accessibility to describe

Decision Support Systems in Urban Planning. Edited by Harry Timmermans. Published in 1997 by E & F N Spon. ISBN 0 419 21050 4

areal differentiation is proposed by Hillier *et al.* (1993). Named relative asymmetry, their space syntax measure takes accessibility as a mean, topological distance from each space to all others in the same spatial system.

A rank of these indicators, according to the complexity of their inner structure, could show the following:

1. Measures that do not distinguish point hierarchy, that is to say, do not differentiate origins (demand points) from destinations (supply points), such as relative asymmetry.
2. Measures that do not distinguish different destinations in terms of their quality, such as the models which consider the distance to the nearest supply point.
3. Measures that do hierarchize supply points although they do not consider increasing or decreasing probabilities of choice derived from chain destinations, such as the measures of consumer welfare.
4. Measures that do handle supply hierarchies as well as plural destinations, such as the multi-stop travel model.

It is rather interesting that, although relative asymmetry and multi-stop travel models are at opposite ends of the list above, they share an important point in common, which is the attention given to the spatial particularities of the system in hand. While the latter try to relate the relative position of supply points to the probability of successful demand trips, the former tackles the issue of grid configuration. Whilst the multi-stop travel model measures the effectiveness of attractants attached to a circulation system, relative asymmetry measures the effectiveness of the circulation system itself, with its possible effects on location of attractants. As a possible measure of the urban spatial structure, it seems clear that the absence of attractants in space syntax models is a serious restriction; on the other hand, it suggests that the multiple movements made possible by the urban grid can generate complex patterns of use. In this direction, multi-stop-type models could well benefit from a morphological specification of grid configuration. By adding to users' choice of supply locations, already measured by the multi-stop device, a dimension of route choice, a new model structure could be achieved.

Space centrality indicators can be seen as a first bridge between these different families of models, to the extent that they do bring together grid as well as built-form particularities. In this case, built form works as a *proxy* of attractants, giving a first dimension of their uneven distribution and effect on spatial systems. In this chapter, the idea of combining grid configuration and attractants is developed further and a new measure, named *spatial convergence*, is proposed.

A NOTE ON SPACE CENTRALITY

The first idea structuring space centrality is that every built-form unit is reachable from every other built-form unit through a sequence of public spaces. Consequently public spaces fall on the path between every pair of *built-form units* (BFU) and so they are central in relation to them, as illustrated in Fig. 7.1. Considering an uneven distribution of BFUs and a multiplicity of paths between each pair, it is then assumed that some public spaces will be more central than others in the whole linkage of all possible pairs of BFUs in a given system.

The second idea essential to spatial centrality is the indissolubility between built form and public space, in the sense that tension is created by built form and channelled through public spaces; no tension is generated without built form and no tension is distributed without public spaces. Considering the two basic system's components (built form and public space) and one fundamental relationship between them, adjacency, it is possible to represent such a system as an urban graph, in which each dot is a unit of space (built and open ones) and each edge is an adjacency. The result is a galaxy (Kruger, 1979) with a constellation of public spaces loaded with small constellations of built-form units, as suggested in Fig. 7.2. Such a graph is then processed in the following way:

1. Identify all shortest paths between all possible pairs of built-form units. The shortest paths are topologically determined, that is to say, spaces linking BFUs are taken irrespective of their actual length and counted as one step. The shortest path between two built-form units will be the one with least steps.
2. Assign to each space belonging to the shortest path(s) between each pair of BFUs a unit of weight, signalling its role in providing reachability from one to another.

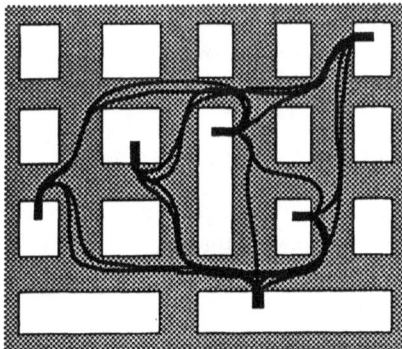

Fig. 7.1 An example of the reachability scheme proposed by the theory, in which every built-form unit is reachable from every other through a multiplicity of public space paths, is shown here.

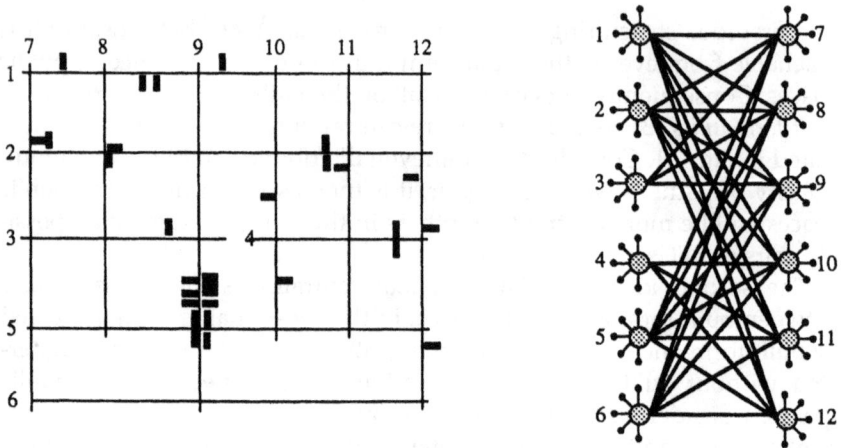

Fig. 7.2 Construction of an urban graph, expressing the reachability scheme, from usual urban maps. Each stippled circle represents a public space, each dot represents a built-form unit and each edge stands for an adjacency.

3. Sum up all units of weight assigned to each space after all pairs of BFUs are processed. The result shows the relative centrality of all spaces of the system; high figures report spaces heavily assigned to paths between pairs, being more central than ones ranked low.

It is clear that axial lines support a varied number of BFUs throughout the system, according to their length, number of land plots, density and height of buildings, etc. Consequently even not considering, at this stage, the actual activities housed inside each building, the dimensions of spatial differentiation are considered. Spatial centrality measured through such a procedure can be consistently correlated to some aspects of urban spatial structure, as described in Krafta (1994).

THE MEASURE OF SPATIAL CONVERGENCE

Spatial convergence is defined as a particular form of space centrality, in which built-form units are distinguished by their demand/supply nature (residential/service), as well as by the attractiveness each of those activities attains in the urban system. In this version, each dot of the urban graph representing a built-form unit will be labelled as an 'origin' or a 'destination', restricting the choice of possible pairs between which to search for shortest paths, and to proceed with any other calculations. The objectives are as follows:

1. Identify the supply points which are most central in respect of both their position in relation to demand points and their size variety, to which the urban system converges.
2. Rank the demand points in relation to their spatial opportunities, that is to say, their relative accessibility to facilities located at supply points. Such a rank will reflect the position of each demand point in relation to the convergence cones of the system.
3. Complementary to the above, it can be required that the model identifies any potential new supply points, that is, those demand points which, because of their relative position, also have spatial privileges and so are potentially qualified for supply points.

ASSUMPTIONS

It is assumed that:

• Each built-form unit houses one activity.
• Residential activity is rated at attractiveness 'zero', while the attractiveness of the several service activities will be parametrized by indicator of service size (within specific groups) and kind (among diverse groups). Weighted in this way, built-form units will orient relationships between demand and supply points, as well as form spatial clusters of supply activities. It is, then, assumed that demand satisfaction is a probabilistic function of the size and variety of supply points (Arentze *et al.*, 1994).
• The functional link between a demand point *i* and a supply point *j* is mediated by the reachability of *j* from *i* and the eventual presence of other supply points in the shortest path between *i* and *j*, in the same way as it is mediated by the size and variety of supply points, as described above. Consequently, distance weakens the functional relationship between *i* and *j* in the same way as the eventual occurrence of other supply points located on the shortest path between them does so, as illustrated in Fig. 7.3.

SPECIFICATION

The determination of reachability is made from every demand point to every supply point, with the usual identification of all shortest paths, and spaces engaged in them. The first step is to process the usual reachability of the system, which is done by the procedure of identifying all possible pairs of demand–supply points, determining the shortest paths between them, and listing all spaces belonging to those paths. Such a procedure differs from that usually performed for centrality calculations only in that the points are labelled (demand, supply), and reachability is considered only from demand to supply points.

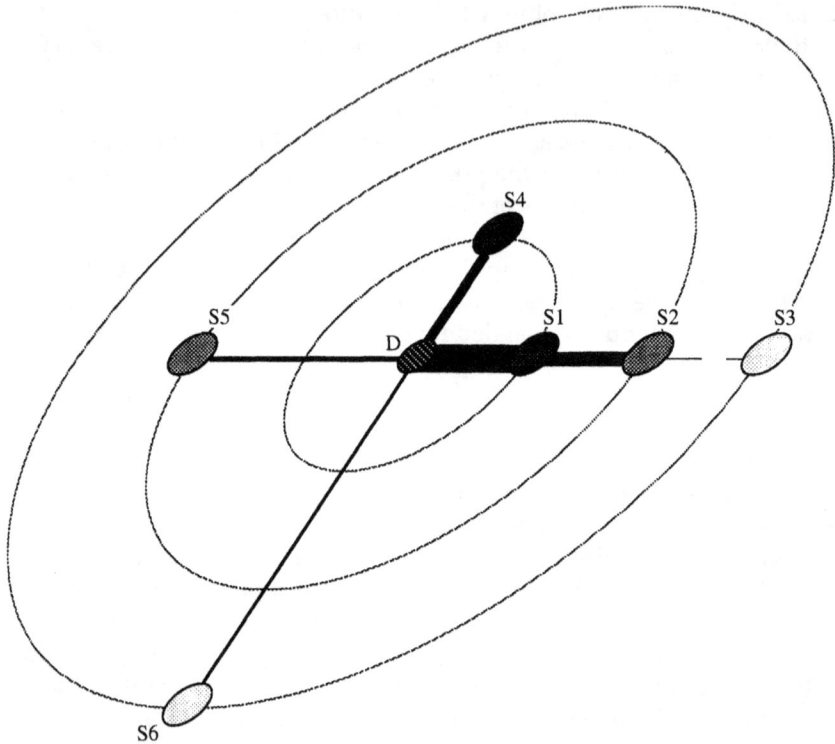

Fig. 7.3 Graphical representation of supply points' hierarchy, based on distance from demand location and relative positioning relationship to other supply locations.

The second step is related to weight assignment. For centrality calculation, a unit of weight is assigned to every pair of built-form units, and then distributed among every space belonging to the shortest paths, each one obtaining a fraction of that unit. In this case, however, two specifications should be introduced. In the first place, because supply points have different statuses, the unit of weight to be shared among spaces must be replaced by a figure reflecting the size of the supply point. For this extent, indicators of size (number of employees, floor area, etc.) could be used. Variety, both within each category of service and among several ones, should also be considered, through the inclusion of a multiplier. In this way, the weighting of two, say, food stores, one of which is twice as big as and offers ten times more product types than the other, would display figures proportional to 1 and 20 respectively.

Secondly, the assignment as such should also be labelled in such a way that the statuses of 'origin', 'destination' and 'link' points are distinguished. The first two are the pair of points being processed; the last is related to all other points which make up the shortest paths, as illustrated in Fig. 7.4.

The third step implies the selective accountancy of all those figures credited to spaces in the process of reachability previously described. Objective 1 at the beginning of this section can be reached by summing up the figures labelled 'origin' for all demand points of the system. The resulting list will rank demand points according to their spatial opportunities in relation to existing facility points. Objective 2 can be reached by summing up all figures credited to supply points. In this case, not only the intrinsic convergence power of each point is considered, but also their relative dominance over other supply points, due to relative position and particular configurational characteristic of public space grid. Finally, objective 3 can be reached by including the figures credited to all points in the calculation. The list containing demand points will point out those which hold highly favourable positions in the spatial system and can be seen as possible alternative supply points.

IMPLEMENTATION

In order to calculate scores for the spatial convergence, as outlined above, a computer program has been created. As described in the flow chart in Fig. 7.5, the algorithm can be run on personal computers and can process quite large networks. The algorithm:

- matches all pairs of demand–supply points;
- goes through the system's connectivity network;
- finds all shortest paths between each pair;
- identifies all spaces belonging to those shortest paths;
- calculates the fraction of weight to be assigned to each space;

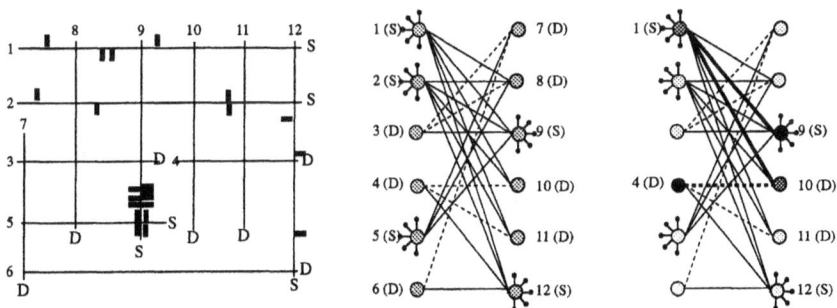

Fig. 7.4 From the urban map (left), an urban graph is constructed (centre) in which spaces are labelled as 'demand' and 'supply'. A third graph (right) shows, for a randomly selected pair of demand–supply points, the diversified point's statuses (origin, destination and link), as well as the supply point's privileges derived from their centrality.

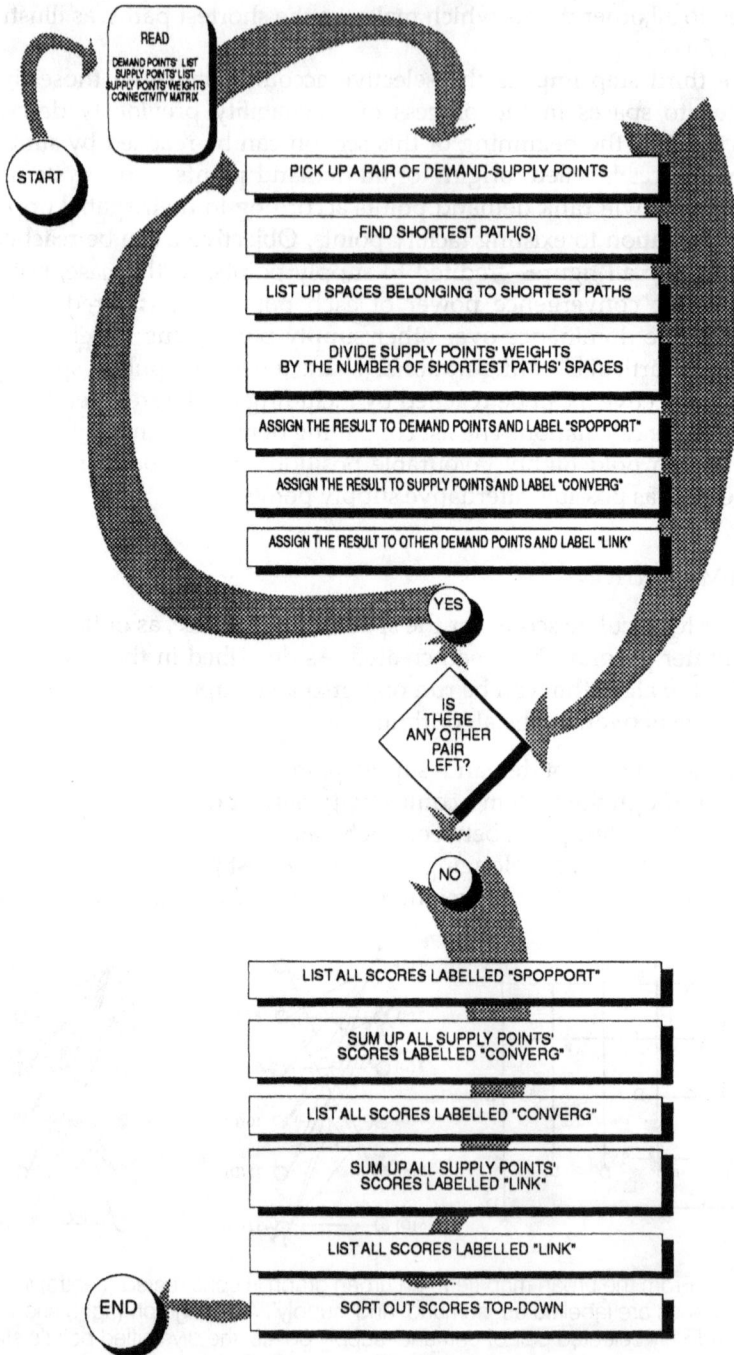

READ
DEMAND POINTS' LIST
SUPPLY POINTS' LIST
SUPPLY POINTS' WEIGHTS
CONNECTIVITY MATRIX

START

PICK UP A PAIR OF DEMAND-SUPPLY POINTS

FIND SHORTEST PATH(S)

LIST UP SPACES BELONGING TO SHORTEST PATHS

DIVIDE SUPPLY POINTS' WEIGHTS
BY THE NUMBER OF SHORTEST PATHS' SPACES

ASSIGN THE RESULT TO DEMAND POINTS AND LABEL "SPOPPORT"

ASSIGN THE RESULT TO SUPPLY POINTS AND LABEL "CONVERG"

ASSIGN THE RESULT TO OTHER DEMAND POINTS AND LABEL "LINK"

YES

IS THERE ANY OTHER PAIR LEFT?

NO

LIST ALL SCORES LABELLED "SPOPPORT"

SUM UP ALL SUPPLY POINTS' SCORES LABELLED "CONVERG"

LIST ALL SCORES LABELLED "CONVERG"

SUM UP ALL SUPPLY POINTS' SCORES LABELLED "LINK"

LIST ALL SCORES LABELLED "LINK"

END

SORT OUT SCORES TOP-DOWN

Fig. 7.5   The model's flow chart.

- assigns the calculated fractions of weight to demand and supply, as well as to intermediate demand and supply points according to their specific labels;
- sums up all partial scores according to objectives 1, 2 and 3 and after all pairs are processed and produces different score sheets, ranking separately demand points according to their spatial opportunity situation, supply points according to their spatial convergence, and demand points according to their spatial convergence.

The program receives data related to demand points, to supply points and to the connectivity characteristics of the spatial system. Regarding the demand side, data refer to the number of points only; from the supply side, data include the number of points and an indicator of each one's size/attractiveness. For the whole system, a connectivity matrix, reflecting the characteristics of the public space network, is included in the data.

INTERPRETATION OF RESULTS

The list labelled '*spopport*' ranks demand points according to their relative spatial opportunity. This means that the accessibility to all supply points in the system is measured for each demand point. The scoring procedure, described above, assigns higher scores to demand points which are nearer to large and varied supply points. The nearness, referred to above, is measured in terms of topological (adjacency) distance, and can be represented by different maps, as explained in the next section. The results are positive figures which compare all demand points within the same system. A relative measure can be introduced which accounts for different-sized systems.

The list labelled '*converg*' ranks supply points according to their spatial convergence. The meaning of this is that each supply point is measured in terms of its: (a) size and variety; (b) capacity of being nearer to demand points; and (c) capacity of falling on the shortest path between demand and other supply points. In this sense, supply points which are in close spatial proximity to demand points, having spatial precedence over other supply points, and being large and varied will be better scored.

The list labelled '*link*' ranks demand points according to their spatial position in the system. It is a classic measure of centrality, in which spaces are scored for their capacity in providing reachability between two others, in this case, between a demand and a supply point. Having high scores, demand points could be interpreted as having 'supply potential', that is, having the spatial condition of being transformed, over time, into new supply points for the system.

SPATIAL AND OPERATIONAL REPRESENTATIONS

Among the several grid representation possibilities – axial (Hillier *et al.*, 1993), point-axial (Kruger, 1989), link (Krafta, 1991) – the first one has been the most suitable in urban morphology cases, for its capacity of retaining the public space's essential quality of connectivity. In effect, by representing a public space grid through a set of axial lines, it is possible to reduce the complexity of its configuration to a basic characteristic – its linear dimension. Axial lines in a grid intercept each other, so they can be further reduced to a graph representation, in which an axial line is expressed by a dot and its connections to other lines expressed by lines.

Applications of centrality measures on axial maps (Krafta, 1994) have proved effective to simulate areal differentiation for intra-urban – that is, very detailed – situations. Results have proved consistently correlated to relevant aspects of urban spatial structure. For spatial convergence cases, however, axial maps present a few problems. First of all, demand as well as supply locations are not precisely determined in axial representation, notably in those cases of regular *'Barcelona ensanche* type' grids. Secondly, axial lines could vary their built form, as well as their activity contents, intensely along their actual extension. Service facilities tend to be located at key points, as far as local urban situations are concerned; similarly, demand locations are better evaluated in terms of their spatial opportunities if a precise spatial definition is given of their locations. Point-axial maps seem to be an acceptable answer to these operational demands.

A point-axial map, also called a 'bunch' map (Kruger, 1989), is a combination of axial and intersection maps. From the former, the point-axial map retains the property of axial connectivity, and from the latter it retains the precise definition of corners. Whilst the axial basic spatial entity is a *line* – represented by a dot in a graph – point-axial maps have a complex basic spatial entity, which is the intersection of two axial lines – the *corner*, also represented by a dot in a graph as exemplified in Figs 7.6 and 7.7. It is complex to the extent that it combines a precise spatial location with axial connectivity: each corner is taken as adjacent to all others along the segments of axial lines intersecting at it. For point-axial maps, the entity represented by a dot in the graph has a precise spatial location – the crossing point of at least two axial lines – although it can have far-reaching connectivity.

Within-place activity aggregation is made at corners according to each one's influence radius. Quantification of supply activities is related to two factors:

1. The actual size of each one, measured in terms of selling area, number of employees, or other relevant indicators.
2. The variety of activities, measured by a multiplier, a parameter applied on the first indicator. Regulation of parameters could be made by the

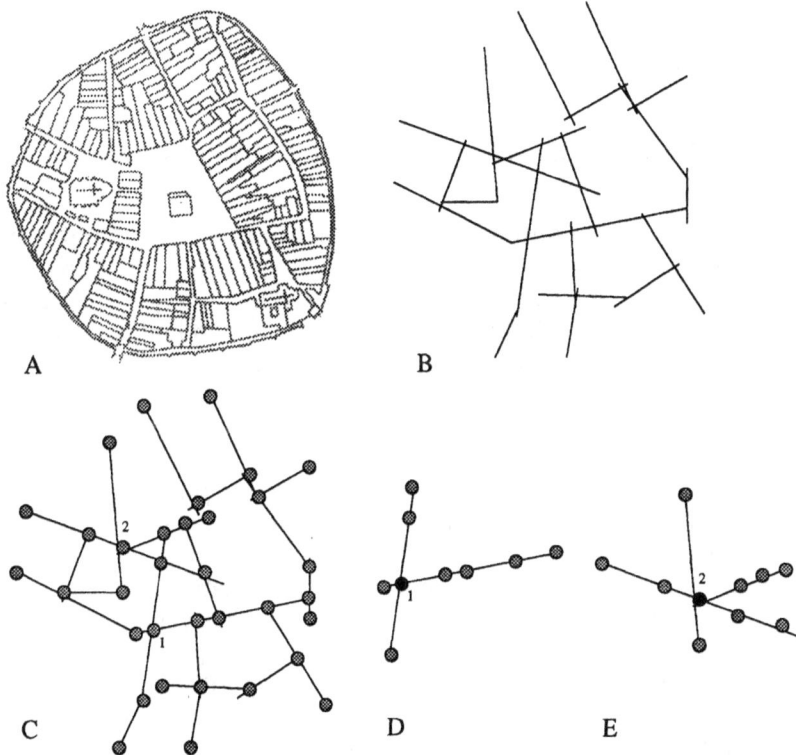

Fig. 7.6   The Czech new mediaeval city of Unicov: its survey map (A), axial map (B), point-axial map (C) and the 'bunches' for locations '1' and '2' (D and E).

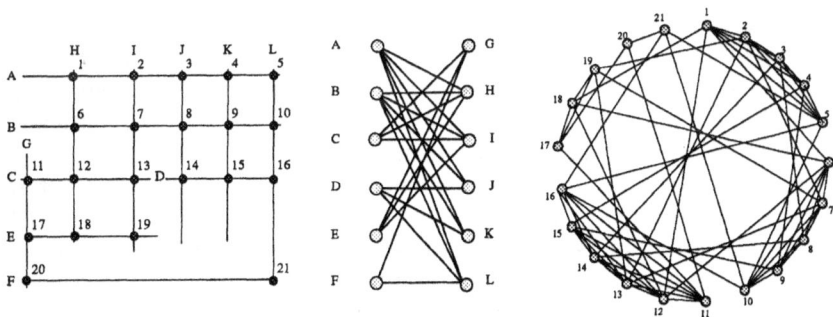

Fig. 7.7   An axial/point-axial map and the corresponding axial and point-axial graph representations.

usual calibration processes, and oriented by correlation with independent variables of urban spatial structure, such as pedestrian or
vehicular flows.

LIMITATIONS AND CONSISTENCIES OF THE PROPOSED INDICATORS

Comparatively, spatial convergence calculations based on axial and point-
axial maps have proved similar, in the sense that the relative distribution
of points in a relief map describes similar relief. However, point-axial convergence exhibits a much more precise spatial description, as axial lines
are detailed in their inner differentiation and displayed accordingly.
Figures 7.8 and 7.9 show such a relative distribution: for the axial version
of the convergence measure, lines, standing for entire, long streets, are
selected; for the point-axial version of it, each dot represents one intersection of two lines, and these are selected according to their relative condition in the system. Similar descriptions occur with the spatial opportunity
measure for demand areas, in which points representing precise locations
are ranked for their relative accessibility to supply locations.

The indicators have equally shown acute responsiveness to discrete
changes in the spatial, as well as the functional, configuration of systems.
Measure applications to settings varying the composition of the grid and
supply locations' profiles have produced diverse results, showing the
ability of the model to respond to discrete changes. In a test area of more
than 100 spaces, an increase in size of one supply point by 1% was
enough to produce altered results throughout the system, with changes
detected in several points' scores. For the same system, an increase of 2%
in the same supply point's size was enough to determine changes in
some points' relative positions. Similarly, changes in grid configuration
have been detected by the model, provided that an altered connectivity
matrix results from such a change.

Tests on the consequences of whether or not the deterrent effect of distance should be considered in the model were performed for several test
areas. The results both for dimensionless (adjacency-based) and Cartesian
(metric, straight-line distance between the pair of points) grid systems
were similar and did not alter the ranking of spaces within the system
considered. Tests were performed on areas configured as orthogonal,
slightly deformed grids, in which the distribution of lines and corners is
fairly regular. In these cases the sequential ordering of lines and corners
could roughly reproduce the distribution of distances between points and
so produce correlated results. It is however expected that grids with a
greater degree of deformation should distort such a correlation.

Limitation of the use of the model may derive from the grid representation. In effect, point-axial maps tend to configure very large graphs,

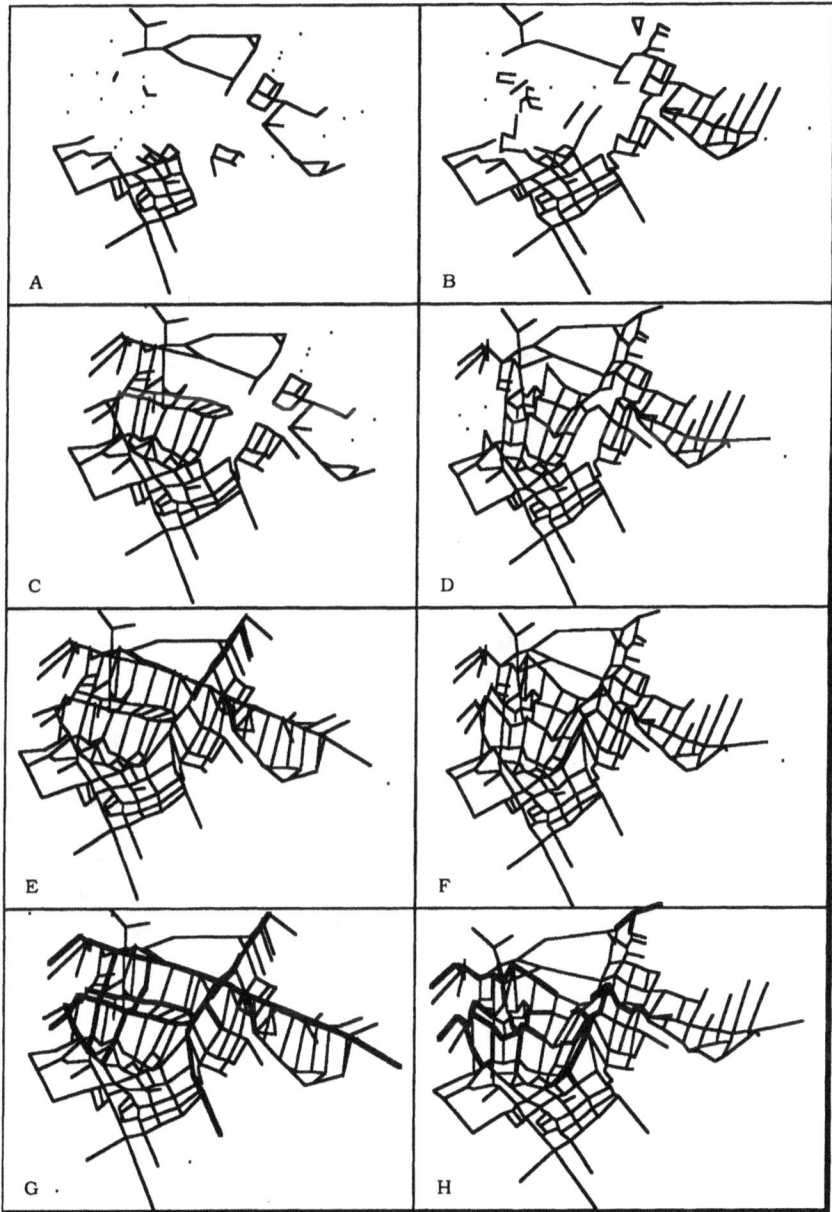

Fig. 7.8 A series of sliced 'relief' maps showing a test area's results for axial (left) and point-axial (right) representations, and the correspondence between the two, with finer detail given by the latter.

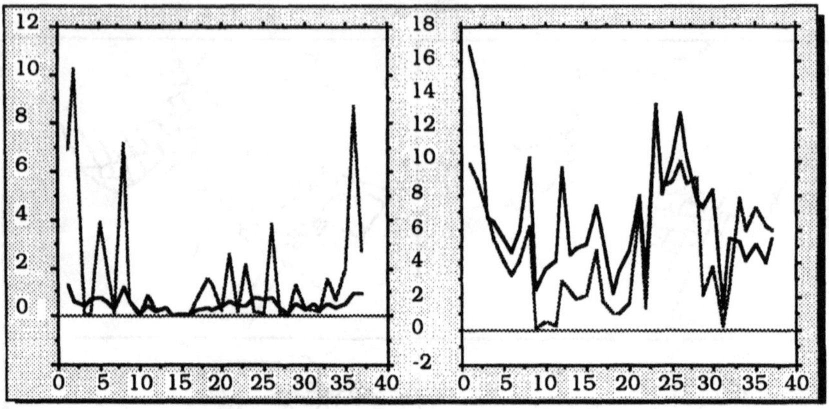

Fig. 7.9 Plotting of two test areas' measurements based on axial (lower lines) and point-axial (upper lines) representations, for corresponding system's spaces. The horizontal axis holds ordered spaces, and the vertical axis contains convergence measure values.

with hundreds of dots and thousands of edges. Although the algorithm itself has shown the capacity to handle such large data with economy (hundreds of pairs on an ordinary PC, and several thousands on a Cray supercomputer), the preparation of files is time-consuming and affords plenty of opportunities for error.

Another limitation in the use of the model is derived from the spatial representation. Handling intra-urban, very detailed, systems poses difficulties to the system's delimitation and boundary identification. In centrality measures (Krafta, 1991) the effects of different-sized systems and boundaries were explored with satisfactory results. The model did not present problems in representing different-sized areas, whereas boundaries were achieved by considering natural barriers (connectivity cut-off) and axial extensions outside the area. In point-axial maps and spatial convergence models, tests for system size effects remain to be done; boundary definitions should also be revised.

CONCLUSIONS

The proposed model differs from previous ones in the following ways:

1. It takes a probabilistic approach to the user's choice among alternative supply locations. No supply point is excluded *a priori* from the user's choice, although they are considered in a context in which proximity and relative position increase the chance of being chosen. Standing near to demand locations as well as falling along the route between demand and other supply locations are essential for the success of supply locations.

2. It considers the probability of supply location to satisfy facility demand related to the size and variety of that supply location, similarly to the method suggested by Arentze *et al.* (1994). To this extent, the attractiveness of supply locations associated to the relative positions constitutes a powered network to which demand locations converge unevenly. To each demand location the model computes trips to all supply locations, weighting each one according to relative position and attractiveness.

3. It describes spatial configuration carefully and gives to it great importance, in the sense that all routing possibilities are examined and weighted accordingly.

4. The algorithm enables simultaneous measures of convergence, opportunity and potentiality to be taken into account. They correspond, respectively, to a systematic evaluation of supply locations, through which attractors associated to spatial configuration are related to demand locations; a demand locations evaluation which measures their relative position to supply locations; and finally the supply potentiality of demand locations.

As a decision support instrument, spatial convergence seems to be able to offer support to planning management problems, giving a systematic evaluation of urban situations as well as assessing the expected performance of virtual ones, from the point of view of the qualified distribution of urban facilities in relation to residential areas.

The model operation can be inserted into a GIS platform. Being fed by essentially spatial information, the model can benefit from data management facilities encountered in GIS applications, which could also offer the possibility to interact with other impact assessment measures. To this extent, it can interact with other indicators within a complex GIS environment, giving a comprehensive assessment of urban investment alternatives.

REFERENCES

Arentze, T., Borgers, A. and Timmermans, H. (1994) Multistop-based measurements of accessibility in a GIS environment, *International Journal of Geographical Information Systems*, vol. 8, no. 4, pp. 343–356.

Hillier, B., *et al.* (1993) Natural movement: or, configuration and attraction in urban pedestrian movement, *Environment and Planning B*, vol. 20, pp. 29–66.

Krafta, R. (1991) *A study of intra-urban configurational development in Porto Alegre – Brazil*, Unpublished PhD thesis, University of Cambridge.

Krafta, R. (1993) Avaliação do impacto de alguns instrumentos urbanísticos sobre o desenvolvimento configuracional urbano, *Anais do Seminário Internacional sobre avaliação dos instrumentos de intervenção urbana*, Universidade de São Paulo.

Krafta, R. (1994) Modelling intra-urban configurational development, *Environment and Planning B*, vol. 21, pp. 67–82.

Kruger, M.J.T. (1979) An approach to built-form connectivity at urban scale: system description and its representation, *Environment and Planning B*, vol. 6, pp. 67–88.

Kruger, M.J.T. (1989) On node and axial maps: distance measures and related topics, *European Conference on Management and Representation of Urban Change*, Cambridge, UK.

Integrating constrained cellular automata models, GIS and decision support tools for urban planning and policy-making

8

Guy Engelen, Roger White and Inge Uljee

INTRODUCTION

Since the beginning of the 1990s, the field of planning has witnessed a change as the *ad hoc* management solutions of the 1980s are gradually taken over by new systematic and strategic planning approaches (Breheny, 1994). To illustrate this point we could mention the ACT-VILL initiative launched in 1994 by the European Communities (1994) 'in the framework of the preparation of new programmes, coordination of national policies, and their coordination with Community policies, technological monitoring and strategic analysis...'. To serve this purpose, the initiative launched five studies '...to deepen our understanding of the difficulties of cities and the elaboration of a diverse portfolio of technological options...', and aimed for the development of 'new "urban concepts", instruments for the integration of cities, simulation models, intra- and trans-urban networks' and 'evaluation of technological options, ...'.

Since the late 1960s and early 1970s, a period in which the development of elaborate mathematical models for urban and regional planning applications boomed, new scientific and technological developments have considerably changed the fields of spatial modelling and urban

Decision Support Systems in Urban Planning. Edited by Harry Timmermans. Published in 1997 by E & F N Spon. ISBN 0 419 21050 4

planning. The elaboration of new scientific paradigms based on such phenomena as complexity, self-organization, chaos and fractals has generally emphasized the fact that exact prediction in complex socioeconomic or socioenvironmental systems is not possible. Rather, such systems have to be studied as integral entities: their intrinsic detail matters, and their success resides in their level of complexity. As a result a new breed of models has been developed that treats socioeconomic systems as integrated systems, and treats them with a true care for their rich and complex behaviour. The main purpose of the models is to serve as thinking tools, to help the user learn about the nature and dynamic behaviour of the real-world system and to find out how it is critically bounded, rather than to make definite statements about the future state of the system modelled. The work of modellers and spatial scientists today also benefits from the revolution that has taken place in the computer and information sciences, leading to desktop computer systems with capabilities that could only be dreamed of 20 years ago.

These changes open new perspectives for scientists in the field of urban and regional planning, and are an incentive to develop new instruments designed to render planning tasks that previously were extremely time-consuming and expensive accessible to almost any planner or policy-maker in the field. In our effort to build practical instruments for urban and regional planning, we develop new urban simulation models and embed them in decision support environments. In this framework, advantage is taken of the benefits that geographical information systems (GIS) bring to the planning community. In this chapter, we report on our ongoing work.

GIS = DECISION SUPPORT SYSTEMS FOR URBAN PLANNING?

Over the last decade, researchers have made considerable progress in improving the capabilities and usefulness of geographical information systems for urban planning (Webster, 1993, 1994), and GIS, in its current form, is an appropriate support tool for urban planners in some of their decision-making tasks. This is certainly the case for tasks that require the detailed and accurate knowledge of the detailed location of physical objects, such as utilities planning (e.g. pipelines, electricity lines), cadastre and engineering applications. But, while GIS has been quite successful in planning applications in such areas as resource management and rural planning, its appearance on the urban and regional planning scene has been much more hesitant (Couclelis, 1991). From its conception, GIS – in theory at least – combined the great merits of spatial database management systems, graphical data manipulation, mapping and cartographic modelling. However, 'missing almost entirely are non-localised spatial notions such as spatial organization, configuration, pattern, spatial process, spatial dynamics, restructuring, transformation, change. Yet these are all notions that are central in urban and regional studies, and they underlie urban and regional planning especially at the strategic level' (Couclelis, 1991, p. 15). In more technical terms Jankowski and Richard (1994, p. 339) conclude that 'current GIS analysis is based on simple spatial geometric processing operations such as overlay comparison, proximity measures, and buffering. It does not provide optimization, iterative equation solving, and simulation capabilities necessary in planning.'

For systems as complex and as dynamic as cities, performing acts of planning without having reasonable ideas on how activities, land uses and the spatial interactions will change as the result of the intrinsic growth potential and planning interventions seems a somewhat futile exercise. Hence, it is a major shortcoming of today's GIS systems not to offer the possibility of dynamic and spatial modelling in the preparation and evaluation of urban policies. This is a view supported by many authors (e.g. Batty, 1991a; Eastman *et al.*, 1993). However, there is also the view among many that providing modelling capabilities within GIS is not so much an issue, and that GIS should remain foremost a system for data storage, display and overlay analysis (e.g. Brimicombe, 1992).

Over the past several years, we have implemented DSS (decision support systems) for urban planning and policy-making. To this end we created new urban simulation models, incorporating GIS, and enhanced them with decision support capabilities. In this framework, advantage is taken to the extent possible of the benefits offered by GIS, such as data management, data transformation, data visualization, cartographic modelling and spatial analysis. On the rich GIS data layers, dynamic socioeconomic and socioenvironmental models are built that treat the urban space as consisting of a two-dimensional matrix of small cells, typically 200 to 500 metres on the side. Specifically, the city is represented by means of a constrained cellular automaton model, in which the cell states represent the key land uses of the city. A number of additional tools allow the models to be used in a decision support context and permit the design, analysis and evaluation of policy interventions in the urban system. Both intra-urban and inter-urban or regional applications have been developed. In the following sections, the different components and applications will be discussed in more detail.

CELLULAR AUTOMATA MODELS

Cellular automata (CA) get their name from the fact that they consist of *cells*, like the cells on a chessboard, and that cell states may evolve according to a simple transition rule, the *automaton*. The study of cellular automata goes back to the late 1940s when von Neumann and Ulam gave birth to the field (Fredkin, 1991). After rather slow progress in the 1960s and 1970s CA gained gradually more attention in several scientific disciplines, most particularly in physics, mathematics, computer science and biology (artificial life). At present an important and rapidly growing body of knowledge on the behaviour and capabilities of CA exists.

Cellular automata raised, until very recently, only limited interest in the geographical community, and this despite the fact that Tobler (1979) referred to them as 'geographical models'. Generally speaking, most applications remained rather theoretical (e.g. Couclelis, 1985, 1988, 1989; Phipps, 1989); the potential usefulness was being discussed and demonstrated, but no particular model was being applied and tested. Fredkin's remark that 'CAs can deal naturally with Euclidean space-time, but finding CA systems that model aspects of the real physical world is work in progress' (Fredkin, 1991, p. 256) seems relevant in this context. Recently interest in CA among spatial scientists has been growing rapidly and many new applications are under development. Possibly they agree with Fredkin that: 'What is true is that most serious attempts to find a way of incorporating a property of nature into the CA environment have met with progress: today we see ways of incorporating dozens of characteristics of the real world into CA models' (Fredkin, 1991, p. 256). Examples of applications include among others: the modelling of urban and regional development (White and Engelen, 1993, 1994; White *et al.*, 1997; Engelen *et al.*, 1993a, b, 1995; Batty and Xie, 1994; De Moura Campos, 1992); forest fires (Green, 1990); epidemics (Green, 1993); starfish outbreaks (Bradbury *et al.*, 1990); and lava flows (Young and Wadge, 1990).

The best-known and most studied cellular automata model is Conway's 'Life' (Gardner, 1970). It is defined as follows:

1. A two-dimensional Euclidean space (in principle infinite) is divided into an array of unit squares called *cells*.
2. Cells are in one of two *states*: alive or dead.
3. The state of a cell can change because of the state it is in, and because of the state of the cells in its *neighbourhood*. In 'Life' the neighbourhood consists of the eight cells surrounding the centre cell.
4. To decide on the state of the cell in the next iteration, *transition rules* are applied to each cell and its neighbourhood. For 'Life', the rules have a biological sense to them and are as follows:
    (a) a dead cell surrounded by three live cells, will become alive (= *reproduction*);
    (b) a live cell will stay alive if it has two or three live neighbours;
    (c) otherwise it will die because of *isolation* if it has fewer than two live neighbours, or *overcrowding* if it has four or more.
5. Time progresses uniformly, and at each *discrete time* step, all cells change state simultaneously.

Transition rules can be qualitative (as in 'Life'), quantitative or a combination of both. Rules are in general deterministic (as in 'Life') but may contain stochastic elements (Lee *et al.*, 1991; White and Engelen, 1993). If all rules apply in an identical manner to all the cells of the grid, as they do in deterministic CA, then spatial stationarity is assumed (Tobler, 1979). Further, spatial isotropy (Tobler, 1979) is assumed within the neighbourhood if the exact positioning of the neighbours in the neighbourhood is not considered in the formulation of the transition rule. For diffusion processes the latter often will not apply, as the position within the neighbourhood and contiguity of cells in specific states is of importance.

Given an initial state for all the cells in the grid and transition rules that apply to the neighbourhood, the dynamics of the system will unfold. It has been shown that models, such as 'Life', which in their definition are very simple, may show in reality a very complex and rich behaviour, and, although the transition rules are defined within the spatial extent of the (micro)neighbourhood only, they are capable of generating spatial patterns that are macroscopic in nature. The macroscopic patterns generated vary from totally ordered to totally chaotic with a number of intermediate and transient states in between both extremes (e.g. Wolfram, 1986; Langton, 1992; McIntosh, 1991).

CONSTRAINED CELLULAR AUTOMATA MODELS

Some researchers have used 'Life', or model formulations derived from it, to represent geographical phenomena (Casti, 1989; Batty and Xie, 1994; Roy and Snickars, 1993). However, to build models that represent more practical geographical problems, it seems that more complex CA are required and that their dynamics need to be constrained. Complexity is used here as defined by Fredkin (1991, p. 255): 'some combination of: a large number of states per cell, a complex CA (transition) rule, neighbourhood (spatial connectivity and dimensionality), boundary condition or initial condition'. In the remainder of this section we will discuss the characteristics of a generic constrained cellular automata model which we have developed over the past several years and which has been applied to intra-urban (White and Engelen, 1993, 1994; White et al., 1997) and inter-urban (Engelen et al., 1993a, b, 1995) cases.

THE CELL STATES

Geographers traditionally have studied geographical systems in terms of a physical, environmental space within which a relatively large number of agents interact. Likewise, most dynamic spatial models of socio-economic systems describe the behaviour of at least three to four spatial agents, representing groups of residents and investors or employees in major economic sectors such as commerce, industry and agriculture (e.g. White, 1977; Allen and Sanglier, 1979; Clarke and Wilson, 1983). On the other hand, cellular geographical models based on 'Life' describe geographical systems in terms of two or three agents only: occupied versus non-occupied land (Batty and Xie, 1994), vacant land or land inhabited by black or white residents (Casti, 1989). To deal more realistically with interaction mechanisms such as segregation, diffusion, clustering and agglomeration, or repulsion and attraction, the introduction of more cell states is a useful extension. For example, in the application of our CA model to Cincinnati (see later section), cells can be in any of seven states, each representing actual land uses: vacant, commercial, industrial, housing, river, railroad, road. In the application of the model to a Caribbean island, 12 land uses are considered. Obviously raising the number of states (k) in the CA will increase, in theory at least, the number of possible state transitions of each cell (k^2 including transition to the same state), and defining the transition rules of the model will be more cumbersome. However, in practical modelling cases, a substantial number of transitions are physically unlikely or even impossible. In the example of Cincinnati, it is impossible for a road cell to change into a river cell in a model that does not include flooding as a transition mechanism. We have learned from our applications that elaborate models can run successfully with a number of transition rules in the order of $2k$.

THE NEIGHBOURHOOD

Flow and diffusion processes will require spatial contiguity to take place, since 'the interactions consist of point to point spread: one sick person infects another; one burning tree ignites another; water currents carry starfish larvae from one reef to another; and seeds spread from one site to another' (Green, 1993). Hence, they can be represented in a model defined in terms of the Moore neighbourhood, consisting of the eight nearest cells. For example, in a CA model representing the flow of lava down the flanks of a volcano, the lava front will extend from a front cell to one of its immediate neighbouring cells because of the gravity and other forces acting upon the lava (Young and Wadge, 1990). Socioeconomic interactions take place over distances extending beyond the nearest neighbours, and even to represent rather local interaction processes, a neighbourhood of a larger size than the immediate neighbours is required because interactions generally change, even over short distances. For example, commercial activities cluster into shopping centres because of agglomeration benefits over short distances, but create voids in between because of competition over longer distances. In our applications we use circular neighbourhoods with radius of a maximum of six cells, covering an area of 113 cells (including the centre cell). Owing to the discrete nature of the cellular space, all 113 cells lie in one of 19 discrete distance zones (rings) around the centre (including the centre cell on ring 1), and the transition rules are defined in terms of these rings.

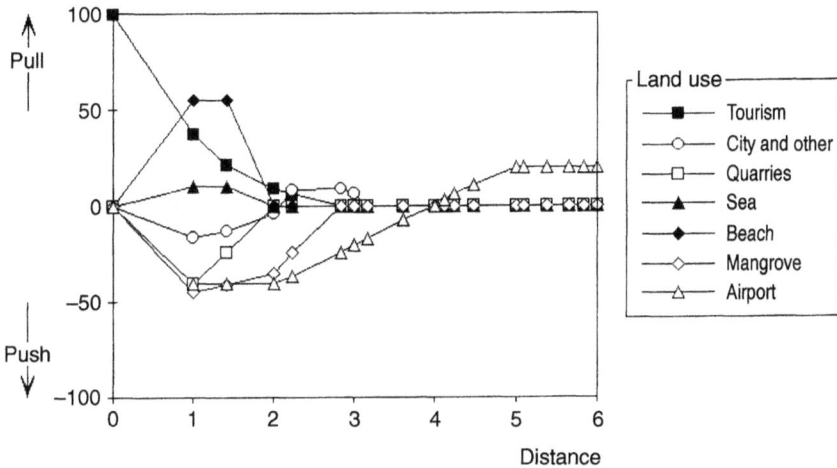

Fig. 8.1 The cellular automata transition rules for 'tourism' used in the island model of a later section.

THE TRANSITION RULES

As mentioned earlier cellular automata transition rules can be qualitative, quantitative or combinations of both, and they can be deterministic or stochastic. They will determine the new state of the cell in the grid on the basis of the states of the cell itself and the cells in its neighbourhood. In our CA model, the transition rules represent in a general way locational preferences and spatial interaction mechanisms, including push and pull forces and agglomeration or competition effects. They are written as distance functions. For each possible interaction between pairs of cells in a different state, transition weights are entered for the 19 concentric rings around the centre cell. This means, in theory at least, a total of $19k^2$ weights that need to be entered. As mentioned earlier a great number of these weight coefficients will be equal to 0, due to the fact that not all interactions take place over the full radius of the neighbourhood (e.g. the effect of a railway on industry) or because some spatial agents will be indifferent to the location of others. Thus, our Cincinnati model consists of seven states, 14 rules and 179 weights, while the island model consists of 12 states, 25 rules and 176 weights. Figure 8.1 shows the rules for the land use 'tourism' as they are used in the island model (see later section).

In conclusion, for the definition of our transition functions, we assume spatial isotropy within the neighbourhood, and define transition weights solely for sets of cells – specifically all the cells located on the same concentric circle – rather than individual cells.

For each cell, the potential for transition to each active cell state z is calculated as follows:

$$P_z = vS_z A_z N_z \qquad (8.1)$$

$$N_z = \sum_d \sum_i (w_{z,y,d})(I_{d,i}) \qquad (8.2)$$

$$v = 1 + [-\ln(\text{rand})]^a \qquad (8.3)$$

Here P_z is the potential for transition to state z; S_z is the suitability of the cell for state z, with $0 \le S_z \le 1$, and if $N_z < 0$ then S_z is replaced by $(1 - S_z)$; A_z is the accessibility of the cell for state z, given by

$$A_z = 1/(1 + D/a_z) \qquad (8.4)$$

with D the Euclidean distance from the cell to the nearest cell of the transportation network and a_z the coefficient expressing the importance of good accessibility for state z, and if $N_z < 0$ then A_z is replaced by $(1 - A_z)$; N_z is the neighbourhood effect; $w_{z,y,d}$ is the weighting parameter applied to cells in state y in distance zone d; $I_{d,i} = 1$ if cell i in distance ring d is in state y, otherwise $I_{d,i} = 0$; v is a stochastic disturbance term, where $(0 < \text{rand} < 1)$ is a uniform random variant, and a is a parameter that allows the size of the perturbation to be adjusted.

Once all transition potentials P_z have been calculated, cells will change to the state for which their potential is highest until the demand for cells in that state is met (see later subsection for more details).

THE CELLULAR SPACE

Cellular automata models such as 'Life' evolve in an isotropic, homogeneous cellular space. Except for purely theoretical problems (e.g. White and Engelen, 1993), spatial problems are set in spaces that have idiosyncrasies and heterogeneities at all levels of detail. The detailed representation of space as well as the simulation regime of cellular automata permit us 'to add in all sorts of much more realistic assumptions, about boundaries, shapes, and histories, in a straightforward way, that may well be precluded in an analytic formulation' (Krieger, 1991). We have introduced idiosyncrasies on the level of the individual cells of the cellular space. The apparent similarity of cellular spaces with raster-based GIS systems led us to define these in terms of geographical factor maps (Wright, 1990) and derived suitabilities for each of the land use functions modelled. This allows us to introduce physical, environmental, institutional and historical characteristics in socioeconomic models at a high level of spatial detail (variable S_z in equation (8.1)). In addition, the accessibility of the cell is introduced (variable A_z in equation (8.4)). This is an expression of its nearness to the transportation network.

FORCING THE DYNAMICS

An initial spatial configuration on a grid of cells, a neighbourhood and transition rules are in principle sufficient to cause a cellular automaton to evolve over time, possibly indefinitely, and most of the theoretical work done in the field consists precisely in the analysis of the patterns thus generated. However, socioeconomic systems are shaped by interaction processes that take place at different geographical scales, some of which are very local and within the reach of the neighbourhood, some of which are beyond the reach of the cellular space of the modelled system. This problem is dealt with in the work of Roy and Snickars (1993) and Batty and Xie (1994). The latter develop on the basis of 'Life' a model that takes into consideration phenomena beyond the reach of the neighbourhood through the introduction of larger geographical entities called *fields* and *regions*. In order to incorporate the dynamics caused by long-range processes, we have integrated in our cellular automata models more traditional dynamic models, which in the most generic case, are regionalized (see penultimate section). In the simulation context, the latter will calculate the overall growth of the system as a result of its internal 'macro'-dynamics and its exchanges with the world outside, and will 'force' this growth, as a constraint, upon the cellular model. The cellular model will, on the basis of its 'micro'-dynamics, allocate the growth to specific cells and will return this information to the macro-model and thus affect the macro-dynamics. Practically speaking, the macro-level model will generate at each iteration the total number of cells in each state T_z. To allocate those, the cellular model calculates the potentials for all cells to change to each state and ranks them from highest to lowest. Starting with the first value in this list, the T_z cells with highest potential for transition to state z are selected. Thus, a cell will change to the state z for which its potential P_z is highest, unless P_z is not among the T_z highest, in which case the cell might change to a state z' for which its transition potential P_z' is among the T_z' highest.

   We conclude this section with the remark that the introduction of idiosyncrasies on the level of the individual cells and the forced global dynamics are non-traditional characteristics of cellular automata models. Hence they have been given little attention in cellular automata research so far. Both can influence the dynamics of cellular automata profoundly, and it goes without saying that many fundamental questions still remain to be researched in the future.

AN INTRA-URBAN AND AN INTER-URBAN EXAMPLE

In the previous section, we introduced a constrained cellular automata model that can be applied to a wide range of geographical applications. It can be graphically schematized as in Fig. 8.2. It consists of three components: At the macro-level (Fig. 8.2, top), a global (see following two subsections) or a regionalized (see penultimate section) dynamic interaction model is used which calculates growth coefficients as the result of 'macro'-dynamics. These growth coefficients are fed into the cellular model (Fig. 8.2, middle) which will allocate them spatially on the basis of its 'micro'-dynamics. The link between both levels is bi-directional in that the cellular model will return information to the macro-level and thus influence processes at that level. The models at both levels get their data from the same geographical database (Fig. 8.2, bottom), in fact from a custom-designed GIS able to exchange information with commercial GIS packages. Two examples developed with this model will be discussed in the remainder of this section. The first concerns an intra-urban application to the city of Cincinnati. The second is an inter-urban application to a hypothetical island in the Caribbean. For more detail on both applications we refer to the references in the text.

CINCINNATI

The application to Cincinnati (White *et al.*, 1997) is a natural and immediate follow-up on work done on purely theoretical urban structures. In this earlier version of the model, basic questions of evolving urban form were being researched in a fully homogeneous cellular space of 40 by 40 cells. The macro-level dynamics were read in as constant growth coefficients. Cells could be in any of four states representing urban land uses: vacant, industrial, commercial or residential. In the deterministic cellular automata transition rules a stochastic parameter was introduced (v in equation (8.1)) to represent the uncertainty in locational decisions and spatial interactions. The sensitivity of the model to this stochastic parameter was tested and urban structures were generated ranging from highly simple to completely random with intermediate forms that assume a reasonable degree of complexity. To measure the level of complexity of the urban patterns, their fractal dimension was calculated and compared with values observed for real cities (Frankhauser, 1991). From these comparisons, the conclusion was drawn that constrained cellular automata models are capable of generating urban forms comparable to real-world examples.

These promising results led us to further analyse the capability of cellular automata models on more practical cases, such as the city of Cincinnati. The aim of the Cincinnati model (White *et al.*, 1997) is to find out (i) whether the CA modelling framework, at least in principle, is capable of realistically simulating observed growth, and (ii) whether it is capable of generating realistic spatial patterns and clusters of activity. Further, the experiment is designed to study the introduction of idiosyncrasies in

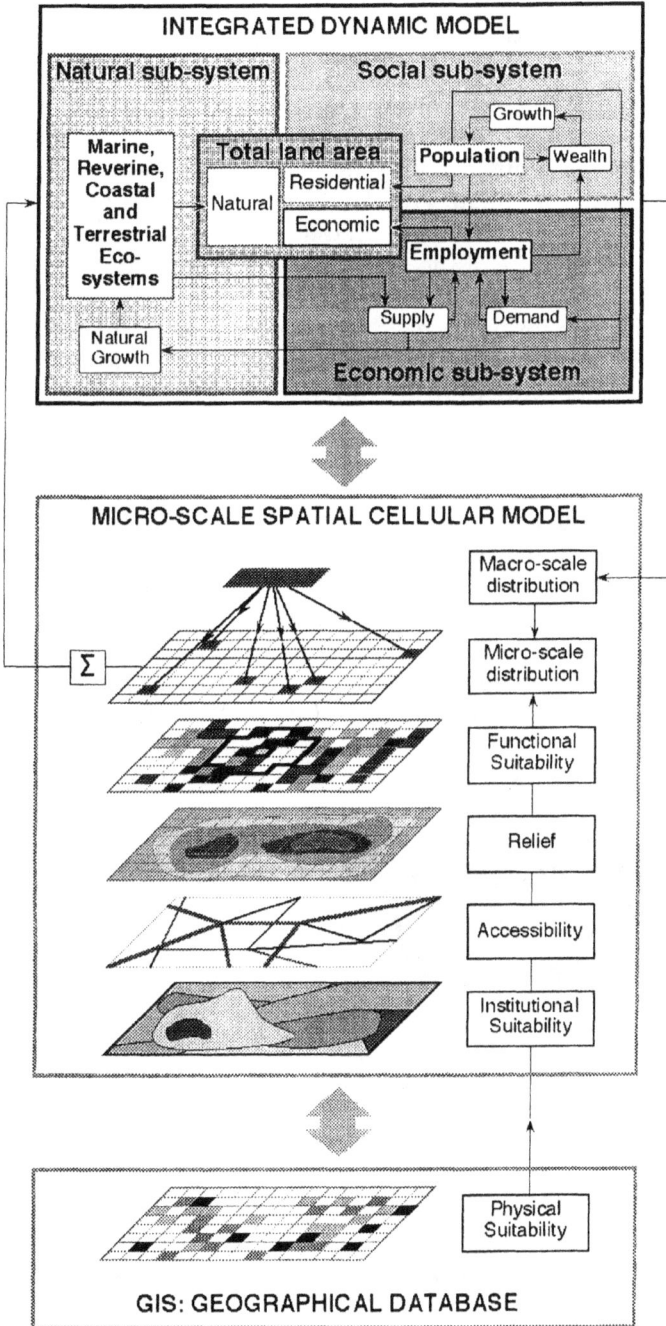

Fig. 8.2   Schematic representation of the three components of the model. At the macro-level (top) the island model is depicted (see later section).

the urban CA model and the development of urban structures in heterogeneous cellular spaces. Cincinnati was chosen as an example because of the existence of an atlas of urban land use in US cities for 1960 (Passonneau and Wurman, 1966). The cities in the atlas are represented on a 250 m raster of 80 by 80 cells. The size of Cincinnati in 1960 was such that not only the centre but also the periphery of the city is reasonably contained within the map. We also dispose of a map representing the land use of the city in 1915, and used it as an intermediate time point to verify the performance of the simulator. The major features of the transportation network (roads and railroads) together with the variable suitability of the area for industrial development (essentially determined by slope of land) are included in the simulation as inhomogeneities in the cell space. The network of roads and railways and the industrial suitability are shown in Fig. 8.3.

Figure 8.4 shows a typical simulation run over 50 iterations (120 years). The dates on the maps are approximate. In the absence of a map, the initial condition is an approximation of how land use in the city could have been around 1840. The overall growth of the city is fed in externally by means of a simple growth model. A constant growth of 7% per iteration for each of the three land use categories (industry, commerce, housing) is used, which results in the correct amount of cells for each land use in 1960. The purpose of the exercise was not to accurately reproduce the history of Cincinnati. The latter would have required a much more sophisticated upper-level model, much more reliable intermediate data and more calibration effort. Also, the use of a model to recreate an urban history of

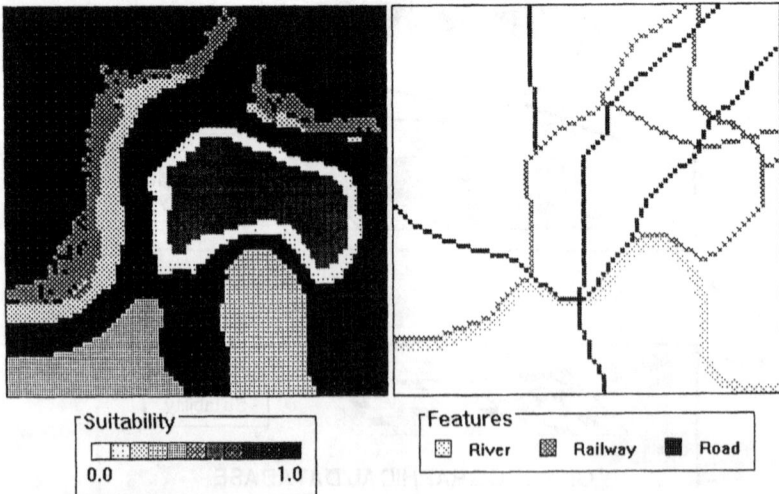

Fig. 8.3 Suitability of land for industry (left) and the transportation networks (right) used in the Cincinnati simulations.

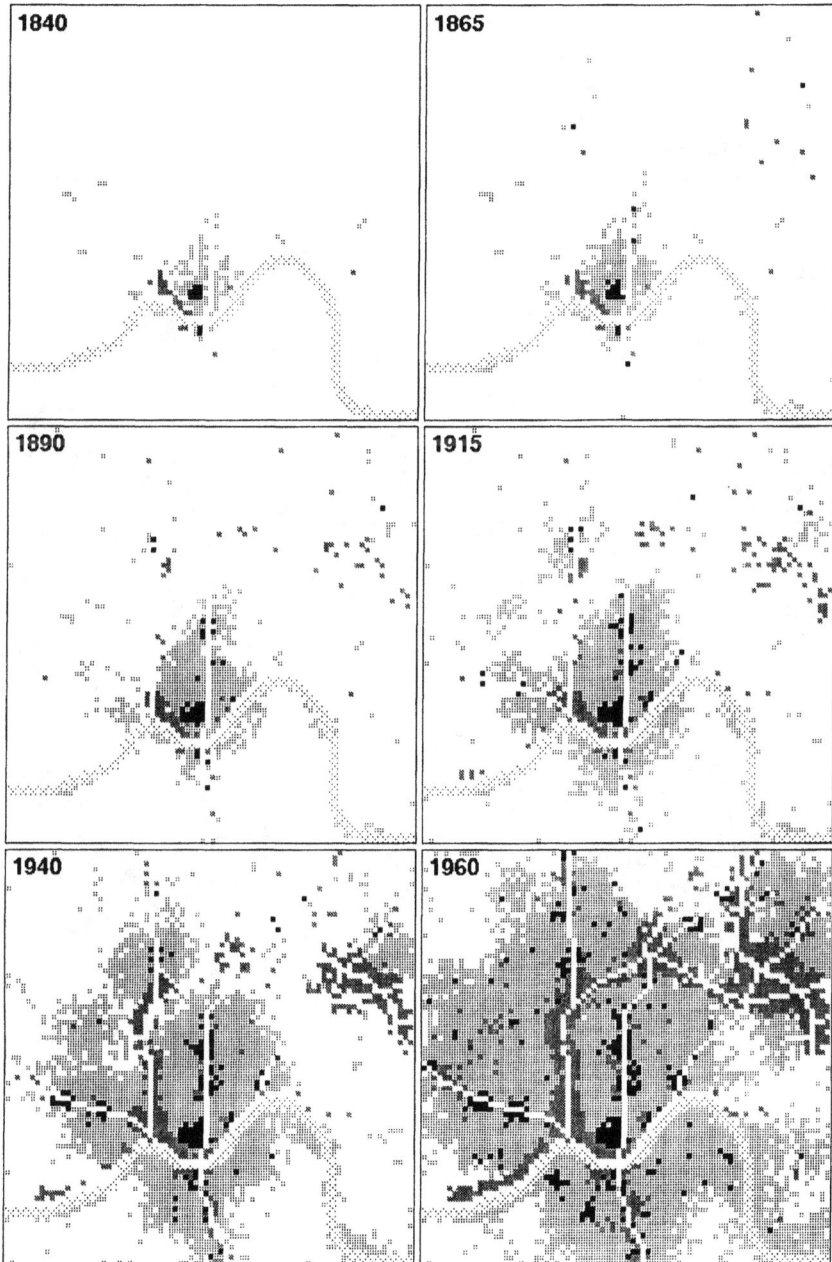

Fig. 8.4   A typical simulation run of the Cincinnati model. The dates on the maps are approximate. (See Fig. 8.5 for the key.)

over a century cannot be more than academic. Simulations were run with different values for the stochastic parameter (v), and with or without suitabilities (S_z) and the transportation system (A_z). From the analysis of different simulation runs, and their comparison with the actual city in 1960 (Fig. 8.5) we concluded (White *et al.*, 1997) that cellular automata models can reproduce urban form in a reasonably realistic manner and that they are capable of generating urban structures and clusters of a size beyond the radius and reach of the neighbourhood. Inhomogeneities, entered as

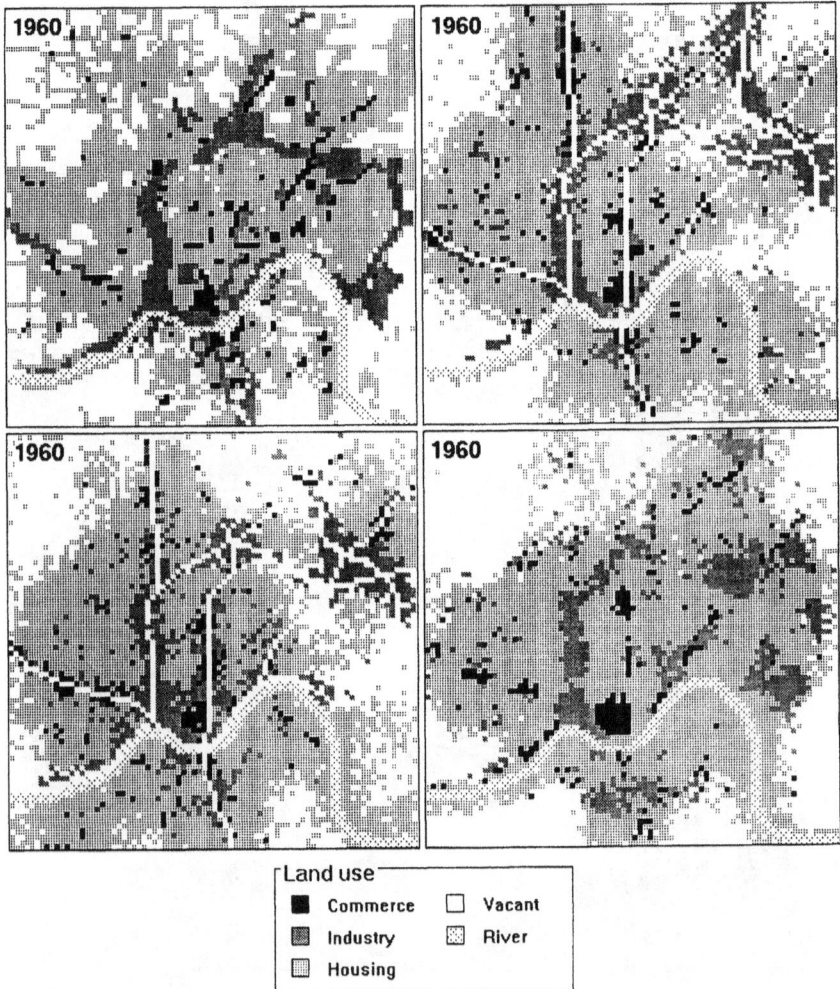

Fig. 8.5 The actual land use in Cincinnati in 1960 (top left) and the final state (1960) of the simulation runs: stochastic variant of the run shown in Fig. 8.4 (top right); simulation without suitabilities but with transportation network (bottom left); and simulation without network but with suitabilities (bottom right).

land features (i.e. river cell, railway cell), land suitabilities (i.e. slopes, soils) or accessibilities (nearness to the transportation system) structure the urban space. They have a stabilizing effect on the model in that they restrict the possible patterns of urban development.

As a next logical step in this series of urban simulations, we are now applying the model to simulate the detailed growth of the City of St. John's, Newfoundland, Canada. The aim of this exercise will be to learn more about the difficulties of developing and running constrained CA models in practical urban modelling exercises. Also, we will apply the knowledge gained from work done with the island model and replace the simple macro-level model that generated the overall growth in the above example with the standard spatial interaction-based urban dynamics model which we have begun to develop in Ren and White (1993); see also White and Engelen (1994).

A CARIBBEAN ISLAND

The second example is an inter-urban problem. It concerns the application of our generic constrained CA model to a prototypical Caribbean island. The Caribbean island model, or in short the island model, is the result of a study commissioned by UNEP (United Nations Environment Programme, Caribbean Regional Co-ordination Unit, Kingston, Jamaica) aiming at the development of a generic model and simulation shell to analyse climate-induced changes in land use and land cover on small islands and low-lying coastal areas in the Caribbean (Engelen *et al.*, 1993a, b, 1995). Climate change is expressed here in terms of sea-level rise and temperature change. Even a superficial analysis of this problem will reveal that phenomena at very different geographical scales will possibly cause land use changes. For instance, a sea-level rise of some 20 cm vertically will result in the flooding and loss of small parts of coastal lands. It will result in the retreat of some human activities and their relocation away from the sea. This might have knock-on effects and cause land use changes throughout. The study of such effects is only possible if a detailed representation of the land use is possible, hence the use of a cellular model seems appropriate. However, temperature changes of about 4°C in Canada, the northern USA or northern Europe might influence considerably the drive of the people to spend their holidays in a warm Caribbean island. This is a phenomenon happening on a intercontinental scale, hence can only be studied by means of a correct representation of the island and its economy as part of a much larger, global, system. Thus forcing the dynamics of the cellular automata model by means of a dynamic, macro-economic, long-range model seems a reasonable means to tackle the full problem.

We have equipped our generic constrained CA model with a more elaborate macro-scale model, capturing the non-local dynamics of the population, the economy and the environment in an integrated fashion (see Fig. 8.2, top). This macro-scale model calculates the amount of land required for various socioeconomic activities, *in casu*: residential, tourism, subsistence agriculture, export agriculture, city activities (commercial and industrial) and mining (of construction materials). It does this by means of four linked modules, handling the environmental, social, macro-economic and land productivity aspects of the problem:

- The *environmental, or natural, module* consists of a set of linked relations representing the expected changes through time of sea level and precipitation, and the effects of those on the suitable land area, precipitation, storm frequency, and external demands for services and goods produced. These relations are entered as semi-qualitative expressions and reflect hypotheses or expert knowledge as it is available today.
- The *social module* models the island demography in terms of a single group. The population grows exponentially as the result of birth, death and migration. The birth rate is specified to follow a long-term structural trend, while the mortality and migration rates have both a structural and a social component. The latter reflects the well-being of the island population and is a function of the employment rate.
- The *economic module* models the island economy by means of a highly aggregated and simplified input–output model, which is updated and solved at each iteration.
- The *land productivity module* takes as an input the growth quantities generated by the linked natural, social and economic modules, expressed as number of people and number of jobs in the various economic sectors, and translates them into the spatial units, or cells, required to house these new people and new jobs. In this calculation it uses information obtained from the cellular model relative to the scarcity and marginality (as determined by suitability) of land.

The four modules are tightly interlinked: (i) the export demands change due to climate-induced changes; (ii) household demand varies with a changing population and its well-being; and (iii) the economic activity influences the growth of the population. But also the linkage of the macro-scale with the cellular model is rather intense, as (iv) the amount of available land changes due to sea-level changes, and (v) available and suitable land influences external demand, as well as (vi) the location and the density of activities. In the linkage of the macro-model and the cellular model, the land productivity module fulfils a key role and its correct calibration is crucial since it matches numbers of the macro-model with land use patches of the cellular model. Indeed, data for the macro-scale model are generally census data, summed or averaged over administrative units and expressed in terms of people, jobs and monetary units. The data for the cellular model are mostly obtained from field observations, remote sensing or maps, and consist in the extent of land use and land cover in a purely morphological sense.

The cellular part of the island model is developed on a rectangular grid of 60 by 70 cells, each covering an area of 500 by 500 m. The same 113-cell neighbourhood is used. Cells are in one of 12 possible states, of which six have their direct counterpart in the macro-scale model: tourism, city functions, local (subsistence) agriculture, export agriculture, quarries (mining construction materials), and housing; one is the natural or vacant state; and five concern land uses and land covers for which dynamics are not governed by the cellular model *sensu stricto*, yet are taken into consideration in the transition rules of the first six land uses mentioned. This latter group consists of: sea, beach, mangrove, coral reef, and airport. The dynamics of sea, beach, mangrove and coral reef are governed by specific rules which depend primarily on the changing sea level in conjunction with the relief of the island. Airport cells remain fixed unless they are moved or replaced by the user of the model.

As commissioned by UNEP we designed an island that resembles a typical small Caribbean island: an area of some 940 km²; flat in the west with highlands (max. 490 m) in the east; sandy beaches as well as rocky shores; coral reefs and mangroves; a windy east coast; an initial population of 24 500; a total of 11 000 jobs in tourism, agriculture (subsistence and export), commerce and industry and construction (in this order of importance); a very open economy depending on the export of tourism and agricultural goods; and importing a wide range of goods and services. Since we talk about a theoretical island, no real calibration has taken place. Parameter values are chosen to reflect as realistically as possible a Caribbean situation for the next 40 years. Net population growth is nearly 2% a year but decreases slowly, and the economy stagnates: the external demand for tourism initially grows but reaches a ceiling after 20 years; external demand for agricultural products initially grows, but starts to decline after 20 years; and the external demand for city functions grows slowly throughout the whole period.

With the initial land use shown in Fig. 8.6 (top), we have run the model under different scenarios relative to climatic change and have shown the effects it has both in terms of a changing economy – shifting towards subsistence agriculture – and in terms of changing land uses throughout most of the territory. The latter specifically causes pressure on marginal land and thus creates direct and indirect problems in terms of aquifer depletion, surface water pollution and erosion, problems that have been reported to exist on real islands in the region (Blommestein, 1993). A typical simulation run is shown in Fig. 8.6, with to the right a temperature rise of 2°C and sea-level rise of 20 cm, and to the left the same simulation without climate change.

All island model simulations have been run with inhomogeneities on the level of the individual cells. They consist in the DEM (digital eleva-tion model) of the island and suitability (S_z) and accessibility (A_z) maps for each of the functions modelled. The transition rules are kept determinis-tic ($v = 1$). We have run simulations with varying sizes of the neighbour-hood and different transition functions. The differences in the generated patterns can be explained as artefacts and specificities of the transition rules used. Running many simulations confirms the conclusions drawn from the Cincinnati simulations, namely that the introduction of the inhomogeneities stabilizes the model strongly.

A MULTI-REGIONAL ISLAND MODEL

The more generic case of the forced cellular automata model is one in which a multi-regional model represents the spatial interactions within and without a number of large regions at the macro-level. This approach is certainly relevant if the dynamics of the modelled system are consider-ably influenced by interaction at the macro-level or if the interaction of the modelled system with the world outside happens primarily through one or some of the macro-regions (i.e. because of a common border with a neighbouring system, region or state, or because of the layout of the transportation system, and the location of harbours and airports). We have stated elsewhere (Engelen *et al.*, 1993a) that our Caribbean island is too small to be subdivided in macro-regions, hence that its dynamics can be modelled adequately by means of a single macro-region forcing the cellular model. Yet, as an experiment, we have regionalized the macro-level model of the island model and have created four regions named West, Central, East and South (see Fig. 8.7, top left). The experiment is primarily meant to get insight into the mechanism required to couple a multi-regional macro-level model with a cellular model, and to get an understanding of the dynamics within the macro-regions on the cellular level. With this purpose in mind, as little as possible has been changed in the island model. This has the advantage of simplicity and allows for comparisons with the single-region version. The following changes have been made:

- In the macro-level model only the land productivity module is changed in such a manner that it no longer calculates the number of new cells to be allocated for the total island, but rather for each of the four regions of the island. This is done in the most straightforward manner possible, which consists in a constant percentage distribution of the total growth among the four regions. The percentages are set for

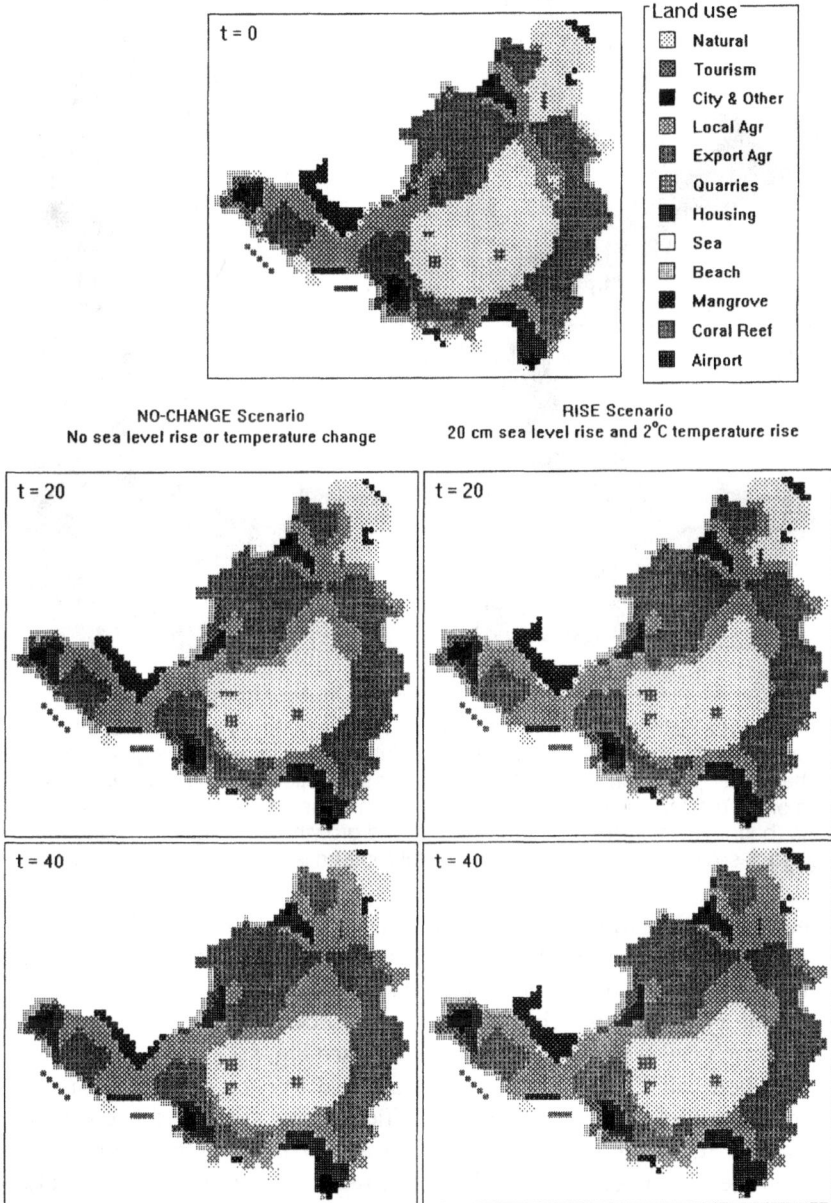

Fig. 8.6 Two simulation runs of the Caribbean island model. The initial condition is shown on top. To the right is the simulation under conditions of climate change. To the left is the same simulation without climate change.

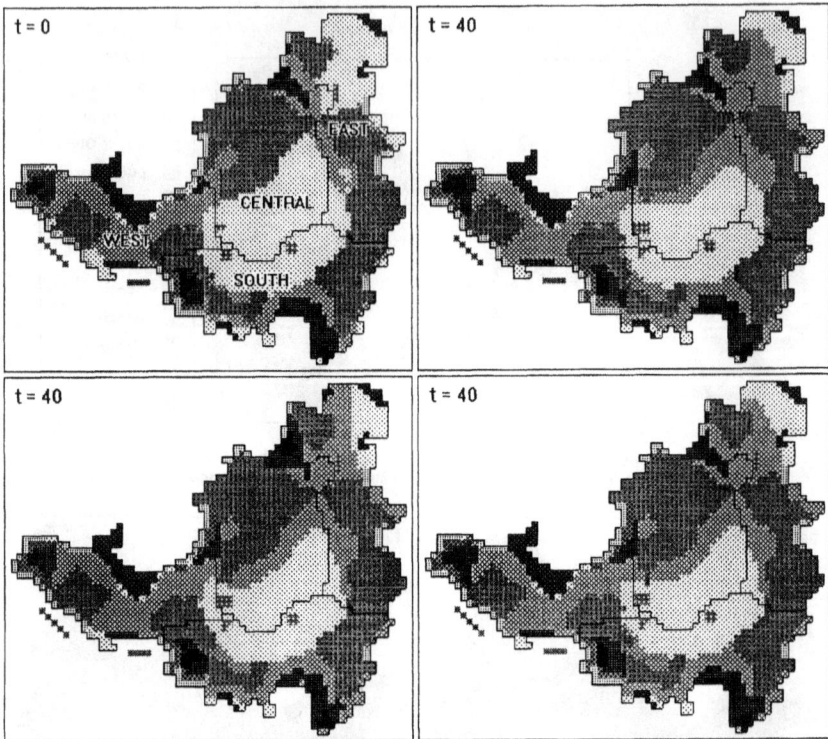

Fig. 8.7   The four-regions Caribbean island model: (a) Initial condition of all simulations (top left). (b) The final state of a simulation run with the one-region version of the model (top right). (c) The final state of a simulation with the four-regions version of the model. The distribution of the growth is the same as in the one-region case (bottom right). (d) Same as (c), but all the growth in 'city' functions and 'housing' goes solely to regions East and Central (bottom left). (See Fig. 8.6 for the key.)

each land use function independently. We fully realize that this is a mechanism unlike spatial interaction, but it has the advantage of being fully under the control of the analyst in this experimental set-up.

- At the cellular level, the island is subdivided into four regions such that each cell is part of only one region (see Fig. 8.7).
- The same allocation mechanism is applied to each of the regions: the macro-model generates growth coefficients for each land use function in each region. For each cell and for each land use, transition potentials are calculated. Borders between regions do not affect the definition or application of neighbourhoods or transition functions. Hence, no special rules apply near the borders. Cells will change to the land use for which their transition potential is highest. If the demand for the specific land use within the region is met, cells might get land uses for which potentials are less than highest.

We have run simulations with both the one-region and the four-regions model with identical parameter settings, on both the macro-level and the cellular level. For the sake of comparison, the simulation results of both models are presented on the level of the four regions (see Fig. 8.7). In the one-region simulations we analysed in more detail the growth of each land use category in each of the four regions. These differ remarkably. Despite the fact that the growth is generated by one and the same model, rather different mixes of activity and histories typify the four regions. Figure 8.8, comparing the West region with its neighbour Central region, is the result of a typical run. West is dominated by local agriculture, but also has relatively high activities in the city and tourism sector. It is a very crowded region, which explains why there is only little expansion in most land use categories in the early stages of the simulation. Central region is very much the export agriculture region of the

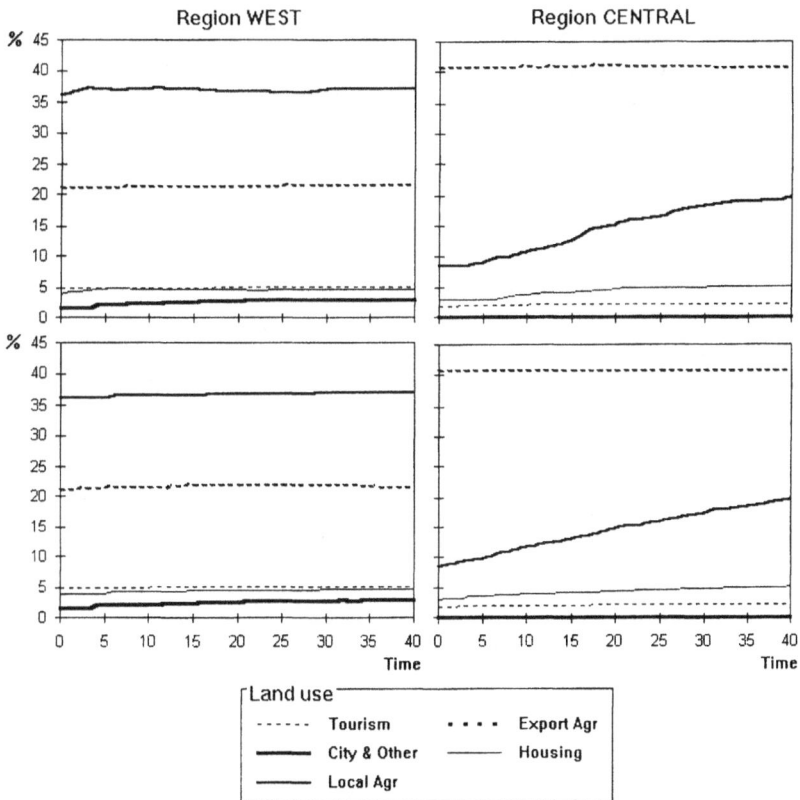

Fig. 8.8 Evolution of the land use in regions West (left) and Central (right) in the one-region version (top) and the four-regions version (bottom) of the Caribbean island model.

island. Except for export agriculture, all activities are undergoing a fairly strong expansion. Early in the simulation, there is still a substantial amount of open space in Central. It is, however, hilly and marginal land, and is rapidly taken in by local agriculture. Notice also in the graphs that the expansion of most land uses in Central is to some extent logistic. This is most noticeable for local agriculture, with a slow start, a steep growth from year 10 onwards for 20 years and finally a slow growth again after year 30 when suitable land is becoming scarce in the region. There are no city functions in Central throughout the full simulation. City functions predominantly concentrate in regions West and South, where also most of the people dwell.

From this one-region simulation we calculated the average growth over the 40-year simulation interval for each of the four regions and for each land use. These coefficients were then used to distribute the overall growth among the regions in the four-regions model. In this way, we can run simulations that end with the same amount of cells for each land use and in each region. Figure 8.7 compares the final states of the one-region and the four-regions simulations. Generally speaking, there is a strong resemblance between both versions of the model. The small differences are mostly due to the fact that, rather than being attracted to a region solely because of the specifics of cells and their neighbourhoods, land uses are now first being distributed over the regions due to the constant growth coefficients and then allocated on the basis of the cellular dynamics. Owing to the imposed location (in one of the four regions) and timing of the location, certain cells get a specific land use earlier or later than in the one-region simulation. This allows patterns to grow that are sufficiently resistant to cause spatial bifurcations, thus changing the history and final outlook of the individual regions and the island as a whole. Apart from these minor deviations, which are in any case artefacts of the particular regionalization of the model, we can state that the fact of having regional borders is not affecting the simulation results. It is because individual cell potentials (P_z) are calculated without regard to the borders, that borders are not affecting location on the cellular level. This demonstrates one of the merits of cellular automata models, namely that they permit the study of the detailed morphological aspects of urban and regional growth, which is not possible with most contemporary spatial modelling approaches (Batty, 1991b). This characteristic is more explicitly demonstrated in the following experiment. Growth coefficients for most land use categories and regions are imposed as explained previously, except for city functions and housing. Growth in city functions and housing is uniquely directed to regions Central and East (50% each). This could be the result of a policy decision, which promotes both regions or forbids growth in any other but the two regions. The question at hand is: Where will such growth take place, and will a possible location take advantage of pull factors in the neighbouring region? Figure 8.7 shows the result of the experiment after a 40-year simulation. One notices that a large city and residential cluster has grown near the coast, right across the border between regions Central and East, where the city and residential functions allocated to region Central cluster with the existing and new city cells of region East. In turn this generates the potential to concentrate housing and attract new city functions.

The four-regions model with which these results were obtained lacks a spatial interaction mechanism and does not respond to the clusters formed. In other words, the cluster in our experiment will not be perceived by the macro-model as a nucleus that will attract more activity to the regions Central and East. If the macro-level model were replaced by a model having the dynamics of more traditional spatial interaction models, such as developed by White (1977), Allen and Sanglier (1979), Clarke and Wilson (1983), Engelen and Allen (1986), Pumain *et al.* (1989), Ren and White (1993) and others, clusters, such as the one created, could indeed set off new flows at the macro-level and be reinforced on the cellular level to generate rather different-looking islands or cities. The loop would thus be closed: the cellular patterns would influence the macro-behaviour, which would cause new events on the micro-level.

TOWARDS A DECISION SUPPORT SYSTEM FOR URBAN PLANNING

Thus far our discussion has focused on the relative merits of a modelling framework, rather than on the user of such a framework in practical planning problems or in policy-making. A model is not very helpful in solving actual planning problems unless it is made available to the end-user in a transparent and responsible manner. One way of doing this is to embed it in a decision support system (DSS) (e.g. Schutzelaars *et al.*, 1994; Janssen, 1992; Kim *et al.*, 1990).

Decision support systems are computer-based information systems that are built to help decision-makers address ill-structured problems by allowing them to *access* and use *data* and *analytic models* (El-Najdawi and Stylianou, 1993). *Access* to models and data is provided by means of the user interface (UI), which – in the state-of-the-art systems at least – is of a graphical nature and is to hide the technical complications of the information system from the end-user. The *data* required to correctly define, analyse and possibly solve the problem are stored in the database management system (DBMS) of the DSS. For planning and other geographical problems, the better solution is to have a GIS take care of data management, since it usually has additional analytical and decision support features (see second section). Finally, the *analytic models* are stored in the model-base management system (MBMS) of the DSS.

Typically decision models, statistical and operations research methods, as well as tools to portray, compare and evaluate different decision alternatives, are part of it. Even more essential in the model base are the domain-specific models capable of grasping the complexities of the system and the problems under study. All the instruments in the model base are of a formal nature, hence exclude decision-making solely based on common sense or intuition. Good formal decision support methods will rather assume that the decision-maker desires to make decisions on the basis of a consistent line of reasoning and will suggest solutions in a way that makes intuitive sense to him (Holtzman, 1989).

Urban and regional planners deal with problems that are somewhat in conflict with one of the basic principles on which DSS rest, namely that decision-making is a normative process: that a definition of optimality can be given and that, in line with this, rules can be developed and actions taken that result in an optimal solution for a stated problem. Urban planning problems are rarely posed in terms of a single goal, rather as a set of different, often contradicting, goals that all should be met where and when possible. This involves 'satisfying' rather than 'optimizing', as there is not a 'unique' or 'optimal' answer to the questions raised; rather different alternative solutions coexist and need to be evaluated. In the given circumstance, simulation models seem very useful, because (Boersma, 1989):

1. They allow the representation of complex situations that are beyond the reach of the operations research methods and analytical tools typically used in DSS.
2. They provide a realistic, plastic representation of the real system, thus allowing the user to get a better insight into the actual decision domain and particular decision situations.
3. They allow the user to forecast alternative and comparable future states, and thus constitute an instrument to investigate the likelihood of a desired situation through experimentation.

From the discussions in the previous sections we may add to this list:

4. Cellular automata simulation models are reasonably well suited to represent the complex dynamics of geographical systems at a high level of spatial resolution.

But simulation is a weak decision technique in the sense that it is not goal-directed, hence 'is not concerned with finding an initial state (along with constraints or conditions of the model itself) that can lead to a given result' (Rothenberg, 1989, p. 79). The user must change the model and run 'What-if?' experiments over and over again with the aim of reaching a predefined goal state, not knowing whether it can be attained anyway. The development and inclusion in the DSS of tools that extend simulation models beyond 'What-if?' in the sense meant by Rothenberg (1989) will be of considerable help to the urban planner and policy analyst.

Little or no commercial simulation software is available for building cellular automata models. In principle, spreadsheet programs are usable, but have their limitations in terms of user-friendliness specifically concerning the introduction of transition rules, initial conditions and macro-level models. We have developed a fairly generic simulation shell that is usable in designing and running constrained cellular automata models as specified in the third section. It features a built-in GIS system and a set of tools allowing the user to develop interactively his or her own application. The user decides on the area to be modelled, its spatial extent and resolution, and the type and number of socioeconomic activities and land uses to be included. He or she will either import a DTM (digital terrain model), a land use map and suitability maps from an existing application (e.g. a GIS), or enter them by means of the built-in 'Land use', 'Height' and 'Suitability' editors. Similarly, the transportation network, the accessibility parameters and the transition rules will be entered or changed by means of graphical editors. The user has access to the macro-level model via a graphical representation of the model. It features the subsystems of the model, their principal components (as boxes) and feedback loops (as arrows) (Fig. 8.2, top). This scheme serves to display the architecture of the model but it is also a graphical interface to the different components of the model. If the appropriate model box is clicked, a dialogue window opens, thus permitting access to the variables and parameters for that part of the model. While the simulation is running, the same windows display the current values of the model variables and parameters. Some of the mathematical expressions (equations) of the model can be switched on or off, but none can be changed. This is a restriction we would like to change in the future, perhaps by including a library featuring interchangeable model components that could be selected, linked and run by the user.

In the shell both levels get their data from a built-in custom-designed GIS system, which can exchange data with commercial GIS packages. The custom-designed GIS has been developed to speed up data exchange, the execution of the simulation model and the presentation of the results. We have successfully exchanged data with the GIS packages IDRISI and SPANS. When linked to such a package, typical GIS operations, such as data entry, data preparation, data quality control and overlay analysis, can be executed by it. Exporting simulation results into the package will allow further analysis including multi-criteria and multi-objective analysis on alternative simulation outcomes (Eastman *et al.*, 1993).

To compare different 'What-if?' runs carried out by the user, comparison tools have been included. They perform cell-by-cell comparisons and display the results on a map, and make statistical comparisons by means of cross-tabulations and the kappa statistic (Monserud and Leemans, 1992). This type of comparison is important when a very detailed analysis of a specific area is required. For the analysis of general trends and long-term changes in land use and land coverage, more general similarities need to be detected and studied. Thus measures are required that can recognize patterns, shapes and contiguity. An example of such a measure is the fractal dimensionality of the land use patterns (White and Engelen, 1993). A tool is included that calculates the fractal dimension of spatial patterns on the basis of different measures. Lastly, a tool has been included that permits the user to run the models in stochastic mode. For each parameter a range rather than a unique value can be defined. At run-time, a value will be chosen randomly in this interval. The model is run a great number of times – as set by the user – and for each land use a probability map is generated, showing for each cell the percentage of runs for which the cell features the particular land use. The resulting probability maps give an indication to the user of areas where specific land uses appear in a more or less consistent manner and may reveal conflicts in the context of sustainability (Engelen *et al.*, 1996). But the same tool is also useful in sensitivity analysis and in the search for spatial bifurcations (White and Engelen, 1997).

This decision support system has been implemented in MS Windows 3 on top-range IBM-compatible PCs equipped with an 80386 or 80486 processor with a minimum of 4 Mb of RAM and preferentially a SuperVGA graphics board and screen. This platform has the great advantage of being widely available, of being cost-effective and of being sufficiently powerful to perform the calculations required within reasonable time limits. The system makes extensive use of the multi-tasking and inter-program communication facilities offered by Windows. This is most explicitly demonstrated in its capability to exchange data at run-time with other Windows applications. For example, switching on a menu option will suffice for it to send model output to a Microsoft Excel 5.0 spreadsheet, which can be used for graphing and further analysis.

CONCLUSIONS

In this chapter we have touched upon a number of considerations and problems related to the use of cellular automata models for solving practical spatial problems. Many problems remain to be solved. We have come to understand that geographical problems are extremely complex and that new scientific concepts, theories, or paradigms can rarely be applied in a straightforward manner. Cellular automata are not different in this respect. They show more than intuitive similarities with geographical systems, in both their definition and dynamic behaviour. They are very simple to define, to implement, even to work with, and yet they exhibit a high level of complexity. Such is their complexity that theoreticians hardly understand the behaviour of 'Life', a two-state cellular automata with eight neighbours and controlled by an extremely simple transition rule. Geographers discovered 'Life' very early on, called it the 'geographical model', but considered it too simple to be used for solving 'real problems'.

We have suggested ways of adding geographical detail to CA models: increasing the number of cell states, increasing the size of the neighbourhood, defining and applying quantitative transition rules, introducing stochastic perturbations in the transition rules, introducing inhomogeneities in the cell spaces, and finally forcing the cellular dynamics. We have run a great number of simulations with such models and we have come to promising results. We have been able to generate realistic urban patterns and we have modelled realistic-looking urban histories. We linked cellular models to GIS, thus benefiting from the 'goodies' of this quickly growing field, but also introduced physical, environmental, historical and institutional details in dynamic spatial models. We integrated cellular models with more traditional dynamic (macro-level) models and could demonstrate how spatial dynamics no longer need to be studied in terms of centroids of sharply dissected (census) areas, but that space can be dealt with such as it really is: continuous. But we do not want to pretend to have all the answers. Essential questions remain to be explored, both from a theoretical and from a practical point of view. To name only a few:

- What is a correct grid size? Are cells to be in the 100–500 m range, or can we apply the same methodology for cells measuring 50 km on the side? Does this require more than changing the definition of the transition functions?
- What is the effect of the grid resolution on simulation results? Do models of the same area, but developed on different grids, produce results that are comparable? Or, is there hardly any resemblance? Gras (1995) did some experiments on this and came to the conclusion that results remain reasonably comparable, but that certainly very short-range interactions are getting lost when the grid gets to be too gross. Should we then try to define 'optimal' grid sizes per land use type? And, is it possible to define a model that mixes grids of different resolution, each representing some land use category?
- What are correct transition rules? Is there a way of deciding on 'good' transition functions for a list of commonly used land use categories?

Who will do the empirical studies required? And, can we calibrate our rules against real-world situations?

- What meta rule should apply to the transition rules? Can a poor subsistence farmer on a Caribbean island stop a multinational hotel chain from turning his land into a holiday resort in the absence of 'strict' planning and building restrictions? How are such differences in economic bargaining power captured correctly in transition rules? And, how are sets of transition rules kept consistent?

It will take time and effort to get past these questions. But surely they need an answer, even a practical answer. Moreover, new tools will need to be developed to render the definition and calibration of cellular automata models easy and transparent. In the decision support environment these will need to be supplemented with new instruments that help in the comparison and evaluation of simulation results. It is essential to have tools capable of comparing spatial patterns on a level of abstraction in between fractal dimensionality and cell-by-cell comparison. Such instruments should be able to distinguish simulation results that are qualitatively similar, meaning that visually compared they look very similar, even if on a cell-by-cell basis they might be very different. This kind of tool would detect essential differences in the structures generated, possibly point to important spatial bifurcations in the modelled system, but neglect minor deviations. Since decision-making involves the final selection of a 'best' alternative from a set, the inclusion of tools that assist in the multi-criteria and multi-objective evaluation of simulation results as well as their ranking against a target or goal state would make the methodology developed much more accessible and useful to the policymaker or the planner in the field.

REFERENCES

Allen P. and Sanglier M (1979) 'A dynamical model of growth in a central place system', *Geographical Analysis*, 11, pp. 256–272.

Batty M. (1991a) 'Computers in planning: old ideas, new tools', *Environment and Planning B*, 18, pp. 135–137.

Batty M. (1991b) 'Generating urban forms from diffusive growth', *Environment and Planning A*, 23, pp. 511–544.

Batty M. and Xie Y. (1994) 'From cells to cities', *Environment and Planning B*, 21, pp. 31–48.

Blommestein E. (1993) *Sustainable Development and Small Island Developing Countries*, ECLAC, Trinidad and Tobago.

Boersma S.K.Th. (1989) *Beslissingsondersteunende Systemen*, Academic Service, Schoonhoven.

Bradbury R.H., van der Laan J.D. and MacDonald B. (1990) 'Modelling the effects of predation and dispersal of the generation of waves of starfish outbreaks', *Mathematical Computing and Modelling*, 13, pp. 61–68.

Breheny M. (1994) 'Reviving reason', *Environment and Planning B*, 21, pp. 139–141.

Brimicombe A.J. (1992) 'Flood risk assessment using spatial decision support systems', *Simulation*, 59, 6, pp. 379–380.

Casti J.L. (1989) *Alternate Realities*, John Wiley & Sons, New York.

Clarke M. and Wilson A.G. (1983) 'The dynamics of urban spatial structure: progress and problems', *Journal of Regional Science*, 23, pp. 1–8.

Couclelis H. (1985) 'Cellular worlds: a framework for modelling micro–macro dynamics', *Environment and Planning A*, 17, pp. 585–596.

Couclelis H. (1988) 'Of mice and men: what rodent populations can teach us about complex spatial dynamics', *Environment and Planning A*, 20, pp. 99–109.

Couclelis H. (1989) 'Macrostructure and microbehaviour in a metropolitan area', *Environment and Planning B*, 16, pp. 141–154

Couclelis H. (1991) 'Requirements for planning-relevant GIS: a spatial perspective', *Papers in Regional Science*, 70, pp. 9–19.

De Moura Campos M. (1992) 'Cellular geography and neural networks, learning socio-spatial dynamics from examples', paper presented at the *NARSC Meeting*, New Orleans, 1992.

Eastman J.R., Kuem P.A.K., Toledano J. and Weigen J. (1993) *GIS and Decision Making*, UNITAR, Geneva, Switzerland.

El-Najdawi M.K. and Stylianou A.C. (1993) 'Expert support systems: integrating AI technologies', *Communications of the ACM*, 36, (2), pp. 55–65.

Engelen G. and Allen P.M. (1986) 'Modelling the spatial distribution of energy demand for the province of Noord Holland: towards an integrated approach', *Sistemi Urbani*, 2/3, pp. 241–261.

Engelen G., White R. and Uljee I. (1993a) 'Exploratory modelling of socio-economic impacts of climatic change'. In Maul G.A. (ed.), *Climate Change in the Intra-Americas Sea*, Edward Arnold, London, pp. 306–324.

Engelen G., White R, Uljee I. and Wargnies S. (1993b) *Vulnerability Assessment of Low-lying Coastal Areas and Small Islands to Climate Change and Sea Level Rise*, Final Report to UNEP CAR/RCU, RIKS Pub. 905000/9379, Maastricht.

Engelen G., White R., Uljee I. and Drazan P. (1995) 'Using cellular automata for integrated modelling of socio-environmental systems', *Environmental Monitoring and Assessment*, 34, pp. 203–214.

Engelen G., White R., Uljee I. and Wargnies S. (1996) 'Numerical modelling of small island socio-economics to achieve sustainable development'. In Maul G.A. (ed.), *Small Islands. Marine Science and Sustainable Development*, American Geophysical Union, Washington DC, Coastal and Estuarine Studies, **51**, pp. 437–463.

European Communities (1994) 'Call for tender relating to studies concerned with cities (code: ACT-VILL)', *Official Journal of the European Communities*, C163, pp. 14–15.

Frankhauser P. (1991) 'Aspects fractals des structures urbaines', *L'Espace Geographique*, pp. 45–69.

Fredkin E. (1991) 'Digital mechanics: an informational process based on reversible universal cellular automata'. In Gutowitz H. (ed.), *Cellular Automata, Theory and Experiment*, MIT Press, Cambridge, Mass., pp. 254–270.

Gardner M. (1970) 'The fantastic combinations of John Conway's new solitaire game Life', *Scientific American*, 223, pp. 120–123.

Gras R.E. (1995) 'GRAZZAVILLE een onderzoek naar de invloed van de resolutie van de cellulaire automaat CITY', Master thesis, Eindhoven University of Technology, Faculty of Architecture, Building and Planning.

Green D.G. (1990) 'Landscapes, cataclysms and population explosions', *Mathematical and Computer Modelling*, 13, pp. 75–82.

Green D.G. (1993) 'Emergent behaviour in biological systems'. In Green D.G. and Bossomaier T.J. (eds), *Complex Systems – From Biology to Computation*, IOS Press, Amsterdam, pp. 24–35.

Holtzman S. (1989) *Intelligent Decision System*, Addison-Wesley, Reading, Mass.

Jankowski P. and Richard L. (1994) 'Integration of GIS-based suitability analysis and multicriteria evaluation in a spatial decision support system for route selection', *Environment and Planning B*, 21, pp. 323–340.

Janssen R. (1992) *Multiobjective Decision Support for Environmental Management*, Kluwer Academic, Dordrecht.

Kim T.J., Wiggins L.L. and Wright J.R. (1990) *Expert Systems: Applications to Urban Planning*, Springer-Verlag, New York.

Krieger M.H. (1991) 'Segmentation and filtering into neighbourhoods as processes of percolation and diffusion: stochastic processes (randomness) as the null hypothesis', *Environment and Planning A*, 23, pp. 1609–1626.

Langton C. (1992) 'Life at the edge of chaos'. In C. Langton *et al.* (eds), *Artificial Life II: Proceedings of an Interdisciplinary Workshop on the Synthesis and Simulation of Living Systems*, Santa Fe Institute Studies in the Science of Complexity, No. 10, Addison-Wesley, Redwood City, pp. 41–92.

Lee Y.C., Qian S., Jones R.D., Barnes C.W., Flake G.W., O'Rourke M.K., Lee K., Chen H.H., Sun G.Z., Zhang Y.Q., Chen D. and Giles C.L. (1991) 'Adaptive stochastic cellular automata: theory'. In Gutowitz H. (ed.), *Cellular Automata, Theory and Experiment*, MIT Press, Cambridge, Mass., pp. 159–180.

McIntosh H.V. (1991) 'Wolfram's class IV automata and a good life'. In Gutowitz H. (ed.), *Cellular Automata, Theory and Experiment*, MIT Press, Cambridge, Mass., pp. 105–121.

Monserud R.A. and Leemans R. (1992) 'Comparing global vegetation maps with the Kappa statistic', *Ecological Modelling*, 62, pp. 275–293.

Passonneau J. and Wurman R. (1966) *Urban Atlas: 20 American Cities*, MIT Press, Cambridge, Mass.

Phipps M. (1989) 'Dynamical behaviour of cellular automata under constraints of neighbourhood coherence', *Geographical Analysis*, 21, pp. 197–215.

Pumain D., Sanders L. and Saint-Julien Th. (1989) *Villes et Auto-Organisation*, Economica, Paris.

Ren J. and White R. (1993) 'The simulation of urban system dynamics in Atlantic Canada 1951–1991', *Canadian Geographer*, 39, pp. 252–262.

Rothenberg J. (1989) 'The nature of modelling'. In Widman L.E., Loparo K.A. and Nielsen N.R. (eds), *Artificial Intelligence, Simulation and Modelling*, John Wiley & Sons, New York, pp. 75–92.

Roy G.G. and Snickars F. (1993) 'City life. A study of cellular automata in urban dynamics', paper presented at the 33rd European Congress of the Regional Science Association, Moscow, August 24–27, 1993.

Schutzelaars A., Engelen G., Uljee I. and Wargnies S. (1994) 'Computer systems that enhance the productivity of public-sector planners', *International Journal of Public Administration*, 17, (1), pp. 119–154.

Tobler W. (1979) 'Cellular geography'. In Gale S. and Olsson G. (eds), *Philosophy in Geography*, Reidel, Dordrecht, pp. 379–386.

Webster J.C. (1993) 'GIS and the scientific inputs to urban planning. Part 1: Description', *Environment and Planning B*, 20, pp. 709–728.

Webster J.C. (1994) 'GIS and the scientific inputs to urban planning. Part 2: Prediction and prescription', *Environment and Planning B*, 21, pp. 145–157.

White R. (1977) 'Dynamic central place theory: results of a simulation approach', *Geographical Analysis*, 9, pp. 227–243.

White R. and Engelen G. (1993) 'Cellular automata and fractal urban form: a cellular modelling approach to the evolution of urban land use patterns', *Environment and Planning A*, 25, pp. 1175–1199.

White R. and Engelen G. (1994) 'Cellular dynamics and GIS: modelling spatial complexity' *Geographical Systems*, 1, pp. 237-253.

White R. and Engelen G. (1997) 'Cellular automata as the basis of integrated dynamic regional modelling', *Environment and Planning B*, **24**, pp. 235–246.

White R., Engelen G. and Uljee I. (1997) 'The use of constrained cellular automata for high-resolution modelling of urban land use dynamics', *Environment and Planning*, **24**, pp. 323–343.

Wolfram S. (1984) 'Universality and complexity in cellular automata', *Physica D*, **10**, pp. 1–35.

Wolfram S. (1986) 'Approaches to complexity engineering', *Physica D*, **22**, pp. 385–399.

Wright J.R. (1990) 'ISIS: toward an integrated spatial information system'. In Kim T.J., Wiggins L.L. and Wright J.R. (eds) *Expert Systems: Applications to Urban Planning*, Springer-Verlag, New York, pp. 43–66.

Young P. and Wadge G. (1990) 'FLOWFRONT: simulation of a lava flow', *Computers and Geosciences*, 16, pp. 1171–1191.

Constructing and consulting fuzzy decision tables

9

Frank Witlox, Theo Arentze and Harry Timmermans

INTRODUCTION

A decision table (DT) is 'a table that represents the exhaustive set of mutually exclusive conditional statements within a pre-specified problem area' (Verhelst, 1980; Lucardie, 1994; Vanthienen and Dries, 1994). It displays the possible actions that a decision-maker can follow according to the outcome of a number of relevant conditions. Table 9.1 shows an example of a DT which evaluates the suitability of a potential location site for a business with respect to the supply of raw materials.

In Table 9.1, four quadrants or parts may be distinguished. The *condition set* (upper left part of the table) consists of all the relevant condition subjects or attributes that have an influence on the decision-making process. In this example, both conditions, C_1 and C_2, in the specified table relate to distances (i.e. C_1 represents the distance (X) to a harbour, and C_2 represents the distance (X) to a railway station). The *action set* (lower left part of the table) contains all possible actions a decision-maker is able to

Table 9.1 A crisp DT evaluating the supply of raw materials

Supply of raw materials				
C_1: distance to harbour	$X < 1000$	$X \geqslant 1000$		
C_2: distance to railway station	–	$X < 250$	$250 \leqslant X \leqslant 450$	$X > 450$
A_1: evaluation supply of raw materials	good R_1	good R_2	medium R_3	bad R_4

Decision Support Systems in Urban Planning. Edited by Harry Timmermans. Published in 1997 by E & F N Spon. ISBN 0 419 21050 4

follow. In Table 9.1, the action set refers to how a potential location site is evaluated in terms of supply possibilities of raw materials. Therefore, action A_1 evaluates these possibilities. The *condition space* (upper right part of the table) specifies all possible combinations of condition states (CS). These condition states represent the relevant sets or categories of possible value outcomes for a particular, given condition. In this example, two condition states, CS_{11} ($X < 1000$) and CS_{12} ($X \geq 1000$), are specified for condition C_1; and three condition states, CS_{21} ($X < 250$), CS_{22} ($250 \leq X \leq 450$) and CS_{23} ($X > 450$), for condition C_2. Note that with respect to the categorization of the conditions, two important logical requirements or constraints must be fulfilled, i.e. *exhaustivity* and *exclusivity*. Exhaustivity means that the DT must account for all possible states that a condition is able to take. The exclusivity requirement refers to the fact that each combination of condition states has to be included in one and only one column of the DT, or in other words, condition state alternatives have to be mutually exclusive. The *action space* (lower right part of the table) contains the categorization of all the possible action states. In Table 9.1, three different action states (i.e. 'good', 'medium', 'bad') are used to evaluate a location site with respect to the supply of raw materials. Finally, any vertical linking of an element out of the condition states with an element of the action states produces a so-called *logical rule*. This logical rule is in fact a simple decision rule.

A major advantage of using a DT (like Table 9.1) is the accuracy with which a choice-maker is able to make a decision. Once the different condition states have been established, evaluation is rather straightforward. This easy evaluation follows from the fact that the condition states are distinct and sharply defined. If, for instance, $C_1 = 1100$ (within CS_{12}) and $C_2 = 230$ (within CS_{21}), the DT concludes that the location site is evaluated as 'good' in respect of the supply of raw materials (i.e. decision rule R_2). In addition to this inherent characteristic, crisp DTs also have other advantages when compared to other qualitative choice modelling techniques (i.e. decision plan nets). We mention among others: the validation and verification issue, the ability to account for 'spreading', the ability to allow for the use of multiple evaluation categories, the advantage of providing a better overview of the decision structure, the capacity to permit optimalization procedures, the ability to allow for the use of subtables, and the power to account for a normative aggregation (Witlox, 1995).

However, it would be wrong to suggest that the DTs have no specific disadvantages. A major drawback, as also noted by Timmermans and van der Heijden (1987), is the lack in the DT technique of being able to allow for measurement errors and omitted variables. Furthermore, it may be argued that, due to the sharpness of the boundaries between two exactly defined condition states, decision-making becomes too rigid and inflexible to be still deemed realistic. The implications of the latter characteristic can easily be illustrated in Table 9.1. Take, for instance, condition C_1 with its two associated condition states, CS_{11} ($X < 1000$) and CS_{12} ($X \geq 1000$). According to decision rule R_1 of the DT, a potential location site is evaluated as 'good' with respect to the supply of raw materials, if the distance between a harbour and a location site is less than 1000 m. A question that arises from the above statement is whether it is realistic to assume that a decision-maker is able to assert that a distance of 999 m between a harbour and a potential location site implies a 'good' evaluation, while 1 m further away, a second variable, i.e. the distance to a railway station, needs to be evaluated in order to assess the location site with respect to the supply of raw materials? Clearly, the answer here is 'no'. The state transition of condition C_1 will occur more or less continuously and gradually. There exists a certain vagueness or fuzziness in the delineation of different condition states. As a result, we have to redefine the crisp condition states in order to reflect the gradual transition between both condition states. Obviously, an identical line of thought can be developed for the three condition states of condition C_2.

A possible solution to the redefinition problem is found in the concept of *fuzzy sets* in the definition of the condition states.

FUZZY SETS

The fuzzy set theory was introduced by Zadeh (1965) to deal with problems in which the absence of sharply defined criteria is involved. In particular, fuzzy sets aim at mathematically representing the vagueness intrinsic in linguistic terms and approximate reasoning.

Zadeh (1965) defined a fuzzy set as 'a class of objects with a continuum of grades of membership'. This fuzzy set is characterized by a *membership function* (also called truth or indicator function) which assigns to each object of the set a grade of membership ranging from 0 (non-membership of the set) to 1 (full membership of the set). More formally, a fuzzy set is defined as follows (Zadeh, 1965, 1975):

> In a universe of discourse U, a fuzzy set A of U is characterized by a membership function $\mu_A: U \rightarrow [0, 1]$ which associates with each element u of U a real number $\mu_A(u)$ in the interval $[0, 1]$, with $\mu_A(u)$ representing the grade of membership of u in A.

Following the above definition, $\mu_A(u) = 0$ implies non-membership, $\mu_A(u) = 1$ means full membership, and $0 < \mu_A(u) < 1$ signifies partial membership or intermediate degrees of membership. Obviously, the nearer the value of $\mu_A(u)$ to 0 (1), the lower (higher) the grade of membership of u in A. Also, gradual transition follows from partial degree of membership of the set.

A fuzzy set is characterized by a membership function which assigns to each object of the set a degree of membership ranging from 0 (non-membership of the set) to 1 (full membership of the set). Classifying membership functions is by no means an easy task. This is partly explained by the fact that the choice of a membership function is (i) context-dependent (i.e. devised for a specific, individual problem), and (ii) for a same context, dependent on the observer (different observers have different opinions). Thus, there exists a great deal of variation. Here, it is not our intention to make a complete literature coverage on membership functions. This would lead us too far, and moreover is done elsewhere (e.g. Dubois and Prade, 1980; Dombi, 1990; Turksen, 1991; Kerre, 1993; Cox, 1994; Tzafestas, 1994). However, the most representative standard forms of membership functions that have been advanced to represent fuzzy concepts are the S, L and π curves (see also Figs 9.1 and 9.2).

The S curve is defined in terms of only three parameters: the zero membership value (α), the complete membership value (γ) and the inflection point (β). It is used to represent increasing concepts like 'long', 'old', 'rich', 'tall', 'heavy', etc. The S membership function for $u \in \mathbb{R}$ is specified as follows (Sanchez, 1986; Hellendoorn, 1990):

$$S(u; \alpha, \beta, \gamma) = \begin{cases} 0 & \rightarrow \quad u \leq \alpha \\ 2[(u-\alpha)/(\gamma-\alpha)]^2 & \rightarrow \quad \alpha < u \leq \beta \\ 1 - 2[(u-\gamma)/(\gamma-\alpha)]^2 & \rightarrow \quad \beta < u \leq \gamma \\ 1 & \rightarrow \quad u > \gamma \end{cases}$$

It follows from the above specification that only within the domain of $[\alpha, \gamma]$ are partial degrees of membership possible. This is because all values of x lower than α imply zero membership, whereas all values of u beyond γ imply full membership. The inflection point, $\beta = (\alpha + \gamma)/2$, is the point with degree of membership equal to 0.5. By determining the values of α and γ for a certain concept, the S curve is established.

The L curve is also a non-linear function that can be parametrized. It is used to represent decreasing notions such as 'short', 'young', 'poor', 'low', 'light', etc. In fact, an L curve is the complement of an S curve. Therefore, the L membership function for $u \in \mathbb{R}$ is equal to:

$$L(u; \alpha, \beta, \gamma) = [1 - S(u; \alpha, \beta, \gamma)]$$

Finally, the symmetric π membership function results from a continuous linking of an S membership function and its reflected image (i.e. the L curve) resulting in a bell-shaped function. The π membership function depends on two parameters: the value from the domain around which the function is centred (γ), and the bandwidth parameter (β). The bandwidth parameter is twice the distance between the inflection point and the centred value. It is used to represent fuzzy numbers and 'about' or 'close to' representations. More formally, the π membership function for $u \in \mathbb{R}$ is specified as follows (Hellendoorn, 1990):

$$\pi(u; \beta, \gamma) = \begin{cases} S(u; \gamma - \beta, \gamma - \beta/2, \gamma) & \to u \leq \gamma \\ 1 - S(u; \gamma, \gamma + \beta/2, \gamma + b) & \to u \geq \gamma \end{cases}$$

Note that the inflection points of the π curve are defined by γ and β, namely ($\gamma \pm \beta/2$). Also, the endpoints are determined from the specification of the π curve's parameters as ($\gamma - \beta$) on the left-hand side and ($\gamma + \beta$) on the right-hand side. The width of the curve depends on the value of β (Cox, 1994).

Having reviewed some typical membership function specifications, we now turn our attention to the integration of fuzzy sets and DTs. This will result in the construction of a so-called *fuzzy decision table* (FDT).

CONSTRUCTION OF A FUZZY DECISION TABLE

A fuzzy decision table (FDT) is an extended version of a crisp DT in order to deal with imprecise and vague decision situations. The extension amounts to the introduction of fuzzy sets in the condition space and/or action space of the crisp DT.

The construction of an FDT usually involves the following steps (Francioni and Kandel, 1988; Vanthienen and Dries, 1994):

1. Definition of conditions, condition states, actions and action states for a specific choice problem.
2. Substitute, where necessary, crisp condition and/or action states with fuzzy sets.
3. Specification and estimation of fuzzy membership functions.
4. Specification of the problem in terms of fuzzy decision rules.
5. Construction of the FDT.
6. Check for completeness, contradictions and correctness.
7. Simplification, optimization and depiction of the FDT.

It is evident that the first step in the construction of a DT, be it crisp or fuzzy, starts with the definition of the conditions and actions and their associated states that have an influence on the decision problem. Different techniques exist to determine the relevant conditions and actions (Witlox, 1995). However, the point of interest here concerns the actual definition of the condition and action states. In this first stage, all condition and action categorizations are assumed to be crisp so that, in a later stage of the construction process (i.e. step 2), only those crisp categorizations that are deemed too stringent may be replaced by their fuzzy sets equivalents. In other words, it is not necessary to substitute all crisp categorizations with fuzzy sets, but only those the decision-maker views as too strict or too sharply defined. In practice, this substitution applies only to continuous variables (interval variables). Therefore, building an FDT will usually start with the construction of the crisp case.

In the second step, all those crisp condition and action states that prove to be too stringent are substituted with fuzzy concepts, more particularly, fuzzy sets. In other words, for condition C_1 in Table 9.1, condition state CS_{11} ($X < 1000$) is replaced by the fuzzy set 'short' distance, and CS_{12} ($X \geq 1000$) by the fuzzy set 'long' distance. Consequently, for condition C_2 with its associated crisp condition states, CS_{21} ($X < 250$), CS_{22} ($250 \leq X \leq 450$) and CS_{23} ($X > 450$), the fuzzy sets 'short', 'about average' and 'long' distance can be specified, respectively.

The third step involves the specification and estimation of the membership functions. This process is often called 'fuzzification'. In our example, membership functions need to be specified for three different types of fuzzy linguistic notions: (i) 'short' being a decreasing notion, (ii) 'long' being an increasing notion, and (iii) 'about average' being a fuzzy number or an 'about' or 'close to' representation.

First, a concept like 'short distance' (i.e. an intrinsic decreasing notion) is best represented by a decline curve as it is evident that shortness is inversely proportional to distance. Therefore, the fuzzy set 'short' is best represented by means of an L curve. Secondly, the concept 'long distance' is an intrinsic increasing notion because it stands to reason that longness is proportional to distance. Consequently, the concept is best represented by a growth curve (i.e. an S curve), being the complement of a decline curve. Thirdly, a concept like 'distance is about average' can be represented by means of a bell-shaped curve. We opt here to use the π curve.

All three selected membership function representations (L, S and π curves) are non-linear and parametric functions. The latter characteristic implies that we have to further specify, and if necessary estimate the parameters of the different membership functions (Table 9.2). In Table 9.2, the membership functions for the different fuzzy condition states of

Table 9.2 Specification membership functions for C_1 and C_2

Membership function specification condition C_1		Membership function specification condition C_2		
C_{11} short	C_{12} long	C_{21} short	C_{22} about average	C_{23} long
$L(X; \alpha, \beta, \gamma)$ $= 1 - S(X; \alpha, \beta, \gamma)$	$S(X; \alpha, \beta, \gamma)$	$L(X; \alpha, \beta, \gamma)$	$\pi(X; \beta, \gamma)$	$S(X; \alpha, \beta, \gamma)$
$\alpha = 750$	$\alpha = 750$	$\alpha = 150$	–	$\alpha = 350$
$\beta = 1000$	$\beta = 1000$	$\beta = 250$	$\beta = 200$	$\beta = 450$
$\gamma = 1250$	$\gamma = 1250$	$\gamma = 350$	$\gamma = 350$	$\gamma = 550$

conditions C_1 and C_2 are specified. The parameters of these membership functions are here arbitrarily defined.

Figures 9.1 and 9.2 illustrate in a graphical way the membership functions specified in Table 9.2. Note from Figures 9.1 and 9.2 that, although both conditions C_1 and C_2 are evaluated in terms of a continuous variable X (representing a distance), the domain (i.e. $[\mathfrak{R}_i, \mathfrak{R}_j]$) of the different

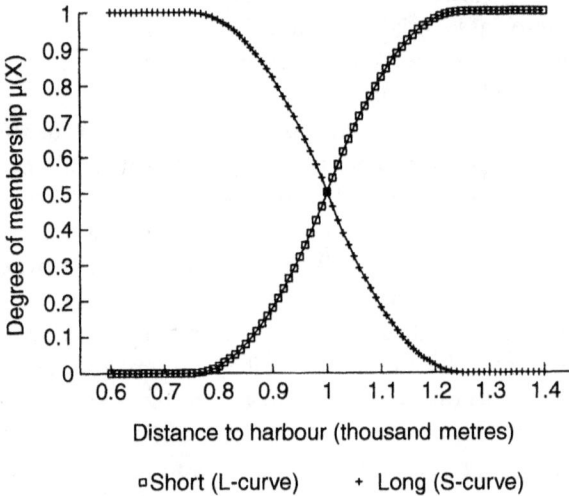

Distance to harbour (thousand metres)

□ Short (L-curve)   + Long (S-curve)

Fig. 9.1   Fuzzy sets for the concept 'distance to harbour' (combined).

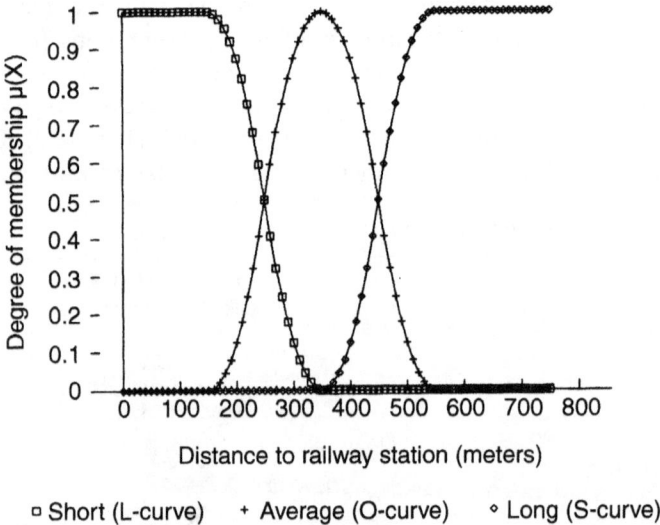

Distance to railway station (meters)

□ Short (L-curve)   + Average (O-curve)   ○ Long (S-curve)

Fig. 9.2   Fuzzy sets for the concept 'distance to railway station' (combined).

associated fuzzy sets, in which partial degrees of membership are possible, is limited. The domain (or support) of a fuzzy set is the set of all the elements whose membership degrees are greater than 0 and smaller than 1.

In theory, the input values for conditions C_1 and C_2 (both expressing a distance) could be equal to any number ranging from 0 to ∞. However, for the decision-maker, this entire range of possible condition values is not assumed fuzzy. There exist certain ranges of distance that can be categorized on a crisp basis. For instance, in our decision problem, it is evident that all distances below, say, 100 m will never be associated with the fuzzy set of 'long' distances; hence, the associated membership value will always be equal to 0. As such, there is nothing fuzzy about this kind of distance categorization; and, no doubt other ranges of distances can be uncovered that categorize as easily. The problem, therefore, is to know where crisp categorization ends and fuzzy categorization starts. In other words, in which interval of distances does categorization become fuzzy? This is indicated by the domain of the fuzzy set. In the case of the L and S curves, the domain is equal to $[\alpha, \gamma]$ or [750, 1250]. The domain of the π curve ranges from $[\gamma - \beta, \gamma + \beta]$ or [150, 550]. All values of X outside these respectively specified domains result either in a zero or a full membership of the associated fuzzy set. Obviously, by altering the parameters of the membership function, the domain of the fuzzy set will automatically change as well.

The fourth step deals with the specification of the choice problem in terms of fuzzy decision rules. A fuzzy decision rule is established, by analogy with the crisp case, by vertically linking the elements of the condition space with the elements of the action space. However, an important difference with crisp decision ruling is that in an FDT the elements of the condition and action spaces are fuzzy sets. Thus, a fuzzy decision rule (i.e. a fuzzy 'if...then...' rule) combines and modifies fuzzy sets.

In view of the integration of fuzzy sets and DTs, it seems evident that the intersection operator – one of the standard Zadeh min/max fuzzy set operators – would be the most common form of operator used to construct a fuzzy decision rule. The primary reason is that DTs are based on conjoint ('AND') decision rules and that the fuzzy intersection operator is the equivalent of the logical AND operation. However, applying the intersection operator also means that both the exclusivity and exhaustivity properties could be violated. Therefore, the product operator is advanced as an alternative (Dubois and Prade, 1980; Francioni and Kandel, 1988).

The fifth step deals with the actual construction of the FDT on the basis of the defined fuzzy decision rules. The result is shown in Table 9.3. The DT depicted in Table 9.3 is the fuzzy extension of the crisp DT depicted in Table 9.1. In Table 9.3, action A_1 appears as a fuzzy set. This implies that in an FDT a decision (here, the question whether or not the location site is suited for the supply of raw materials) cannot be taken by

Table 9.3 An FDT evaluating the site's suitability in respect to the supply of raw materials

Supply of raw materials				
C_1: distance to harbour	short		long	
C_2: distance to railway station	–	short	about average	long
A_1: evaluation supply of raw materials	good (1.0) R_1	good (0.9) R_2	medium (0.5) R_3	bad (0.1) R_4

merely checking all the decision rules in search of a 'perfect' match. Instead, the degree of matching between the given condition combination and each column should be assessed. As a result, more than one action configuration may be chosen, but each with a degree in [0, 1].

Translated to our decision problem, the classification of a site in respect of the supply of raw materials to, for instance, R_2, is expressed as a *degree* of membership, whereby 0 implies that the location site does not belong to R_2, and 1 signifies that the location site is a full member. Obviously, it goes without saying that in addition to these two extreme (crisp) evaluations, all partial or gradual degrees of membership are also possible outcomes. The numbers in brackets associated with the action states of A_1 are to be interpreted as scores or codes (not membership function values) that allow us to further differentiate between different action states. These scores will be used later when calculating weighted averages (see below).

It can also be seen that when condition C_1 is evaluated as being 'short', condition C_2 becomes irrelevant in the decision-making process. This is indicated by the so-called 'don't care' entry (denoted '–') in Table 9.3. Because a 'don't care' entry cannot possibly influence the outcome of the decision-making process, it is assumed to be equal to 1. As such, it has no effect when the product operator is used.

The sixth step examines the FDT with regard to the requirements of completeness, contradictions and correctness. Here, some similarity can be noted with the crisp case. First, the check for completeness verifies whether the FDT contains decision rules which have empty action states. In other words, in an incomplete FDT certain condition combinations will not lead to a decision in terms of an action configuration. If this is observed, it should be rectified at this stage. Stated more formally, the check for completeness implies that the sum of the membership values over all condition state alternatives is greater than or equal to 1. Secondly, the FDT is controlled for contradictions. In the crisp case, checking for contradictions implied making sure that no two actions which exclude one another must be executed at the same time. Usually, such a contradiction occurred as a result of violating the exclusivity property (i.e. each combination of condition states has to be included in one and only one column of the DT) when defining the condition states of the DT. In an FDT, the exclusivity property is interpreted in terms of membership function values. It is no longer required that there exists one and only one perfect match between a combination of condition states and an action state. The degree of matching between a column in the FDT and a given condition configuration is a value in [0, 1]. As the nature of fuzziness allows for some overlap between states, there should be no problem. Stated more formally, the exclusivity property is fulfilled if the sum of the membership values over all condition state alternatives is smaller than or equal to 1. Thirdly, the notion of correctness can be determined in a similar way to that of the crisp case. That is, it can be checked by the knowledge engineer whether the FDT reflects the ideas of the expert.

The seventh and final step concerns the simplification, optimization and depiction of the FDT. This process proceeds according to the principles of the crisp case (see Lucardie, 1994; Vanthienen and Dries, 1994; Witlox, 1995).

In sum, the construction of an FDT proceeds mainly according to the steps of the crisp case. However, some extensions are needed. First, it is necessary to define the fuzzy sets which will be introduced in the condition and/or action spaces of the crisp DT. Secondly, the associated fuzzy membership functions must be specified and estimated. Thirdly and finally, some provisions need to be made in order to handle fuzzy decision rules.

It should be clear that, in addition to these extensions, other important contrasts exist between a crisp and fuzzy decision table. For one, the fuzzy decision output differs substantially from the 'all-or-nothing' crisp decision output. Note that the decision output follows from the consultation of the DT.

CONSULTATION OF A FUZZY DECISION TABLE

It is evident that crisp DTs produce crisp decision outputs. This property was deemed to be one of the major strengths of applying the crisp DT formalism. However, it was also noted that the greatest weakness of crisp decision-making is the fact that crisp DTs are unable to take into account imprecision and vagueness that abound in human decision-making. Crisp DTs only appear to produce an accurate or non-fuzzy decision output because the imprecision inherent in decision-making is not noticed. By contrast, in an FDT, this imprecision or vagueness is made explicit, resulting in a fuzzy decision output. Although this may seem somewhat self-evident, this property has important implications. For instance, it is no longer required for an FDT to be exclusive in its condition or action states. This implies that, unlike with crisp DTs, a fuzzy decision or action configuration cannot be taken by merely checking with each column of the table to match (perfectly) a given condition configuration. Instead, the degree of membership indicates that the quality of the matching between the given condition combination and each column should be evaluated (Chen *et al.*, 1994). Thus, while in a crisp environment only one action configuration is possible (i.e. an 'all-or-nothing' or a binary $\{0, 1\}$ decision), in a fuzzy environment, more than one action configuration, each with a degree in $[0, 1]$, may be chosen. Note also that the membership function value gives an indication of the degree of precision (or imprecision) with which a decision can be taken.

It is worthwhile to emphasize that as a result of the 'extension principle' (Zadeh, 1975) fuzzy consultation can be made on *crisp* as well as on *fuzzy* decision tables. In other words, a crisp DT is just a special case of an FDT. This is of great significance because this means that existing (crisp) DTs can always be used as a starting point to construct and, in a later stage, consult an FDT. Note also that fuzzy consultations outside the domain of the fuzzy set result in the simple binary crisp decision output.

To illustrate how the consultation of an FDT works and which decision output it produces, we return to our hypothetical example. By taking arbitrary values for the conditions C_1 and C_2, and by processing these values through the FDT depicted in Table 9.3, a fuzzy decision output is obtained. In order to compare the fuzzy results with the crisp output, the same condition values are also processed through the crisp DT (Table 9.1). Three different decision situations are discussed.

SITUATION 1: $C_1 = 1100$ m, $C_2 = 230$ m

Crisp consultation

Given the fact that $C_1 = 1100$ (within the fuzzy domain of CS_{12}) and $C_2 = 230$ (within the fuzzy domain of CS_{21}), the crisp DT concludes that the location site is evaluated as 'good' in respect of the supply of raw materials (i.e. decision rule R_2 in Table 9.1).

Fuzzy consultation

Before being able to proceed to fuzzy consultation, three additional steps need to be taken:

1. Calculation of membership values of condition states
2. Calculation of membership values of action states
3. Determination of the degree of matching

First, the various membership function values for the different fuzzy condition states have to be calculated. These real numbers, $\mu_A(u)$, represent the grade of membership of u in A, with u being the arbitrary chosen distance variable (X) and A denoting a fuzzy condition state. Based on the membership function specifications defined in Table 9.2, the degrees of membership shown in Table 9.4 are obtained.

It can be noticed that the arbitrarily chosen distance of 1100 m for condition C_1 falls within the specified fuzzy domain of both associated fuzzy sets (i.e. $[\mathfrak{R}_i, \mathfrak{R}_j] = [750, 1250]$). Therefore, the associated degrees of set membership may equal any value in the interval $[0, 1]$. Here, as a result of the membership function specification, 1100 m results in a 0.18 membership value with the fuzzy set of 'short' distances and a 0.82 membership value with the fuzzy set of 'long' distances. Apparently, 1100 m inclines more to the fuzzy set of 'long' distances than to the fuzzy set of 'short' distances. This is explained because, in the crisp case, 1000 m formed the absolute boundary determination between the two condition states ($X <$ 1000 and $X \geq 1000$). With respect to condition C_2, it can be seen that a distance of 230 m has a 0.68, 0.32 and 0.00 membership value with the fuzzy sets 'short', 'about average' and 'long' distances, respectively. Once again, note that it is only when the specified distance falls within the domain of the fuzzy set that a partial degree of membership is possible. Outside the domain, set membership will either be equal to 0 or equal to 1. Hence, 230 m has a zero degree of membership in the fuzzy set of 'long' distances.

Note as well that the degrees of membership associated with both conditions sum to unity (i.e. $\mu_{cs11(short)}(X) + \mu_{cs12(long)}(X) = 1$; $\mu_{cs21(short)}(X) + \mu_{cs22(average)}(X) + \mu_{cs23(long)}(X) = 1$). Hence, this property implies that the law of the excluded middle holds, which is an inherent characteristic of the DT formalism.

The second step involves an assessment of the membership values of the action states of A_1 on the basis of the calculated membership values of the different condition states. By definition, an action state in a DT results from a conjunction of different condition states. In an FDT, these condition categorizations are defined as fuzzy sets. Therefore, by applying the fuzzy product operator (referred to as '$\times$'), membership values are found for the various action states of A_1. In Table 9.5, the product operator is used to calculate the membership values of the different action states of A_1, given the fact that $C_1 = 1100$ m and $C_2 = 230$ m.

Table 9.4 Specification membership values for C_1 (1100) and C_2 (230)

C_1	$\mu_{cs11(short)}(X)$	$= L(X; \alpha, \beta, \gamma)$	$= L(1100; 750, 1000, 1250)$	$= 0.18$
	$\mu_{cs12(long)}(X)$	$= S(X; \alpha, \beta, \gamma)$	$= S(1100; 750, 1000, 1250)$	$= 0.82$
C_2	$\mu_{cs21(short)}(X)$	$= L(X; \alpha, \beta, \gamma)$	$= L(230; 150, 250, 350)$	$= 0.68$
	$\mu_{cs22(average)}(X)$	$= \pi(X; \beta, \gamma)$	$= \pi(230; 200, 350)$	$= 0.32$
	$\mu_{cs23(long)}(X)$	$= S(X; \alpha, \beta, \gamma)$	$= S(230; 350, 450, 550)$	$= 0.00$

To illustrate how Table 9.5 is constructed, take, for instance, the action state in the fuzzy decision rule R_2. By applying the product operator, the membership value is equal to 0.5576 (i.e. $C_1 \times C_2 = [(\mu_{c1}(1100)) \cdot (\mu_{c2}(230))]$ $= [(0.82) \cdot (0.68)] = 0.5576$).

Note also that for condition C_2, the 'don't care' entry is substituted for a membership value equal to 1. Clearly, this substitution has no influence on the final determination of the membership values of the different action states of A_1.

The third and final step deals with establishing the overall degree of matching. In this context, matching implies establishing the degree of membership that a potential location site has with the set of location sites that are perfectly suited in respect of the supply of raw materials. Eventually, this will lead to the fuzzy decision output. However, unlike in the crisp case, in a fuzzy environment more than one action configuration may be chosen, each with a degree in the interval [0, 1]. In other words, action states – being also fuzzy sets – overlap each other. This complies with working with multi-dimensional fuzzy rules.

In analogy with Tzafestas (1994), the degree of matching is calculated as a weighted average of the different overlapping membership values and the arbitrary assigned scores. This results in the following:

$$A_1 (C_1 \times C_2) = \frac{(0.18)(1) + (0.5576)(0.9) + (0.2624)(0.5) + (0)(0.1)}{(0.18) + (0.5576) + (0.2624) + (0)} = 0.8130$$

It is found that the location site has a 0.81 membership value with the fuzzy set of perfectly suited location sites. In other words, it is important to note that the match is by no means deemed 'perfect', or else the location site would have a full membership value with the set of perfectly suited location sites. As such, a degree of precision (or imprecision) can be given to the decision alternative. Note also that the product operator possesses the advantage of having a denominator equal to 1.

When comparing the crisp and fuzzy decision outputs, it should be clear that the latter allows for a more subtle decision differentiation than the former. Given the arbitrarily chosen distances for C_1 (= 1100 m) and C_2 (= 230 m), the consultation of the crisp DT resulted in the conclusion that the potential location site was evaluated as 'good' with respect to the supply of raw materials. Actually, this kind of decision output does not really say much about the factual supply possibilities of the location site.

Table 9.5 Specification membership values for A_1 (C_1 = 1100 and C_2 = 230)

C_1 (1100)	0.18		0.82	
C_2 (230)	1.00	0.68	0.32	0.00
A_1 ($C_1 \times C_2$)	0.18	0.5576	0.2624	0.00
	R_1	R_2	R_3	R_4

We simply know that it is 'good', but we do not know how good it is, and, perhaps even more important, whether other location sites exist with a better than good supply potentiality. Clearly, this is because we are unable to make comparisons between location sites that point to an identical crisp action state. The crisp DT evaluates all these locations as functionally equivalent, but makes no further distinction in terms of a degree of matching or ranking order. To illustrate, in our example, all locations that have a harbour within a range of 1000 m were categorized as 'good', regardless of whether the harbour was located within a 100 m, 500 m, or even 999 m radius of the potential location site. Recall that it was exactly this lack of flexibility, typical of working with crisp DTs, that gave cause to the introduction of fuzziness in the decision-making process.

In contrast to the crisp DT output, the FDT concluded that the location site had a 0.81 membership value with the fuzzy set of locations that are perfectly suited to supply raw materials. In other words, the matching is by no means evaluated as 'perfect' because the particular location is not a full member of the set of perfectly accessible location sites. Furthermore, on the basis of this fuzzy decision output, it is possible to compare and rank location sites in terms of their overall calculated membership values, as it is obvious that the higher the membership value, the better the degree of matching, and the more precise we are able to assign the location site to the fuzzy set, and vice versa. Note also that only those locations which have similar membership values are deemed totally functionally equivalent.

SITUATION 2: $C_1 = 1100$ m, $C_2 = 250$ m

Situation 2 differs from the first in that we have slightly altered the distance value of condition C_2. Instead of it being equal to 230 m, C_2 is now equal to 250 m. The distance parameter for condition C_1, however, is left unchanged ($C_1 = 1100$ m). Intuitively, we would expect that such a minor change in input values would have little effect on the overall decision output.

Crisp consultation

Processing the slightly altered distance values through the crisp DT results in the conclusion that the location site's suitability with respect to the supply of raw materials is evaluated as 'medium' (i.e. decision rule R_3). Note that with $C_2 = 230$ m, it was rated as 'good'. This demonstrates again how sensitive crisp DTs react to changes in the parameters of the conditions, and that working with too stringently defined condition categorizations could cause sudden alterations in the decision output.

In addition to these elements, it may also be observed that a condition's influence or relevance on the crisp decision output is at its strongest at the margin between different condition states. It is there that small changes in condition values could lead to a state transition, with the consequence that completely different decision actions will be followed.

Fuzzy consultation

As a result of the change in the value of condition C_2, the degrees of membership of the associated condition states need to be recalculated. Obviously, this will also have its effect on the specification of the membership value of A_1. The results of both mathematical operations are shown in Tables 9.6 and 9.7.

In Table 9.6, it can be seen that with $C_2 = 250$ m, the membership values for the three different fuzzy condition states are 0.50, 0.50 and 0.00, respectively. Note that the distance of 250 m is the inflection point of both the L ('short' distance) and π ('about average' distance) membership curves. In respect to the fuzzy set 'long' distance, 250 m falls outside the fuzzy domain, hence its membership value is equal to 0 (non-fuzzy).

Table 9.7 is constructed on the basis of the membership values ascertained in Table 9.6, and determines the degrees of membership for the different action states of A_1. The degree of matching is equal to:

$$A_1 (C_1 \times C_2) = \frac{(0.18)(1) + (0.41)(0.9) + (0.41)(0.5) + (0)(0.1)}{(0.18) + (0.41) + (0.41) + (0)} = 0.7540$$

Given the fact that C_2 altered from 230 m to 250 m, this results only in a minor change in the fuzzy decision output. It is now established that the particular location site has a 0.75 membership value with the fuzzy set of

Table 9.6 Specification membership values for C_1 (1100) and C_2 (250)

C_1	$\mu_{CS11(short)}(X)$	$= L(X; \alpha, \beta, \gamma)$	$= L(1100; 750, 1000, 1250)$	$= 0.18$
	$\mu_{CS12(long)}(X)$	$= S(X; \alpha, \beta, \gamma)$	$= S(1100; 750, 1000, 1250)$	$= 0.82$
C_2	$\mu_{CS21(short)}(X)$	$= L(X; \alpha, \beta, \gamma)$	$= L(250; 150, 250, 350)$	$= 0.50$
	$\mu_{CS22(average)}(X)$	$= \pi(X; \beta, \gamma)$	$= \pi(250; 200, 350)$	$= 0.50$
	$\mu_{CS23(long)}(X)$	$= S(X; \alpha, \beta, \gamma)$	$= S(250; 400, 500, 600)$	$= 0.00$

Table 9.7 Specification membership values for A_1 (C_1 = 1100 and C_2 = 250)

C_1 (1100)	0.18		0.82	
C_2 (250)	1.00	0.50	0.50	0.00
$A_1 (C_1 \times C_2)$	0.18	0.41	0.41	0.00
	R_1	R_2	R_3	R_4

perfectly suited location sites. In other words, the degree of matching is somewhat decreased (a decline from 0.80 to 0.75), but there is certainly no reason to conclude that the location has only a 'medium' accessibility for supply of raw materials. Therefore, FDTs react more moderately to changes in the condition values than do crisp DTs.

SITUATION 3: C_1 = 500 m, C_2 = 750 m

In the third and final decision situation, C_1 is equal to 500 m and C_2 to 750 m. The purpose of this very particular situation is to illustrate the so-called 'extension principle'. This axiom states that the classical results of crisp (Boolean) logic are recovered from fuzzy set operations when all fuzzy membership grades are restricted to the traditional set {0, 1}. In other words, crisp and fuzzy consultation will lead to identical decision outputs.

Crisp consultation

It can be seen that with condition C_1 being smaller than 1000 m, the crisp DT immediately concludes that the location site is evaluated as having a 'good' potential with respect to the supply of raw materials, regardless of the condition value of C_2. In the crisp DT, this amounts to executing decision rule R_1 in Table 9.1.

Fuzzy consultation

Given a new set of input values, we first recalculate all membership values for the different associated fuzzy condition states. This is shown in Table 9.8.

In Table 9.8, only full and zero membership values occur. This is because both specified condition values (C_1 = 500, C_2 = 750) fall outside the fuzzy domains of the membership functions, which implies that partial or gradual set membership is not possible. The specified condition values are either totally contained in the fuzzy set or totally excluded from it. Here, with C_1 = 500, it is clear that a full membership value is obtained for the fuzzy set of 'short' distances, and a zero membership

Table 9.8 Specification membership values for C_1 (500) and C_2 (750)

C_1	$\mu_{CS11(short)}(X)$	$= L(X; \alpha, \beta, \gamma)$	$= L(500; 750, 1000, 1250)$	$= 1.00$
	$\mu_{CS12(long)}(X)$	$= S(X; \alpha, \beta, \gamma)$	$= S(500; 750, 1000, 1250)$	$= 0.00$
C_2	$\mu_{CS21(short)}(X)$	$= L(X; \alpha, \beta, \gamma)$	$= L(750; 150, 250, 350)$	$= 0.00$
	$\mu_{CS22(average)}(X)$	$= \pi(X; \beta, \gamma)$	$= \pi(750; 200, 350)$	$= 0.00$
	$\mu_{CS23(long)}(X)$	$= S(X; \alpha, \beta, \gamma)$	$= S(750; 350, 450, 550)$	$= 1.00$

value for the fuzzy set of 'long' distances. The latter is the complement of the former (i.e. $\mu_{CS12(long)}(X) = 1 - \mu_{CS11(short)}(X)$). The specified value for condition C_2 (= 750) also falls outside the fuzzy domains of all three defined membership functions. Consequently, all theoretical values less than 0 or greater than 1 are 0 or 1, respectively. No further differentiation will be useful.

A fuzzy consultation on the basis of input values that are specified outside the fuzzy domains of the membership functions results in a crisp decision output (i.e. {0, 1} instead of [0, 1]). This can also been seen in Table 9.9.

Note that whenever a zero membership value for a condition state is obtained, there is no need to further calculate the membership values of all subsequent condition states of that particular condition state, as they will have no influence on the fuzzy decision output. This is because of the nature of the fuzzy set operator used to determine the membership value of the action states. This can easily be verified. In Table 9.9, condition state CS_{12} has a zero membership value. Notice that all three decision rules (R_2, R_3 and R_4), which combine CS_{12} with the three different condition states of condition C_2, result in action states that have a zero degree of membership. This is because the product operator multiplies the membership values of the fuzzy sets. Therefore, the moment a zero membership value for a fuzzy set appears, the fuzzy set operator generates a zero membership value for the consecutive action states.

Finally, the degree of matching is obtained as follows:

$$A_1 (C_1 \times C_2) = \frac{(1)(1) + (0)(0.9) + (0)(0.5) + (0)(0.1)}{(1) + (0) + (0) + (0)} = 1.0$$

The result is a perfect match. In other words, the location site is evaluated as a full member of the set of locations that is perfectly suited to supply raw materials.

In conclusion, the fuzzy decision output: (i) is far more robust than a crisp decision output when it comes to reactions to changes in the condition inputs; (ii) allows for making more subtle comparisons between choice alternatives; and (iii) is able to account for imprecisions and vagueness in the decision-making process.

Although these advantages suggest that FDTs are preferred to the crisp DT formalism, it is worthwhile to point out that some decision

Table 9.9 Specification membership values for A_1 (C_1 = 500 and C_2 = 750)

C_1 (500)	1.00		0.00	
C_2 (750)	1.00	0.00	0.00	1.00
A_1 ($C_1 \times C_2$)	1.00	0.00	0.00	0.00
	R_1	R_2	R_3	R_4

situations do not benefit from the introduction of fuzziness. This primarily concerns decision situations that are intrinsically crisp and demand a crisp decision output. For instance, in legislation, determining whether somebody is an adult involves a crisp decision output (e.g. if $X \geq 18$ years then X is an adult).

CONCLUSIONS AND DISCUSSION

In this chapter, we focused on some methodological issues typical of applying the crisp DT method. In particular, it was argued that in many real-world problems, the use of crisp condition and action states proves to be a too stringent assumption to impose on the decision-maker. In order to solve this problem, we enhanced the crisp DT formalism to incorporate elements from the theory of fuzzy sets as developed by Zadeh (1965).

The fuzzy set theory aims at mathematically representing the vagueness intrinsic in linguistic terms and approximate reasoning. Through the use of the fuzzy sets, ill-defined and imprecise knowledge and concepts can be treated in an exact mathematical way. Fuzzy sets allow for partial or gradual set memberships. This property is reflected in the shape of the membership function. Hence, the choice of the type of membership function and its estimation are most important subjects in fuzzy set theory.

By integrating fuzzy sets in the condition and/or action space of a crisp DT, an FDT is obtained. The construction of an FDT was explained in a step-by-step manner, and illustrated by means of a brief example. The chapter concluded with an assessment of how to use and consult an FDT.

Clearly, a number of additional elements need to be further analysed. First, the locational decision-making problem will have to be modelled by including all relevant location factors. These factors can also be elicited from the decision-makers by means of a decision table structure (including sub-tables). Secondly, the estimation of different membership functions is an issue that needs to be addressed. This ought to enable us to estimate, instead of arbitrarily defining, the various membership function values. Finally, the location analysis should be made two-sided; apart from establishing the characteristics of a potential production environment (i.e. the locational profile), the characteristics of the production requirements put forward by a particular company (i.e. the organizational profile) should be assessed as well.

REFERENCES

Chen, G., J. Vanthienen and G. Wets (1994) *Fuzzy Decision Tables: Extending the Classical Formalism to Enhance Intelligent Decision Making*, Departement Toegepaste Economische Wetenschappen, Katholieke Universiteit Leuven, Leuven.

Cox, E. (1994) *The Fuzzy Systems Handbook. A Practitioner's Guide to Building, Using, and Maintaining Fuzzy Systems.* Academic Press, London.

Dombi, J. (1990) Membership function as an evaluation, *Fuzzy Sets and Systems*, 35, pp. 1–21.

Dubois, D. and H. Prade (1980) *Fuzzy Sets and Systems: Theory and Application.* Academic Press, Boston.

Francioni, J.M. and A. Kandel (1988) A software engineering tool for expert system design, *IEEE Expert*, 3, pp. 33–41.

Hellendoorn, H. (1990) Reasoning with Fuzzy Logic, Ph.D. Thesis, Technische Universiteit Delft, Delft.

Kerre, E.E. (1993) Basic principles of fuzzy set theory for the representation and manipulation of imprecision and uncertainty. In Kerre, E.E. (ed.), *Introduction to the Basic Principles of Fuzzy Set Theory and Some of its Applications.* Communication & Cognition, Gent, pp. 1–158.

Lucardie, G.L. (1994) Functional Object-Types as a Foundation of Complex Knowledge-Based Systems, Ph.D. Thesis, TNO Bouw, Rijswijk.

Sanchez, E. (1986) Medical applications with fuzzy sets. In Jones, A., A. Kaufmann and H.-J. Zimmermann (eds), *Fuzzy Sets Theory and Applications.* Reidel, Dordrecht, pp. 331–347.

Timmermans, H.J.P. and R.E.C.M. van der Heijden (1987) Uncovering spatial decision-making processes: a decision net approach applied to recreation choice behaviour, *Tijdschrift voor Economische en Sociale Geografie*, LXXVIII, pp. 297–304.

Turksen, I.B. (1991) Measurement of membership functions and their acquisition, *Fuzzy Sets and Systems*, 40, pp. 5–38.

Tzafestas, S.G. (1994) Fuzzy systems and fuzzy expert control: an overview, *The Knowledge Engineering Review*, 9, pp. 229–268.

Vanthienen, J. and E. Dries (1994) Illustration of a decision table tool for specifying and implementing knowledge based systems, *International Journal on Artificial Intelligence Tools*, 3, pp. 267–288.

Verhelst, M. (1980) *De Praktijk van Beslissingstabellen.* Kluwer, Deventer and Antwerp.

Witlox, F. (1995) Qualitative housing choice modelling: Decision plan nets versus decision tables, *Netherlands Journal of Housing and the Built Environment*, 10, pp. 209–237.

Zadeh, L.A. (1965) Fuzzy sets, *Information and Control*, 8, pp. 338–353.

Zadeh, L.A. (1975) The concept of a linguistic variable and its application to approximate reasoning. Part I, *Information Sciences*, 8, pp. 199–249.

An optimization method for facility location using a genetic algorithm

10

Yoshitsugu Aoki and Naoto Muraoka

INTRODUCTION

In community-facility planning, the tasks of the planner are to plan the location, size, and building's outlines (such as building volume and room composition) and to manage the facility, which must be fit for the purpose and at the same time reflect the demands of residents in the community. The facility-location problem of where to construct the facility within the community is a particularly important task.

The problem of facility location has been carried out from the points of view of users' convenience, services' efficiency and impartiality. Thus studies on user behaviour and theoretical studies on location have been undertaken. With respect to the studies on user behaviour, it has become clear that the usage patterns can be well predicted from the distances between the users and the facility by using a gravity model or Huff's model (Huff, 1963). It has also become apparent that such patterns can be understood using a spatial-interaction entropy-maximizing model (Wilson, 1970). Studies on location have led, through theoretical studies from the viewpoint of location theory in industry such as the ice-cream vendor model, to the classification and formulation of problems as a mini-sum problem (Weber's problem), a mini-max problem, a median problem or a maximum-coverage problem, depending on differences in evaluation criteria (Ohsawa, 1992). However, it is a difficult task to determine the optimum location within a given area for which facility planning is to be carried out with the

Decision Support Systems in Urban Planning. Edited by Harry Timmermans. Published in 1997 by E & F N Spon. ISBN 0 419 21050 4

existing formulas and methods. Although various methods have been proposed for determining the optimum location in an area, the quantity of computation increases explosively as the number of potential locations increases. The enormous quantity of computation entails much difficulty in actually locating a facility.

Recognizing such conditions, the object of the present chapter is to establish a method which enables us to determine efficiently the optimum location of a facility, whatever the facility-use behaviour and whatever the evaluating criteria for the location of the facility.

The fundamental idea for constructing such a methodology is greatly different from the old way of thinking involving numerical optimization methods. The present study is intended to imitate the fact that living things have evolved through the process of heredity into desirable ones which are best adapted to their environment. This idea, first proposed by Holland (1975), is called a genetic algorithm (GA). The effectiveness and formulation of this algorithm in the allocation problem have been shown by Aoki (1993) in application to a room-allocating problem.

GENERAL PROCEDURE FOR FACILITY-LOCATION PLANNING

Prior to the proposition of a method for determining optimum facility location, we must understand the procedure for determining the location of a community facility. We attempt to grasp in a uniform manner the models that describe the facility-selecting behaviour of users, since, as mentioned above, these models vary according to the kind of facilities. Many different models are proposed, and criteria used for evaluating the goodness of location are rich in variety. Representative facilities classified by characteristics are presented in Table 10.1. From consideration of the procedure for determining a location, it can be seen that, in all cases, the procedure is carried out as shown in Fig. 10.1. That is to say, in the first step, a planner identifies what types of residents will reside in what places in the future, namely, at the target time. In the second step, the planner constructs a model which describes the facility-selecting behaviour of users. In the third step, the planner sets an index or an evaluating model which is used for evaluating performance of the facility. After such preparations have been made, the planner searches for a desirable location. The new proposal therefore must be the proposal of a method which is in accordance with the above procedure for determining the optimum location of facilities.

In an optimum locating method, when the estimation of community population, a model for facility-use behaviour and a model for evaluating facility location are given, the optimum solution must be calculable from these pieces of information.

Table 10.1 Models that describe the facility-selecting behaviour of users, and evaluating methods of facility location

Type of facility[a]	Typical facility	Model that describes the facility-selecting behaviour of users	Evaluating method of facility location
I	Public baths Liquor shop Convenience store	Gravity model or Huff's model	Number of users of the facility *Maximizing*
	Post office	Voronoi diagram	Distance between the farthest residents and the facility *Minimizing*
II	Commercial facility	Gravity model or Huff's model	Number of users of the facility *Maximizing*
	Medical facility	Spatial-interaction model	Total sum of the distances between the facility and the users *Minimizing*
III	Elementary school Junior high school	Voronoi diagram	Distance between the farthest residents and the facility *Minimizing*
IV	Emergency hospital Fire station Police station	Voronoi diagram	Number of residents covered by the facility *Maximizing* Distance between the farthest residents and the facility *Minimizing*
V	City Hall Central Library	–	Distance between the users and the facility whose accumulative frequency in the order of shorter one is over a certain time *Minimizing*

[a]Type I: Facility should be used by as many residents as possible, whose use behaviour depends on the distance between it and them.
Type II: Facility whose use behaviour doesn't always depend on the distance between it and the users.
Type III: Emergency facility.
Type IV: Facility for which one needs to decide the available area.
Type V: Facility is only one in an administrative district.

1st Step
Predicting the population in the planning area

You must predict how many residents are going to be in each division of the area. In this chapter, we divided the objective area into grids, and predicted the population of each grid. We supposed that all residents in the divided area of a grid were in the centre of the grid area, and that the locating point of the facility was also there.

2nd Step
Predicting the behaviour of residents using the facility

In the case of an elementary school, the behaviour of users is dictated by the school's available area. But in the case of a commercial facility, can only be predicted in a probabilistic fashion. We think that there are two kinds of behaviours of residents using the facility. One is that residents use the nearest facility; the other is that they select the facility at random.

3rd Step
Evaluating the facility-locating plan

There are many factors which have an effect on the evaluation of facility location; for example, distance, volume, scale, cost, number of residents using the facility, and so on. Many methods for evaluating facility location have been suggested, and Table 10.1 can be used to select an appropriate method.

4th Step
Optimizing the facility-locating plan

After you formulate the evaluation of the facility location, you maximize or minimize it according to the aim of the planning facility. The optimal facility location shows a principal guideline for facility location planning.

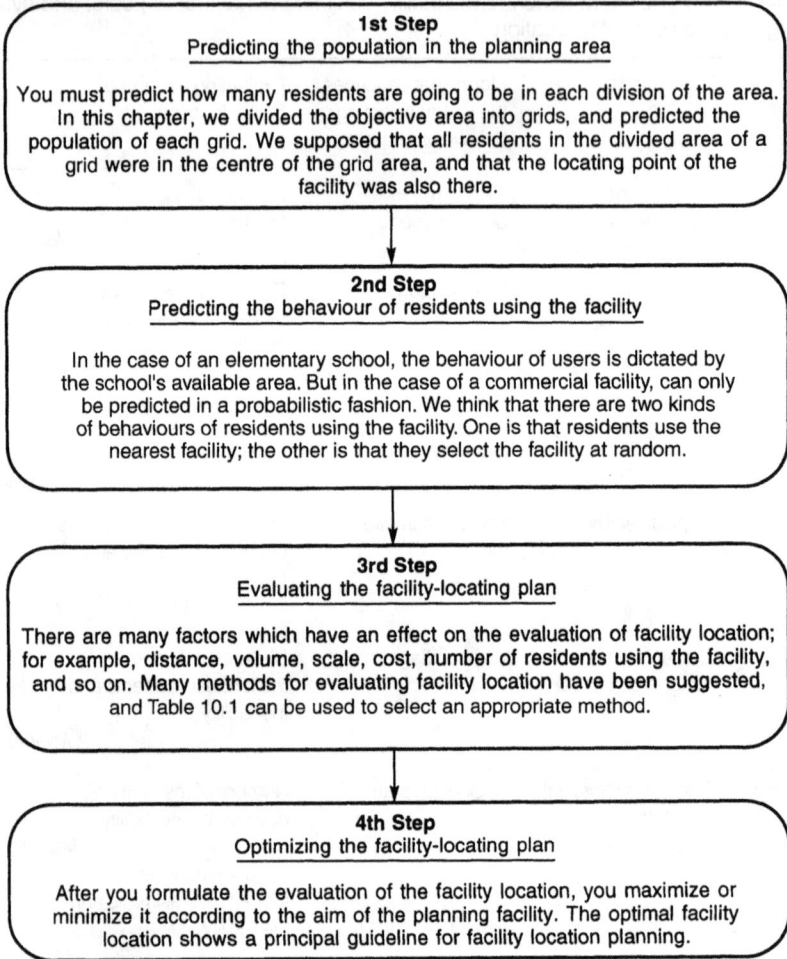

Fig. 10.1   Procedure of planning the facility location.

ALGORITHM FOR LOCATING A FACILITY

CONCEPT OF A GENETIC ALGORITHM

In a GA, all of the fundamental concepts are given 'biological' names. Conditions in a given problem are called an environment. One of the potential solutions, that is, one of the alternative plans, is called an individual; the denotation of an individual by a list of symbols is called a chromosome. The chromosome is composed of fundamental units, which are called genes, and it expresses information on the individual. The degree to which an individual fits itself to its environment is called fitness. The fitness corresponds to an evaluation function in an ordinary problem of optimization. The better the fitness is, the more descendants it leaves. There are two ways in which the next-generation individuals (children) are generated: one is where children are generated by the crossing-over of chromosomes of two individuals (parents); the other is where a child is generated by a mutation in which a part of a chromosome of an individual is altered at random. An individual having low fitness is removed from a set of individuals by selection. As a result, a group of individuals comes closer and closer to the optimum solution as generation after generation is evolved. We carry out optimization by utilizing this phenomenon.

FORMULATION OF A GA FOR SOLVING A FACILITY-LOCATION PROBLEM

What we intend to obtain is one optimum facility-locating plan. Here one of the alternative facility-locating plans and a set of them are put into correspondence, respectively, with an individual in a living population and a group of individuals therein. In this case, since each individual expresses its own information in terms of a chromosome, it is necessary to describe in advance the information on each alternative facility-locating plan in terms of a code called a chromosome.

Next, it is essential to define an evaluation function which is used for evaluating the goodness of facility location, putting the evaluating function into correspondence with the fact that low-fitness individuals are removed.

Furthermore, it is necessary to choose a method for producing a code that expresses a new alternative facility-locating plan, from a chromosome code of the preceding one, using the crossing-over of chromosomes and the mutation of a chromosome.

It is essential to establish in advance a procedure for removing individuals that have been lowly evaluated, from a set of the next generation's individuals described above, namely, the new alternative facility-locating plans. This removal corresponds to what is called selection.

The foregoing is a procedure for formulation of a GA for solving a facility-location problem, and we will now demonstrate how this procedure can be used to locate a facility at an arbitrary point within a domain on a two-dimensional plane. The discussion becomes more simple in the case of node location in a network problem.

DEFINITION OF A CHROMOSOME OF AN ALTERNATIVE LOCATING PLAN

A method for converting the locating plan of a facility to a chromosome representation must be defined so that the coding and the decoding can be carried out in a state where the locating plans of facilities are put into one-to-one correspondence with the chromosome representation. In the present chapter, we propose the following manner of representation for the reason shown in a later paragraph that will describe a mutation.

We consider a rectangular domain that contains a region within which a facility must be located. By equally dividing the rectangular domain lengthwise and crosswise, four smaller rectangular domains are obtained. The four smaller domains thus obtained are called northwestern, southwestern, northeastern and southeastern. These are denoted respectively as (0, 0), (0, 1), (1, 0) and (1, 1). If each smaller domain is again divided in a similar manner into four further smaller domains – northwestern, southwestern, northeastern and southeastern – the location of a facility can be indicated more precisely. If this division is repeated n times according to the need, it follows that the initial rectangular domain is divided into 4^n small rectangular zones (hereinafter called grids), and that the location of the facility can be given. A method for coding a location into two sequences of symbols 0 and 1 is illustrated in the upper part of Fig. 10.2. A process for decoding the two sequences of symbols into the X and Y coordinates of the facility location is shown in the lower part of Fig. 10.2. Thus a location expressed in terms of two sequences of symbols equals a chromosome of an alternative locating plan for one facility. In an alternative locating plan for plural facilities, what is made up by connecting end-to-end the sequences of symbols which express the respective locations of the facilities equals the chromosome of the alternative locating plan for the facilities.

DEFINITION OF AN EVALUATION FUNCTION FOR AN ALTERNATIVE LOCATING PLAN

We set an evaluating index which expresses the goodness of location, according to the characteristics of the facility to be located. A function that is used in the calculation of an evaluating index from information of location is called an evaluation function. In a GA, the value for an evaluating index to each alternative location plan is called fitness, and shows the degree of fitness of an individual to its environment. As shown later on, the higher fitness an individual has, the greater the next generation, because a high-fitness individual has a high probability of reproducing. This means, in location planning, that the more excellent an alternative locating plan is, the more improved alternatives it generates.

In the method proposed in the present chapter, as discussed in the previous section, any evaluation function type is feasible. In order to

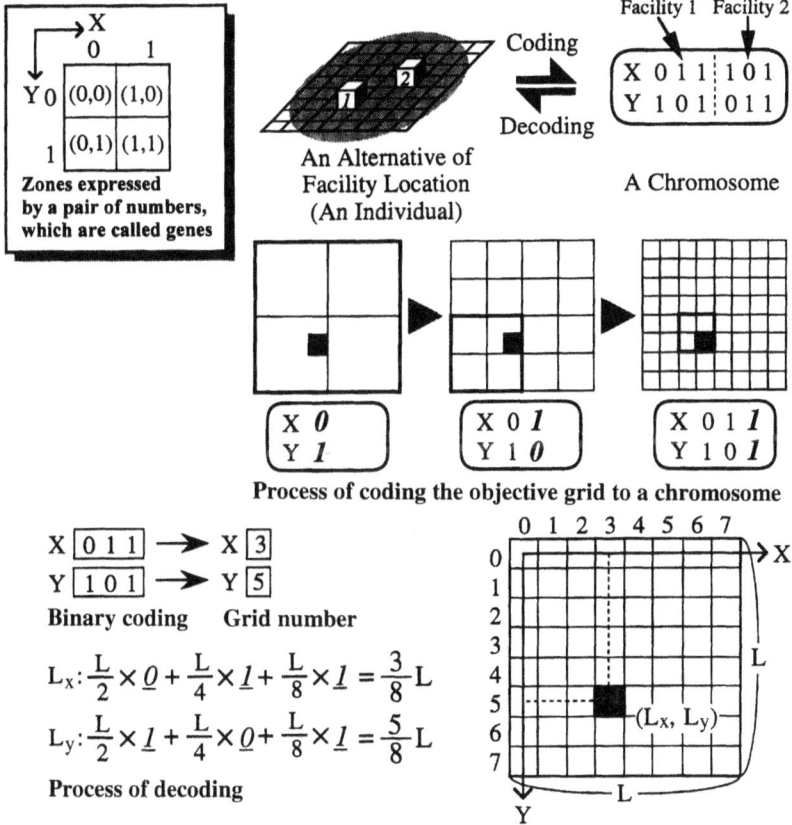

Fig. 10.2   Definition of genes, and the relation between an alternative facility location and a chromosome.

show concretely the feasibility and to take into account also a case where plural facilities are located simultaneously, we define an evaluation function as follows.

We express the total sum of the distances between each facility and users' respective places of residence (hereinafter called the attending distances of users) as a measure of the goodness of location by

$$Q = \sum_i \sum_j d_{ij} x_{ij}$$

where d_{ij} is the distance between place i and facility j (the jth facility) and x_{ij} is the number of residents in place i who use facility j.

In order to calculate the right hand side of the above equation, the following procedure is necessary: For each alternative locating plan, we predict the user choice behaviour for each facility by using a spatial-interaction model; namely, we predict which facility the residents in each divided zone will use. It means that a spatial-interaction model has been chosen as a facility-selecting model in Table 10.1. In this case, the number x_{ij} of the residents in place i who use the jth facility is obtained by solving the following equations:

$$x_{ij} = A_i B_j \exp(-kd_{ij})$$
$$A_i = N_i/[B_j \exp(-kd_{ij})]$$
$$B_j = N_j/[A_i \exp(-kd_{ij})]$$

where k is a constant, N_i is the total number of residents in place i who use facilities, and N_j is the total number of users of facility j. The latter two are given by

$$N_i = \sum_j x_{ij} \text{ and } N_j = \sum_i x_{ij}$$

In this model, since the total number of users of facility j is limited to the maximum number of users which facility j is capable of accommo-dating, the optimum location comes to depend upon the scale of the facility, as shown later. Viewed conversely, location planning is linked with volume or capacity planning. Consequently we come to be able to judge also the appropriateness of a volume plan from the resulting alternative location plan.

GENERATION OF IMPROVED ALTERNATIVE LOCATING PLANS

In the present study, we first generate at random the individuals which represent alternative locating plans. Thereafter, from the first generation of individuals (namely, the alternative location plans at first stage thus generated), we generate individuals in the next generation by methods called, respectively, crossing-over of chromosomes and mutation.

Production of the next generation by crossing-over of chromosomes

Crossing-over has the following meaning: Two individuals are chosen as parents among a group of individuals, and two children are generated by the interchange of corresponding segments of the parents' chromosomes. The possibility that a more excellent individual will be generated is enhanced by imparting a probability to a potential individual, such that the higher the fitness of the potential individual, the higher the probabil-ity that the individual will be chosen as a parent. In the present study, when there are N individuals, the probability P_i that the individual with rank i in terms of the evaluation function will be chosen as a parent has been defined as follows:

$$P_i = 2(N - i + 1)/N(N + 1)$$

Although various methods exist for the crossing-over of the chromosomes of the two individuals thus chosen, a two-point crossing-over method, in which each of the two chromosomes is cut at two points and the corresponding segments of the two chromosomes are interchanged, is adopted in the present study.

Production of the next generation by mutation of chromosomes

We assume that a mutation takes place at random; namely, we choose one individual at random and alter randomly a certain segment of a chromosome that expresses an alternative locating plan. Doing this enables an individual that has not yet reached the true optimum, namely, an individual that is in a state of local optimum, to change and to approach the true optimum.

The consideration of the meaning of such a mutation leads to the realization that it is efficient to roughly determine in the early stages a zone that contains that desired locating position and to search towards the final stages for a better position by varying the position infinitesimally. We have adopted the following method of handling a mutation, which takes advantage of the chromosome notation defined previously and shown in Fig. 10.2. Namely, the method makes use of a characteristic that genes vary in the size of the area which they express, according to their position: Each time a new generation is generated, the mutating point is caused to move from the genes that express a wider area, to the genes that express a smaller area. This enables us to expect the effectiveness of roughly estimating the optimum locating position in the early stages and to narrow down the search domain by moving the mutating point to the genes that express a smaller area, in each of the subsequent stages.

Figure 10.3 shows an algorithm for optimization of facility location by means of the above-described procedure for a GA.

EFFICIENCY TEST OF THE ALGORITHM ON NUMERICAL EXAMPLES

In order to confirm whether the method defined by the algorithm shown in Fig. 10.3 functions efficiently, we investigate the efficiency of the method in advance by applying it to a numerical example of a facility-locating problem. We demonstrate the high efficiency of this method by taking, as an example, a problem as to how to locate n

Set the maximum generation for evolving individuals (G_{max}), and generate N individuals as the initial generation at random by 0 and 1.
In this procedure, we produce many variously located plans without considering the goodness of them.

Evaluate all the individuals

1st
2nd
:
Nth
Order the individuals with the fitness of each one, and give them probabilities according to the rank of each individual.
The probability is necessary for generating improved alternative locating plans in crossing-over procedure.

Crossing-over Procedure

Choose two individuals according to each given probability, and generate two new individuals by crossing-over procedure.
Continue this procedure till $N/3$ new individuals are generated.

Evaluate the new generated individuals

Mutation Procedure

Mutate the individuals from the 1st rank to $N/3$-th one by rewriting some genes of each chromosome randomly.
In this procedure, we generate $N/3$ new individuals.

Mutating Point

1st
2nd
:
$N/3$-th
:
Nth

$N/3$ Higher Fitness Individuals of the Generation

New Generated Individuals

Selection Procedure

Replace the individuals from $2N/3+1$-th rank to Nth one with $2N/3$ new individuals generated in crossing-over and mutation procedure. These N individuals are next generation. In this procedure, the individual of the highest fitness of the generation is taken over to next generation without being killed.

Continue the procedures in ☐ till the generation becomes G_{max}-th generation.
The number of individuals which are evaluated to the last is $N + 2/3 \times N \times G_{max}$.

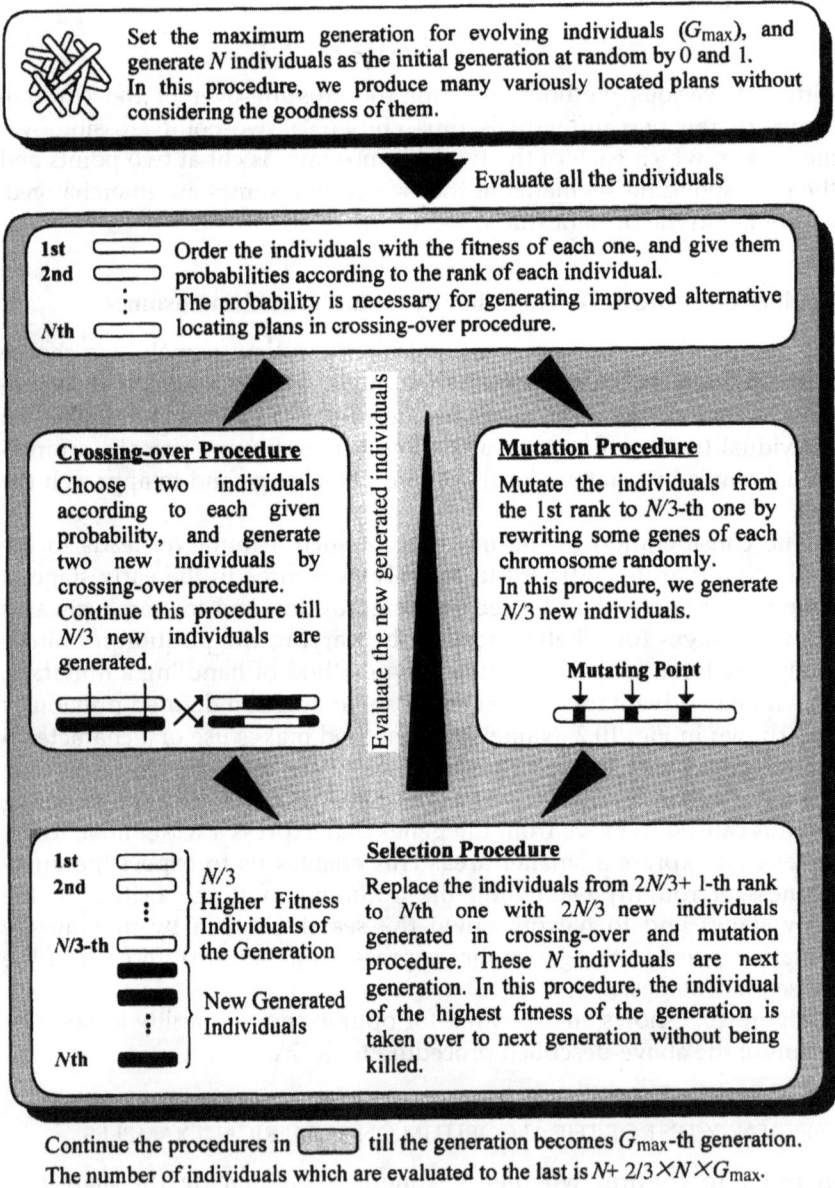

Fig. 10.3   Algorithm for optimization of facility location.

facilities in a district where the population is distributed as indicated in Fig. 10.4.

In the case of $n = 2$, that is, in the locating problem of two facilities, we could obtain, in the eighth generation, the optimum solution which agreed with the solution obtainable from an exhaustive search when individuals were caused to evolve with the flow shown in Fig. 10.3 on condition that the initial number of individuals was 72. In this case, the total number of individuals which was generated and evaluated, including the final generation, was 552. The transition of the value of individuals is shown in Fig. 10.5. From the fact that it was necessary to calculate the evaluations for 32 640 (= $^{256}C_2$) locations in the case of an exhaustive search, it can be seen that the optimum solution was obtained considerably efficiently.

Table 10.2 gives a compilation of the results obtained when the optimum solutions were sought in a similar manner as above in the cases of $n = 3$ and $n = 4$. It is understandable from Table 10.2 that, in the present method, the mere investigation of only a fraction of all the alternative locating plans enables us to obtain the optimum solution, hence it has been shown that the calculating efficiency is high.

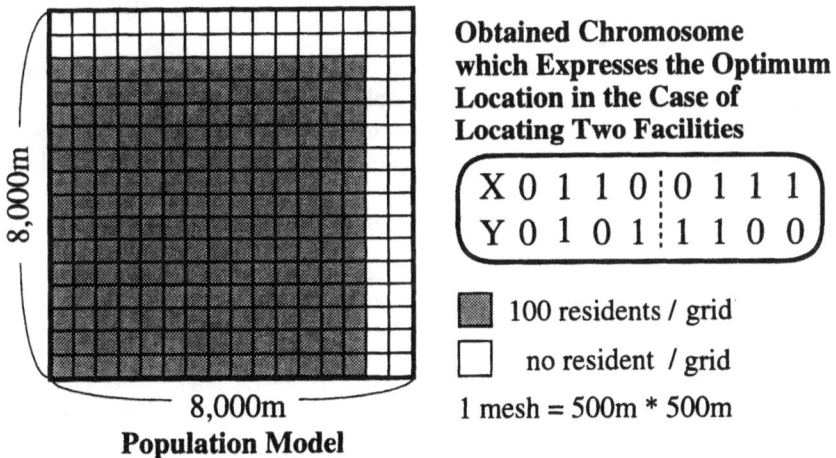

Obtained Chromosome which Expresses the Optimum Location in the Case of Locating Two Facilities

$$\begin{pmatrix} X & 0 & 1 & 1 & 0 & 0 & 1 & 1 & 1 \\ Y & 0 & 1 & 0 & 1 & 1 & 1 & 0 & 0 \end{pmatrix}$$

■ 100 residents / grid

□ no resident / grid

1 mesh = 500m * 500m

8,000m

8,000m

Population Model

Supposing that 50% of residents live within a distance of 1,000m from the facility

Fig. 10.4 Population model for the example problem of locating n facilities.

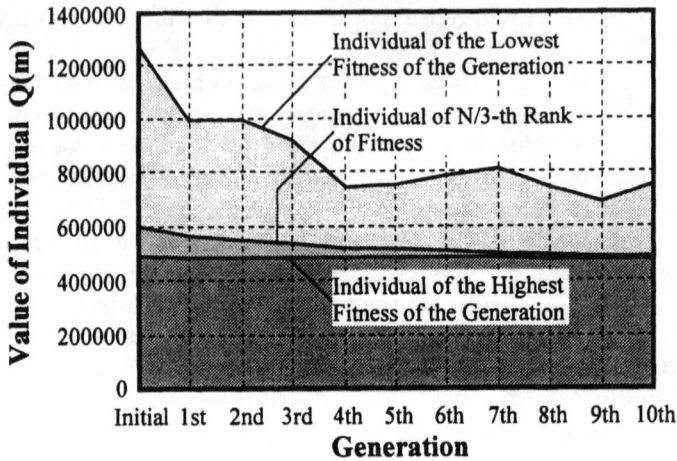

Fig. 10.5 Transition of the value of individuals of each generation.

APPLICATION OF THE METHOD TO ACTUAL COMMUNITY-FACILITY PLANNING

CONDITIONS ON PLANNING A COMMUNITY MEETING FACILITY IN M. TOWN

We investigated concretely the location of facilities by using the present method. The region that became the subject of the present study was M. Town, which is a residential zone and located about 10 km from the central Tokyo business district.

A face-to-face survey was conducted on residents of M. Town in order to extract information as to what public facilities were lacking in the town. Since group activities were popular in M. Town, the rate of use of the meeting facilities was high. Accordingly more meeting facilities

Table 10.2 Obtained chromosome which expresses the optimum location in the case of $n = 3, 4$

n	Obtained chromosome which expresses the optimum location	Generation obtaining the optimum chromosome	Number of individuals evaluated by the generation	Number of feasible alternatives of location
3	X 1 0 1 1 | 0 0 1 1 | 0 1 0 1 Y 0 1 1 1 | 0 1 0 1 | 1 1 0 1	46	2280	2763 520
4	X 1 0 1 0 | 0 0 1 1 | 1 0 1 0 | 0 0 1 1 Y 1 1 0 0 | 0 1 0 1 | 0 1 0 1 | 1 1 0 0	41	2040	174 792 640

should be established. As a result, information that community meeting facilities were lacking was extracted. Thus we demonstrate how to select the sites of new meeting facilities by using the method described in the preceding section.

Table 10.3 tabulates the number of users to be accommodated (hereinafter called the accommodation number) as of April 1994 in each of the existing main meeting facilities and the community population for whom each meeting facility – see Fig. 10.7 for information regarding its location – is intended. In spite of the fact that Meeting Facility 1 was intended for about 1.7 times as many residents as Meeting Facility 3, the accommodation number of Meeting Facility 1 was only about one-third of that of Meeting Facility 3. Accordingly it was necessary to establish one new meeting facility around Meeting Facility 1 in order to make up for a deficiency in the accommodation number of Meeting Facility 1. In this case, from the ratio of the population for whom Meeting Facility 1 was intended to that for whom Meeting Facility 3 was intended, it could be seen that one new meeting facility was needed which had accommodation for users of the order of 310 ≈ [243 × (accommodation number of Meeting Facility 3) × 1.7 × (the ratio of the population for whom Meeting Facility 1 was intended to that for whom Meeting Facility 3 was intended)] – 90 × (the accommodation number of Meeting Facility 1).

OPTIMUM LOCATION OF COMMUNITY MEETING FACILITIES,
IN M. TOWN

On the basis of the preceding consideration, we consider locating one new meeting facility which has accommodation for 310 users. A population distribution in M. Town was obtained prior to determining the optimum location for the meeting facility to be newly established. The area of M. Town was covered by a regular square grid in order to code the location. That is, the district including M. Town was divided into 16 × 16 regular square zones of 500 m square, and the population totals of each grid were obtained. This is shown in Fig. 10.6

It was found from a prior investigation that residents of M. Town did not always use their nearest facilities because the residents frequently moved by car. Consequently the use of meeting facilities by residents was

Table 10.3 Existing main meeting facilities of M. Town in April 1994

	Accommodation number	Community population
Meeting Facility 1	90	12 822
Meeting Facility 2	350	44 088
Meeting Facility 3	243	7 427

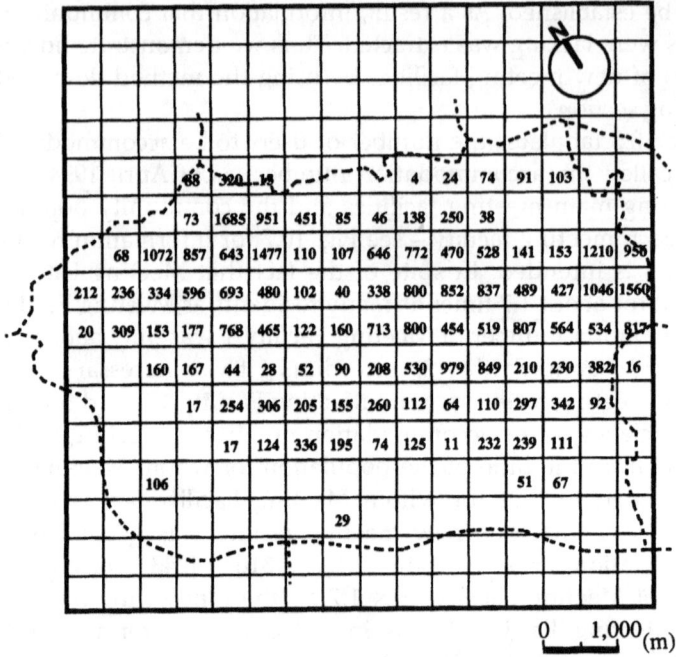

Fig. 10.6 Population of each grid of M. Town in April 1991.

of the type of random facility selection. Then, the meeting facility-selecting behaviour of users could be described in terms of a spatial-interaction model. Hence, for each of the alternative locating plans, the number of residents in grid i who use the jth facility is obtained by using the spatial-interaction model, and the total sum of the distances between each facility and users' respective places of residence (the travelling distances of users) was taken to be an index to the goodness of location.

The location that would minimize this total sum of distances was obtained as the optimum location of the desired meeting facility. The optimum location indicated in Fig. 10.7 was obtained when we caused individuals to evolve with the flow of the algorithm shown in Fig. 10.3 on condition that the initial number N of individuals was 12. The number of individuals that was generated and evaluated up to and including the final generation was 92, which was equal to about one-third of the computational effort of an exhaustive search.

MODIFICATION OF OPTIMUM LOCATING PLAN

The evaluation of the optimum locating plan can be seen from Table 10.4: In Case B in which one new meeting facility that has accommodation for

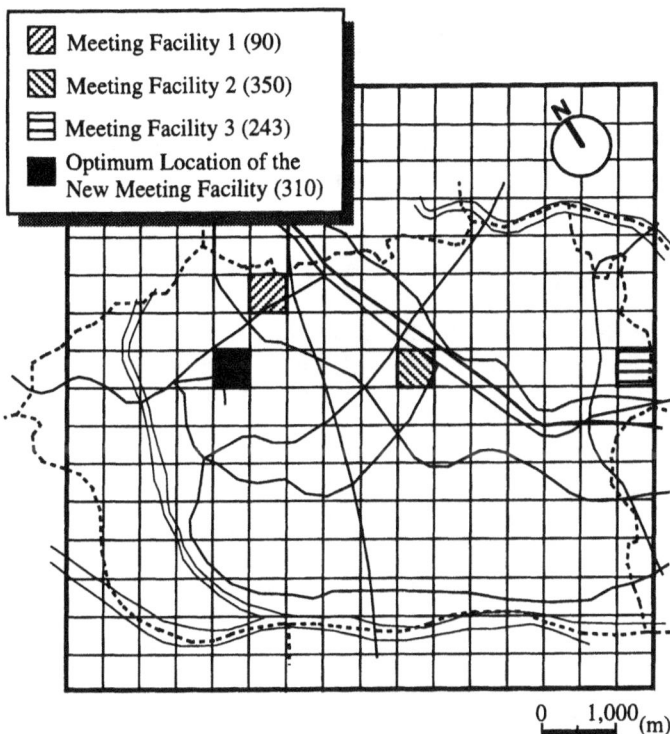

Fig. 10.7 Optimum location of the new meeting facility.

310 users is located at the optimum location (as indicated in Fig. 10.7), the average of the travelling distances of users is shortened by 300 m as compared with that in Case A – *status quo* as of 1994. Thus, we may safely say that it follows that the convenience of the new facility improves.

Since the optimum location obtained by the present method is relatively near Meeting Facility 1, we consider a modified plan in which

Table 10.4 Average travelling distance of users

Case	Total sum of accommodation number, S	Total sum of travelling distance, L (km)	Average travelling distance of users, S/L (km)
A	683	1211	1.772
B	993	1460	1.470
C	993	1557	1.568

Case A: *Status quo* as of 1994.
Case B: Case that the new meeting facility was constructed in the area shown in Fig. 10.7.
Case C: Case that the accommodation number of Meeting Facility 1 changed from 90 to 400 by rebuilding or extending it.

the accommodation number is taken to be $400 \times (90 + 310)$ by the enlargement or new construction of Meeting Facility 1. The evaluation of this plan is shown in Case C. The average of the travelling distance of users in Case C is increased by as much as 100 m as compared with that in Case B of the optimum plan. It can be said, however, that Case C is superior in cost to Case A, since there is no need for newly acquired land cost in Case C.

CONCLUSION

In the planning of facility location, techniques for evaluating the goodness of location have been studied, but a method of simply obtaining the optimum location has not been established. Thus, the results of the studies have not been fully made use of in planning an actual facility location. In the present study, we have developed a method for obtaining the optimum location in which the value for a given evaluating function becomes the best, on the basis of an optimizing technique called a genetic algorithm. We have been able to confirm the effectiveness of the method by applying it to a concrete example of planning a facility location.

This method may safely be said to be a very versatile one, since it is applicable to almost all facility-location problems by simply choosing both an appropriate model of facility-use behaviour and an evaluating index which is incorporated into an evaluation function. Even in the case where there are plural evaluation indices, the respective optimum locations related to them can be quickly obtained. Furthermore, since the number of alternative facility-locating plans to be evaluated is determined not by the number of facilities to be located nor by the number of locations proposed for the facilities, but by the number of initial individuals and the maximum number of generations, the number of alternative facility-locating plans to be evaluated can be held down to surprisingly few. Hence we may truthfully say that the present method is an effective one for solving facility-location problems in which computational effort is enormous and which thus require considerable computer memory. A method of setting the maximum number of generations and the number of initial individuals has not been established yet, and consequently we must set them from experience. Since the maintenance of variety cannot be achieved unless the number of initial individuals is set at a high number, if possible it is necessary to take this into consideration when setting the number of generations and the number of initial individuals. Further research should address this issue.

REFERENCES

Aoki, Y. (1993) Plan optimization and analogy with evolution process, *Summaries of Technical Papers of Annual Meeting, Architectural Institute of Japan* (in Japanese), Tokyo, Japan, September 1993, vol. E, pp. 1129–1130.

Holland, J.H. (1975) *Adaptation in Natural and Artificial System.* University of Michigan Press.

Huff, D.H. (1963) A probabilistic analysis of shopping centre trade area, *Land Economics*, vol. 39, pp. 81–90.

Ohsawa, Y. (1992) Facility location models. *Analytic Models for Architecture and Urban Planning* (in Japanese), Inoue-Shoin, Japan, pp. 136–149.

Wilson, A.G. (1970) *Entropy in Urban and Regional Modeling.* Pion, London.

PART THREE

Application

PART THREE

Towards hybrid technologies for urban design: balancing reliability, power and speed in decision support

11

Joan Antoni Solans and Josep Maria Fargas

INTRODUCTION

We attempt to construct a theory of decision support system design, based on the three independent concepts of reliability, power and speed borrowed from epistemology. We say that a system is *reliable* if a large part of its performance is useful or correct, that it is *powerful* if it performs in a useful way in a variety of situations of interest, and that it is *fast* if its behaviour is consistently dynamic. An arithmetic calculator, for example, is more reliable than a mathematician, but the latter is more powerful. A programming language is as reliable as a calculator, but the calculator is faster.

We use this framework to argue that a successful deployment of decision support technology must take into account the balance between reliability, power and speed. We illustrate this approach with the case of a hybrid system for studying urban transportation issues in the Greater Barcelona Region based on land use, contrasting it with more conventional tools such as traditional geographical information systems or traffic analysis software. The hybrid system is shown to sacrifice the reliability and speed characteristic of commercially available software for a powerful set of computational tools developed specifically for the problem at hand.

Decision Support Systems in Urban Planning. Edited by Harry Timmermans. Published in 1997 by E & F N Spon. ISBN 0 419 21050 4

This trade-off process is formalized using an analysis based on second-order reliability, power and speed concepts. We show that micro-level sacrifices of one of these properties are often inversely correlated with the same characteristics at the macro-level. For example, the relatively slow performance of in-house software components on a given project can result in a high level of dynamism in addressing several related projects.

We extend the design theory outlined above to a methodology for characterizing decision support systems in general, and argue that the hybrid technologies approach is more likely to result in systems reflecting the user's domain knowledge and skills.

CRITERIA AND SCOPE OF THE PLANNING PROBLEM

In planning terms, Barcelona has in many senses the typical polarized structure of a capital town. The Greater Barcelona Region (GBR), locally called Region 1, holds half of the population of Catalonia with about three million people and around 170 municipalities. Economics studies about labour markets (Esteban, 1989) show how these municipalities can be grouped in consecutive rings around Barcelona city, where each ring has a different degree of *labour interrelation* defined in terms of mobility due to work travel. The degree of labour interrelation is defined as the percentage of trips between municipality A and municipality B over all the trips related to municipality A, so as to measure, both ways, the percentage of the working population that lives in municipality A and works in municipality B, and the percentage of jobs of municipality A occupied by people living in municipality B, considering as a base of relationships all the movements with origin and destination within the municipality (internal + entrances + exits). The application of these criteria to the GBR leads to the definition of a system of markets and sub-markets according to a scheme with a central area of influence defined by Barcelona and its metropolitan area as one market centred in Barcelona and with a medium radius of about 35 km. The first metropolitan ring polarized by Barcelona is characterized by several metropolitan subsystems with strong residence–labour relationships and services with the metropolitan centre and also by the fact that the municipalities inside the ring have stronger links among themselves than with those outside it. The rest of the greater metropolitan area is organized with more autonomous markets, which, while being part of the global metropolitan market, constitute clear urban systems with daily residence–labour relationships around cores like Sabadell and Granollers and act as sub-centres or cities of second order with strong relationships with the capital.

One of the most important planning goals of the railroad analysis model, commissioned by the Planning Department of Catalonia

(Regional Autonomous Government), is to decentralize the railroad network. The railroad network has a tremendous impact in the municipalities' relationships in terms of residence–labour mobility, and thus in terms of the *territorial functional balance*. From the point of view of railroad traffic, the Catalan railroad network, called the Catalan 8, is also totally polarized by Barcelona city, especially at the greater metropolitan level, and behaves like a star with a shape of a stretched out figure 'eight'. Figure 11.1 shows the existing and proposed railroad network for the GBR. A more particular goal of the railroad analysis model is to assess the potential use of the railroad network in the future based on land use. To carry out the study, a dynamic computer model was designed ensuring compatibility with the current technology used at the Planning Department based on Intergraph GIS and network analysis software and workstations with Oracle relational databases. The model uses the land use data of the Land Use Plan (LUP) aggregated at the municipal level, shown in Fig. 11.2 (Solans *et al.*, 1990). The hypothetical horizon of the study was fixed at year 2005, which has to do with the time validity of the LUP for the GBR. The railroad network that the traffic analysis model studies is based on the present network of the GBR with the complement of added segments and a specialization of the different railroad lines into 'regional' lines (RENFE, the state level lines) with few stops and 'metropolitan' or commuter lines (FFCC, the local government ones). In terms

Fig. 11.1 Greater Barcelona Region, municipalities and railroad network.

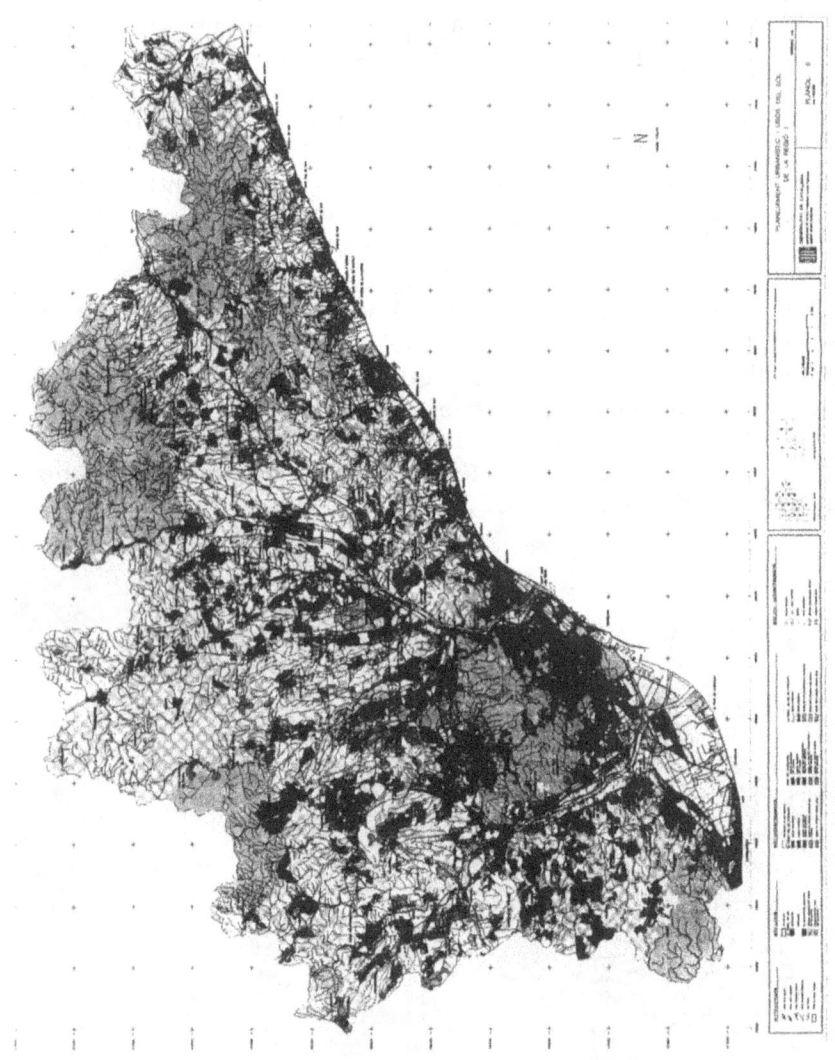

Fig. 11.2 Greater Barcelona Region Land Use Plan, Planning Department of Catalonia.

of the model, the stops of Barcelona are represented as only one special stop with special features, as we will explain later.

HYPOTHESIS OF THE RAILROAD TRAFFIC ANALYSIS MODEL

As explained above, the model uses the data of the LUP that was carried out by the Planning Department for the GBR. The LUP states for each planning sector its land categories, land use and intensity of use (see Fig. 11.2). All this data has been aggregated at the municipal level to simplify the first prototype of the analysis model. In particular, the data about current planning law and programmed land (that is, with growth expectations) are the ones that have been considered to get for each municipality its total population and its potential number of jobs under the horizon of year 2005. The map in Fig. 11.3 shows the distribution of population in 1991 for the GBR and its relationships with the proposed railroad network. It is interesting to note how the natural topography corridor, called the Vallès corridor, corresponds to the topology of the railroad network and to the distribution of population. Owing to the fact that the metropolitan area of Barcelona with its 27 municipalities has a big metropolitan park in the middle, the Collcerola mountain, naturally surrounded by communication infrastructures, the proposed first railroad ring parallel to the coast takes advantage of this natural configuration, and just the

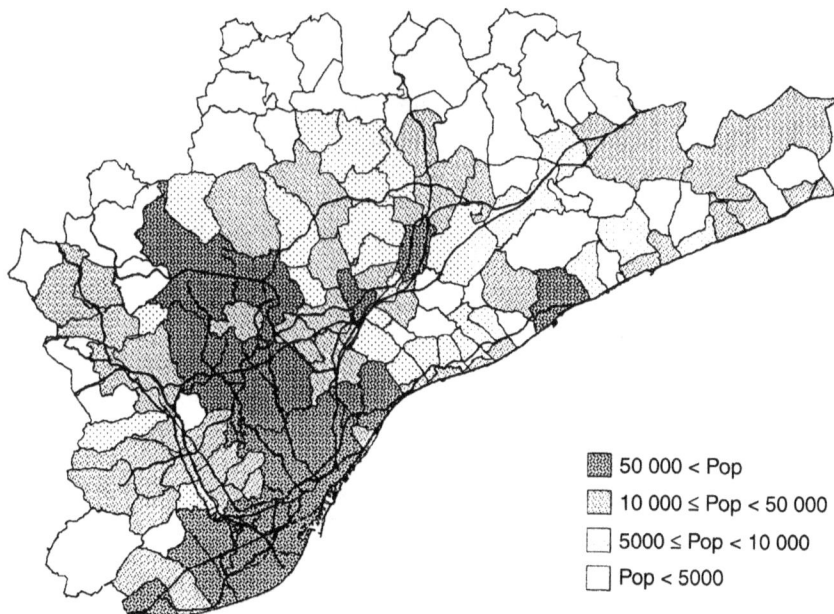

Fig. 11.3   Greater Barcelona Region, distribution of population in 1991.

addition of small segments of railroad lines was needed to complete the axle, part of which is now being used only by freight trains. This option was never carried out before because of the great attraction and polarization force of Barcelona city over the whole Catalan network. In terms of the second ring, a completely new line was designed to connect the metropolitan sub-centres like Sabadell, Terrassa and Granollers. This second ring has the potential of growing until the sea to the east and reaching Mataró, the biggest coastal sub-centre of the GBR, this way closing the ring. This option was not considered for several reasons like budget, strategic priorities, strong difficulties of topography and timetable.

We defined an index of mobility related to motorization level (1 for municipalities with high mobility, 2 for medium, 3 for low, and a special level of mobility for Barcelona named B) and the type of labour offer for each municipality (i.e. industrial, services or central services). Table 11.1 shows the distribution of population by levels of mobility and labour sector that is used by the system and that can be dynamically changed according to user needs or future potential changes and adjustments. This table is used to determine the distribution of the active population by industrial workers, service and central service ones according to each level of mobility. Figure 11.4 shows the distribution of population as a function of the distance to location of work by levels of mobility, and it illustrates how far the different segments of population travel according to the duration of the trip. To set up the index of mobility for each municipality, we used the census data origin–destination matrices for obliged mobility of 1991, and we adjusted the index by hand and municipality-by-municipality according to the criteria and knowledge of each of the different territorial experts of the Planning Department, so as to configure the municipalities data table, part of which is shown in Table 11.2. On top of the municipal data, the model includes extra-municipal nodes like the SEAT automobile factory at Martorell, the airport, the F1 circuit at Montmeló, the TGV high-speed train station, etc., that are distinguished by an asterisk in the municipalities data table (Table 11.2). Each municipality and extra-municipal node has a connection with one or more than one railroad stations to which it contributes with a specific percentage of its population. These connections are used to obtain the total population

Table 11.1 Distribution of active population by levels of mobility and labour sector

Sector	Level 1	Level 2	Level 3	Level B
Industrial	34%	48%	57%	60%
Services	32%	32%	23%	40%
Central services	34%	20%	20%	0%

of the model, the stops of Barcelona are represented as only one special stop with special features, as we will explain later.

HYPOTHESIS OF THE RAILROAD TRAFFIC ANALYSIS MODEL

As explained above, the model uses the data of the LUP that was carried out by the Planning Department for the GBR. The LUP states for each planning sector its land categories, land use and intensity of use (see Fig. 11.2). All this data has been aggregated at the municipal level to simplify the first prototype of the analysis model. In particular, the data about current planning law and programmed land (that is, with growth expectations) are the ones that have been considered to get for each municipality its total population and its potential number of jobs under the horizon of year 2005. The map in Fig. 11.3 shows the distribution of population in 1991 for the GBR and its relationships with the proposed railroad network. It is interesting to note how the natural topography corridor, called the Vallès corridor, corresponds to the topology of the railroad network and to the distribution of population. Owing to the fact that the metropolitan area of Barcelona with its 27 municipalities has a big metropolitan park in the middle, the Collcerola mountain, naturally surrounded by communication infrastructures, the proposed first railroad ring parallel to the coast takes advantage of this natural configuration, and just the

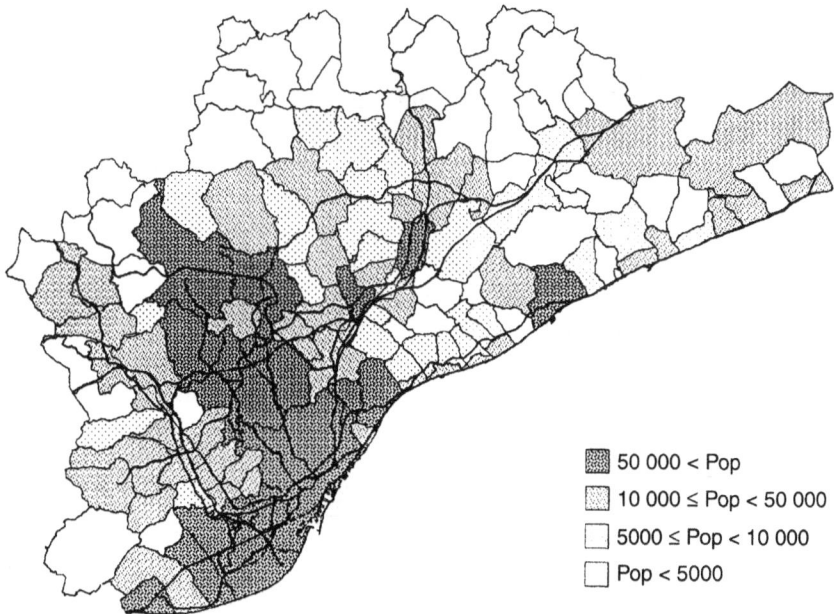

Fig. 11.3   Greater Barcelona Region, distribution of population in 1991.

addition of small segments of railroad lines was needed to complete the axle, part of which is now being used only by freight trains. This option was never carried out before because of the great attraction and polarization force of Barcelona city over the whole Catalan network. In terms of the second ring, a completely new line was designed to connect the metropolitan sub-centres like Sabadell, Terrassa and Granollers. This second ring has the potential of growing until the sea to the east and reaching Mataró, the biggest coastal sub-centre of the GBR, this way closing the ring. This option was not considered for several reasons like budget, strategic priorities, strong difficulties of topography and timetable.

We defined an index of mobility related to motorization level (1 for municipalities with high mobility, 2 for medium, 3 for low, and a special level of mobility for Barcelona named B) and the type of labour offer for each municipality (i.e. industrial, services or central services). Table 11.1 shows the distribution of population by levels of mobility and labour sector that is used by the system and that can be dynamically changed according to user needs or future potential changes and adjustments. This table is used to determine the distribution of the active population by industrial workers, service and central service ones according to each level of mobility. Figure 11.4 shows the distribution of population as a function of the distance to location of work by levels of mobility, and it illustrates how far the different segments of population travel according to the duration of the trip. To set up the index of mobility for each municipality, we used the census data origin–destination matrices for obliged mobility of 1991, and we adjusted the index by hand and municipality-by-municipality according to the criteria and knowledge of each of the different territorial experts of the Planning Department, so as to configure the municipalities data table, part of which is shown in Table 11.2. On top of the municipal data, the model includes extra-municipal nodes like the SEAT automobile factory at Martorell, the airport, the F1 circuit at Montmeló, the TGV high-speed train station, etc., that are distinguished by an asterisk in the municipalities data table (Table 11.2). Each municipality and extra-municipal node has a connection with one or more than one railroad stations to which it contributes with a specific percentage of its population. These connections are used to obtain the total population

Table 11.1 Distribution of active population by levels of mobility and labour sector

Sector	Level 1	Level 2	Level 3	Level B
Industrial	34%	48%	57%	60%
Services	32%	32%	23%	40%
Central services	34%	20%	20%	0%

Table 11.3   Stations data table

Station	Population	Jobs	Mobility	Labour sector	Comment
1	6 000	510	1	Ind.	First node of the model
...					
57	11 675	11 675	1	Cen.	
58	21 536	5 291	1	Ind.Cen.	
59	10 768	2 646	1	Ind.Cen.	
60	5 384	1 323	1	Ind.Cen	
61	0	0	0		
62	14 917	3 183	2	Ind.Ser.	
63	27 155	5 330	2	Ind.Ser.	
64	0	0	0		Extra-municipal node
65	20 366	3 998	2	Ind.Ser.	
66	14 558	3 301	2	Ind.Cen.Ser.	
...					
81	190 000	∞	1	Ind.Cen.Ser.	Barcelona node
...					
243	50 800	15 180	2	Ind.Ser.	Last node of the model

FUNCTIONING OF THE ANALYSIS MODEL

The railroad traffic analysis model of the GBR is based on the Intergraph GIS software of the Planning Department. It uses the GBR Land Use Plan base maps (see Fig. 11.2), databases and topology tables to determine, predict and display the population served by the lines, the population attracted and generated by each municipality, the potential number of travellers on each segment of railroad line, and the location of railroad stations (see Figs 11.5 and 11.6). The geo-referenced databases of municipalities were complemented with the knowledge of the Planning Department experts about predicting the potential population of each municipality for the year 2005 based on land use, its number of potential jobs, the type of labour offered and the level of mobility, as shown in Fig. 11.4 and Tables 11.1–11.3.

The attraction–generation computer model works with three modules, each one of which does the following tasks:

The first module assigns destinations to each origin or station, calculating the smallest time of the trip or the distance covered for each pair of origin and destination points. This module considers the points of the network where turns are not allowed, it penalizes in time the transfers of railroad lines – from metropolitan lines to regional lines and vice versa – and it takes into account the different speeds of the trains in the metropolitan and regional lines. Some of the transits without stops and through specific stations, for example through Barcelona, are also penalized in time. The structure of the system database is such that the links

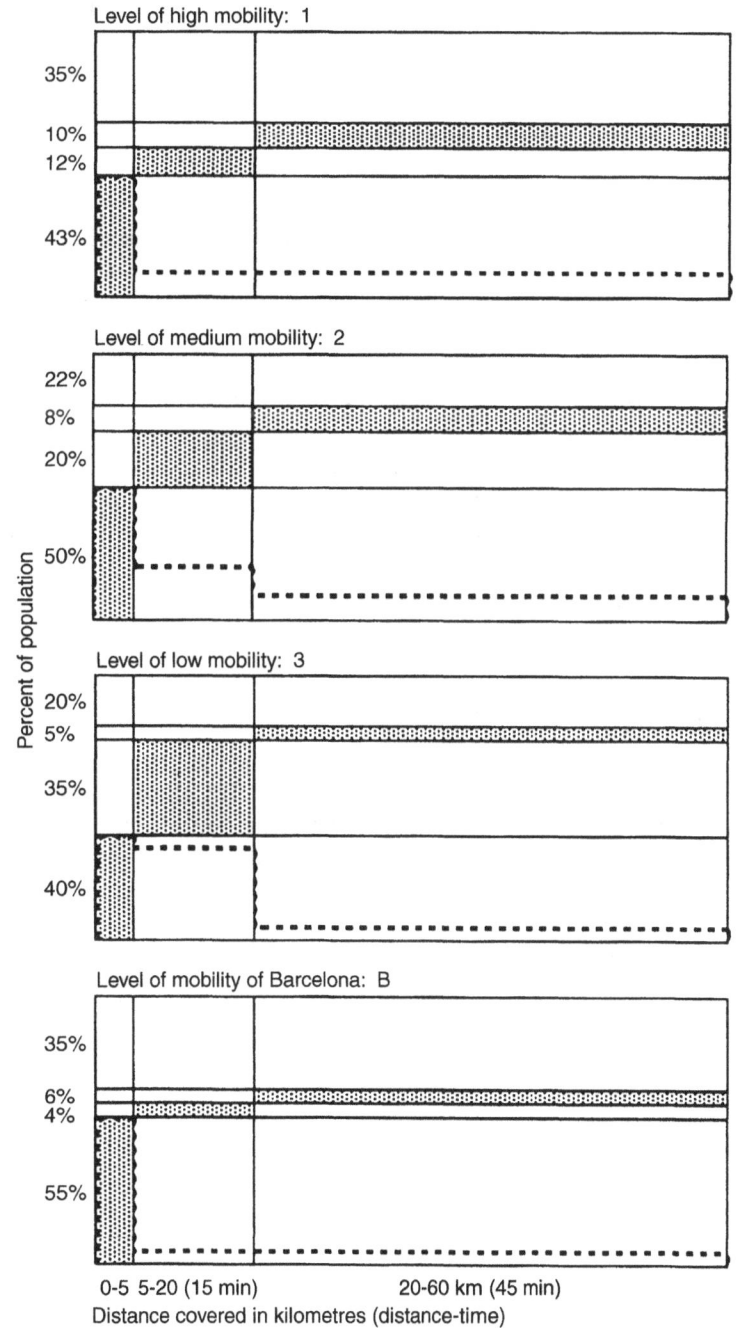

Fig. 11.4   Distribution of population as a function of the distance to location of work by levels of mobility.

and number of jobs, the average index of mobility and the labour offer for each railroad station as shown in the stations data table, part of which is shown in Table 11.3. The number of trips generated by Barcelona city has been considered a special category or level of mobility, as shown in Fig. 11.4. Seasonal traffic (i.e. the coastal traffic generated by beaches in summer) has also been included in the final total numbers for each municipality.

The extra-municipal nodes data contains information about generated and attracted trips instead of data about population and number of jobs. The load of the model network with the generated and attracted data outside the GBR was obtained from 1991 census data and the number of tickets sold by RENFE and FFCC. This data about traffic generated outside the GBR is represented by different extra-municipal nodes at the end of each railroad line, considering the end of the railroad line to be the intersection of the line with the limit of the GBR.

Data about travellers attracted and generated by the airport has been processed from 1987 origin and destination matrices published by the Transportation Department of the local government (Batlle, 1989). The number of potential travellers going from the airport to each of the stations of Barcelona is considered as the number of travellers generated by the airport, and the number of travellers going from each station of Barcelona to the airport is considered as the number of travellers attracted by the airport.

The number of trips generated by Barcelona has been extrapolated from 1987 origin and destination matrices by adding all the trips of all the stations going out from Barcelona. On the other hand, at the level of the analysis model, Barcelona city is considered with an infinite attraction or capable of absorbing all the trips having Barcelona as destination, as shown in Tables 11.2 and 11.3 (Barcelona is station 81).

The model uses this data to generate different graphical and numerical statistics such as the number of trips for each railroad segment and the typical origin–destination matrix. The attraction–generation table, part of which is shown in Table 11.14, summarizes the 143 × 143 origin–destination matrix of daily trips between railroad stations (extra-municipal nodes are also included in the table as stations at the limit of the GBR). According to the results of the model, this matrix has a total number of 112 million trips per year, from which 65.5 million correspond to the FFCC or metropolitan lines and 46.5 million to the RENFE or regional lines for the year 2005. The classical diagram maps of the railroad traffic network loads (Figs 11.5 and 11.6) show the load of potential annual trips for each railroad segment (in thousands) and the generated and attracted trips by each municipality and extra-municipal node.

Table 11.2 Municipalities data table

Municipality	Population	Jobs	Mobility	Labour sector	Station number and distribution (%)		
Sant Climent de Llobregat	2 577	510	2	Ser.	35 60%	44 40%	
* Outside R1 (Castelldefels)	6 000	0	0		8 100%		
Castelldefels	54 197	6 388	2	Ind.Ser.	24 78%	16 22%	
Gavà	46 336	9 737	2	Ind.Cen.Ser.	34 25%	31 55%	27 20%
* Aeroport (El Prat de Ll.)	11 675	11 675	1	Cen.	57 100%		
El Prat de Llobregat	67 888	13 325	2	Ind.Ser.	63 40%	70 30%	65 30%
Barcelona	190 000	∞	1	Ind.Cen.Ser.	81 100%		
Sant Quirze del Vallès	14 917	3 183	2	Ind.Ser.	62 100%		
Sabadell	208 464	53 224	2	Ind.Cen.Ser.	67 30%	68 40%	74 30%
Cerdanyola del Vallès	64 100	10 973	2	Ind.Cen.Ser.	69 35%	71 35%	72 30%
Ripollet	31 414	5 693	2	Ind.Ser.	79 100%		
Ullastrell	8 064	360	3	Ind.	45 100%		
La Llagosta	13 685	3 648	2	Ind.	86 100%		
Martorelles	6 019	3 161	2	Ind.	89 100%		
Santa Maria de Martorelles	800	100	2	Ser.	89 100%		
Montornés del Vallès	13 379	5 939	2	Ind.	97 100%		
Montmeló	9 297	4 221	2	Ind.	97 65%	99 35%	
Granollers	63 260	22 061	2	Ser.	104 50%	109 50%	
Barberà del Vallès	33 737	11 350	2	Ind.Cen.	80 40%	77 30%	76 30%

Fig. 11.5 Diagram map of the railroad traffic network loads.

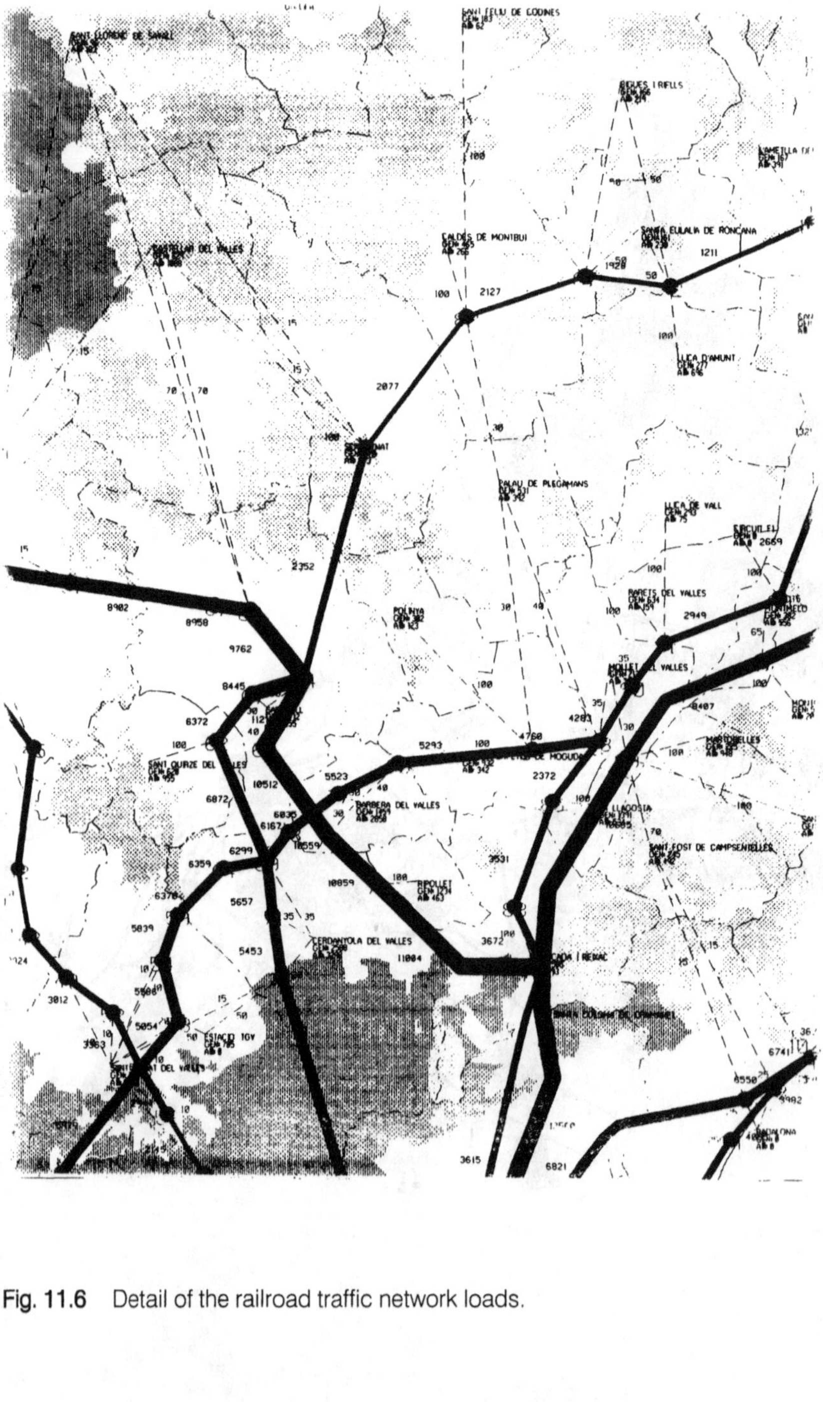

Fig. 11.6 Detail of the railroad traffic network loads.

Table 11.4 Attraction–generation table

Station	Population	Travellers			Number of jobs		
		Potential	Real	Real/Pot.(%)	Potential	Real	Real/Pot.(%)
1	6 800	1 496	595	40	510	0	0
...							
57	11 675	2 569	1 565	61	11 675	798	7
58	21 536	4 738	2 778	59	5 291	1 310	25
59	10 768	2 369	1 290	54	2 646	2 645	100
60	5 384	1 184	580	49	1 323	1 323	100
61	0	0	0		0	0	
62	14 917	3 508	2 031	58	3 183	3 181	100
63	27 155	6 387	3 188	50	5 330	2 729	51
64	0	0	0		0	0	
65	20 366	4 790	2 434	51	3 998	3 998	100
66	14 558	3 424	1 641	48	3 301	3 297	100
67	62 539	14 709	7 661	52	15 967	8 057	50
68	83 386	19 612	9 971	51	21 290	6 183	29
69	22 435	5 277	3 189	60	3 841	3 843	100
70	20 366	4 790	2 465	51	3 998	3 993	100
71	22 435	5 277	2 602	49	3 841	3 843	100
72	35 382	8 322	4 919	59	7 260	7 267	100
73	0	0	0		0	0	
74	62 539	14 709	7 545	51	15 967	6 966	44
75	0	0	0		0	0	
76	10 121	2 380	1 256	53	3 405	1 072	31
77	10 121	2 380	1 528	64	3 405	3 409	100
78	10 701	2 517	1 245	49	2 617	2 611	100
79	31 414	7 389	4 033	55	5 693	1 296	23
80	13 495	3 174	1 995	63	4 540	4 554	100
81	190 000	41 800	19 004	45	$\infty \geqslant$46 614	46 614	
...							
143	50 800	11 948	1 942	16	15 180	2 377	16
Total	2 507 254	622 021	321 379	52	620 970	321 390	48

between the data of the municipalities and the data of the stations can be changed dynamically.

The second module uses the matrices of population distribution by levels of mobility and labour sector and the matrices of population distribution as a function of the distance to the location of work by levels of mobility to assign to each destination the total number of travellers that it can absorb from each origin. One important criterion of this module is the fairness of the loads assignation process between competing origins guaranteeing that the order in which the program does the assignation does not affect the results of the analysis. There are also second-order criteria that can be changed such as the ratio of the number of travellers absorbed by a destination and the total number of travellers generated by competing origins to fill the same destinations. The model is characterized by the fact that it also guarantees that travellers of a certain labour sector will travel to destinations where they will find jobs of the same labour sector. Extra-municipal nodes are processed in an additional phase so as to make sure that the totality of its generated and attracted trips will load the network.

The third module uses the results of the first two modules to distribute the loads corresponding to each origin–destination pair to the railroad line segments that join the points with the shortest path. The model does not consider any capacity limit of the railroad lines. This module can also be used to produce other syntheses of data about the anterior modules, like, for example, to produce the origin–destination matrix already mentioned, to compare the volumes of types of trips by labour sector, and to analyse the through-traffic of a station in relation to the traffic whose destination is that station.

RELIABILITY, POWER AND SPEED

In terms of global evaluation of the computer system we created and, in general terms, of expert systems for design and planning, we would like to borrow, from the literature on epistemology, the concepts of *reliability*, *power* and *speed*, as general measures of performance (Goldman, 1986) and with the special interpretation and application to design that Papazian (1991) does in his thesis.

We say that a system is *reliable* if a large part of its performance is useful or correct; that it is *powerful* if it performs in a useful way in a variety of situations of interest; and that it is *fast* if its behaviour is consistently dynamic. An arithmetic calculator, for example, is more reliable than a mathematician, but the latter is more powerful. A programming language is as reliable as a calculator, but the calculator is faster. Reliability will be the degree to which a system produces 'good' (or 'acceptable') designs. Note that a system which always produces the same (good) design is completely reliable. Power will be the range of different (good) designs that a system can produce. A system which is capable of producing many different kinds of designs, none of which are good designs, is powerful, but not reliable at all. Speed will be a measure of how fast the system produces a design, a response. We will use the term *dynamism* as a measure of responsiveness or spontaneity. A system may internally enumerate all possible designs and eliminate ones which are unsatisfactory. Such a system is reliable and powerful but it looses out on dynamism.

We would like to claim that 'good' expert systems must find the right balance between these three or four terms so as to avoid being inappropriate either because they are *over-designed* and thus too expensive in terms of time, money and effort, or because they are too trivial and thus inaccurate or incomplete. One of the reasons why it is very often difficult to find the right balance between reliability, power and speed in expert systems for design and planning is due to the fact that the expert knowledge must be rediscovered while building the modelling system and also to the fact that it varies as a function of the scale of the problem at hand.

The most important constraints of the railroad analysis model were to design a computer system to be used dynamically and under the changing conditions of land use and planning cycles. To ensure these conditions, the computer model had to be compatible with the Intergraph GIS facilities of the Planning Department. In addition to this and due to the fact that the modelling system was required to make predictions about the potential use of the railroad network based on land use expectations of development defined by the GBR Plan, we were forced to design specific software rather than using standard software of traffic analysis which could not satisfy the requirements we needed and was difficult to make compatible with the rest of the Department software.

We would like to argue that the modelling system we designed, although it is not as reliable as commercially available traffic analysis software, is very powerful since it answers most of the planning questions that interest the Planning Department and it produces statistics very valuable to build 'What-if?' scenarios. Commercial software might not need serious adjustment phases so as to be used consistently, but the software we designed had to be adjusted and tested before systematically using it for the whole region. In terms of power, standard traffic analysis software was incapable of using multiplicity of factors or different parametric functions to define a variable according to different intervals, as we needed for example to define duration of trip (or distance covered) to work as a function of the distribution of population per labour sector and level of mobility. For standard traffic analysis software it was certainly easy to use general relationships at the level of origin–destination matrices (i.e. from all origin nodes with industrial workers to all destinations with industry), but these relationships were lost at the point of the analysis itself since only the information about the origin–destination pairs is retained (i.e. from A to B, where A and B are specific stations). One solution to use this commercially available software was to define as many origin–destination matrices as there were different labour sectors that we wanted to model (i.e. one matrix for industrial workers, another for service workers who only travel to Barcelona, etc.), assuming that the final combined matrix, as a simple addition of these independent matrices, would not affect or change the final network analysis due to the effects of network overload, which cannot be taken into account in this solution. Consequently, as opposed to traditional traffic analysis software, we can claim that our model was more powerful. A special feature of our model was the capacity to carry out unpredictable consequences and future uses at the technical and political levels. The system can be used to establish priorities of new railroad line construction; to develop specifically directed land use policies to readjust the territorial balance as a function of the railroad network; to better inform and support political decisions on infrastructures; to make potential railroad use predictions; to generate new needs and thus be able to expand (we have developed another expert system that can be used in conjunction, which automatically simulates dynamic train graphs to study the impact of different types of trains on existing train schedules like high-speed trains on commuter train schedules); etc.

The analysis model also performs very well in terms of dynamism since it was designed to be used dynamically, as opposed to standard software. Not only was the analysis model able to regenerate all its tables and graphs from the many possible levels of changes – from different topology, municipalities data and trains constraints to different distributions of population tables, etc. – but also it was able to include very easily slightly different types of data like the extra-municipal nodes and, due to its modularity, different network analysis algorithms. On the other hand, the system we designed was very slow. This was partially due to the many (computing/hardware) platform compatibility constraints we had and partially due to the fact that speed was not a priority, since we had to solve memory allocation and storage problems and implement lexical scoping. We would like to generalize that the relatively slow performance of in-house software components on a given project can result in a high level of dynamism in addressing several related projects, as our analysis model shows.

We think we found a good balance between the factors since we reached all our goals in such a way that now the system will be expanded to all the Catalonia railroad network for studying the other three subsystems of the network, the relationships among them at the regional and state scale, and the impact of the addition of high-speed lines and new connections both in terms of topology and in terms of potential use.

We would also like to argue in favour of what we call hybrid models, models that combine different levels of knowledge captured either by algorithms or by exhaustive databases more or less built by hand. In the early phases of the analysis model design, we had to carry out two very long and tedious sessions with the different territorial experts of the Planning Department to fine-tune the algorithms and to capture the municipalities data. For example, the index of mobility was adjusted by hand and municipality-by-municipality according to the criteria and knowledge of each of the different planners. This process proved to be very useful, efficient and dynamic, although, as we mentioned before, the price we had to pay, compared to using standard available software, was a longer adjustment phase of the model behaviour.

Finally, we would like to point out our conviction that developing expert systems without exhaustively drawing out knowledge from other different paradigms so as to make easier the task of computer modelling, will generate better design and decision tools. As pointed out at the beginning of the chapter, the relationships between the planning point of view and the economics one are obvious and complementary, but implementing literally the algorithms and functions to design the system would have led us to a less flexible model, more than this, a misleading model, since the economics data results would then have been interpreted in planning terms with the possibility of inaccurate interpretations (Fargas, 1991). In the future, we think it might be very interesting to use the statistics that the model generates (namely the origin–destination matrix and the maps of top ten nodes of highest centrality in terms of time and distance, not included in this chapter) to test it, as well as to find out the relevance of the railroad communications, in terms of the economic concepts pointed out before like self-containment, self-sufficiency and functional balance at the level of the territory. Thus, the hybrid system is shown to sacrifice the reliability and speed characteristic of commercially available software for a powerful set of computational tools developed specifically for the problem at hand.

REFERENCES

Batlle, L. (1989) *El Transport Ferroviari a Catalunya*, Institut Català per al Desenvolupament del Transport, Generalitat de Catalunya, Barcelona.

Esteban, M. (1989) *Distribució de la Mobilitat per Treball a la Regió Metropolitana de Barcelona, Anàlisi dels Mercats de Treball*, Àrea Metropolitana de Barcelona, Barcelona.

Fargas, J.M. (1991) *Designing Rules: Heuristics of Invention in Design*, SMArchS-MCP Thesis, School of Architecture and Planning, Massachusetts Institute of Technology, Cambridge, Mass.

Goldman, A. (1986) *Epistemology and Cognition*, Harvard University Press, Cambridge, Mass.

Papazian, P. (1991) *Principles, Opportunism and Seeing in Design: A Computational Approach*, SMEECS-SMArchS Thesis, Department of Computer Science and School of Architecture and Planning, Massachusetts Institute of Technology, Cambridge, Mass.

Solans, J.A. *et al.* (1990) *Mapa i Base de Dades de Planejament Urbanístic i Usos del Sòl de la Regió I*, Direcció General d'Urbanisme, Generalitat de Catalunya, Barcelona.

GIS and decision support systems for local authorities in Malaysia

12

Ahris Yaakup, Foziah Johar and Nor Azina Dahlan

INTRODUCTION

Despite the fairly widespread recognition of the benefits of GIS for local authorities, its adoption by local planning authorities in Malaysia has not been particularly encouraging. The reluctance of local authorities to accept the challenge to embrace the technology is due mainly to lack of support from the management level, lack of in-house expertise with which to make use of the system and the high cost of GIS. On the other hand, local authorities are now faced with increasingly complex urban problems and inevitably urban planners have to come up with better solutions. Of late, there have been enormous improvements in the price and performance of computer hardware and functionality of software packages, such that a wide range of specific demands for the management, analysis and presentation of data can now be met in a cost-effective manner. A direct consequence of these new opportunities has been the rapid growth in the number of users developing the urban planning and monitoring applications. This chapter examines the functions of a local authority and indicates areas in which GIS as a decision support tool can be most effective.

LOCAL GOVERNMENT IN MALAYSIA

The Malaysian administrative system is divided into three major hierarchies: federal government, state government and local government.

Decision Support Systems in Urban Planning. Edited by Harry Timmermans. Published in 1997 by E & F N Spon. ISBN 0 419 21050 4

Level of high mobility: 1

35%

10%
12%

43%

Level of medium mobility: 2

22%
8%
20%

50%

Percent of population

Level of low mobility: 3

20%
5%

35%

40%

Level of mobility of Barcelona: B

35%

6%
4%

55%

0-5 5-20 (15 min)   20-60 km (45 min)
Distance covered in kilometres (distance-time)

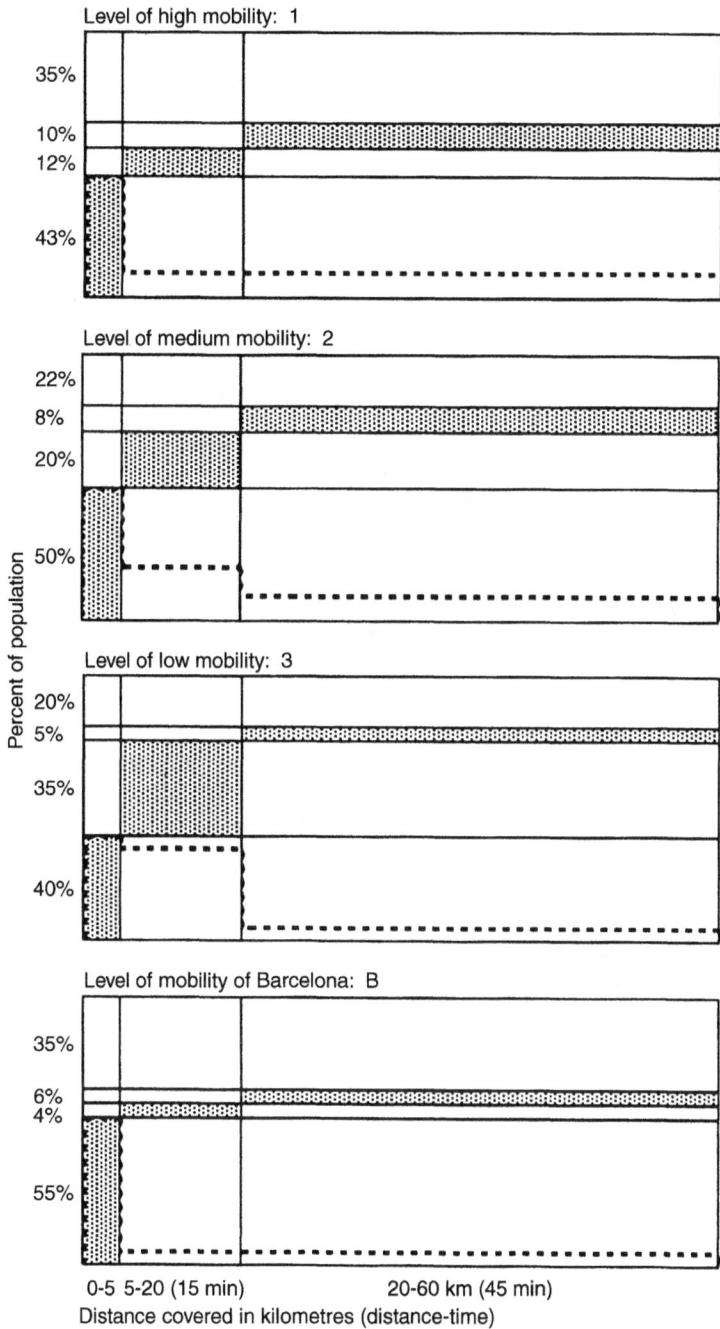

Fig. 11.4   Distribution of population as a function of the distance to location of work by levels of mobility.

and number of jobs, the average index of mobility and the labour offer for each railroad station as shown in the stations data table, part of which is shown in Table 11.3. The number of trips generated by Barcelona city has been considered a special category or level of mobility, as shown in Fig. 11.4. Seasonal traffic (i.e. the coastal traffic generated by beaches in summer) has also been included in the final total numbers for each municipality.

The extra-municipal nodes data contains information about generated and attracted trips instead of data about population and number of jobs. The load of the model network with the generated and attracted data outside the GBR was obtained from 1991 census data and the number of tickets sold by RENFE and FFCC. This data about traffic generated outside the GBR is represented by different extra-municipal nodes at the end of each railroad line, considering the end of the railroad line to be the intersection of the line with the limit of the GBR.

Data about travellers attracted and generated by the airport has been processed from 1987 origin and destination matrices published by the Transportation Department of the local government (Batlle, 1989). The number of potential travellers going from the airport to each of the stations of Barcelona is considered as the number of travellers generated by the airport, and the number of travellers going from each station of Barcelona to the airport is considered as the number of travellers attracted by the airport.

The number of trips generated by Barcelona has been extrapolated from 1987 origin and destination matrices by adding all the trips of all the stations going out from Barcelona. On the other hand, at the level of the analysis model, Barcelona city is considered with an infinite attraction or capable of absorbing all the trips having Barcelona as destination, as shown in Tables 11.2 and 11.3 (Barcelona is station 81).

The model uses this data to generate different graphical and numerical statistics such as the number of trips for each railroad segment and the typical origin–destination matrix. The attraction–generation table, part of which is shown in Table 11.14, summarizes the 143 × 143 origin–destination matrix of daily trips between railroad stations (extra-municipal nodes are also included in the table as stations at the limit of the GBR). According to the results of the model, this matrix has a total number of 112 million trips per year, from which 65.5 million correspond to the FFCC or metropolitan lines and 46.5 million to the RENFE or regional lines for the year 2005. The classical diagram maps of the railroad traffic network loads (Figs 11.5 and 11.6) show the load of potential annual trips for each railroad segment (in thousands) and the generated and attracted trips by each municipality and extra-municipal node.

Table 11.2 Municipalities data table

Municipality	Population	Jobs	Mobility	Labour sector	Station number and distribution (%)					
Sant Climent de Llobregat	2 577	510	2	Ser.	35	60%	44	40%		
* Outside R1 (Castelldefels)	6 000	0	0		8	100%				
Castelldefels	54 197	6 388	2	Ind.Ser.	24	78%	16	22%		
Gavà	46 336	9 737	2	Ind.Cen.Ser.	34	25%	31	55%	27	20%
* Aeroport (El Prat de Ll.)	11 675	11 675	1	Cen.	57	100%				
El Prat de Llobregat	67 888	13 325	2	Ind.Ser.	63	40%	70	30%	65	30%
Barcelona	190 000	∞	1	Ind.Cen.Ser	81	100%				
Sant Quirze del Vallès	14 917	3 183	2	Ind.Ser.	62	100%				
Sabadell	208 464	53 224	2	Ind.Cen.Ser.	67	30%	68	40%	74	30%
Cerdanyola del Vallès	64 100	10 973	2	Ind.Cen.Ser.	69	35%	71	35%	72	30%
Ripollet	31 414	5 693	2	Ind.Ser.	79	100%				
Ullastrell	8 064	360	2	Ind.	45	100%				
La Llagosta	13 685	3 648	3	Ind.	86	100%				
Martorelles	6 019	3 161	2	Ind.	89	100%				
Santa Maria de Martorelles	800	100	2	Ser.	89	100%				
Montornès del Vallès	13 379	5 939	2	Ind.	97	100%				
Montmeló	9 297	4 221	2	Ind.	97	65%	99	35%		
Granollers	63 260	22 061	2	Ser.	104	50%	109	50%		
Barberà del Vallès	33 737	11 350	2	Ind.Cen.	80	40%	77	30%	76	30%
* Circuit F1 (Montmeló)	0	0	0		99	100%				
Vilanova del Vallès	3 022	650	2	Ind.	109	100%				
* Estació TGV (Sant Cugat)	2 350	0	0		58	50%	72	50%		

Table 11.3   Stations data table

Station	Population	Jobs	Mobility	Labour sector	Comment
1	6 000	510	1	Ind.	First node of the model
...					
57	11 675	11 675	1	Cen.	
58	21 536	5 291	1	Ind.Cen.	
59	10 768	2 646	1	Ind.Cen.	
60	5 384	1 323	1	Ind.Cen	
61	0	0	0		
62	14 917	3 183	2	Ind.Ser.	
63	27 155	5 330	2	Ind.Ser.	
64	0	0	0		Extra-municipal node
65	20 366	3 998	2	Ind.Ser.	
66	14 558	3 301	2	Ind.Cen.Ser.	
...					
81	190 000	∞	1	Ind.Cen.Ser.	Barcelona node
...					
143	50 800	15 180	2	Ind.Ser.	Last node of the model

FUNCTIONING OF THE ANALYSIS MODEL

The railroad traffic analysis model of the GBR is based on the Intergraph GIS software of the Planning Department. It uses the GBR Land Use Plan base maps (see Fig. 11.2), databases and topology tables to determine, predict and display the population served by the lines, the population attracted and generated by each municipality, the potential number of travellers on each segment of railroad line, and the location of railroad stations (see Figs 11.5 and 11.6). The geo-referenced databases of municipalities were complemented with the knowledge of the Planning Department experts about predicting the potential population of each municipality for the year 2005 based on land use, its number of potential jobs, the type of labour offered and the level of mobility, as shown in Fig. 11.4 and Tables 11.1–11.3.

The attraction–generation computer model works with three modules, each one of which does the following tasks:

The first module assigns destinations to each origin or station, calculating the smallest time of the trip or the distance covered for each pair of origin and destination points. This module considers the points of the network where turns are not allowed, it penalizes in time the transfers of railroad lines – from metropolitan lines to regional lines and vice versa – and it takes into account the different speeds of the trains in the metropolitan and regional lines. Some of the transits without stops and through specific stations, for example through Barcelona, are also penalized in time. The structure of the system database is such that the links

Fig. 11.5 Diagram map of the railroad traffic network loads.

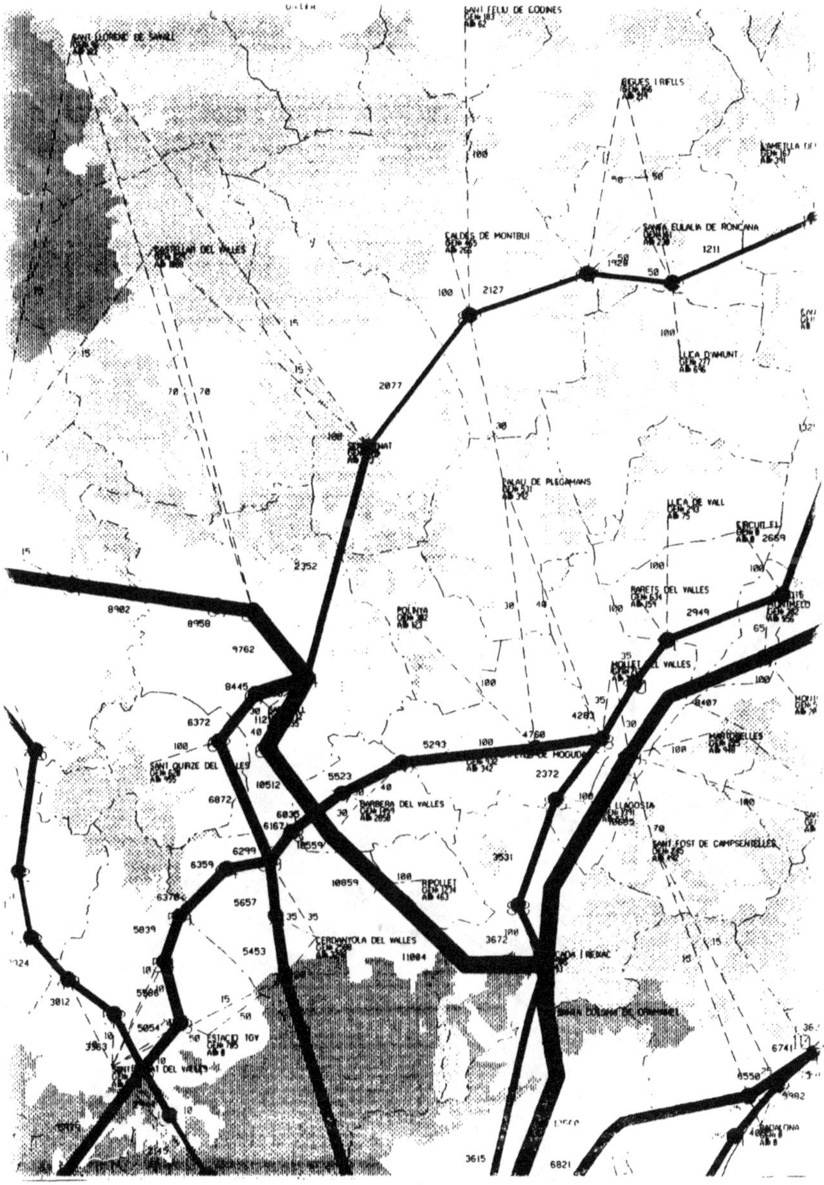

Fig. 11.6 Detail of the railroad traffic network loads.

Table 11.4 Attraction–generation table

Station	Population	Travellers			Number of jobs		
		Potential	Real	Real/Pot.(%)	Potential	Real	Real/Pot.(%)
1	6 800	1 496	595	40	510	0	0
...							
57	11 675	2 569	1 565	61	11 675	798	7
58	21 536	4 738	2 778	59	5 291	1 310	25
59	10 768	2 369	1 290	54	2 646	2 645	100
60	5 384	1 184	580	49	1 323	1 323	100
61	0	0	0		0	0	
62	14 917	3 508	2 031	58	3 183	3 181	100
63	27 155	6 387	3 188	50	5 330	2 729	51
64	0	0	0		0	0	
65	20 366	4 790	2 434	51	3 998	3 998	100
66	14 558	3 424	1 641	48	3 301	3 297	100
67	62 539	14 709	7 661	52	15 967	8 057	50
68	83 386	19 612	9 971	51	21 290	6 183	29
69	22 435	5 277	3 189	60	3 841	3 843	100
70	20 366	4 790	2 465	51	3 998	3 993	100
71	22 435	5 277	2 602	49	3 841	3 843	100
72	35 382	8 322	4 919	59	7 260	7 267	100
73	0	0	0		0	0	
74	62 539	14 709	7 545	51	15 967	6 966	44
75	0	0	0		0	0	
76	10 121	2 380	1 256	53	3 405	1 072	31
77	10 121	2 380	1 528	64	3 405	3 409	100
78	10 701	2 517	1 245	49	2 617	2 611	100
79	31 414	7 389	4 033	55	5 693	1 296	23
80	13 495	3 174	1 995	63	4 540	4 554	100
81	190 000	41 800	19 004	45	$\infty \geqslant$ 46 614	46 614	
...							
143	50 800	11 948	1 942	16	15 180	2 377	16
Total	2 507 254	622 021	321 379	52	620 970	321 390	48

between the data of the municipalities and the data of the stations can be changed dynamically.

The second module uses the matrices of population distribution by levels of mobility and labour sector and the matrices of population distribution as a function of the distance to the location of work by levels of mobility to assign to each destination the total number of travellers that it can absorb from each origin. One important criterion of this module is the fairness of the loads assignation process between competing origins guaranteeing that the order in which the program does the assignation does not affect the results of the analysis. There are also second-order criteria that can be changed such as the ratio of the number of travellers absorbed by a destination and the total number of travellers generated by competing origins to fill the same destinations. The model is characterized by the fact that it also guarantees that travellers of a certain labour sector will travel to destinations where they will find jobs of the same

labour sector. Extra-municipal nodes are processed in an additional phase so as to make sure that the totality of its generated and attracted trips will load the network.

The third module uses the results of the first two modules to distribute the loads corresponding to each origin–destination pair to the railroad line segments that join the points with the shortest path. The model does not consider any capacity limit of the railroad lines. This module can also be used to produce other syntheses of data about the anterior modules, like, for example, to produce the origin–destination matrix already mentioned, to compare the volumes of types of trips by labour sector, and to analyse the through-traffic of a station in relation to the traffic whose destination is that station.

RELIABILITY, POWER AND SPEED

In terms of global evaluation of the computer system we created and, in general terms, of expert systems for design and planning, we would like to borrow, from the literature on epistemology, the concepts of *reliability*, *power* and *speed*, as general measures of performance (Goldman, 1986) and with the special interpretation and application to design that Papazian (1991) does in his thesis.

We say that a system is *reliable* if a large part of its performance is useful or correct; that it is *powerful* if it performs in a useful way in a variety of situations of interest; and that it is *fast* if its behaviour is consistently dynamic. An arithmetic calculator, for example, is more reliable than a mathematician, but the latter is more powerful. A programming language is as reliable as a calculator, but the calculator is faster. Reliability will be the degree to which a system produces 'good' (or 'acceptable') designs. Note that a system which always produces the same (good) design is completely reliable. Power will be the range of different (good) designs that a system can produce. A system which is capable of producing many different kinds of designs, none of which are good designs, is powerful, but not reliable at all. Speed will be a measure of how fast the system produces a design, a response. We will use the term *dynamism* as a measure of responsiveness or spontaneity. A system may internally enumerate all possible designs and eliminate ones which are unsatisfactory. Such a system is reliable and powerful but it looses out on dynamism.

We would like to claim that 'good' expert systems must find the right balance between these three or four terms so as to avoid being inappropriate either because they are *over-designed* and thus too expensive in terms of time, money and effort, or because they are too trivial and thus inaccurate or incomplete. One of the reasons why it is very often difficult to find the right balance between reliability, power and speed in expert systems for design and planning is due to the fact that the expert

knowledge must be rediscovered while building the modelling system and also to the fact that it varies as a function of the scale of the problem at hand.

The most important constraints of the railroad analysis model were to design a computer system to be used dynamically and under the changing conditions of land use and planning cycles. To ensure these conditions, the computer model had to be compatible with the Intergraph GIS facilities of the Planning Department. In addition to this and due to the fact that the modelling system was required to make predictions about the potential use of the railroad network based on land use expectations of development defined by the GBR Plan, we were forced to design specific software rather than using standard software of traffic analysis which could not satisfy the requirements we needed and was difficult to make compatible with the rest of the Department software.

We would like to argue that the modelling system we designed, although it is not as reliable as commercially available traffic analysis software, is very powerful since it answers most of the planning questions that interest the Planning Department and it produces statistics very valuable to build 'What-if?' scenarios. Commercial software might not need serious adjustment phases so as to be used consistently, but the software we designed had to be adjusted and tested before systematically using it for the whole region. In terms of power, standard traffic analysis software was incapable of using multiplicity of factors or different parametric functions to define a variable according to different intervals, as we needed for example to define duration of trip (or distance covered) to work as a function of the distribution of population per labour sector and level of mobility. For standard traffic analysis software it was certainly easy to use general relationships at the level of origin–destination matrices (i.e. from all origin nodes with industrial workers to all destinations with industry), but these relationships were lost at the point of the analysis itself since only the information about the origin–destination pairs is retained (i.e. from A to B, where A and B are specific stations). One solution to use this commercially available software was to define as many origin–destination matrices as there were different labour sectors that we wanted to model (i.e. one matrix for industrial workers, another for service workers who only travel to Barcelona, etc.), assuming that the final combined matrix, as a simple addition of these independent matrices, would not affect or change the final network analysis due to the effects of network overload, which cannot be taken into account in this solution. Consequently, as opposed to traditional traffic analysis software, we can claim that our model was more powerful. A special feature of our model was the capacity to carry out unpredictable consequences and future uses at the technical and political levels. The system can be used to establish priorities of new railroad line construction; to develop

specifically directed land use policies to readjust the territorial balance as a function of the railroad network; to better inform and support political decisions on infrastructures; to make potential railroad use predictions; to generate new needs and thus be able to expand (we have developed another expert system that can be used in conjunction, which automatically simulates dynamic train graphs to study the impact of different types of trains on existing train schedules like high-speed trains on commuter train schedules); etc.

The analysis model also performs very well in terms of dynamism since it was designed to be used dynamically, as opposed to standard software. Not only was the analysis model able to regenerate all its tables and graphs from the many possible levels of changes – from different topology, municipalities data and trains constraints to different distributions of population tables, etc. – but also it was able to include very easily slightly different types of data like the extra-municipal nodes and, due to its modularity, different network analysis algorithms. On the other hand, the system we designed was very slow. This was partially due to the many (computing/hardware) platform compatibility constraints we had and partially due to the fact that speed was not a priority, since we had to solve memory allocation and storage problems and implement lexical scoping. We would like to generalize that the relatively slow performance of in-house software components on a given project can result in a high level of dynamism in addressing several related projects, as our analysis model shows.

We think we found a good balance between the factors since we reached all our goals in such a way that now the system will be expanded to all the Catalonia railroad network for studying the other three subsystems of the network, the relationships among them at the regional and state scale, and the impact of the addition of high-speed lines and new connections both in terms of topology and in terms of potential use.

We would also like to argue in favour of what we call hybrid models, models that combine different levels of knowledge captured either by algorithms or by exhaustive databases more or less built by hand. In the early phases of the analysis model design, we had to carry out two very long and tedious sessions with the different territorial experts of the Planning Department to fine-tune the algorithms and to capture the municipalities data. For example, the index of mobility was adjusted by hand and municipality-by-municipality according to the criteria and knowledge of each of the different planners. This process proved to be very useful, efficient and dynamic, although, as we mentioned before, the price we had to pay, compared to using standard available software, was a longer adjustment phase of the model behaviour.

Finally, we would like to point out our conviction that developing expert systems without exhaustively drawing out knowledge from other

different paradigms so as to make easier the task of computer modelling, will generate better design and decision tools. As pointed out at the beginning of the chapter, the relationships between the planning point of view and the economics one are obvious and complementary, but implementing literally the algorithms and functions to design the system would have led us to a less flexible model, more than this, a misleading model, since the economics data results would then have been interpreted in planning terms with the possibility of inaccurate interpretations (Fargas, 1991). In the future, we think it might be very interesting to use the statistics that the model generates (namely the origin–destination matrix and the maps of top ten nodes of highest centrality in terms of time and distance, not included in this chapter) to test it, as well as to find out the relevance of the railroad communications, in terms of the economic concepts pointed out before like self-containment, self-sufficiency and functional balance at the level of the territory. Thus, the hybrid system is shown to sacrifice the reliability and speed characteristic of commercially available software for a powerful set of computational tools developed specifically for the problem at hand.

REFERENCES

Batlle, L. (1989) *El Transport Ferroviari a Catalunya*, Institut Català per al Desenvolupament del Transport, Generalitat de Catalunya, Barcelona.

Esteban, M. (1989) *Distribució de la Mobilitat per Treball a la Regió Metropolitana de Barcelona, Anàlisi dels Mercats de Treball*, Àrea Metropolitana de Barcelona, Barcelona.

Fargas, J.M. (1991) *Designing Rules: Heuristics of Invention in Design*, SMArchS-MCP Thesis, School of Architecture and Planning, Massachusetts Institute of Technology, Cambridge, Mass.

Goldman, A. (1986) *Epistemology and Cognition*, Harvard University Press, Cambridge, Mass.

Papazian, P. (1991) *Principles, Opportunism and Seeing in Design: A Computational Approach*, SMEECS-SMArchS Thesis, Department of Computer Science and School of Architecture and Planning, Massachusetts Institute of Technology, Cambridge, Mass.

Solans, J.A. *et al.* (1990) *Mapa i Base de Dades de Planejament Urbanístic i Usos del Sòl de la Regió I*, Direcció General d'Urbanisme, Generalitat de Catalunya, Barcelona.

GIS and decision support systems for local authorities in Malaysia

12

Ahris Yaakup, Foziah Johar and Nor Azina Dahlan

INTRODUCTION

Despite the fairly widespread recognition of the benefits of GIS for local authorities, its adoption by local planning authorities in Malaysia has not been particularly encouraging. The reluctance of local authorities to accept the challenge to embrace the technology is due mainly to lack of support from the management level, lack of in-house expertise with which to make use of the system and the high cost of GIS. On the other hand, local authorities are now faced with increasingly complex urban problems and inevitably urban planners have to come up with better solutions. Of late, there have been enormous improvements in the price and performance of computer hardware and functionality of software packages, such that a wide range of specific demands for the management, analysis and presentation of data can now be met in a cost-effective manner. A direct consequence of these new opportunities has been the rapid growth in the number of users developing the urban planning and monitoring applications. This chapter examines the functions of a local authority and indicates areas in which GIS as a decision support tool can be most effective.

LOCAL GOVERNMENT IN MALAYSIA

The Malaysian administrative system is divided into three major hierarchies: federal government, state government and local government.

Decision Support Systems in Urban Planning. Edited by Harry Timmermans. Published in 1997 by E & F N Spon. ISBN 0 419 21050 4

Local government has different patterns and organization: City Hall for Kuala Lumpur, City and Town Councils for the state capitals and big towns (13 cities and towns), and District Councils (80 districts). In 1976, the Local Government Act 1976 (Act 171) was passed by the Parliament, providing a consolidated legal framework for local authorities. Act 171 enables the local authority to undertake a wide range of functions, thus changing the narrow field of operation accepted in the past. Part XII offers an immense choice, permitting involvement in practically all services at the local level. The authority will provide for controlled and well-managed public places, environmental control, collection of taxes on premises, and issuance of licences for commercial, industrial and other activities. Particularly important are powers to acquire land in the general interests of the public, to develop industrial estates and to enter into joint ventures with other local authorities, and even with the private sector.

The planning powers of local authorities are similarly set out, not in the Act but in the allied Town and Country Planning Act 1976 (Act 172). According to Clause 5(1) of the latter, 'Every local authority shall be the local planning authority for the area of the local authority', thus, conferring a primary physical planning responsibility at the local level. These extensions materialized in the form of a development plan, which will be prepared by the local authorities for the purpose of organizing, controlling and planning the development and use of land and buildings in their area. The development plan will be in two parts, namely the structure plan (which provides broad-base development policies) and the local plan (which translates these policies on to Ordnance Survey maps).

It is clear that development at the local level will involve a lot of policies and implementation decisions which have to consider the cost and benefit to every level of town dwellers. The interdependence between investments and their environment, and the need to integrate all groups of inhabitants in urban society under decent living conditions, would be the prime concerns of urban planners and managers at local level. Information systems have to be created to monitor, assess and administer the complex spatial realities of urban areas for both large metropolises and the small and medium towns that structure the regions (de Bruijn, 1990).

Owing to the wide range of activities, over the years, the local authorities have amassed a huge amount of information. A substantial portion of this information is geographical in nature, such as the layout of housing schemes, roads and drainage systems, the composition and distribution of population, the distribution of land use and so forth. Unfortunately, these data are often inaccessible even to the local council administrators. The main reason is that the database management system is based on a manual filing system which makes retrieval of information very difficult and time-consuming. To alleviate the problem, a number of local authorities employ a computer database system such as Data Base IV, Filemaker,

Statistical Analytical System or Statistical Package for Social Scientist. While these systems help tremendously in information retrieval and analysis, they do not handle spatial data very well. Thus, jobs assigned to the system are quite limited to routine retrieval.

INFORMATION SYSTEMS FOR LOCAL AUTHORITIES

Given the dynamic nature of planning and management, it is particularly important to have a well-conceived information system which can serve as the eyes and ears of large planning processes. It provides for the monitoring and surveillance of compliance with planning regulations and it serves as an early warning system with regard to sources of friction, imbalances, shortfalls and failures in the process of urban planning and management. Up-to-date and reliable information is therefore needed at municipal level to facilitate administrative procedures, policy planning and plan implementation. It is required for forecasting, modelling and evaluation of the current situation and changes that are in progress.

Much of the planning and management at local level has to do with the use of land and how the different types of land use relate to one another. Spatially referenced data including parcel boundaries, buildings on site and ownerships of lands and buildings are a fundamental part of an information-based approach to urban planning and management. This information combined with socioeconomic data, such as census data or natural and environmental data, provides more meaningful information for planners and decision-makers.

This approach also brings increasing rationality to the decision-making process. Since the geographical information is stored and processed in its primary form, analysis can be more quantitative and rational. The modelling stage that is called for in the urban planning process requires planners to make explicit their criteria for the selection of alternative programmes. This encourages the selection of objective criteria, based on real data about the area under study.

Another reason for improvement being required is the quest for efficiency. The advent of corporate planning and the continued squeeze on local authority expenditure has led local authorities to examine critically whether service delivery is efficient and effective. Indeed, this has become one of the fastest developing areas of policy planning within local government (Barrett and Masters, 1985).

DESIGN AND IMPLEMENTATION OF GIS AT LOCAL AUTHORITY LEVEL IN MALAYSIA

Faced with rapid growth, there is constant pressure on most towns in Malaysia to improve services while reducing costs, and to be more efficient and effective in their daily operations and management activities. Recognizing the fact that 70–80% of the information and activities with which a local authority is concerned are location-dependent (Yaakup, 1991), a geographical information system (GIS) is required to address these problems. Land and building, for example, are the primary sources of income; utilities, such as schooling, hospitals and economic development incentive are provided by defined geographical area. A GIS provides the tools to manage and use information concerning land and other phenomena which are geographically referenced.

Design of a local authority information system should be based on an understanding of how municipal operations and planning are carried out. Municipal functions or tasks, and the types of data which support them, comprise the vital elements involved in operations and planning in local authorities. The tasks and the supporting data will provide the fundamental framework upon which a conceptual model of geographical data entities and their relationships can be developed (Table 12.1).

The required GIS activities and needs of a department in local government show several areas of common interest including:

1. a centralized base map generation and maintenance function;
2. automated update of files from operational transactions;
3. access to a comprehensive database of parcel- and building-related data;
4. a commonly used parcel and building identification system;
5. access to a database of information concerning land and building development activities throughout the towns;
6. a capability to analyse and assess tax and licensing;
7. a capability to analyse community facility service areas and site suitability.

The conceptual model of GIS for local authorities in Malaysia is based on the land parcel as the central entity in the GIS (Figure 12.1). The model represents the basic component of the local authority in a manner that most easily translates into some of the newer technology involving relational databases and graphic information (maps). The components of this model include the following:

1. A Geographic Index – this provides the location and spatial relationships for geographic entities at the block level of geography (planning unit).
2. The Cadastral and Land Record Database – this provides the location and spatial relationship information for geographic entities at the cadastral or parcel level of geographic and non-graphic information for the parcels, e.g. lot number, which would be used as a unique identifier for an individual parcel.

Table 12.1 The functions of local authorities and the required GIS application

Functions of local authority	GIS application
Development plan preparation (structure/local plan)	Forward data mapping Backward data capture • storage and retrieval of land information • planning application and trend of development Interactive data modelling • site selection • environmental impact analysis • modelling of land suitability for development • network model • isoline model
Development control/planning application/building plan	Backward data capture • district and zone management • storage and retrieval of land information/detailed land title • notices • tracking of application and trend of development
Control of river and streams	Forward data mapping/Backward data mapping • comparison of available data on level of pollutants at predetermined points or relationship among land uses • network model
Maintenance of roads, drains facility, etc.	Forward data mapping/Backward data mapping • information system on maintenance date according to zones, establish priority area, etc.
Garbage collection	Forward data mapping/backward data mapping • optimum route, identification of problem area/point, maintenance according to zone
Control of housing development/ squatters	Forward data mapping/Backward data capture • inventories of owners, value, housing density, problem areas, etc. • management of zones and land • notices
Taxation and licensing	Forward data mapping/Backward data capture • storage and retrieval of land/building information • interactive data modelling

3. The Geodetic Control Database – this provides the geographic reference framework for the model, the data in this database being used to register new map data into the system and to improve the positional accuracy of the existing data, when possible, i.e. State Plane Coordinate is used for this purpose.
4. Other related information – including building, administrative, environment, engineering and planning information.

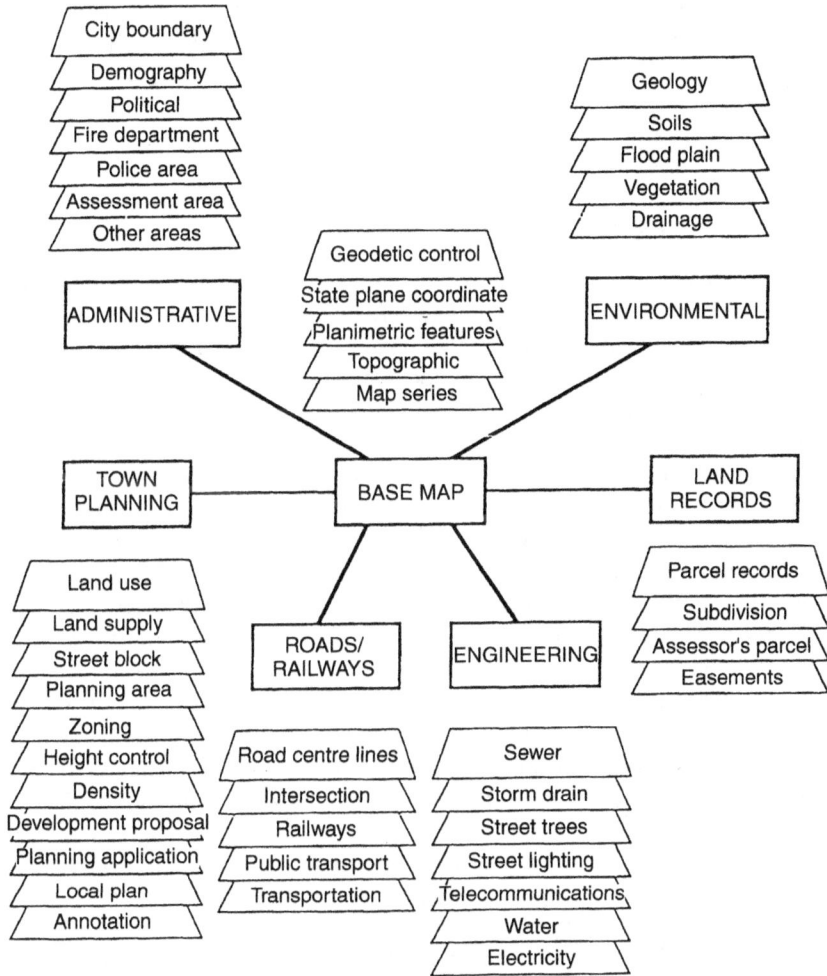

Fig. 12.1   Suggested local authority data model. (Source: Yaakup, 1991.)

The model therefore includes a geographic reference framework, the linkage of geographic and non-graphic parcel-related data, the possibility of overlays and system access in both graphic (map-related) and non-graphic (e.g. queries and text output) forms. The model should also allow an integration of three levels of geography – street network level (including data aggregation areas of block size), the parcel/lot level and building level. These linkages are accomplished by direct overlay of the graphic data or by linkage established within the GIS structure. Finally this approach would allow a core of basic geographic/cartographic data to be established, with the flexibility to add new data or access the database in different ways, depending on application requirements. It would provide direct control of the data that is required by a number of users, and a development approach that is based on information resources management.

EXAMPLE OF GIS APPLICATION FOR LOCAL AUTHORITIES IN MALAYSIA

ASSESSMENT OF RATES AND LICENSING

As mentioned earlier, local authorities not only maintain cleanliness and public health but are also responsible for providing public services and amenities. In return, the public are subjected to various taxes. These taxes are a source of income to local authorities, and property taxes, namely assessment rates, are a major income to the authorities. The primary argument, therefore, is that assessment rates form the major source of income for a local authority, and any improvement to the present administration of assessment rates could improve revenue collection, which in turn could improve provision of services to the community. Presently, local authorities which employ the database systems can easily provide a list of premises that have paid their rates, but they cannot however show where those who have not paid or those in arrears are located. If these are known, the collection of assessment rates can be efficiently administered. The implementation of GIS has shown that a local authority not only increases revenue in terms of rates but can improve the administration of assessment rates tremendously. In this exercise, information that is required includes owner's name, location of premises, dates of assessment, rates levied and rates in arrears. In building up the GIS for Temerluh Local Authority (Fig. 12.2), information on the use of buildings has been included for the purpose of licensing policies (Hashim *et al.*, 1994).

In the above example, GIS will mainly be used to retrieve data. Combined with other databases, the local authority GIS can also be used to determine property value, i.e. by constructing land value maps. Such maps will indicate, among other things, the growth pattern, the market preference, the use of buildings and the potentiality of an area. The distribution of values is therefore useful to valuers, planners, estate agents, property developers, the local authority and those who deal with real estate (Husin and Hashim, 1992). The present database systems in the Malaysian property valuation institutions and the local authorities are incapable of producing land value maps. The main weakness of such systems is that, while they are able to handle descriptive data, they are incompetent in dealing with spatial data (Husin and Said, 1991). As such, land value maps are constructed manually. A list of property values is first generated by the computer and subsequently the values are

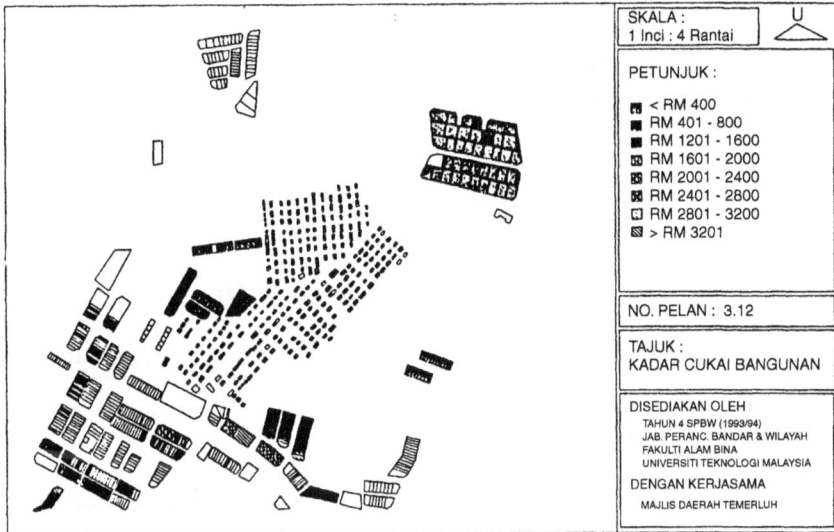

SKALA :
1 Inci : 4 Rantai

PETUNJUK :

- < RM 400
- RM 401 - 800
- RM 1201 - 1600
- RM 1601 - 2000
- RM 2001 - 2400
- RM 2401 - 2800
- RM 2801 - 3200
- > RM 3201

NO. PELAN : 3.12

TAJUK :
KADAR CUKAI BANGUNAN

DISEDIAKAN OLEH
TAHUN 4 SPBW (1993/94)
JAB. PERANC. BANDAR & WILAYAH
FAKULTI ALAM BINA
UNIVERSITI TEKNOLOGI MALAYSIA
DENGAN KERJASAMA
MAJLIS DAERAH TEMERLUH

Fig. 12.2   GIS for assessment of tax and licensing. (Source: Hashim *et al.*, 1994.)

transferred manually onto a layout plan. This method is obviously time-consuming and laborious. It is therefore no surprise that land value maps are rarely constructed. A local authority GIS which records the transaction of properties can produce land value maps which show the land value of transacted properties. However, if GIS is to be useful in this respect, it cannot just rely on transacted properties, since it means that such a land value map would be historical in nature. A comprehensive land value map has to illustrate the land value distribution for all properties, regardless of whether they have been transacted or not. In addition, it must also be capable of portraying past, present as well as future land value distributions. By incorporating multiple regression analysis (MRA) into the GIS, a regression-based land value model can be derived. The regression model may then be used to simulate the values of the unsold properties and forecast property values in the future (Husin and Hashim, 1992).

DEVELOPMENT CONTROL

The present system of development control is by the granting or refusal of planning permission for development. Under the Malaysian planning legislation, the authority to grant or refuse planning permission is the local planning authority of the area to which the proposed development relates. Recent directives required that certain planning applications shall be accompanied by a *development proposal report*, which includes a written statement and a plan to (i) describe the present condition of the land which is the subject of the development, and (ii) describe the proposed development, in particular how it would be likely to have a significant effect on the built environment. In most cases, a development proposal report involves a technique for the systematic compilation of expert quantitative analysis and qualitative assessment of a project's land use and development viability. This includes its effect on the surrounding area. The results should be presented in such a way as to enable the importance of the predicted results, and the scope for modifying or mitigating them, to be properly evaluated by the relevant decision-making body before a planning application decision is made. Information required for a development proposal report would therefore include the following major aspects:

1. Status of land and restrictions.
2. Land use analysis and intensity of development. This includes land use zoning, population density zoning, limit of height, plot ratio and plinth area, and predetermined public area.
3. Analysis of issues and potential of site. This includes site location, existing drainage system, topography and slope, existing road system, existing land use, natural features which must be preserved and development potential.
4. Analysis of surrounding development. This includes infrastructure, type, intensity and facilities of the surrounding area.
5. The policies of the structure plan and local plan regarding the sites.

In addition, the planning proposal should also observe the planning standards or other policies which may be imposed from time to time.

In an era of increasing urban problems, the development proposal report is seen as one of the tools to assist the authority in carrying out their functions. The urban system can no longer be confined to simple land use and traffic concepts. The planner's conception of the urban system must extend to include a host of social, political and economic variables. The mixture of problems which must all be resolved together creates a situation in which many alternatives must be tried, combined, improved and tested by analysis, by experiment and by public discussion. The information system therefore must expand correspondingly if anything like effective understanding and control is to be achieved. The development of GIS provides a tool which can contribute to a much clearer understanding of real planning problems as well as prescriptive planning scenarios to enhance the quality of urban planning and control.

In preparing the development proposal report for the development of a squatter area, the Kuala Lumpur City Hall developed a squatter GIS. The squatter GIS has been extensively interrogated to generate several alternative solutions to the problems. Various scenarios which take into account the socioeconomic characteristics of squatters, the constraints of physical layout, the availability of land and land suitability for different kinds of development have been generated (Fig. 12.3). To determine the economic efficiency of each alternative, cost–benefit analyses have been incorporated into the evaluation process. Having prepared the evaluation model, the operation was accomplished within a short time-frame using database management techniques and computer mapping of the results. In this way, the resulting scenarios which incorporate the cost–benefit factor can be modified rapidly to suit the requirements of the solution (Yaakup and Healey, 1994).

In a planning agency, information users range from professionals who prepare alternative plans and policies to decision-makers who decide on policies and the final plans. For people who prepare policy options, the problems of complex GIS command sequences and the difficulty of combining information from different applications are especially important. Facility in the use system is of particular importance to decision-makers. This type of user is concerned with being able to weight or evaluate policies. This factor should be taken into account in developing the user interface. The squatter GIS has been developed to accommodate the requirements of this group quite reasonably. The development of powerful, flexible, yet easy-to-use programming languages and a sophisticated

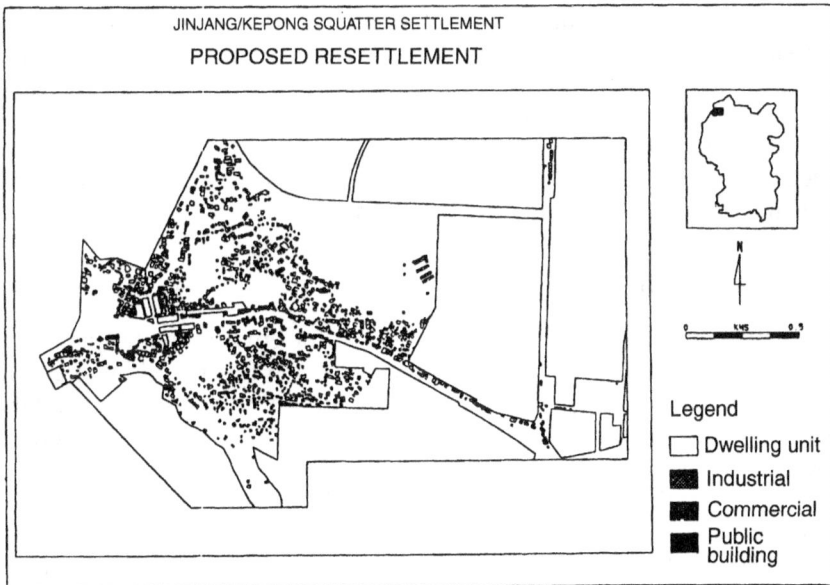

Fig. 12.3 GIS for squatter settlement planning and management. (Source: Yaakup, 1991.)

screen management facility has enabled the decision-makers to interact with the system. Thus, GIS is more than a retrieval system. It has allowed analysis of a wide range of data sets in new ways and has highlighted relationships which might otherwise have been overlooked.

URBAN CONSERVATION

Of late, there has been widespread concern regarding the effects of rapid urbanization on the character of Malaysian towns and cities. Although Malaysian architectural heritage rarely dates back more than a century, the urban areas are filled with an array of pre-war (the 1948–1960 Malayan Emergency Period) buildings from which the distinct character- istics of most Malaysian towns were derived. These pre-war buildings are most vulnerable in the context of being demolished to make way for the urban high-rise development due their strategic location. It is therefore essential that this valuable architectural heritage is retained for posterity. GIS has been developed to become a tool in decision-making for local authorities who have to deal with a complex set of criteria for the pur- pose of urban conservation (Yaakup *et al.*, 1994). It essentially starts with the selection of criteria of priority buildings for conservation upon which the database is designed. The capability of GIS in selecting and retrieving a large volume of data will be utilized in analysing specific development in the realm of urban conservation. Using the integrated planning approach, other information will be integrated into the database, includ- ing land use allocation and urban renewal programmes, by which the future planning scenario can be anticipated. This will help in assessing impacts of redevelopment based on the predicted and anticipated growth pattern of the area concerned. GIS has been used in a model of selection criteria developed to form the basis and rationale for urban con- servation in a local authority area (Fig. 12.4).

ENVIRONMENTAL MANAGEMENT

GIS have become of increasing significance for environmental planning and assessment in recent years. One main reason for this is the need, in environmental planning, to compare a great number of area-related data describing the affected natural resources and their sensitivity related to the effects of impacts. Because GIS can be used to overlay these, it repre- sents a highly efficient instrument for such planning tasks.

Environmental impact assessment (EIA) has been defined as an activ- ity or process designed to identify and predict the impact on the biogeo- physical environment and on people's health and well-being of legislative proposals, policies, programmes, projects or operational proce- dures and to interpret and communicate information about impacts. In

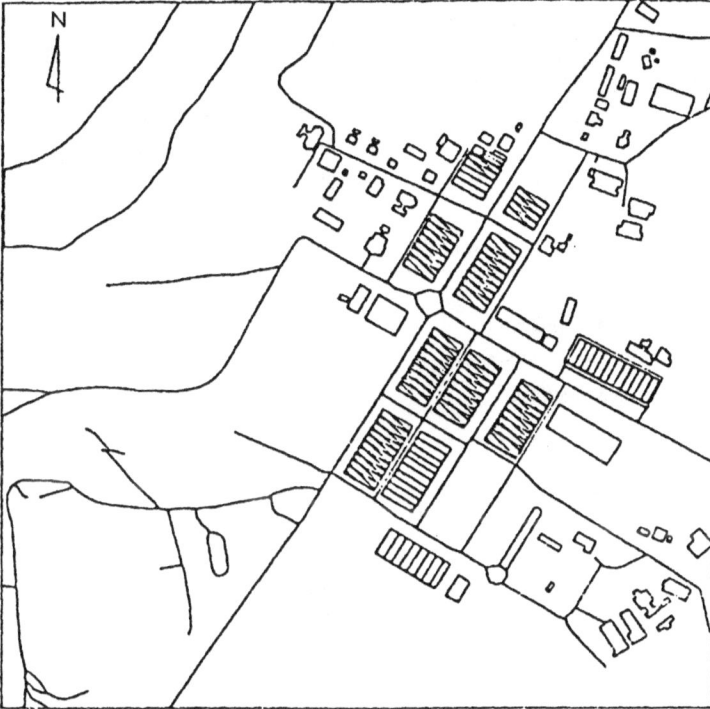

Fig. 12.4 Urban heritage GIS. (Source: Yaakup *et al.*, 1994.)

principle, this exercise could be done by conventional methods, but the drawback with this is the very time-consuming nature of the manual work involved. Environmental impact studies use very large databases of natural resource and land use data and normally different alternatives of impacts have to be assessed (Schaller, 1990). The results of several alternative impacts on natural resources and human well-being have to be modelled using different methods such as distribution models, pollution models, changes of land use, behaviour models, etc. (Fig. 12.5). In connection with impact models, GIS are very useful tools to carry out such sophisticated work, because after having the resources and socioeconomic databases, changes in land use or type of physical and human impacts can be modelled easily and quickly, and results can be presented in the form of high-quality graphic or tabular presentation (Jusoh and Othman, 1994).

Another area of GIS application to environmental quality at the local authority level is the maintenance of cleanliness and waste disposal collection. It is proven that waste disposal collection and management improved tremendously using spatial informatics, integrating GIS and DSS (van der Meulen, 1993). This GIS task is one of the interesting and positive applications of GIS at local authority level in Malaysia.

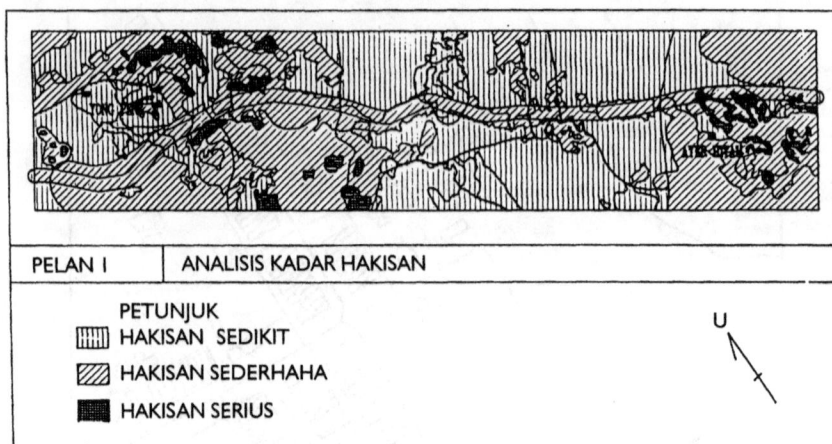

PELAN I	ANALISIS KADAR HAKISAN

PETUNJUK
- ▥ HAKISAN SEDIKIT
- ▨ HAKISAN SEDERHAHA
- ▦ HAKISAN SERIUS

Fig. 12.5 GIS for environmental impact assessment. (Source: Jusoh and Othman, 1994.)

GIS AND DSS APPLICATION FOR LOCAL AUTHORITIES IN MALAYSIA: ISSUES AND FUTURE DEVELOPMENT

Since the early 1980s, there have been major breakthroughs in the cost, speed and data storage capacity of computer hardware and software. With computer costs still dropping, with the emergence of powerful portable machines, and with the possibility of massively increased network bandwidths, enabling a larger and larger segment of society to connect up, the prospects for new types of computer use in problem-solving and policy domains, such as planning and urban design, have never been more promising (Yeh and Batty, 1990). These trends in the development of computer technology have indeed benefited developing countries. The application of GIS will inevitably influence the existing structure and the practice of planning in local authorities. As such, a critical evaluation of GIS applications should be given priority before adopting such a system. Success or failure in the adoption depends on a variety of human, organizational and technical factors (Campbell and Masser, 1992).

The range of GIS applications in local government is considerable, extending from properties assessment and licensing to development control and preparation of development plans. Various implementations of GIS projects have demonstrated that GIS is an important tool in local planning, but that it cannot itself do the planning or solve problems in development and management. There are limited means for applying GIS in devising planning scenarios, in allocating urban investment and in evaluating development proposals. Many issues which remain unresolved in the design and use of GIS should not deter or slow its adoption and the exploitation of its capabilities. According to Brail (1990) the problems with GIS as a support tool for planning arise on three levels, i.e. little projective capacity, no internal evaluative ability and limited user-friendliness. The examples on GIS applications, however, have shown that these problems can be minimized, if not overcome. GIS capabilities should be explored and integrated with other applications, such as a decision support system (DSS) based on mathematical modelling, an expert system (ES) based on logical reasoning and an operational planning model, with the aim of developing planning support systems. There is a need for a planning support system that can meet the diverse requirements of planning and management at local government level. Since the development of planning support systems is still ongoing in research organizations, the use of GIS at local government level is confined to graphic visualization, data management and the basic function of GIS. Another issue to be addressed is the development of an interactive user interface to further enhance the use of GIS for planning and management at local authority level. This will attract more non-expert users to use GIS before developing a more ambitious planning support system.

Another important issue in the implementation of GIS and DSS at local authority level is the overall information management strategy which takes account of data availability, computing capabilities and management requirements. Without well developed information management strategies it is likely that major problems will arise in relation to GIS utilization. There will be mismatches between information needs and data availability as well as between data collection and information processing. The implementation and application of GIS and DSS therefore take a much longer time and it costs more to develop the database before the application can be demonstrated and evaluated. This situation is worse when the local authority itself has relatively little experience on which to base its formulation of managerial needs. Thus the development of reasonable quality of spatial and non-spatial data is essential in adopting the GIS and DSS.

Another requirement for an effective use of GIS and DSS at local authority level in Malaysia is the personal commitment of individuals at all levels of the local authority with respect to overall leadership, general awareness and technical capabilities. Successful GIS and DSS utilization depend on clear leadership and a commitment from senior staff who are aware of the potential opened up by GIS and DSS for urban planning and management. Lack of awareness and technical capabilities in a small local authority is one of the reasons why they prefer to adopt the 'wait and see' attitude in implementing GIS and DSS compared to large municipalities. Small local authorities are seldom willing to implement GIS and

DSS since they have limited budget and lack of personel to implement the systems.

If GIS systems for urban planning are to be sustainable and really effective, they should form part of a wider local authority information system concept. A section responsible for developing and updating the different databases should be set up. It would serve as a source of information to cater for other sections responsible for strategic and local planning, development control and enforcement. Eventually, the local information system may take the technical form of a multi-node networking environment. This would enhance computer awareness among the staff within departments as well as among the decision-makers.

The strategy to be applied for effective system management is the use of an incremental approach to system design. It may begin with a simple forms-driven data system, move on to thematic mapping and a single-purpose GIS and then on to a comprehensive, multipurpose GIS. This step-by-step strategy provides a valuable opportunity for accumulating the practical experience needed for increasingly more ambitious efforts. More importantly, it allows the practical value of the system to be demonstrated early and in turn helps to ensure the political and management support needed to continue the long-term development effort by which a larger system can be developed.

Training/education is another essential component to ensure the smooth transfer of GIS technology. Sophisticated GIS requires trained and experienced technicians to operate and maintain the system, and, more importantly, sophisticated planners, analysts and managers to determine what type of information should be collected and to interpret and use the information that these systems produce. At present the planning process in developing countries is best served by concentrating on available GIS toolkits. Planners should focus their attention on the application of the systems and let the system specialists further develop the system themselves by giving suggestions as to what is needed.

CONCLUSION

With the continued development of computer technology, there is a major opportunity for developing countries to use it to manage the allocation of scarce resources in a rapidly changing environment. The quality of spatial planning and decision-making can be upgraded when available and valid data are handled in an advanced manner with the aid of computers. GIS and DSS can support spatial planning and decision-making because it offers relatively quick response on analytical questions and monitoring issues. Some of the important functions include the ability to retrieve information rapidly and efficiently, to model different future scenarios and to evaluate alternative solutions generated by various modelling procedures.

The implementation of GIS and DSS, however, involves far more than hardware and software decisions. Effective implementation rests on a thorough and systematic evaluation encompassing planning, operational, organizational, institutional, personnel, financial and technical aspects. GIS and DSS are still developing areas. To optimize GIS use, more research and attention need to be directed towards organizational and institutional issues, as well as developing GIS and DSS for planning purposes.

REFERENCES

Barrett, S.M. and Masters, R.J. (1985) 'Information Systems for Policy Planning'. In England, J.R. *et al.* (eds), *Information Systems for Policy Planning in Local Government*, Longman, Harlow, Essex, pp. 2–13.

Brail, R.K. (1990) 'Integrating GIS into Urban and Regional Planning: Alternate Approaches for Developing Countries', *Regional Development Dialogue*, Vol. 11, No. 3, pp. 63–77.

Campbell, H. and Masser, I. (1992) 'The Impact of GIS on Local Government in Great Britain'. In Rideout, T. (ed.), *Geographical Information Systems and Rural Planning*, Planning and Environment Study Group, Institute of British Geographers, Edinburgh, pp. 1–10.

de Bruijn, C.A. (1990) 'New Systems, Other Methods: The Introduction of LIS and GIS in Urban Planning', *Regional Development Dialogue*, Vol. 11, No. 3, pp. 95–119.

Hashim, A., Aman, R., Parlan, N. and Yaakup, A.B. (1994) 'GIS Application in Assessment of Tax and Licensing: A Case of Mentakab', Unpublished Research Report, Department of Urban and Regional Planning, Universiti Teknologi Malaysia, Johor Bahru, Malaysia.

Husin, A. and Hashim, M.G. (1992) 'The Construction of Land Value Maps Using GIS and MRA: A Case Study of Residential Properties in Johor Bahru, Malaysia', Unpublished Research Report, Universiti Teknologi Malaysia, Johor Bahru, Malaysia.

Husin, A. and Said, M.N. (1991) 'Geographic Information System and its Application to Local Authority: A Pilot Study of Majlis Daerah Kulai', paper presented at *Continuing Professional Development Talk: Information Technology – Its Role on Property Development*, National Valuation Institute (INSPEN), Bangi, Selangor, 15–16 June.

Jusoh, R. and Othman, A. (1994) 'GIS Application for Environmental Impact Assessment', Unpublished Research Report, Department of Urban and Regional Planning, Universiti Teknologi Malaysia, Johor Bahru, Malaysia.

Schaller, J. (1990) 'Geographical Information System Applications in Environmental Impact Assessment'. In Scholten, H.J. and Stillwell, J.C. (eds), *Geographical Information Systems for Urban and Regional Planning*, Kluwer Academic, Dordrecht, pp. 107–117.

van der Meulen, G.G. (1993) 'GIS Based Routing and Monitoring of Solid Waste Collection, A PC Based Operational Approach Applied to Chiang Mai, North of Thailand', *Proceedings of GISDECO '93, Second Seminar on GIS and Developing Countries, The Practice of GIS Applications: Problems and Challenges*, Utrecht, The Netherlands, 10–11 June 1993.

Yaakup, A.B. (1991) 'Application of GIS for Urban Planning and Management: A Case Study of Squatter Settlement Planning in Kuala Lumpur, Malaysia', Unpublished Ph.D. Dissertation, Department of Geography, University of Edinburgh, Edinburgh.

Yaakup, A.B. and Healey, R.G. (1994) 'A GIS Approach to Spatial Modelling for Squatter Settlement Planning in Kuala Lumpur, Malaysia', *Environment and Planning B: Planning and Design*, Vol. 21, pp. 21–34.

Yaakup, A.B., Johar, F., Idid, S.Z.A. and Mun, Y.W. (1994) 'GIS for Integrated Planning Decision for Conserving the Malaysian Urban Heritage', paper presented at *Asia GIS/LIS AM/FM and Spatial Analysis Conference*, Hong Kong, 28–31 March 1994.

Yeh, A.G.O. and Batty, M. (1990) 'Guest Editorial', *Environment and Planning B*, Vol. 17, pp. 369–374.

Using the 'ALLOT' model in land use decision-making

13

Elise Bright

INTRODUCTION

The 'ALLOT' ('A Land Location and Optimization Technique'; name and programming are copyrighted) model is a flexible computer model which has been designed to develop economically and environmentally sound alternative land development patterns in a short period of time. ALLOT has the potential to drastically change the way that land use planning is conducted, since it has the capability to allow the incorporation of a wide variety of previously ignored environmental characteristics and up-to-date land use patterns.

ALLOT, which is written in the SAS programming language and runs on any IBM-compatible PC (286 or higher), contains two major parts. The first part employs a GIS database to conduct land suitability analysis for the area. It then produces maps showing the most suitable areas for various land use types. The second part appears to be unique in the field of computerized land use planning models. It combines the results of the suitability analysis with forecast demand for various land use types to produce 'optimum' future land use patterns. The model is capable of quickly allocating a wide variety of forecast demands for various categories of future land uses, allowing easy comparison; thus, it is a powerful land use planning tool. Also, because its allocation decisions are based on community goals and objectives, scenarios reflecting priorities ranging from protection of wildlife habitat to attraction of industry can be realized.

The model has been successfully applied in several real-world situations. First, three alternative future land use patterns were developed for

Decision Support Systems in Urban Planning. Edited by Harry Timmermans. Published in 1997 by E & F N Spon. ISBN 0 419 21050 4

a 105 000 acre rural area surrounding Richland–Chambers Lake near Corsicana, Texas, USA. The area had rural characteristics and was lacking infrastructure, but a large influx of people was expected as the lake was filled (Bright, 1989).

The success of this effort led to a decision to test its use as a method for facility siting (using landfill siting as an example) in the same geographic area. The siting was also done without sacrificing optimum utilization of the land; this was achieved by involving future demand for all land use types in the calculations (Nazem, 1990).

Finally, we had the opportunity to apply the model to a largely undeveloped highway corridor in the city of Southlake, Texas. In this case, the city residents and officials held widely differing views of the future they desired for their community, with options ranging from attracting large amounts of high-technology industry to developing most of the corridor with large-lot single-family homes (Bright, 1991).

Since then, the model has been used in industrial park siting, site planning and land use planning. Using some of these applications as examples, this chapter explains the methodology used in the ALLOT model.

STEP ONE – LAND SUITABILITY ANALYSIS

PURPOSE

Numerous physical and environmental factors must be taken into account when determining the 'optimal' use for land. Thus it is a complex process, because truly optimal land use decisions must be based on evaluations of private-sector economics, environmental impacts and public costs. In the marketplace, this determination is largely based on private-sector economic factors which do not reflect the total costs and benefits of development (Nehman *et al.*, 1975).

An example of how incomplete a picture of total cost is conveyed by market value (Ortolano, 1984) can be found if one looks at floodplains. Although the land may appear good for development from an economic point of view, the cost of downstream flooding is not paid by the developer, nor is the value of lost wildlife and urban open space, nor the cost of flood damage to homes. Another example is the provision of public services and facilities needed to serve a new development (water lines, highway widening, etc.), the cost of which is not always charged to the developer. There are many other examples which could be given to illustrate the imperfections of relying solely on the private market economy to determine optimal land use patterns.

Thus it is clear that realization of optimal land use patterns (with 'optimal' defined as land use patterns which maximize total net benefits) requires systematic use of information that often is not reflected in marketplace decisions (McHarg, 1969), such as data on physical environmental characteristics and public infrastructure. The importance of considering the physical environment when developing land has been emphasized for more than a century by many well known professionals, including George P. Marsh, Frederick Law Olmsted, Sir Patrick Geddes and Benton McKaye (Mumford, 1961). However, a formal methodology was lacking until the development of land suitability analysis.

DEFINITION

This technique is based on the idea that existing land use patterns, availability of infrastructure and presence of certain environmental features will indicate the intrinsic suitability of a parcel of land for various uses (Schneider and Amanullah, 1984). This system should produce development patterns that reduce environmental damage and lower public costs, while still allowing development to occur (Mutunayagam and Bahrami, 1986).

Land suitability analysis is a process through which planners assign land to future use categories in such a way that the overall pattern has a logical relationship among the categories and is in harmony with the natural and built environment. Therefore, very large amounts of input data must be synthesized and mapped for each parcel of land. An overlay technique is typically used for this data collection and analysis (Anjomani, 1984). Originally, the mapping and overlaying was done by hand using tracing paper and shades of grey to indicate suitability, but this is quite tedious to accomplish and can be very inaccurate. Thus the overlaying principle has been translated into computer analysis, using additive numerical weighting systems (US Environmental Protection Agency, 1989).

DEVELOPMENT OF THE MODEL

The model as it currently operates is the product of more than two years of research, programming and testing. The process began as an effort to develop a computer model that could be employed by a class of graduate students who were attempting to develop the Richland–Chambers Lake Area Plan. The theory and logic of land suitability analysis were culled from the literature, then translated into SAS programming. This was done because GIS software for accomplishing this was not yet readily available at an affordable cost.

The programming for the suitability portion of the model proved to be easy when compared to programming the demand-based pixel selection for future uses. Numerous technical difficulties were encountered, particularly when attempting to keep track of remaining demand as the model completed its iterations. After more than a year of study and programming late into many nights, the correct solution was found.

For extra assurance, a test data set was employed that was small enough to allow hand computation of the correct allocations, iteration by iteration. This data set was then fed into the model to see whether the same results were obtained. Finally, the order in which the model analysed and allocated each future land use category was changed and the model run again; when identical pixel selection occurred, we knew that it was working correctly. Figure 13.1 illustrates the model's development.

A review of the current GIS literature (Antenucci *et al.*, 1991; Cassettari, 1993; Fraser Taylor, 1991; Maguire *et al.*, 1991; Mather, 1993; Obermeyer and Pinto, 1994) has revealed that software which accomplishes the land suitability portion of the model is now commonplace, although the author believes that the use of pre-set weights is a very inappropriate feature which greatly reduces the validity of the models, for reasons explained elsewhere in this chapter. An extensive search revealed no model which successfully accomplishes the demand allocation that is the central feature of the second half of the model described in this chapter.

THE ALLOT MODEL – PREPARATION OF THE INPUT DATABASE

In all cases in which the ALLOT model has been employed, a raster-based GIS input database was first established using readily available software such as dBase or FoxPro. The study area was divided into square pixels of uniform size, and the information on each land characteristic relative to each pixel was stored in a file with one record per pixel and one field per characteristic. The file was then converted to ASCII format for use as input into the model, which is written in SAS.

Obtaining the greatest possible resolution and accuracy of the database is important; therefore, the area under study should be divided into the largest number of pixels that the researcher can reasonably manage, depending on time and computing capabilities. Where a single pixel falls into two categories – for example, it may contain two different soil types – a uniform classification policy must be established.

The following characteristics were selected for study based on the requirements for land suitability analysis, the attributes of the study area, and professional expertise regarding what factors are the greatest determinants of total public cost and benefit with respect to land development:

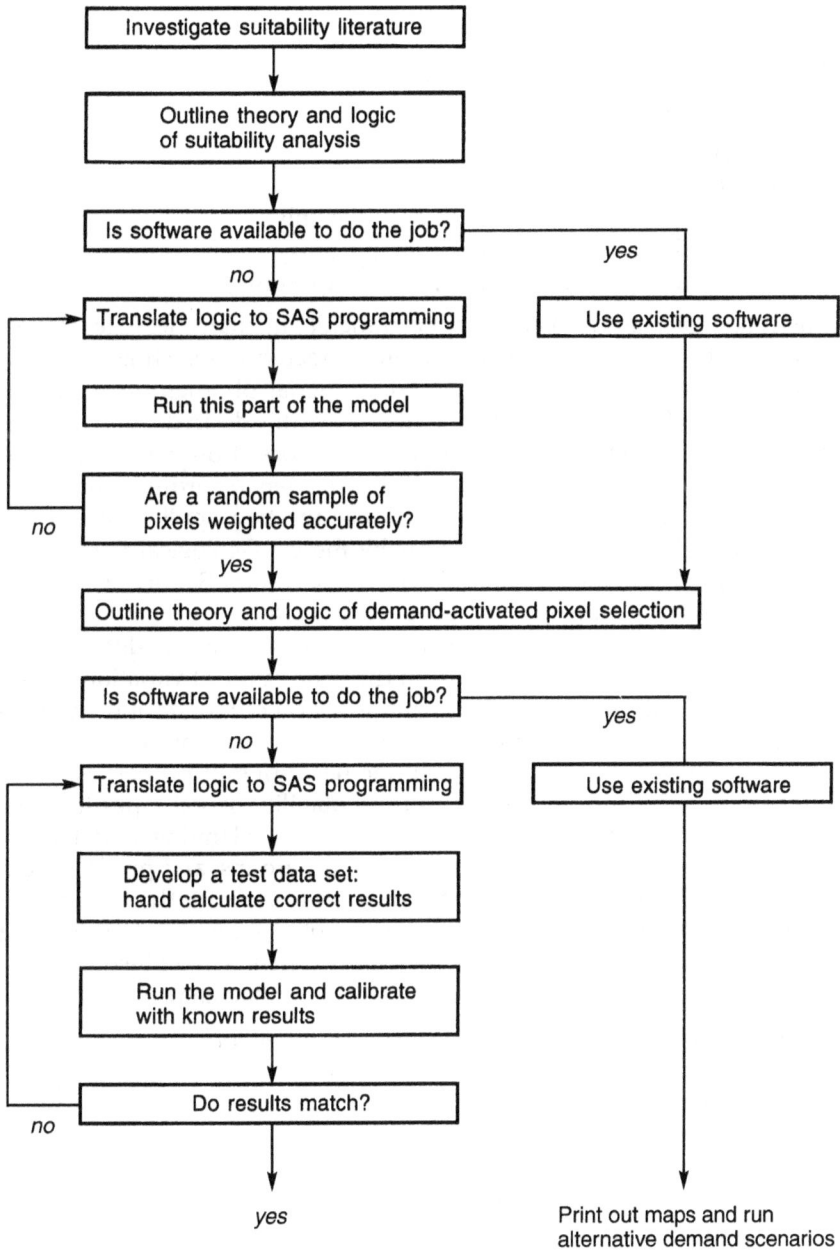

Fig. 13.1 Development of the 'ALLOT' model.

1. Slopes
2. Soils
3. Tree coverage
4. Road access
5. Visual features
6. Existing land use
7. Floodplains and wetlands
8. Proximity to water lines
9. Depth to bedrock (landfill siting example only)
10. Noise levels (highway corridor example only)
11. Land ownership (highway corridor example only)

Selection of characteristics can be difficult. In many less developed nations, data is simply not available on characteristics such as depth to bedrock. Some data can be generated via aerial photography, satellite imagery or field surveys, but in other cases the desired data may be unavailable. Characteristics should be selected based on data availability and on input from experts and community leaders regarding what characteristics are most important to them. For the two applications of the ALLOT model discussed here, reports by the US Geological Survey, US Army Corps of Engineers and US Soil Conservation Service were very useful in collecting data on many land characteristics.

Each land characteristic, in the course of analysis, was divided into different groups. This was done based on the wide range of variation within each characteristic and its particular influence on economic and environmental costs of different types of development. For example, there are many soil types in Nature, and each one has different properties; these differences create wide variations in the suitability of soil types for various development types. For both the land use planning and landfill model applications, soil was divided into eight groups, and pixels located in any of these groups were given a number to indicate the type of soil throughout the computation. The same sort of grouping and numbering was employed with all the other land characteristics. To illustrate, here are the categories used for the 'existing land use' characteristic:

1. Vacant pixels near existing public or institutional uses
2. Vacant pixels near existing single-family uses
3. Vacant, near multi-family existing uses
4. Vacant, near commercial uses
5. Vacant, near industrial
6. Vacant, near airport
7. Developed pixels
8. All other pixels

Group numbers for each of the land characteristics were then loaded into the database fields for each of the records (one for each pixel) in the study area. For example, in the Richland–Chambers landfill study, this involved entering nine items of data for each of 4506 records. After completion of this step, maps can be produced by converting the database to ASCII and using any readily available mapping software (the two examples presented here used SASGRAPH©).

The next step involved quantifying the relationship between each of these land characteristics and their suitability for various future uses. Thus, future land use categories had to be selected. The land use categories for the Richland–Chambers examples are as follows:

1. Low-density residential
2. Medium-density residential
3. High-density residential
4. Multi-family residential
5. Commercial
6. Industrial
7. Recreational
8. Public and institutional
9. Agricultural and vacant
10. Landfill (landfill siting example only)

The addition of depth to bedrock to the list of land characteristics and the addition of landfill as a future land use category illustrate the ALLOT model's flexibility; the user can easily tailor the list of input factors to individual needs. In the Southlake study, an 'estate residential' category was added and 'high-density residential' was removed, since large-lot homes were more prevalent there.

WEIGHTING – PURPOSE AND PITFALLS

The mechanism for quantifying the relationship between the existing land characteristics and the future land use categories is the use of weights. A weight is assigned to each grouping of each present land use characteristic, for each category of future land use. The weight reflects the suitability of each land characteristic grouping for that particular future land use category. For example, if pixel x was predominantly steep slope, the weight for commercial land uses would be low, while the weight for estate land uses would be high.

Using logically developed methods of weight assignment is essential, and errors here are responsible for much faulty analysis in the field (Anderson, 1987). If great care is not taken in establishing a consistent weighting system that accurately reflects both community goals and expert opinion, then the results of any model will be severely flawed. Here is a summary of major pitfalls to avoid.

(a) Community goals and objectives must be accurately reflected in the weighting system. For example, in Southlake the community had a strong preference for low-density, single-family residential development in undeveloped areas, with multi-family housing confined to areas close to the highway or to existing commercial nodes. The weights assigned to the relationship between the future land use category of multi-family housing and the present land characteristics of 'close to highway' and 'close to commercial' were, therefore, very high.

(b) Expert opinion (including legal advice) must also be reflected in the weighting system. Again using the Southlake study as an example, legal experts advised us that aircraft noise must be treated as a 'knockout factor': that is, if high noise levels were present, then a pixel simply could not be selected for residential use no matter how suitable it might be in every other way; the legal consequences of allowing residential development in these areas would be too severe. Thus, the weights relating the future land use categories of residential development to the existing land characteristic of high aircraft noise were set extremely low (the lower the weight, the less likely the computer would select that area for that use). Unfortunately, the most suitable areas for residential development in every other way proved to be in the high-noise areas; thus calibration of the model showed that, in order to achieve the desired removal of these parcels, noise weights had to be given much more importance than any other factor (their importance in the analysis had to be increased by a factor of 10). This is an excellent example of how expert opinion should be reflected in weighting.

(c) Mathematical errors should be avoided when combining weights into an overall score. Criticism of the methods used by McHarg and others (Hopkins, 1977) should be heeded, and exaggerated differences among areas that may result from multiplication (except in rare cases such as the noise factor explained above) should be avoided. The problems of multiplying by zero or multiplying a positive by a negative number should not be forgotten either. The issue of how heavily to weight community goals versus expert opinion must also be settled here. Should an expert's view of the importance of noise be more valued than the community's desire to locate multi-family housing in a noise zone, for example? Finally, the importance of ensuring internal mathematical consistency cannot be over-emphasized; every weight must be cross-checked with all others to be certain that it is indeed a true reflection of the relative value and importance of that characteristic for that future use, when considered in relation to all other weights.

EXAMPLE – THE ALLOT MODEL

In all cases, the given weights varied from 1 to 9 (with the exception of noise in the Southlake study, see above). When a pixel was found to fall into a grouping of a given land characteristic which was rated best for any future land use category, the value of 9 was assigned to that pixel for that future use. When a pixel was found to be neither good nor bad for any specific land use category and land characteristic, then the value of 5 was assigned to it. Values below 5 indicated a pixel's degree of unsuitability for future land uses.

It is important to note here that, according to the theory of suitability analysis as discussed by Hopkins (1977), McHarg (1969) and others, the range of numbers employed as weights is not important, as long as it is large enough to reflect variations in importance (for example, a range of 1 to 3 probably would not be sufficient), the range is correctly employed and the pitfalls discussed in the previous section are avoided. If weights from 1 to 9 are employed for all land characteristics, this implies that all are equally important. Thus varying weight ranges may need to be set for each characteristic in order to accurately reflect community goals, as discussed in the previous section.

The weights for each group of land characteristics and each category of future land use are entered into the model as input data; next, the model distributes the weights to each pixel according to the land characteristic grouping code previously entered for it. Thus, the Richland–Chambers land use planning model had 72 numbers assigned to each pixel at this point in the model, and the landfill siting model had 90 numbers for each of the 4506 pixels (see Table 13.1). This automated weight assignment saves hundreds of hours of time over the hand-drawn overlay method used in the past. The only limit to the number of land characteristics, future land use categories, or pixels that can be handled by the model is that imposed by the capacity of the computer being used. Some older PCs may take hours to run it if more categories, characteristics or pixels are used than were employed in these examples.

The model then adds all the weights associated with each land use category for each pixel, resulting in a total of nine weights for the Richland–Chambers example (and ten for the Southlake example) for each pixel. Each of these weights represents the overall suitability of that pixel for a single future land use category. The value of these total weights can range from 10 to 90 in the Southlake example, since each overall weight results from adding the individual weights assigned to each of the land characteristics. This automated adding is another area where the model saves large amounts of time over the hand method, and also produces more accurate results.

The results of this assignment and adding process are stored in an output data file. At this point land suitability analysis is completed and maps can be produced using SASGRAPH (after sorting the data set, dividing the weighted scores into groups, and assigning a dot pattern to each

Table 13.1 Example of additive weighting for a single pixel – Pixel number 3021[a]

Land characteristic	Group number	Weights assigned for								
		REC	LDR	MDR	HDR	MULR	COM	IND	PUB	AGR
Soil	8	9	9	9	7	6	5	9	1	9
Slope	3	9	9	1	7	5	5	7	3	3
Trees	4	9	1	1	7	8	8	1	1	1
Visual	3	9	1	9	5	8	8	3	5	5
Floods	5	9	1	1	1	1	1	1	7	4
Roads	4	1	9	9	9	9	9	9	5	9
Water lines	5	1	5	9	9	9	7	7	5	5
Existing land use	8	1	5	9	8	9	9	5	5	1
Depth to bedrock	2	1	9	5	5	5	5	5	5	9
Totals		49	49	53	58	60	57	47	37	46

[a] If there was demand for all uses, this pixel would be selected for multi-family use. If demand for multi-family had been met already, it would be selected for whichever future use it had the highest score and for which there was demand.

Key:
REC = recreational use
LDR = low-density residential use
MDR = medium-density residential use
HDR = high-density residential use
MULR = multi-family residential use
COM = commercial use
IND = industrial use
PUB = public use
AGR = agricultural use

group) to show those areas that are most suitable for each of the future land use categories (see Table 13.1).

IS THIS AN OPTIMAL SOLUTION?

These maps could be considered as representing optimal future land use patterns, but the author contends that they are optimal only in a strict mathematical sense: they show the areas which received the highest scores for each future land use category. However, there is no comparison among the land use categories for any given parcel, and no consideration of demand. As Anjomani (1987) pointed out, for real-world applications one cannot ignore demand; difficult decisions about how to use a parcel which is highly rated for several uses must be made, and allocations must be made for parcels which are highly rated for uses for which there is little demand (Anjomani and Saberi, 1988). It is useful to recall at this point that the author's definition of 'optimal' land use is not based solely on compatibility with the natural and built environment. An optimal pattern is considered to be that which satisfies demand for use of the land in a manner that minimizes total public cost (including direct cost, such as provision of roads, and indirect cost, such as adverse environmental impacts) and maximizes public benefit (direct and indirect).

Some examples may be useful to illustrate this point. The city of Houston, Texas, is built almost entirely in an area in which the soils are very unsuitable for construction, and much of the area is subject to flooding. Likewise, much of the city of New Orleans, Louisiana, is built on former wetland areas. A simple land suitability analysis of these areas would no doubt have resulted in a recommendation that neither city be built at all, since natural limitations made the areas best suited for use as nature reserves or parks. Unfortunately, this approach ignores the obvious demand for development in these areas; therefore, a planner using land suitability analysis to justify a recommendation that these areas be used as parks – which is an 'optimal' (mathematically) future land use for these areas – would lose credibility, and possibly employment as well. Worst of all, the real contribution that land suitability analysis can make to planning for growth in these sensitive areas would be lost, due to an over-emphasis on mathematically simple ideas of optimization. Instead, the market would be allowed to determine land use patterns. This has in fact happened in both cities, with the result that they are some of the most unplanned and visually/naturally destructive examples of urban growth in America. Similarly, in the ALLOT study area, suitability analysis showed that nearly all of the area was best for use as landfill. Clearly a more detailed effort, using mathematics to select optimal land use patterns based on real-world demand, was needed if this type of analysis was to be anything but an idealistic, and somewhat laughable, exercise in basic addition. For this reason, the second half of the ALLOT model was developed. The output data set from the land suitability analysis is used as the input data set into this allocation portion.

STEP TWO – ALLOCATING FUTURE LAND USE

First, the data set is sorted based on values in the first future land use category, forcing those pixels with the highest suitability scores for that future land use category to the top of the column.

Next, the optimization model compares across columns (each column represents suitability weights for one future land use category) pixel by pixel, testing for the highest land suitability weight in each pixel. If the land use category being processed had the highest value in the pixel and demand for that land use category had not been met, then the pixel is selected for that future land use; otherwise, the pixel is left for selection for whatever category it may rank more highly for.

When demand for any land use category is met, the computer sets the weight for that land use category for all remaining pixels to zero; thus unwanted but highly rated pixels for the filled land use category are freed for selection for another category (Fig. 13.2). The process is repeated until demand for all future land uses has been met. This requires the computer to sort through all the pixels as many times as the number of land use categories.

Perhaps the most interesting and unique feature of this model is its ability to easily accommodate different demand scenarios. A range of demand forecasts should be developed prior to running the model; very high or low ones can even be included for political reasons. In the Richland–Chambers examples, forecasts of population were developed for the study area using several established population- and employment-based techniques; the result was a range of forecasts that reflected professional inability to accurately predict a narrow range of growth for this largely undeveloped area around a newly formed lake. The model proved to be ideal in handling this uncertainty, since it allowed easy production of a future land use plan for each extreme forecast as well as the middle range, thus allowing the client to monitor growth trends and switch from one optimal land use pattern to another that better fitted emerging trends.

In the Southlake example, accepted forecasting methodology was combined with community vision and political goals to produce five

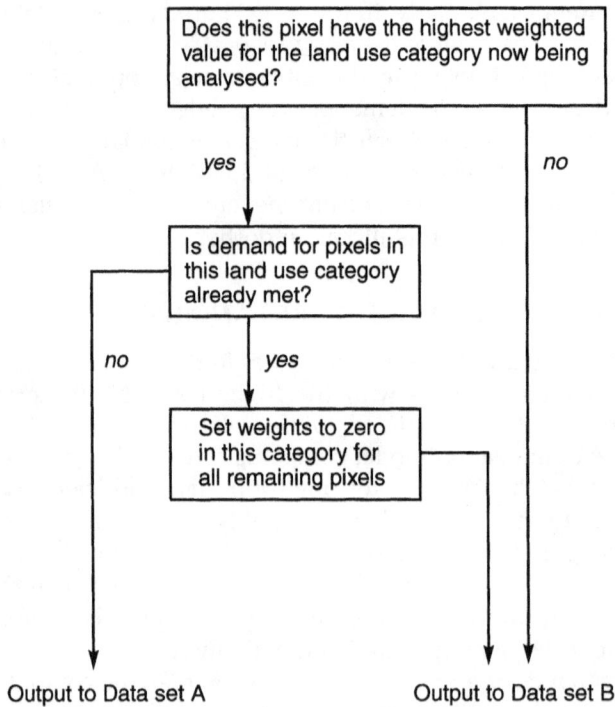

Fig. 13.2   Decision tree.

alternative future land use mixes. Some alternatives reflected the community's desire to become a high-tech centre, while others incorporated the professionals' view that multi-family housing was needed even though the elected officials did not support it. By being able to easily change the results to reflect different goals, the model helped to defuse one of the biggest stumbling blocks in planning, namely the need to adjust desired visions of the future to reality and the reluctance of public officials to do so. We were able to say, for example, that we seriously doubted that their vision of a high-tech centre without multi-family housing will be realized, but if it is, then alternative scenario 3 shows the optimal land use pattern to follow. If their hopes prove to be unrealized, then alternative scenarios 2 and 4 provide them with optimal land use patterns based on what we believe the range of demand will probably be. Alternative scenario 5 should be followed if economic disaster occurs and even our moderate optimism proves to be unwarranted; alternative scenario 1 is the optimal pattern for unexpectedly high growth in non-high-tech areas, with much multi-family demand included. They should adopt the one they hope to achieve, and zone their property, plan their streets and utilities accordingly; but monitor trends over time to be sure that their desired pattern is really occurring; if not, switch to one that is a better fit.

The output of ALLOT is an ASCII data set allocating each pixel to a future land use category. These results were fed into a SASGRAPH program to produce maps of future land use patterns; however, the data set can be used as input into any compatible mapping software. The five alternative future land use patterns developed for Southlake are shown in Figs 13.3 to 13.7.

ANALYSIS OF RESULTS

RELATING MULTIPLE FUTURE USE CATEGORIES TO DEMAND

If future demand for all of the land use categories had not been involved in the analysis, the computing procedure would have been significantly simpler: all the model would have needed to do would have been to allocate suitable pixels for one use – for example, landfill purposes – without paying attention to the rest of the land use categories and the number of pixels being allocated. Unfortunately, the output from this approach would have been incorrect: the result would have been a map showing only the areas that are good for landfills, and this is not what one would consider the best use of the land or optimized land use planning. Optimization can be achieved only when all of the land use categories are involved in the calculation and the demand for each one has been determined. A map illustrating only those areas that are most suitable for landfills means little for two reasons. First, the same areas might be even better suited for apartments or industry. Secondly, consider a case in

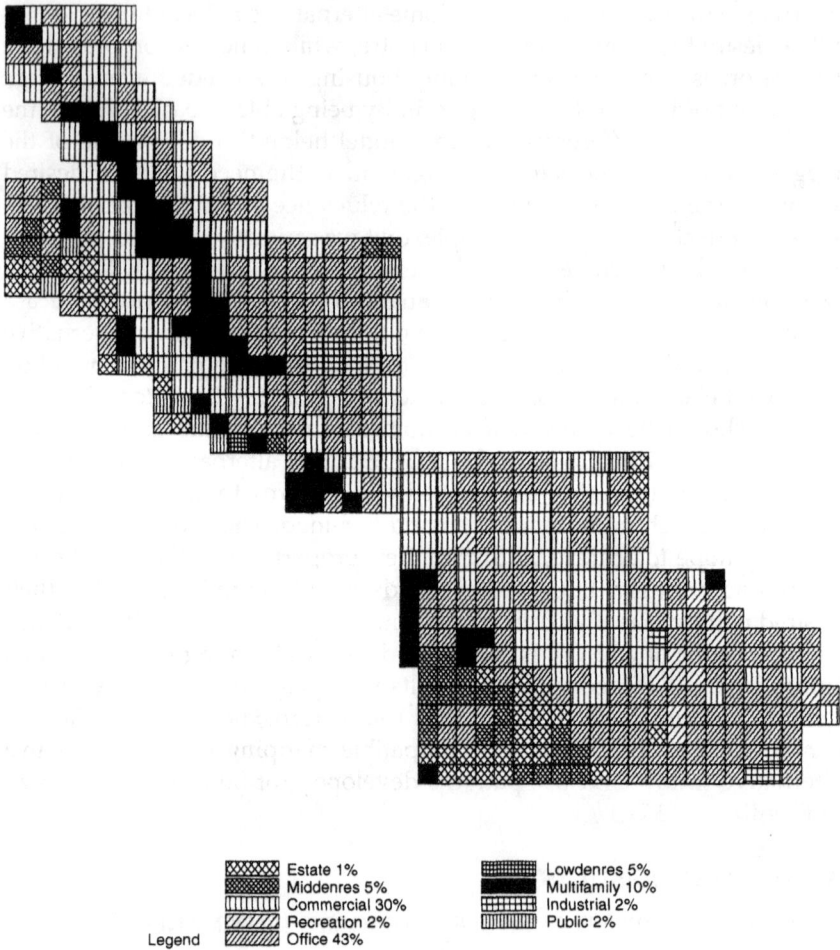

	Estate 1%		Lowdenres 5%
	Middenres 5%		Multifamily 10%
	Commercial 30%		Industrial 2%
	Recreation 2%		Public 2%
Legend	Office 43%		

Fig. 13.3   Southlake scenario 1.

which there will be very low future demand for landfill sites, but nearly all of the area is ideally suited for landfills. In this case, reserving most of the area for landfills cannot be considered as optimal land use allocation, because the act of reserving so much land for an unneeded purpose will push those uses for which there is significant demand into very undesirable areas (assuming that there is enough acreage available for them at all). Since it specifically addresses this issue, the ALLOT model is different from any other model with which the author is familiar.

On the other hand, involving future demand increases the complexity of the modelling and computation procedure. For this reason, a great deal of time was spent on programming the model so that its counter would respond correctly to the needed number of pixels for each land

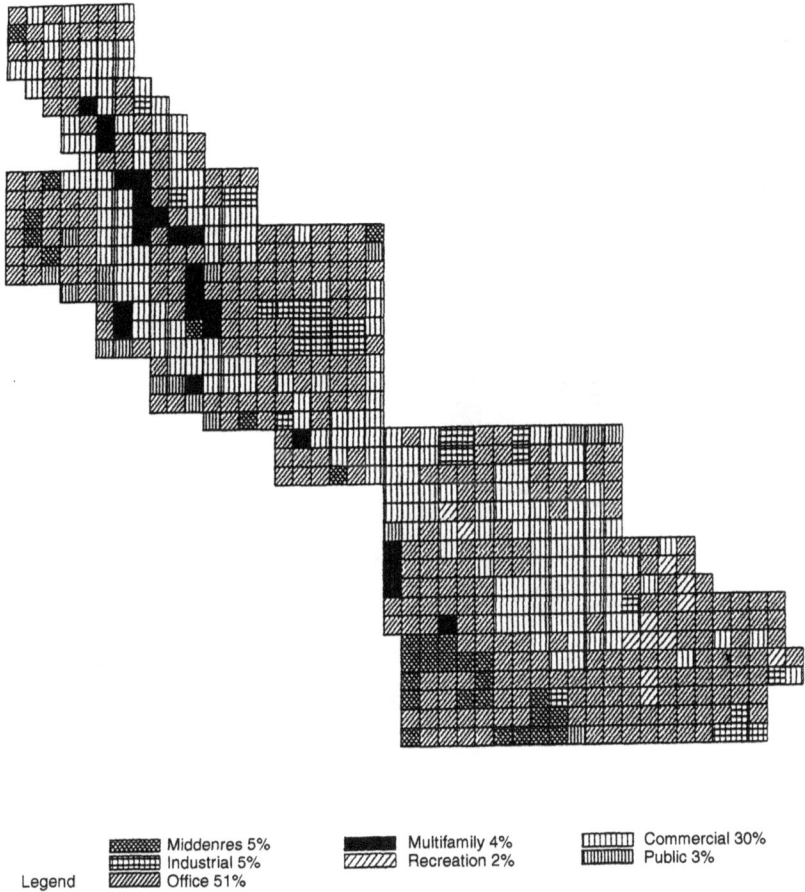

Fig. 13.4 Southlake scenario 2.

use category and select the exact number. Keeping track of the number of allocated pixels to any land use category, and comparing it with the demand throughout the different category sorts of the model, is the most difficult part of the construction of ALLOT. Nevertheless, as a result of intensive programming, the model successfully selected the suitable pixels for each land use category based on future demand.

FUTURE APPLICATIONS

Future applications of this model could be widespread. It is cheaper to use than some GIS systems, which can require purchase of tens of thousands of dollars worth of computer hardware (Gordon, 1985). Although there are PC-based GIS systems available for less than $200 which can complete the tasks performed by Step One of the ALLOT model, all those

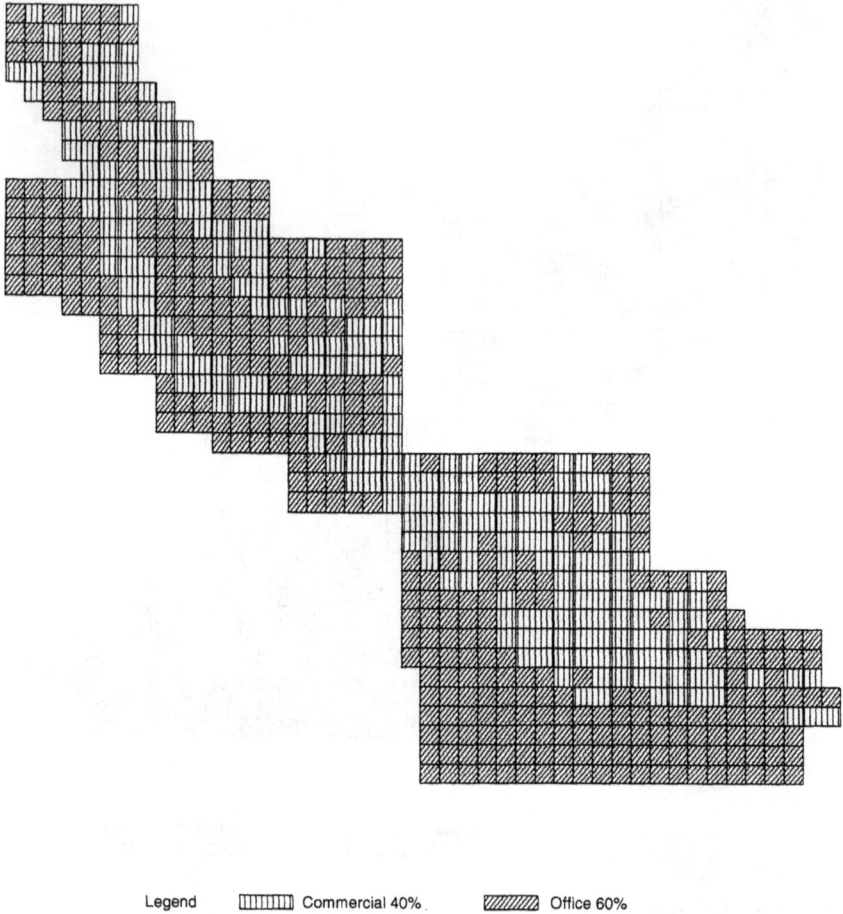

Legend [[[[[[[[]]]]] Commercial 40%   ▨▨▨▨ Office 60%

Fig. 13.5 Southlake scenario 3.

with which the author is familiar contain pre-established weights which are quite difficult to modify. If these weights do not conform to the goals and objectives of the local community (and since they are built in to the software, an exact correspondence is highly unlikely), then the resulting plans will probably not be acceptable to area residents. However, if the reader prefers to employ another PC-based GIS system for Step One, they can certainly do so, and still use the results as input for Step Two if the original system is raster-based and the output file is in ASCII.

The unique contribution of this research lies in the model's ability to allocate many alternative patterns of future land use. Carver (1991) provides a framework for the integration of methods of decision analysis with GIS, and Janssen and Rietveld (1990) apply multi-criteria analysis

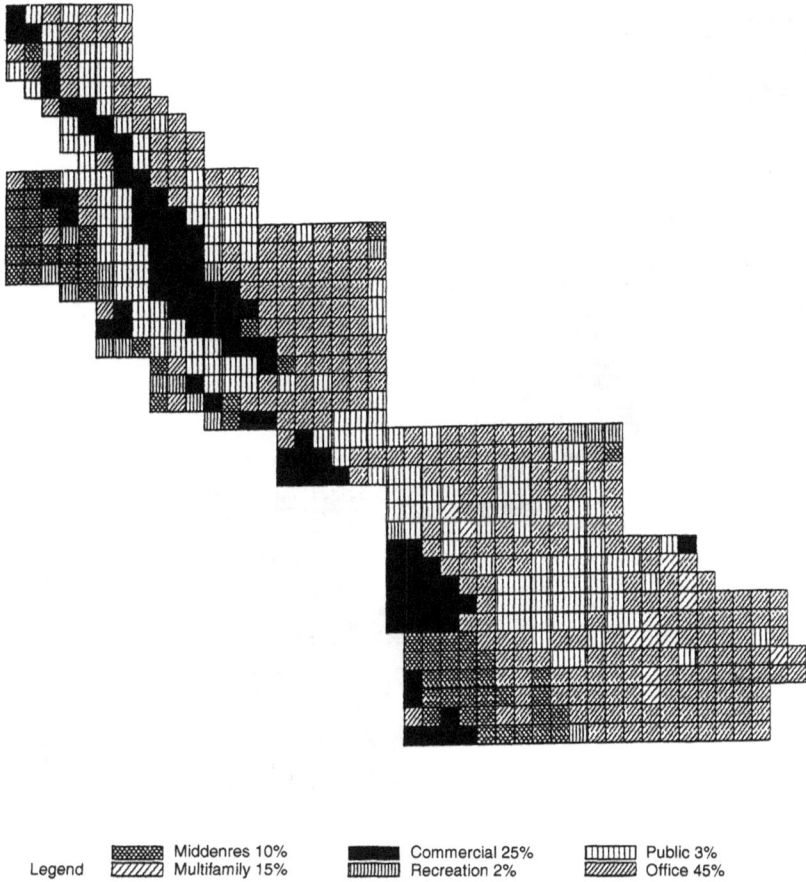

Legend

| | Middenres 10% | | Commercial 25% | | Public 3% |
| | Multifamily 15% | | Recreation 2% | | Office 45% |

Fig. 13.6 Southlake scenario 4.

and GIS to agricultural land use in the Netherlands. However, neither the author nor any colleagues consulted know of another model which fuses demand for all types of specified future land uses with the results of suitability analysis (Eastman *et al.*, 1993). Although valuable, those enhancements currently available focus on one land use category only and thus are subject to the difficulties discussed earlier in this section.

This feature frees planners from trying to forecast growth patterns exactly; rather, a wide variety of alternative forecasts can quickly be mapped and future plans generated to fit unpredictable trends, saving planners many hours of work. Growth patterns that would occur without government planning can also be mapped, if weights and land characteristics that reflect only the private developer's thinking are selected, in order to make a case for planning by vividly illustrating the total cost of undirected, market-controlled growth.

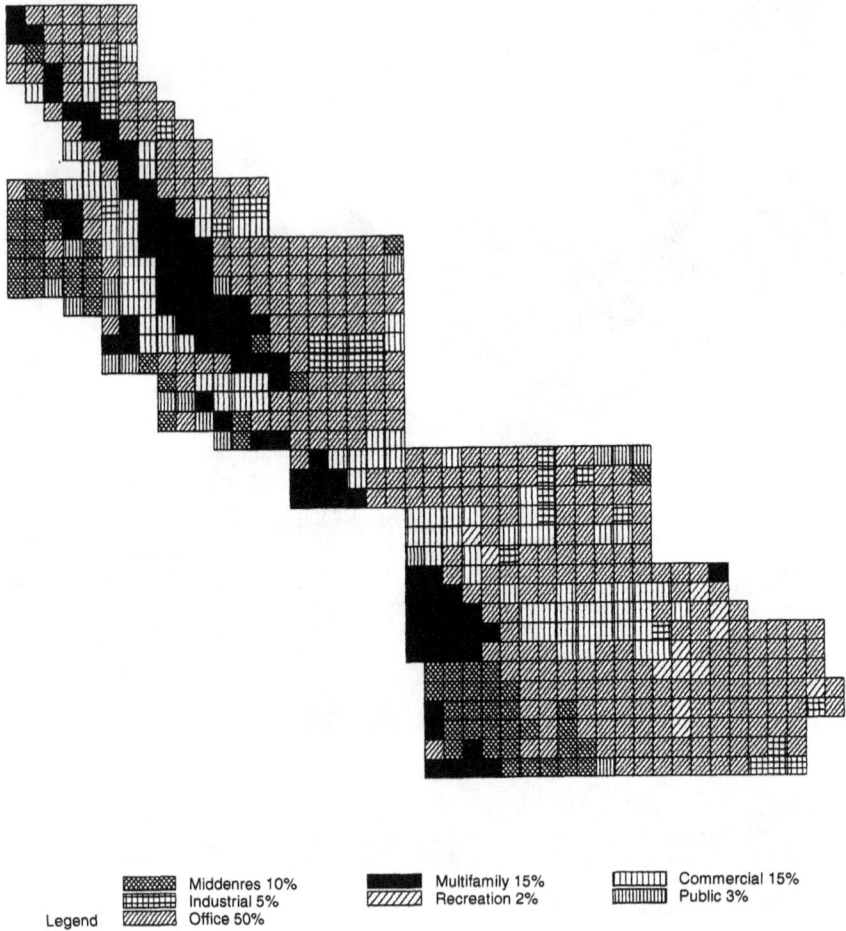

Legend

▨ Middenres 10%	■ Multifamily 15%	▥ Commercial 15%
▤ Industrial 5%	▨ Recreation 2%	▥ Public 3%
▨ Office 50%		

Fig. 13.7 Southlake scenario 5.

Finally, the model can be an invaluable site selection tool, particularly for LULUs (locally unwanted land uses) such as landfills (Melachrinoudis and Cullinane, 1985), since it provides a clear mathematical rationale for site selection. Thus in many applications, it is surely an improvement over present techniques.

POSSIBLE WEAKNESSES

Despite these assets, there are some points which may appear to be significant constraints or failings, yet in reality if the weighting is correctly done they do not appear to operate in practice.

First, there is no overt mechanism for assuring compatibility between future land uses. To rectify this, an iterative loop would have to be added to the programming to compare land use allocations of adjacent pixels with some built-in criteria for incompatibility, reallocating those that conflict.

Secondly, there is no built-in mechanism for searching for large parcels or parcels with specific shapes, which are required for certain uses such as roads or airports. For example, although a given pixel may be ideally suited for airport use, it is useless unless it is contiguous to other well-suited pixels and together they are of a shape that can accommodate the facilities. This issue should be addressed by attaching high weights to those pixels which are surrounded by other similar pixels. For example, if the residents and experts have indicated that an ideal airport site would be at least one mile from any residential areas, have slopes of 0–3%, lack trees, have no wetlands, etc., then when the weights are assigned to certain categories those pixels which possess those characteristics themselves and are next to another pixel in the same category could be weighted highly for airport use. This method would produce clusters of pixels very well-suited for airport use, from which one could be selected that best fitted the desired shape. Since only one airport is needed per area, that use (and the selected pixels) should then be removed from the model and a second run completed, so planners can see what use should be allocated to those areas which are well-suited for airport use but were not selected.

EVIDENCE FROM REAL-WORLD RESULTS

However, in reality neither of these have proved to be serious problems for several reasons. First, the model is designed to operate on a regional or city-wide scale; thus the size of each pixel is usually large enough (15 acres or more) to accommodate most land uses as well as providing buffering among incompatible uses when they do appear next to each other. However, even those applications at the site level have produced sound land use patterns, as described in the final paragraph below.

Secondly, land uses that are incompatible with each other usually have radically different 'ideal' locations anyway: for example, a waste incinerator should be placed in a flat area near a road suitable for heavy truck traffic, with soils designed for heavy structures, very little vegetation, poor wildlife habitat, industrial-size utilities available, etc., whereas residential uses are best suited for much different land characteristics. Very seldom do these characteristics change completely from one pixel to the next; far more often, one characteristic will change slightly while the others remain the same from pixel to pixel, causing only a slight change in the total weighted scores for each future land use among adjacent pixels. As one would expect, neither incompatibility between future land uses nor scattering/lack of contiguity constraints have been problems in any of the applications so far, probably because the weights reflected these different 'ideal' siting requirements and thus produce a natural separation of these uses, along with clustering of pixels well-suited for a given use and a gradual change in use from low-density residential to medium- to high-density to light commercial to heavy commercial to light industrial to heavy industrial, rather than a change from residential to industrial among adjacent pixels.

Finally, as the literature of suitability analysis and land use planning points out from the writings of McHarg (1969) on, these issues do not necessarily mean that the land use patterns produced are less than optimal. To illustrate, consider the smallest site analysed so far using this method: a 330 acre parcel which was divided into pixels only a few feet in size. Among the future uses to be sited were roads and parking lots, both of which required use of contiguous parcels of specific shapes located near future uses in need of access by autos. Additionally, about a third of the site was to be left in its natural state, so no access was warranted. The mapping produced some isolated parcels identified as 'best for parking' or 'best for road', but in general, and somewhat to our surprise, a clear 'best' routing for the road emerged, clusters 'best for parking' appeared, and nearby pixels were identified as best for development rather than for preservation. Not every parcel along the route appeared as 'best for road' or 'best for parking', but the vast majority did. Thus although the 'optimal' use was impossible for every pixel, on the whole the most optimal roadway and parking areas were selected by the model. This is really not surprising if one thinks about the way that both infrastructure and natural features occur and change gradually over given distances. If future modifications prove to be needed, the work of Brookes (1993), who developed a new component for the IDRISI GIS that takes shape into account in identifying land uses, can be of assistance.

ACKNOWLEDGEMENTS

The author would like to acknowledge the work of Ian McHarg, Lewis Hopkins and Ardeshir Anjomani, all of whom pioneered concepts upon which this research built. Also, the dedication of Mr J. Jerry Luor and many other graduate students in the School of Urban and Public Affairs is very much appreciated; they helped make this model a useful applications tool as well as an interesting scholarly exercise.

References 249

REFERENCES

Anderson, L.T. (1987) Seven Methods for Calculating Land Capability/Suitability, Planning Advisory Service Report No. 402, American Planning Association, Chicago.
Anjomani, A. (1984) The overlaying map technique: problems and suggested solutions. Journal of Planning Education and Research, 4(2), 111–219.
Anjomani, A. (1987) Large Scale Land Use Planning and the Interactive Approach: Land Use Planning for a Lakeside Area I, Institute of Urban Studies, University of Texas at Arlington.
Anjomani, A. and Saberi, A. (1988) Large Scale Land Use Planning and the Interactive Approach: Land Use Planning for a Lakeside Area II, Institute of Urban Studies, University of Texas at Arlington.
Antenucci, J.C. et al. (1991) Geographic Information Systems: A Guide to the Technology, Chapman & Hall, New York.
Bright, E.M. (1989) Richland–Chambers Lake Area: A Vision of the Future, Institute of Urban Studies, University of Texas at Arlington.
Bright, E.M. (1991) Land Suitability Analysis: Highway 114 Corridor, Southlake, Texas, Institute of Urban Studies, University of Texas at Arlington.
Brookes, C.J. (1993) A Region-Growing Approach to Integrating Shape into Multi-Criteria Evaluation in GIS, Unpublished M.Sc. Dissertation, Leicester University, England.
Carver, S.J. (1991) Integrating multi-criteria evaluation with GIS. International Journal of Geographical Information Systems, 5(3), 321–339.
Cassettari, S. (1993) Introduction to Integrated Geo-information Management, Chapman & Hall, London.
Eastman, J.R., Toledano, J., Weigen, J. and Kyem, P.A.K. (1993) Participatory multi-objective decisionmaking in GIS. In Proceedings of Auto-Carto 11, American Society for Photogrammetry and Remote Sensing, Bethesda, Maryland, pp. 29–45.
Fraser Taylor, D.R. (ed.) (1991) Geographic Information Systems: the Microcomputer and Modern Cartography, Pergamon Press, Oxford.
Gordon, S.I. (1985) Computer Models in Environmental Planning, Planners Press, Chicago.
Hopkins, L.D. (1977) Methods for generating land suitability maps: a comparative evaluation. Journal of the American Institute of Planners, October, pp. 386–400.
Janssen, R. and Rietveld, P. (1990) Multicriteria analysis and GIS: an application to agricultural land use in the Netherlands. In Scholten, H.J. and Stillwell, J.C.H. (eds), GIS for Urban and Regional Planning, Kluwer, Amsterdam, pp. 146–163.
Maguire, D.J., Goodchild, M.F. and Rhind, D.W. (eds) (1991) Geographical Information Systems: Principles and Applications, Longman, Harlow, Essex.
Mather, P.M. (ed.) (1993) Geographical Information Handling: Research and Applications, John Wiley & Sons, New York.
McHarg, I. (1969) Design with Nature, Doubleday Natural History Press, Garden City, NY.
Melachrinoudis, E. and Cullinane, T.P. (1985) Locating an undesirable facility within a geographical region using the maximum criterion. Journal of Regional Science, 25(3), 115.
Mumford, L. (1961) The City in History, Harcourt, Brace & World, New York.

Mutunayagam, N.B. and Bahrami, A. (1986) *Cartography and Site Analysis with Microcomputers*, American Planning Association, Chicago.

Nazem, P. (1990) *Municipal Waste Management Plan and Application of GIS in Landfill Site Selection*, School of Urban and Public Affairs, University of Texas at Arlington.

Nehman, G., Griffin, J.M. and Duke, K.M. (1975) Land use and environmental planning. *Let's Plan Our Use of the Land*, 7(1), 1–21.

Obermeyer, N.J. and Pinto, J.K. (1994) *Managing Geographic Information Systems*, Guilford Press, New York.

Ortolano, L. (1984) *Environmental Planning and Decisionmaking*, John Wiley and Sons, New York.

Schneider, D.M. and Amanullah, S. (1984) *Computer-Assisted Land Resources Planning*, Planning Advisory Service Report No. 339, American Planning Association, Chicago.

US Environmental Protection Agency (1989) *Geographic Information Systems Handbook*, US Government Printing Office, Washington, DC.

Neighbourhood management, performance measuring and decision-making

14

Jos Smeets

INTRODUCTION

Among managers of the built environment, interest in quality is rapidly increasing. Because of the continuously increasing pluriformity of household types and styles of living, it is realized that the quality of products which are offered (dwellings and neighbourhoods) should also be differentiated. Quality is, according to ISO 9000: 'the whole range of properties and characteristics of a product or a service which are important for the compliance to set requirements or obvious needs'. From this definition it can be derived that a product in itself does not have quality, but that the (potential) user defines the quality by his or her judgement of that particular product. If this definition of quality is applied to the built environment, it must be concluded that the quality of dwellings and neighbourhoods (the meso-scale) is a complex one. After all, users base their judgement on a great number of criteria, not only because dwellings and neighbourhoods are composed of various parts, but also because they perform different functions (see also Rapoport, 1989).

The complexity of quality of the built environment is due to the number of relevant quality aspects rather than to the complexity of separate aspects. These aspects, relating to form, function and technic, are in general very specifically expressible in numbers, visible or describable in

Decision Support Systems in Urban Planning. Edited by Harry Timmermans. Published in 1997 by E & F N Spon. ISBN 0 419 21050 4

words. Consequently quality at the meso-scale can be discussed more objectively than the ISO definition has superficially suggested.

The performance concept which formed a central point of departure in our research on housing in Waalwijk offers possibilities to substantiate the subjective and related components of quality, and forms an important instrument in communication between users and suppliers of the built environment.

The core of the performance concept is the way of thinking in terms of results for the users, instead of in terms of the means brought into action by the experts. A performance has the characteristic that its level can be recorded objectively within certain agreements. The most important condition is that these results are quantifiable and verifiable. Working with the performance concept does place great demands on the methods of measurement used (RGD, 1992).

Although the performance concept was developed initially for the preliminary and implementation stages of the construction/building process, it is also applied more and more in the management and occupancy stages. In the occupancy stage the performance concept is used to determine the quality of dwellings and neighbourhoods. Quality is here defined as the measure to which the supplied performance fits the demanded performance. Should there be, in any case, a mismatch between supplied and demanded performance, then management intervention will be necessary.

PERFORMANCE MEASUREMENT

The complexity of the built environment forces us to differentiate in regard to quality. First, a differentiation into 'technical', 'functional' and 'spatial–visual' quality is possible (Stevens, 1994):

- The *technical quality* deals especially with the performances of the building materials and building components.
- The *functional quality* is determined by matters such as functionality, comfort, safety and adaptability.
- The *spatial-visual quality* encompasses performances in the field of architectural and urban design qualities. Specifically these 'soft' quality aspects are under-exposed in many measuring systems. Matters such as architectural image, spatiality and design quality are difficult to measure objectively.

Another way of structuring the complex quality is a differentiation into 'object levels': 'dwelling', 'building' and 'environment'. The product performances offered by the manager can be structured as follows (Boekhorst and Smeets, 1990):

- The *dwelling* is characterized by a sphere of influence that encompasses the private territory of individual households, including all matters belonging to them, like the size of the dwelling, the number of rooms, the level of rents, the dwelling type and the view from the dwelling.

- The *building form* relates to all aspects of shared use of the living environment in order to reach the dwelling, like the entrance to the building, the entrance hall, the staircases and galleries, etc. – in short, the semi-public parts of the living environment.
- The *physical environment* and the *location* are concerned with all physical aspects of the public parts of the living environment, like the access roads, shops and other facilities, greens, parking facilities, etc.
- The *social environment* concerns the way in which occupants/residents behave with each other and with their environment, whether they take each other into account, social cohesion, negligence, etc. – in short, the living behaviour.

In practice, many diverse points of view are combined. Thus aspects of functionality, comfort and security can be shown on the level of the dwelling.

From the managerial point of view, the object levels are most appropriate: in a structure of scale levels it is clear who has management responsibility. On the dwelling and building level, it is the housing manager and/or the occupier. On the level of the environment, the local government is the most important manager.

The data required to substantiate this performance can be identified by means of a checklist. Part of the data is already available from the current dwelling information system; for the other part, additional data collection is necessary. In this research this additional data collection has already taken place by means of panels of experts. The checklist used consists of the different main aspects (dwelling, housing type, physical environment, social environment) and is structured in partial aspects. At each partial aspect the performances are described in measurable terms, and substructured in five performance levels. Figure 14.1 shows a part of this checklist.

A so-called 'neighbourhood profile', constructed on the basis of an extensive checklist, comprises a large amount of information which can be graphically represented. It 'shows' the offered performances of all main and partial aspects (Fig. 14.2).

THE HOUSING PERFORMANCE RATE (HPR)

To make it possible to compare the profiles of neighbourhoods among each other, the profile is converted into a score, the so-called Housing Performance Rate (HPR). In calculating this HPR, a number of weighting factors are used. As Rapoport (1989) argues, needs, preferences and choice provide the best framework for considering housing and neighbourhoods. For calculating these weighting factors, the results from

1. Dwelling level

The presence of insulation in the dwelling
	cavity-/roof-/glass pane insulation
	cavity-/roof insulation
	cavity- and glass pane insulation or roof- and glass pane insulation
	glass pane insulation or cavity insulation or roof insulation
	no insulation

2. Building level

Access to the dwelling
	dwelling with own access
	front door in shared hall
	front door to controlled gallery
	front door to open gallery
	others

3. Environment level

Traffic safety at main access roads
	no traffic unsafe situation within 1000 m
	no traffic unsafe situation within 500 m
	no traffic unsafe situation
	one traffic unsafe situation
	several traffic unsafe situations

Visual attractiveness of public space
	design and material attractive
	design or material attractive
	neutral attractivity
	design or material unattractive
	design and material unattractive

Fig. 14.1   Part of a checklist – a specimen.

market research on housing in the same town are used (Pott and Smeets, 1993).

This market research shows that, as motives for moving house, characteristics on the dwelling level are more important than those of the living environment. On the dwelling level, specifically 'size', 'number of rooms' and 'private outside space' are mentioned. On the neighbourhood level, 'traffic safety', 'social security', 'playground provision' and 'quality of the road service' play a relatively large role. This results in the following weighting factors:

1. On the *dwelling level*. The dwelling quality is regarded as most important and gets a weighting factor of 3. This forms a more important

Dwelling level   --   ++
Construction quality
Physical quality
Dwelling quality
Heating
Hot water supply
Insulation
Total dwelling size
Size of living room
Size of the kitchen
Location of kitchen
Size of master bedroom
Number of bedrooms
Sanitation
Presence of balcony
Access to dwelling
Store space
Private outside space

Neighbourhood level   --   ++
Physico-spatial quality
Character of the design
Quality of road surface
Quality of sewer
Quality of green area
Quality of play area
Security of public space
Appearance of public space
Shopping facility
Education facility
Social cultural provision
Social cultural provision-adolescence
Quality of structural greens
Quality of playground facilities
Safety at main access roads
Safety at residential roads
Noise disturbance
Parking facility
Environment disturbing activities
Influencing dwelling/non-dwelling
Need for professional support
Need for community work
Corresponding life style
Sense of insecurity
Image

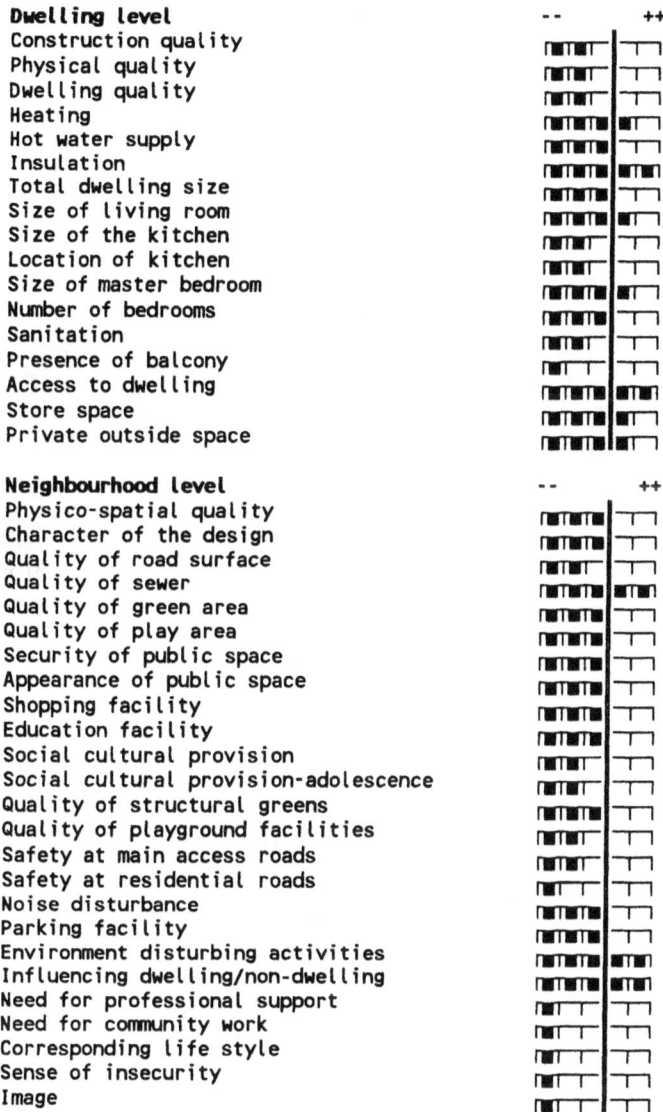

Fig. 14.2   Profile of a dwelling estate. (Source: Maussen and Smeets, 1993.)

house-moving motive than aspects concerning the neighbourhood. Additionally, on the level of the dwelling, 'total floor area', 'size of the master bedroom', 'number of bedrooms' and 'private outside space' are weighted extra heavily (factor 4). These characteristics appear to be of great importance for the house-moving motives according to the market research.

2. On the *building level*. Building quality aspects get a weighting factor 2. Here the quality of 'access' gets an extra weight (factor 2).
3. On the *level of the neighbourhood*. Neighbourhood quality aspects get a weighting factor 1. Here 'quality of road service', 'quality of playground provision', 'safety of public space', 'traffic safety' and 'sense of insecurity' get extra weight (factor 2). These points also appear to be mentioned relatively frequently as house-moving motives.

Here the point of departure is that if an estate has scored on all partial aspects, a 'performance level 3', then the HPR will be 1, whereby the standard score is the total of weighted scores at the quality level 3.

If on all partial aspects the minimum performance level is scored (total weighted scores minimum), then the score is 0.32. If on all partial aspects the maximum performance level 5 is scored (total weighted scores 590), then the score is 1.66.

This HPR can be compared with market and price technical data. By doing this, an insight may appear in the relationship among the market position, price and the delivered or offered product performance (Smeets, 1993).

Figure 14.3 shows the position matrix of the single-family houses of the housing association in Waalwijk. The estate 8.4, of which the profile is

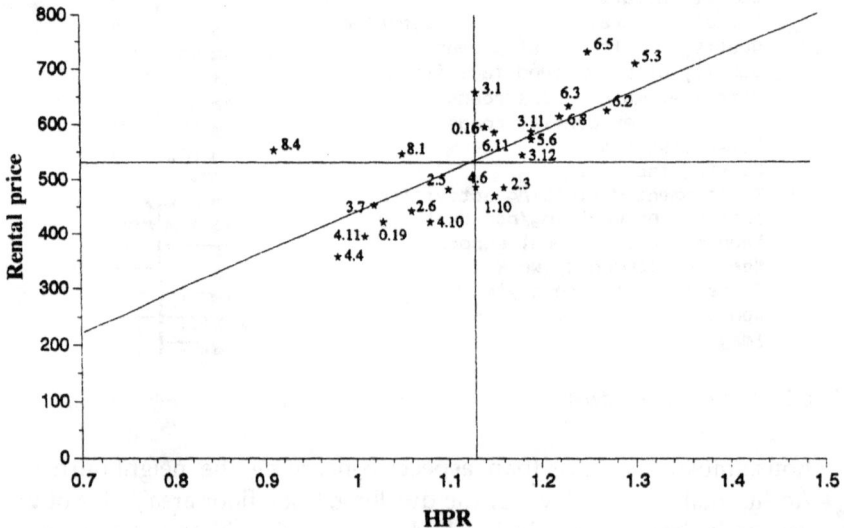

Fig. 14.3 Position matrix: single-family houses. (Source: Maussen and Smeets, 1993.)

shown in Figure 14.2, has an HPR of 0.91 and a rent of more than 500 guilders per month. This low performance can be attributed to the environmental characteristics (see also the estate profile in Fig. 14.2): the poor quality of playground facilities and road service, traffic 'unsafety' in residential roads and on access roads, insufficient social-cultural facilities, sense of insecurity and negative image. Additionally, on the dwelling level the size of the kitchen, position of the kitchen and the sanitary facilities scored low. Moreover, neighbourhood 8.4, of all neighbourhoods, has the shortest occupancy period.

DIFFERENTIATION ACCORDING TO TARGET GROUP

We have seen already that quality is determined by the degree to which the offered and demanded performances in the occupation phase are matched. The demanded performance, however, differs according to the occupant's group.

Research among tenants of tenant-housing in Etten-Leur shows that a correlation exists between supplied performance and appreciation. Even the 'soft' performances show such a correlation. For example, in the neighbourhoods that perform well in design and use of materials of the public space, a significantly higher percentage of dwellers appreciates the dwelling environment as 'attractive' or 'beautiful' rather than in neighbourhoods that perform only moderately in this particular aspect (Bladel-Oudijk and Pott, 1994).

This study also shows that the correlation between supplied performance and appreciation differs by target group. As for the aspects of vandalism and traffic safety, for example, two-person households over 35 years of age and households with young children are substantially more 'sensitive' than average. The majority of these target groups are only satisfied at a very high level of supplied performance.

To make this differentiation of the demand side manageable, suppliers of housing, for example, are increasingly working with target groups. Also these demands can be represented by profiles. These 'demand profiles' are different, depending on target group. The target groups differ in required level of performance, as well as in weight that they place on certain aspects.

In the research, target-group differentiation is realized which fits in the possibilities of building society operating at the site (Maussen, 1994). The differentiations are:

A. one- and two-person households of 18–24 years age group
   starter households
B. one- and two-person households of 25–34 years age group
C. one- and two-person households of 35–44 years age group

D. multi-person households of 18–34 years age group
  single-parent families
  families
E. multi-person households of 35–44 years age group
  single-parent families
  families
F. multi-person households of 45–54 years age group
  single-parent families
  families
G. one- and two-person households of 55–64 years age group
  seniors/empty-nesters
  more or less persons in need of care
H. one- and two-person households over 65 years age group
  seniors/elderly people
  persons in need of (intensive) nursing

During the matching operation the number of quality criteria are kept limited. Specifically, only those dwelling and housing characteristics are taken into account which are of decisive importance for the moving-house behaviour. Table 14.1 represents part of the demand profiles and Table 14.2 part of the applied weights.

Based on the matching operation of demand and supply, suitable product–market combinations (PMC) can be calculated. From this

Table 14.1 Part of the preference profiles according to target group

Assessment criteria	Target groups							
	A	B	C	D	E	F	G	H
Accessibility	1	1	1	4	4	4	1	1
Layout of dwelling	–	–	–	–	–	–	2	4
Interior finishing	3	3	4	3	4	4	4	4
Size of living room	2	2	4	4	4	4	3	3
Number of bedrooms	2	2	3	3	4	4	3	3

Table 14.2 Weighting factors according to target group

Assessment criteria	Target groups							
	A	B	C	D	E	F	G	H
Accessibility	3	3	5	5	5	5	5	5
Layout of dwelling	–	–	–	–	–	–	10	10
Interior finishing	3	5	5	5	5	5	5	5
Size of living room	5	5	10	10	10	10	10	10
Number of bedrooms	10	10	10	10	10	10	10	10

Source: Maussen (1994).

matching it appears clearly that this housing complex is more suitable for the target groups A, B and C than for the remaining target groups. The housing market research, however, shows that contrarily other target groups are over-represented.

IMPLEMENTATION

Housing and neighbourhood as a meso-scale contains four functions (Hortulanus, 1995):

- It is an area that is inhabited, used and experienced.
- It occupies a stipulated place in a hierarchy of neighbourhoods.
- It is a planning and administrative unit for the local authority and a frame for representation of interest of the residents.
- It represents a certain economic value.

The discussed method is related to the first three functions. First and foremost it 'visualizes' the problems and their variation in content and importance in relation to different types of inhabitants. Moreover it offers instruments for structuring the problem and the discrepancy between the present situation and desirable state, i.e. the goals (see also Arentz *et al.*, 1995).

The available information is of importance in strategic decision-making. Important elements of this method in the field of housing management and neighbourhood planning are the identification of target groups, the product–market combinations and the internal strength–weakness analysis. Especially in exercising the strength–weakness assessment and in constructing product–market combinations, the method is extremely useful.

Based on this analysis, strategic choices can be made. If necessary, the supplied and demanded performance can be brought up-to-date by 'reprogramming' the built environment on the meso-scale.

Construction and/or social measures, separately as well as in combination with each other, can then improve the relative position of the neighbourhood (Smeets, 1994). As a result of the study, measures have already been taken in neighbourhood 8.4. The allocation policy has been adjusted and a functional-spatial re-implementation has taken place. The correction possibilities on dwelling level, however, are very restricted.

Also the communication function of the performance concept is obvious. It makes quality negotiable. Specifically formulated performances prevent interpretation differences. In Waalwijk the results of the survey have served as a framework for discussions between the municipality and the corporations on the one hand and the neighbourhood tenants on the other.

So, working with the performance concept not only offers advantages in measuring the built environment, checking the standards for different target groups and determining possible interventions, but also benefits the communication between suppliers (managers) and users.

REFERENCES

Arentze, T., A. Borgers and H. Timmermans (1996) Design of a view-based DSS for location planning. *International Journal of Geographical Information Systems*, **2**, pp. 219–236.

Bladel-Oudijk, G.M. and M. Pott (1994) *Waarderingsonderzoek Woonstichting Etten-Leur*. Interface, Eindhoven.

Boekhorst, F. and J. Smeets (1990) *Naar een Kwaliteitsbesturingssysteem in het Kader van Strategisch Woningbeheer*. Stichting Instituut, Interface, Eindhoven.

Hortulanus, R. (1995) *Stadsbuurten. Een Studie over Bewoners en Beheerders in Buurten met Uiteenlopende Reputaties*. VUGA Uitgeverij, 's-Gravenhage.

Maussen, S. (1994) *Produktmarktcombinaties als instrument voor strategisch voortraadbeheer*, Technische Universiteit, Eindhoven.

Maussen, S. and J. Smeets (1993) *Woningmarktonderzoek Gemeente Waalwijk*, Deel 3: *Woningmarktpositie Woningcomplexen*. December.

Pott, M. and J. Smeets (1993) *Woningmarktonderzoek Gemeente Waalwijk*, Deel 1 en 2. Interface, Eindhoven.

Rapoport, A. (1989) Environmental quality and environmental quality profiles. In *Proceedings of Quality in the Built Environment Conference*, Open House International, July, pp. 75–83.

RGD (1992) *Rijksgebouwendienst: Rijksgebouwendienst-prestatiecontracten*. RGD, Directie Ontwerp & Techniek, Den Haag.

Smeets, J. (1993) Housing tenancy, data management and quality control. In Timmermans, H. (ed.), *Design and Decision Support Systems in Architecture*. Kluwer Academic Dordrecht, pp. 27–37.

Smeets, J., (1994) Strategisch woningbeheer en informatievoorziening. Instrumenten voor marktpositionering en ingreepplanning. In *Handboek Stedelijk Beheer*. VUGA Uitgeverij, 's-Gravenhage.

Stevens, R. (1994) Measuring occupancy performance of real estate with the REN-method. Paper at *2nd Design and Decision Support Systems in Architecture and Urban Planning*, Vaals, The Netherlands, August 15–19.

Design tools in an integrated CAD–GIS environment: space syntax as an example

15

Jan Teklenburg, Harry Timmermans and
Aloys Borgers

INTRODUCTION

At the intra-urban scale level, both urban designers and urban planners participate in the process of creating and maintaining the urban environment. This process is not straightforward in the sense that first planning agencies make their decisions and then, subsequently, designers shape the physical environment according to those decisions. The process is much more circular: planning decisions are affected by the existing urban form; designers create environments that may weaken or strengthen planning decisions; and subsequent planning decisions can weaken or strengthen the intentions of an urban design.

Although it is not possible to draw an exact line between planning and design (planners create 'designs', urban designs for large areas are sometimes as global as 'planning designs'), it is felt that urban design's major concern is with the *physical aspects of urban form*, i.e. the distribution of built forms and open spaces across an urban area. The focus of urban planning is much more on the *use of urban form*, i.e. the distribution of functions and actual behaviour of users across the urban area.

Communication between planners and designers is often a problem. For designers, it seems hard to relate the distribution of built forms and open spaces to its effect on the distribution of functions and actual behaviour of groups and individuals. The effects of the distribution of functions on the intentions of the design regarding the distribution of actual behaviour are not easily accessed by designers. On the other

Decision Support Systems in Urban Planning. Edited by Harry Timmermans. Published in 1997 by E & F N Spon. ISBN 0 419 21050 4

hand, planners often do not recognize the effect of the distribution of built forms and open spaces on (the distribution of) functions and actual behaviour. The problem of miscommunication seems to be adversely affected by the fact that designers and planners use different task environments. This is true even now that fast computer techniques have become readily available for both parties. Designers typically use computer-aided design (CAD) software, whereas planners focus on the use of geographical information systems (GIS). CAD is really a drawing and design aid. The emphasis is on *graphical* information and elements (points, lines, polylines, areas, three-dimensional modelling). GIS focus on spatial *data* and therefore much more on *topology* than on the underlying graphical information. CAD packages typically are poor in handling data, and GIS often have poor graphical interfaces. Because of the latter GIS are not very attractive to designers. And because of the poor data-handling capabilities CAD software is not attractive to planners.

In order to improve communication between designers and planners, both problems have to be accessed. It is necessary to develop languages or tools that address planners and designers alike. At the same time there is a need for some kind of integration of their distinct task environments. In an ideal situation, designers and planners would at least for some part use the same tools in an integrated task environment, thus being able to access each other's data and graphical information. In our opinion the quality of urban environments would benefit from an improved communication between the two parties.

This chapter is organized as follows. First, in the next section we focus on a common tool. There is hardly any need for an integrated task environment without the possibility of a common tool. We do not theoretically discuss the possibility of common tools, but propose a particular tool: *extended 'space syntax' models*. In the third section we discuss the architecture of integrated CAD–GIS environments. In the fourth section we focus on the implementation of a space syntax engine in a particular CAD–GIS environment provided by AutoCAD/AutoCAD Data Extension. The linking from this environment to the AutoCAD/ArcCAD and the ARC/INFO environment is discussed.

EXTENDED SPACE SYNTAX MODELS

The goal of space syntax models is to relate the description of urban morphology to actual behaviour, mostly movement. Fundamental to all models is the *graphical representation* of urban areas. In their original version (Hillier and Hanson, 1984, space syntax models only relate to the urban *morphology*. The extended models proposed in this chapter include the distribution of functions across an urban area. The link between morphology and functions is made through the graphical representation, which is the *axial map* of an urban area.

MORPHOLOGICAL MODELS

All space syntax models start with representing an urban area by its axial map. An axial map of an urban area is constructed in two steps. First, the total space of the area is divided into private (or non-public-accessible) space and public-accessible space. Secondly, in the public-accessible space the least set of the longest lines is drawn so that all spaces in the area are covered and every 'island' of private or non-public-accessible space is surrounded by lines. These lines are called *axial lines*. The set of axial lines is called the *axial map* of the urban area. Figure 15.1 shows two examples of the plan of an urban area and the corresponding axial map. (For a detailed description of the procedure, see Hillier (1989), Hillier and Hanson (1984), Hillier *et al.* (1987a, b) and Teklenburg *et al.* (1992, 1993b).) The space syntax axial map differs from other axial representations (e.g. Krafta, 1994) in that the construction of the map is less arbitrary, the map does not contain buildings nor built-form units, and the axial lines do not necessarily coincide with the pattern of streets and squares of the urban area (the second example in Fig. 15.1).

Having constructed the axial map, it is possible to compute centrality measures for each line of the axial map. These can be computed at: (i) the *local level*, the centrality of a line with regard to its intersecting lines; (ii) the *global level*, the centrality of a line with regard to all the other lines of the axial map; and (iii) the centrality of a line with regard to the *carrier space*, that is the urban fabric surrounding the study area.

Most researchers concentrate on centrality measures at the global level and relate these to pedestrian or vehicular traffic. Examples of measures at the global level based on smallest topological distances are 'real relative asymmetry' based on a diamond-root graph (Hillier and Hanson, 1984; Hillier *et al.*, 1987a), 'real relative asymmetry' based on a corner-of-a-grid graph (Krüger, 1989) and the 'integration score' (Teklenburg *et al.*, 1993b). These three measures have different values, but corresponding distributions across the lines of an axial map. A centrality measure at the global level based on shortest routes between all possible pairs of lines is 'choice' (Hillier *et al.*, 1987a; Peponis *et al.*, 1989). In fact 'choice' is a particular version of 'centrality' as proposed by Krafta (1994), with one built-form unit for each axial line. Krafta's 'centrality' differs from space syntax measures because of the inclusion of the number of built-form units and therewith elements of non-public space.

Now the hypothesis is that central urban spaces (represented by their axial line) have greater *accessibility*, and therefore will show greater numbers of people using those spaces. The use of a space is typically

Plan

Axial map

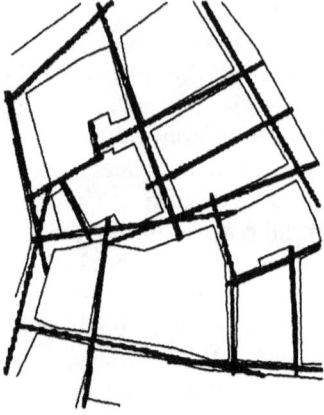

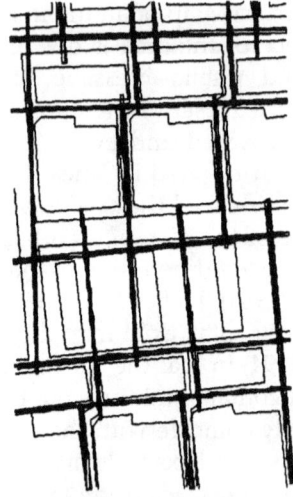

Example 1

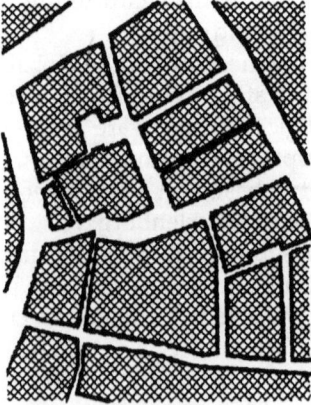

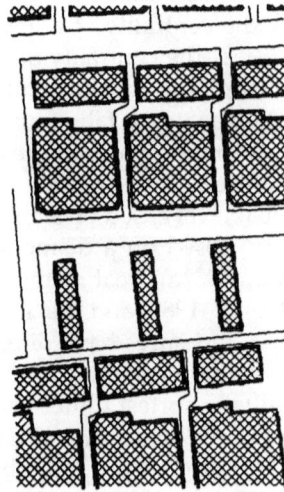

Example 2

Fig. 15.1   Construction of axial map.

measured by pedestrian movement. However, relating the above centrality measures to movement is troublesome because of (i) the effect of the surrounding urban fabric on movement within the area, and (ii) possible edge effects. The impact of the surrounding urban fabric affects the correlation between centrality and movement because it turns some axial lines (not necessarily the central ones) into supply points for pedestrian traffic. Because of the edge effect, axial lines near the edge of the study area may not be very central to the axial map of the study area, when in fact they are very central to the larger area of which the study area is a part. Generally these problems are solved by 'embedding' the study area: centrality measures are computed for a large area while the correlation with movement is researched for the 'core' of the larger area. Deciding on the size of the embedding area is cumbersome, and to date no general solution has been found. Krafta (1994) proposes the most systematic approach by deciding on the core area, and then embedding all lines that are directly connected to the core (one-step embedding), embedding all lines as close as two steps from the core (two-step embedding), and so forth. However, it is not clear whether this procedure will lead to some general conclusion on the number of steps that embedding should include.

For a number of reasons we prefer a different solution to this problem. We take a weighted sum of centrality measures at the different levels (local, global, carrier space), and relate this weighted sum to the use of public space (static and moving users). We reserve the word *integration* for such weighted sums. As integration measures include centrality towards the carrier space, the possible effect of the surrounding urban fabric on use within the area is covered. The same inclusion reduces the edge effects substantially. A further advantage of the integration concept is that different weights can be calibrated for different user groups. Very important is the possibility of easily extending integration measures by other (weighted) variables of axial lines, thus allowing for the *extended space syntax models* we will discuss in the next section. Now the equation for (not extended) integration measures typically takes the form:

$$R^{\text{user group}} = \beta_1(\text{local centrality}) + \beta_2(\text{global centrality}) + \beta_3(\text{carrier space})$$
(15.1)

Table 15.1 summarizes the correlation coefficients of a number of centrality/integration measures against movement (or use). Except for $R^{\text{vehicular}}$ (which refers to privately used motor cars), the centrality/integration measures are related to pedestrian movement. The ranking value (an integration measure with weights based on theoretical considerations about the influence of the carrier space, cf. Teklenburg *et al.* (1992), R^{adults} and R^{children} include bicyclists. The weights of the $R^{\text{user group}}$ integration measures are calibrated over a large number of Dutch neighbourhoods.

Table 15.1 Performance of integration/centrality measures against movement

Measure	Study	Correlation	Notes	Data collection
Integration score	24 Dutch neighbourhoods	0.43[1]		Moving observer
Ranking value	24 Dutch neighbourhoods	0.44[1]	[1]Mean 24 areas	Stratified sample; random within strata; covering whole length of lines; observations in two directions; moving and static users
R^{adults}	24 Dutch neighbourhoods	0.46[1]		
$R^{vehicular}$	23 Dutch neighbourhoods	0.52[2]	[2]Mean 23 areas	Spearman's r
$R^{children}$	12 Dutch neighbourhoods	0.30[3]	[3]Mean 12 areas	
Real relative asymmetry	Hillier et al. (1993)	0.49[4]	[4]King's Cross movement	Moving observer
		0.74[5]	[5]King's Cross log movement	Non-random sample; mix of integrated and segregated lines; covering lines partially; observations in one direction; moving users
		0.54[6]	[6]City of London log movement [4-6]Embedded by not systematically defined catchment area	
	Peponis et al. (1989)	0.70[7]	[7]Sub-areas embedded	
		0.64[8]	[8]Whole towns	
		0.50[9]	[9]Sub-areas not embedded [7-9]Mean multiple areas, square root movement	Pearson's r
Choice	Peponis et al. (1989)	0.48[10]	[10]Mean of table 3, pp 52–53, square roots of choice and movement	
Centrality	Krafta (1994)	0.82[11]	[11]Mean four areas, two-step embedding	Pearson's r
		0.51[12]	[12]No embedding	
		0.73[13]	[13]One-step embedding	
		0.75[14]	[14]Two-step embedding	
		0.71[15]	[15]Three-step embedding [12-15]Single area	

The table shows that, when areas are not embedded, most measures give similar results. Embedding seems to improve correlations, but as there is no general solution for the problem of how many steps embedding should include, one cannot be sure that this improvement is due to morphological characteristics or to features special to the area (such as the distribution of functions). It should be mentioned that Krafta's 'centrality' measure includes built-form units, and therewith (in a very rudimentary way) references the functional layout of the urban areas.

When looking at the distribution of integration measures across an axial map, it is possible to decide on the most accessible spaces (for a particular user group). In new developments, functions (like retailing) or other attractors can be planned along these spaces, thus strengthening the relationship between accessibility because of the layout and attractiveness because of the distribution of functions across the area. In existing areas the fit or misfit between layout and distribution of functions can be examined. This might give directions for further development. Morphological space syntax models can handle changes in layout very well (it is easy to manipulate an axial map); they have major problems however with changes in the distribution of functions. A change in distribution of functions does not affect integration measures. Moreover, when one needs to assess not only accessibility or attractiveness, but also real changes in use because of changes in layout or distribution of functions, we need models with better predictive quality. We expect that including elements of the distribution of functions in space syntax models will lead to such improvement.

INCLUDING DISTRIBUTION OF FUNCTIONS

The relation between morphological accessibility, pedestrian movement and presence or location of shops is the topic of a number of studies. Peponis *et al.* (1989) found that in a number of Greek towns correlations between centrality measures and pedestrian movement tend to be better when shops are open in 26 out of 42 areas. In the remaining areas correlations tended to decline with shops open. Out of 32 areas centrality measures at the global level outperform measures at the local level when shops are open in 13 areas (against the local measures showing stronger correlations when shops are closed), the remaining cases showing no difference for shops open or closed. They also found that the orientation of sub-areas, as can be seen by pedestrian movement, towards the 'whole town' is not affected by shops being open or closed. These are indications that morphological accessibility is an important contributor to movement patterns. They do not give insight however into the relationships between centrality measures and distribution of shops. Hillier *et al.* (1993) found that in most cases the logarithm of movement results in better correlations between movement and centrality measures. It appears that precisely the lines with shops adjacent to them show very high movement rates and are responsible for the outliers in the correlation analysis. When these 'shopping lines' are excluded, not taking the logarithm of movement gives about the same result as taking the logarithm and including the 'shopping lines' (Hillier *et al.*, 1993). In our opinion, on the one hand this indicates strong evidence for the attractor function of shops, and on the other hand (as precisely the lines with shops allocated to them are responsible for the outliers) it means that there is no linear relationship between the location of shops and centrality measures. In a study in a Dutch town centre (Teklenburg *et al.*, 1993a) it was found that the axial lines with the highest integration values do not necessarily coincide with the distribution of shops. It is shown that, at least in this case, the pattern of pedestrian flows coincides much more with the location of shops than with the integration values.

These studies provide evidence for the attractor function of shops. We hypothesize that this attractor function extends to all possible functions in an urban area. Including the distribution of functions in space syntax models might very well improve their predictive quality with regard to movement. On the other hand, this inclusion affects the match–mismatch analysis provided by the morphological models. Thus a strong distinction has to be made between the morphological and the extended models. Morphological models are appropriate for analysis of layouts of urban areas, their match with distribution of functions or the potential of public spaces for allocating functions to them. The major advantage of morphological models is the possibility of analysing the effects of *changes in layout*, which can be done by manipulation of the axial map. These models are powerful tools for urban designers, and can be used by location planners in their first search for possible locations. City planners can make good use of the match–mismatch analysis when looking for directions of further urban development. In subsequent planning phases, when changes in layout are no longer an option and decisions have to be made on the exact locations of particular functions, the stronger predictive quality of the extended models provides a tool to location planners in their search for optimal locations. This difference in planning phase coincides with information available on the distribution and nature of the functions in an urban area. In the more global phase, when morphological models are appropriate, decisions on distribution and nature of functions are global and intentional. In subsequent planning phases the decisions get more into detail, and the extended models become more relevant.

The use of space syntax as a design and planning tool is really augmented by the extension of the original morphological models. It offers a tool for designers and planners in subsequent planning and design phases. It offers *the same tool* to planners and designers. This can enhance communication between both parties, making designers more aware of the impact of the effects of the distribution of functions on the use that will be made of their design, and at the same time making planners more aware of the influence of urban morphology on the potentials for distributing functions across an area and on the actual behaviour in that area.

Planners and designers share the same axial map, and both have access to the functional layout of an area, when this functional layout is related to the lines of the axial map.

Krafta (1994) uses built forms as a proxy of attractors. His model can be seen as a first extension of space syntax with the effect of the uneven distribution of functions across an area. Such an extension, however, is not sufficient to fulfil the needs of a design tool that addresses both designers and planners, as it does not offer the possibility of entering detailed information about the nature and distribution of functions in the detailed planning phase. Therefore we prefer to weigh axial lines for functions that are allocated to them. A major advantage of putting weights on axial lines is that these weights can be calibrated by taking use (or movement) as dependent, and functions and integration (or centrality) measures as independent variables. Now equations for the integration value typically take the form:

$$R^{\text{function}}_{\text{user group}} = \gamma_1 \left(R^{\text{user group}}\right) + \gamma_2 \left(\text{function 1}\right) + ... + \gamma_n \left(\text{function } n - 1\right) \quad (15.2)$$

Different parties in the process of urban planning and design may wish to use different space syntax models, appropriate to their specific needs and the specific planning and design phase they are working at. They may wish to use models based on integration measures, or models based on centrality measures. They may wish to use different weights for functions, include or exclude certain types of functions. As information in subsequent planning phases differs, the global or detailed character of the information available should be addressed in the choice of a particular model. This means that any implementation of space syntax models has to be open-ended and should include a module in which the users can specify the model they wish to use. The open-ended character is fundamental to the goal of space syntax models: to serve as a design and planning tool that addresses designers and planners alike, and therewith enhances communication between the parties involved in the process of urban planning and design.

There is a practical advantage in implementing extended space syntax models in existing software, which is already in use with the parties involved in the process of urban planning and design. Designers typically use CAD software, whereas planners focus on GIS. It would favour the use of space syntax models if they are implemented in an environment that addresses both CAD and GIS. Recent developments in integrated CAD–GIS environments offer such a possibility.

INTEGRATED CAD–GIS ENVIRONMENTS

The integration of CAD and GIS is not always achieved by integrating the software. Schuur (1994) shows an example of an integration of CAD and GIS in a planning laboratory setting, which basically consists of two connected workstations, one for CAD and one for GIS. The idea behind this is that CAD (design, conceptual thinking) and GIS (analysis, analytical thinking) skills and expertise are found in different persons, and that these persons should communicate. The integration of both systems consists of the output of a design process being the input of a GIS analysis and vice versa. This way plan-making is a spiralling process of alternating analytical and design phases. This type of integration is shown to be appropriate when one single agency, including designers and planners alike, is involved in the plan-making process. It does not seem very suitable, however, when more than one planning and/or design agency is involved. When intra-urban development is at stake, in most cities the latter is the case. The opposite, a single, integrated 'plan-making system', does not seem attractive either. The advantages of a flexible, modular tool environment should be preserved.

Dave and Schmitt (1994) show an example of a modular tool environment. They use an existing CAD (AutoCAD) as the graphical interface for their system. This discharges them from maintaining a graphical database, which is taken care of by the CAD. They prefer to extend the CAD with a database-representation scheme and database-query operators over the use of a GIS, as GIS are appropriate for two-dimensional data that do not change much over time, but do not support three-dimensional modelling and efficient handling of data that can change rapidly. The system they propose contains three modules: (i) a graphical database (the CAD), (ii) a database and (iii) a data-query. The advantage of the system is that the *flexibility* of the CAD is maintained fully, while on the other hand drawing and spatial data are combined, thus allowing some kind of analysis in the design process. However, as both the database and the data-query are specific to their application, the system seems appropriate for a single design agency, but does not allow easy exchange of spatial and graphical data with other design and planning agencies. Such a system does not fundamentally enhance communication between parties in the process of urban planning and design.

Designers need the advances of a CAD, but may not need all of the analytical tools provided by the GIS. On the other hand planners may use the analytical tools of the GIS, but have little need for the possibilities offered by a CAD graphical database. The extra costs of a GIS may be too large for designers who do not make full use of the analytical tools provided by it. They would be satisfied with the GIS database, and a simple program making it possible to connect this database to their drawings. Planners who do not really need the sophisticated graphical interface of a CAD (and do not want to pay the extra costs for it) would be satisfied

with a simple program allowing them to read in the graphical information after it has been changed by a design agency. This calls for an architecture of the integrated CAD–GIS environment that contains four
modules: (i) the CAD, which provides a graphical database and drawing
tools; (ii) the GIS database, which should preferably have the possibility to
be accessed by a 'standard' database program, as in that case designers do
not need to buy a GIS in order to manipulate the record themes (i.e. entity
properties) of the GIS database; (iii) the GIS analytical toolkit, available to
planning agencies; and (iv) a module that interconnects the three modules
mentioned above – we call such interconnecting modules *engines*.

Before we discuss the architecture of such engines, we have to address
the problem of lacking flexibility in traditional geo-relational GIS. The
problem in these GIS is that the topology which is needed to connect
graphical information (like lines, points, areas) to spatial data is a static
representation of spatial relationships at a moment in time (Owen, 1993).
When graphical information changes, the cumbersome process of building the topology has to be repeated, the overlaying of layers has to be
redone, and queries and calculations have to be re-executed. The procedures that must be followed to perform analytical studies have always
been dictated by the functionality of the GIS (Owen, 1993) and not by the
nature of the problem at hand. For these reasons, users of GIS feel the
need for more flexibility. There is a need for *dynamic* GIS. A number of
authors propose object-oriented GIS for this purpose (Boursier and Faiz,
1993; ter Haar, 1993; Owen, 1993). Graphical and spatial data should no
longer be stored in separate databases, but in one object-oriented database. At the same time flexibility of GIS should be enhanced by using on-
line topology and dynamic function triggers (ter Haar, 1993; Owen, 1993).
This means that changes in graphical information results in the automatic
execution of a number of functions like automated rebuilding of topology,
automated overlaying of layers and automated re-execution of queries.

To maintain the flexibility of CAD, the integration of CAD and GIS
calls for dynamic GIS. The call for dynamic systems becomes even
stronger when shared tools like space syntax are considered. In a traditional geo-relational GIS one of the major advantages of space syntax
models, the ease of manipulating the axial map, would become practically impossible. Unfortunately dynamic (object-oriented) GIS are not yet
commercially available. The same is true for reliable object-oriented database software.

The solution to make the interconnecting *engine* dynamic has major
advantages. Parties in an integrated CAD–GIS environment are not
obliged to wait for dynamic systems to become available, but can still use
the traditional CAD, GIS and a relational database. The new software is
the interconnecting engine. By implementing the common tools (like the
extended space syntax models) in dedicated GIS that perform the engine

function, extra costs would be minimized. The use of the common tool provides the different parties in the process of urban planning and design with the dynamic interface which is needed to really enhance communication.

A further advantage of a modular architecture based on an interconnecting, dynamic engine containing common tools is that full CAD and GIS functionality is maintained. In a space syntax context this means that in the CAD environment three-dimensional designs can be constructed on top of the two-dimensional space syntax analysis. In the GIS environment, the results of space syntax analysis can be overlaid on thematic maps or other GIS analysis.

The implementation of a dynamic space syntax engine still faces major problems. To be dynamic the engine needs its own database management, while using the graphical CAD database, the GIS relational database and the GIS topology as input. Changes in graphical information have to trigger changes in the relational database and the GIS topology. Changes in the relational database have to be reflected on the drawing database, and have to trigger re-execution of, at least a part of, the overlays and the queries. It does not seem a good idea to have all these triggers function without any intervention by the user of the system. The interface of the engine should include the possibility of user decision on the triggers to be executed, save or discard data and/or topology from earlier analysis. At the beginning of each session, the user will have to answer questions about what drawing, what database and what topology should be used as input to the engine. At the closing of each session, it should be possible to save information to user-defined drawing, database and topology. The same possibility should, as the user wishes, be offered while a session is in progress. A solution has still to be found to what kind of files should be needed to transport information from one party to another. At least it is clear that the information files, when the space syntax engine is available, should be capable of triggering functions in separate CAD, GIS and relational databases.

IMPLEMENTATION IN AN AutoCAD/ADE ENVIRONMENT

As interconnecting engines have to update drawing databases, relational databases, GIS topology, overlays and queries, they cannot be software-independent. In our research we focus on AutoCAD for the CAD module, ARC/INFO for the GIS module, and dBASE for the relational database module. Using these three software environments has major advantages. The use of AutoCAD in computer-aided design is widespread. AutoCAD offers excellent possibilities of writing extended applications, thus making the graphical database accessible to non-AutoCAD functions and software. We prefer the use of AutoCAD Development

System over the use of AutoLISP, as the first is a C-language and can be used to communicate with GIS and database software. AutoLISP is a programming language designed especially for communication with the AutoCAD graphical database, and lacks the universal nature of the C-language. By using AutoCAD Data Extension (ADE) it becomes possible to link external databases to an AutoCAD graphical database. Sometimes the AutoCAD/ADE combination is considered a fully equipped GIS in itself (Wittreich, 1995), but its analytical tools are restricted to editing (internal and external) databases, overlay analysis and buffering. Even more, the AutoCAD/ADE combination links *graphical* entities to data (there is no topology) and lacks clean and build functions. A major advantage of the AutoCAD/ADE combination is that a number of graphical databases can be queried simultaneously, thus making AutoCAD drawings smaller and easier to organize. Transport of drawing files, when exchange of data between different parties in urban planning and design is needed, can be kept to a minimum.

ARC/INFO is a widely used GIS, and available in a PC version. Its record themes are stored in dBASE-compatible files, thus making them accessible to the AutoCAD/ADE combination. Some users may prefer the AutoCAD/ArcCAD combination over the use of ARC/INFO, as this gives direct access to a number of ARC/INFO functions in an AutoCAD drawing environment. In fact ArcCAD is an ARC/INFO-compatible GIS using the AutoCAD graphical database and the AutoCAD user interface. ArcCAD GIS coverages are completely interchangeable with ARC/INFO coverages.

ADE can handle a number of relational database formats. But as both ARC/INFO and ArcCAD store their record themes in dBASE-compatible files, the choice for dBASE as the relational database module becomes inevitable. The dBASE file format may be considered the standard for relational database management, and most software packages can handle this type of file.

The space syntax engine contains four modules: (i) the object-oriented, dynamic database; (ii) the space syntax definition module; (iii) the (user-interfaced) dynamic trigger module; and (iv) the overall user interface.

The space syntax engine uses its own, temporary database. This database is dynamically defined and object-oriented. It is input from the graphical database, the relational database and the GIS coverage files. Each of these (or a combination) can be replaced by transport files, which contain both data and dynamic triggers. At user-defined moments the information from the dynamic database is updated to the graphical database, relational database, the GIS coverage files and/or transport files. At this time the dynamic trigger module performs a number of update functions automatically. Some other functions will be executed when user-defined and interfaced. The temporary database contains the lines of the axial map as objects. Centrality measures (computed at the first input of the axial map) are attributes of the objects. The computation is re-executed automatically when the user makes changes to the axial map. If the user has indicated the relationship of the axial map to the carrier space, and has defined a specific space syntax model, $R^{user\ group}$ integration measures are computed (with automatic triggered re-execution) as well. The user can define functions connected to the lines. The functions are defined as attributes of the objects. The definition may vary from global (demand location–supply location) to detailed (e.g. type of function, floor space). The definitions can be read in from the relational database, or entered using the overall space syntax interface. When function definitions are entered, and the user has specified a specific space syntax model, $R^{user\ group/function}$ are computed as attributes of the objects. Re-execution of the computations when the axial map is manipulated and/or function definitions are changed is user-interfaced. The temporary database should also have the possibility to contain building blocks and street sections as objects. The distribution of functions and the functions themselves are attributes of these objects. This second type of object can be related to the first type (axial lines). This process is user-interfaced and can be used instead of the direct function definition of axial lines, thus making data management more flexible.

The dynamic trigger module has two functions: (i) the update to the databases mentioned in the above paragraph, and (ii) the automated or user-interfaced execution of updating the dynamic database when changes in the graphical data urges rebuilding of topology. This module keeps track of topology and interacts with the GIS coverage files (or their transport file replacement).

The space syntax definition module affords the definition of the space syntax model that should be used for the analysis. In this module the user decides on the graphical elements to be used (construction of the axial map). The axial map can be read in from the graphical database, a GIS coverage file or constructed using the CAD. The module affords the definition of centrality or integration measures (including weights for each centrality level). How the information about the distribution of functions should be connected to the axial map, and what functions in what detail to include, is user-defined. The space syntax definition module is the main interface between user, temporary database, CAD, GIS and relational database.

The overall user interface will be implemented in two ways. First, the user interface is a *separate* module which links (when available) the CAD, the database files, the GIS coverage files and the GIS. From this interface it is possible to access (and interchange between) the CAD, the GIS and the three modules of the space syntax engine. Secondly, the interface is *within* the AutoCAD/ADE environment. This interface operates on graphical database and relational database. There is no need for the database program to be present. The interface uses AutoCAD and ADE procedures and functions as much as possible, adding a number of functions needed to perform space syntax analysis and export ARC/INFO-compatible GIS coverages. The latter requires that clean and build functions are implemented in this second interface. This second interface is much more software-dependent than the first one, but gives parties using only AutoCAD/ADE faster access to the space syntax engine. Because of the restricted analytical tools in the AutoCAD/ADE environment, we consider this of major importance.

CONCLUSION

This chapter proposes the use of common planning and design tools in an integrated CAD–GIS environment. It is shown that extended space syntax models have strong possibilities of enhancing communication between different parties in the process of urban planning and design. To allow common use of the tool we suggest connecting CAD and GIS by dynamic interfaces called *engines*. An architecture for such a space syntax engine in the AutoCAD/AutoCAD Data Extension environment with links to AutoCAD/ArcCAD and ARC/INFO environments is developed.

ACKNOWLEDGEMENT

This research is supported by the Technology Foundation (STW). AutoCAD®, AutoLISP®, AutoCAD Development System™ and AutoCAD Data Extension™ are (registered) trademarks of Autodesk Inc. ArcCAD™ and ARC/INFO® are (registered) trademarks of Environmental Systems Research Institute Ltd. dBASE® is a registered trademark of Ashton Tate, a division of Borland International Inc.

REFERENCES

Boursier, P. and S. Faiz (1993) A Comparative Study of Relational, Extensible and Object-Oriented Approaches for Modelling and Querying Geographic Databases. In Harts, J., Ottens, H.F.L. and Scholten, H.J. (eds), *EGIS '93, Conference Proceedings, Fourth European Conference and Exhibition on Geographical Information Systems*, Genoa, Italy, March 29 – April 1, EGIS Foundation, Amsterdam, pp. 764–772.

Dave, B. and G. Schmitt (1994) Information Systems for Urban Analysis and Design Development *Environment and Planning B: Planning and Design* 21, pp. 83–96.

Hillier, B. (1989) The Architecture of the Urban Object. *Ekistics* 56, No. 334/335, pp. 5–21.

Hillier, B. and J. Hanson (1984) *The Social Logic of Space.* Cambridge University Press, Cambridge.

Hillier, B., R. Burdett, J. Peponis and A. Penn (1987a) Creating Live, Or, Does Architecture Determine Anything. *Architecture and Behaviour* 3, pp. 233–250.

Hillier, B., J. Hanson and J. Peponis (1987b) Syntactic Analysis of Settlements. *Architecture and Behaviour* 3, pp. 217–231.

Hillier, B., A. Penn, J. Hanson, T. Grajewski and J. Xu (1993) Natural Movement: Or, Configuration and Attraction in Urban Pedestrian Movement. *Environment and Planning B: Planning and Design* 20, pp. 29–66.

Krafta, R. (1994) Modelling Intraurban Configurational Development. *Environment and Planning B: Planning and Design* 21, pp. 67–82.

Krüger, M.J.T. (1989) On Node and Axial Grid Maps: Distance Measures and Related Topics, *European Conference on Management and Representation of Urban Change*, Cambridge, UK.

Owen, P.K. (1993) Dynamic Function Triggers in an On-Line Topology Environment. In Harts, J., Ottens, H.F.L. and Scholten H.J. (eds), *EGIS '93, Conference Proceedings, Fourth European Conference and Exhibition on Geographical Information Systems*, Genoa, Italy, March 29–April 1, EGIS Foundation, Amsterdam, pp. 1249–1256.

Peponis, J., E. Hadjinikolaou, C. Livieratos and D.A. Fatouros (1989) The Spatial Core of Urban Culture. *Ekistics* 56, No. 334/335, pp. 43–55.

Schuur, J. (1994) Analysis and Design in Computer-Aided Physical Planning. *Environment and Planning B: Planning and Design* 21, pp. 97–108.

Teklenburg, J.A.F, H.J.P. Timmermans and A.F. van Wagenberg (1992) The Distribution of Use of Public Space in Urban Areas. In Gross, M.D. and Arias E.G. (eds), *Equitable and Sustainable Habitats, Proceedings of the 23th Annual Conference of the Environmental Design Research Association*, pp. 56–65.

Teklenburg, J.A.F, H.J.P. Timmermans and A.W.J. Borgers (1993a) Changes in Urban Layout and Pedestrian Flows. In *Environmental Issues, Proceedings of Seminar A held at the PTRC Transport, Highways and Planning Summer Annual Meeting*, University of Manchester Institute of Science and Technology, 13–17 September. PTRC Education and Research Services, London, pp. 97–108.

Teklenburg, J.A.F, H.J.P. Timmermans and A.F. van Wagenberg (1993b) Space Syntax: Standardised Integration Measures and Some Simulations. *Environment and Planning B: Planning and Design* 20, pp. 347–357.

ter Haar, P.W. (1993) Dynamic Analysis for Dynamic Problem. In Harts, J., Ottens, H.F.L. and Scholten, H.J. (eds), *EGIS '93, Conference Proceedings, Fourth European Conference and Exhibition on Geographical Information Systems*, Genoa, Italy, March 29 – April 1, EGIS Foundation, Amsterdam, pp. 746–753.

Wittreich, W.P. (1995) Is the AutoCAD Data Extension a GIS? *GIS World* 8, No. 5, p. 30.

Three-dimensional CAAD modelling: technical constraints and local planning attributes as parameters for conceptual design support and evaluation

16

Ashraf Ismail and Kevin McCartney

INTRODUCTION

It is essential to distinguish between computer-aided design (CAD) and computer-aided architectural design (CAAD), in particular when discussing issues related to the domains of urban or local planning. CAD is scarcely used in the planning departments of the local planning authorities (LPAs) in the UK in the form of GIS (Ismail, 1995b). This is evident in the design and local planning process, where computerization has not taken place. Such packages do not provide the full range of 2D and 3D functions to accommodate visualization. There has been an expressed demand for the utilization of CAAD in those departments to explore visualization techniques in conjunction with the GIS. Contemporary academic research, which involves the domain of urban or local planning and CAAD, continues to over-exploit the qualitative aspects of visualization: exploring rendering techniques, animation, perception, recognition

Decision Support Systems in Urban Planning. Edited by Harry Timmermans. Published in 1997 by E & F N Spon. ISBN 0 419 21050 4

and description of existing or historical structures. This is expressed in the application of ready-made CAAD software packages, which are often explored beyond their limits.

This chapter describes research that explores the 3D-CAAD models to assist in managing the urban built environment and evaluating the conceptual design based upon quantitative and qualitative parameters. There are two assumptions that have been tested and validated. First, there is a structured pattern for generating complex models that would require modelling support based upon technical 'constraints'. Secondly, a model can be used for conceptual design evaluation and decision support based upon a set of parameters (i.e. objects' attributes), identified from the local planning practice in the UK. As a result of the analysis and testing of various modelling case studies, a theoretical framework was developed, namely the '3D-CAD Modelling Paradigm', which consists of three distinguishable components: (i) implementation, (ii) validation, and (iii) modelling process. The paradigm is also a practical framework for managing the process of developing 'product' and 'target' models (Ismail, 1995a). Moreover, this chapter expands on the paradigm and elaborates on the concepts of modelling and decision support. Two prototypes are presented here, the Modelling Shell and DS-CAAD, to illustrate a possible application of the parameters. The prime concern of this chapter is to demonstrate the process of parametrization, which is part of the 'implementation' as described in the 3D-CAD modelling paradigm (Ismail, 1995b).

MODELLING AND THE TECHNICAL CONSTRAINTS

Modelling exercises were carried out to establish the structural pattern of generating complex models. These differed in scale, from small objects to large urban models, which contained different levels of detail. The results revealed that any assumed functional and complex model should be developed according to appropriate aims, objectives and practical modelling process. The completed modelling work focused on the practical aspects of modelling and defined eight fundamental parts (Ismail, 1995c). These are listed here as follows:

1. Abstraction; to establish a framework and protocol.
2. The product model; to conceptualize the role of final model.
3. Procedural refinement; to assess the abstraction and conceptualization.
4. Model and components' hierarchy; to define a detailed framework for components.
5. Performance; to evaluate the adopted procedures and the model role.
6. Logical data exchange; to consider their aspects.
7. Information transfer; to prepare a plan.
8. Front-end users; to reconsider their needs.

Apart from the eight fundamentals that influence the process of modelling, there are other technical or logical factors that have significance on the quality of result (i.e. product models). Those factors or 'constraints' could be utilized to provide modelling support. This is to assist the novice users and the decision-makers during or even prior to the development of models. It is assumed that the interaction between the modelling 'constraints' could suggest the possibilities of achieving the required models. However, users should be aware of the modelling process to assess such possibilities of achieving a 'target' or a 'product' model. Table 16.1 lists the constraints together with their means of measurement or description. They are described in more detail below.

Model form

The complexity of a model is identified according to its presumed functions. There has to be a general awareness of the modelling criteria (i.e. the reasons for modelling) to determine the objectives. Once these are defined, it should be possible to select a model form that corresponds to the suggested aim.

Model type

If this modelling constraint is to be used for support, novice users must be able to differentiate between the suitability of every type and comprehend their limitations. Since this requires a special expertise, the support should incorporate advice on different modelling types available to the enquirer. For example, preference could be expressed in pursuing a complex model accompanied by high quality of rendering output. As a result

Table 16.1 Technical or logical parameters for modelling support

Constraints	Measurement and/or description
1. Model form	Blocks, detailed and complex
2. Model type	Wire, solid, rendered, animated, real time, etc.
3. Model size	Object, building, site and urban.
4. Time (for modelling and resources)	Hour, day, week, etc., and number of available users
5. Processor speed	MHz, compatibility test with modelling (co-processors)
6. RAM (hardware memory)	MByte, efficiency for handling the required modelling
7. Storage capacity (hardware memory)	MByte, GByte, availability for holding large models
8. Swap file (application memory)	MByte, GByte, availability for background processing
9. Modelling applications	Flags (method of searching for the applications)
10. Platform	Flags (methods of searching for operating systems)

of the interaction of the prescribed modelling constraints in the Modelling Shell, the user could be informed about the limitations of achieving such a model. The support could then be strengthened in the form of suggestions. In this case, the user may re-evaluate his or her needs and probably be satisfied with a smaller scale of model, less rendering quality, or a combination of similar alternatives. In this case, he or she should be able to determine which of these suggestions are nearest to the objectives. Therefore, the user's knowledge is important in defining the modelling objectives.

Model size

Novice users tend to be over-ambitious in defining the size of models. Their initial goals are often never achieved, not due to their lack of creativity, but as a result of technical incompetence. They tend to carry out modelling tasks irresponsibly to achieve the so-called large or complex model. Then, they discover that it cannot be achieved due to some technical limitations (i.e. processor speed or the technique adopted for constructing the model). Understanding the model size as a modelling 'constraint' does not necessarily mean the visually perceived size (i.e. small, medium, large, etc.) or judging it by its file size in bytes. It encompasses understanding of modelling 'optimization' by carefully selecting the appropriate entities and resourcefully constructing the model's components. For example, 'abstraction' and 'the hierarchical composition' of a model should provide typological information to indicate objects' dependences. Therefore, the modelling paradigm provides a framework to assist the users in defining the requirements of the 'target' model. Consequently, the user would be better informed when selecting an alternative model size.

Time

This is a comprehensive management tool and pertains to the organization of human resources. A senior decision-maker, with partial knowledge of modelling, should be able to make informed decisions about the possibilities of constructing a model within a given timescale, based either upon the client's brief or upon his or her own tacit knowledge. A number of options should be available. Therefore, the timescale would require interaction with other parameters such as: number of users, number of available modelling applications and their platform, and the model's information (form, type and size).

Processor speed

The speed influences the modelling process and the performance of any sizable model. It is possible to predict the performance of the final model.

However, some users do not have the privilege of making such decisions, usually proven wrong, resulting in an 'idle model'. They need to be supported before engaging in the modelling tasks. Consequently, a number of problems have to be resolved: If the processor speed can support the modelling process, would it be possible to manipulate the requested model? If not, would a different size or form of model be sufficient to fulfil the modelling criteria? The user has to assess these predicaments.

Hardware and software memory

Users need to be informed about the hardware and software configurations to support their modelling tasks. Needless complications often hinder the modelling process due to the lack of sufficient hardware memory or incorrect configuration, resulting in data loss. The support should aim at preventing any mishaps and should run concurrently with the modelling tasks. Such information should be presented in a user-friendly format. Concurrence is vital to assist the user in monitoring the process of modelling and during configuration of the modelling environment as and when needed, not as a result of system failure.

Modelling application and platform

Novice users tend to select modelling applications based upon personal preferences. On the contrary, the choice should be made based upon the objectives of modelling. The required support would be beneficial if a variety of modelling applications reside on a number of modelling systems. The decision-maker should be able to consult the Modelling Shell about the availability of applications that can fulfil the formerly defined objectives. The feedback should indicate analysis representing the status of the modelling application(s): availability and suitability. The Modelling Shell would need to interact with all the above modelling constraints to provide the assumed performance.

The former description of the modelling process and constraints gives an indication of the type of support envisaged in a technically oriented modelling support application. Three different users could benefit from such application: the decision-maker, novice and expert users. A later section of this chapter describes the prototype and suggests an approach for the interaction of the constraints.

A PRAGMATIC APPROACH TO LOCAL PLANNING

This section outlines the role of modelling for a specific domain. It was assumed that, in producing 3D-CAAD models to implement evaluation and support during the process of development of a conceptual design, a number of parameters need to be identified. It is suggested here that the appropriate evaluation should not solely be devoted to the visual analysis. Initial stages of evaluation could be based upon the legislative and other physical (quantifiable) measures found at the local planning scale and, in particular, in supplementary planning guidance (SPG).

There are reasons for adopting this approach. First, architects are not only responsible to their clients, nor can they alone determine the type of development to be constructed at a particular site. Secondly, their design proposals submitted are scrutinized by the local planning authorities (LPAs) appointed to safeguard the community interest and the built environment. Thirdly, part of the planners' analysis is to ensure compliance with rules and regulations. These are described and illustrated in statutory and non-statutory documents, respectively, devised to inform and regulate the planners as well as the architects. Therefore, it was decided and argued that the parameters for conceptual design evaluation are better identified from local planning practice, rather than relying solely on the architects' design vocabulary, which is limited to personalized interpretations often biased towards some aesthetic considerations. The question of the suitability of SPG for provision of design information and the effectiveness of SPGs as guidance documents have been considered for critical examination in the research. The process of building design can be a tedious task, let alone the complexities of its computerization, especially the process of obtaining planning permission or building approval. Even with an experienced architect, the process of obtaining planning permission lasts several months. There is therefore a clear advantage in being able to ensure compliance with regulations before entering the process for obtaining full planning permission.

The supplementary planning guidance (SPG) comprises documents produced by the LPAs to explain, in general terms, the design considerations either applicable to the city or relevant to a particular site. Currently, there are three types of such documents, each of which is produced to cover particular design and planning aspects. LPAs have adopted various terms or titles to describe the documents and the information they contain. In the research, it is argued that the SPGs are hybrids of three types, described as follows:

- First, the design guides are manuals that identify standards to promote good design practice. The aim of such documents is to put forward a clear and constructive statement of the LPA policies for general guidance. An example of the most popular type of design guide was produced by the County Council of Essex (1973) entitled 'A Design Guide for Residential Areas'. The guide presents design ethics of physical and visual analysis in both text and graphics format. This is usually used by the designer or the project architect for small and large developments.

- Secondly, the design briefs are normally leaflets or pamphlets to present a particular design issue in general terms. There are examples from several planning authorities that indicate specific instructions for development and building control procedures. The majority cover design considerations for small developments, building improvement and/or conservation of areas or particular features.
- Thirdly, site development briefs are usually presented in a report format and describe a specific site and indicate the design requirements and relevant considerations in question, leaving the aesthetic decisions to the designer. However, in some cases, building materials are clearly described and expected to be used. Planning and design policies are usually documented also graphically on the site maps. Occasionally a section devoted to the presentation of the proposed design schematics is included, together with the description of the planning application procedures.

In addition, the design and local planning process has two predicaments. First, the production and management of the design and local planning information in the process are predominantly linear. This is represented in design generation, followed by acquirement of statutory approval and then construction taking place. The benefits of adopting a heuristic approach, which characterizes the process of information feedback from the various designers, is not exploited in managing, capitalizing upon and capturing the knowledge. Such a heuristic working environment would better inform the users about the incremental development of design or the built environment. Unfortunately, after the construction of building design, such knowledge is typically dispersed. There are no adequate systems in practice to capitalize upon the produced design and planning knowledge for management of a future project.

Secondly, when architects alongside their design team and the planners are involved, communication can be complicated by each member holding different interests and design vocabularies. These apparent gaps in communication may never be resolved without standardizing some of the practical aspects of design and the local planning process. Bjork (1992) and van Nederveen and Tolman (1992) suggested that there might be advantages in standardizing the process of modelling and the representation of its associated data. Beheshti (1990) also suggested that there could be benefits from automating relevant aspects such as administration, planning and coordination of project information. Utilizing the 3D-CAAD models as a system or a platform for retaining and managing such knowledge should be implemented in such a way that would interest each stockholder, and provide direct access to a variety of practical and relevant information. The model should provide standardized and analogous information suitable for carrying out three tasks:

1. Designers and architects may wish to design and evaluate their concepts based upon the local planning parameters.
2. Planners may explore, visualize and analyse alternatives of their design concepts that are usually expressed in the site development briefs.
3. The planners alternatively could have total control of the system for managing the urban built environment by means of quantified analysis and visualization.

To develop such a complex system, it is essential: (i) to define the knowledge or the parameters that govern evaluation and support; (ii) to demonstrate a shared consensus in the proposed methodology (Guba and Lincoln, 1989); and (iii) to propose a methodological framework for its implementation as a point of departure from the process of parametrization. Consequently, it would be possible to describe and assess the role of optimized 3D-CAAD models. Furthermore, a working relationship between the parameters could be formulated to assist in identifying the basic requirements for its implementation. The potential of exploiting 3D-CAAD models could be expressed in the identification of parameters and a method for their interaction that appropriately describe design and local planning. Beheshti (1990) stresses that the automation of similar processes should reflect what is carried out in the 'real world'. However, this may require certain modifications and does not necessarily suggest the production of an entirely new method for work.

IDENTIFYING THE LOCAL PLANNING PARAMETERS

Completed field studies (i.e. questionnaires and interviews) which covered almost 30% of the planning authorities in England provided the major statistical work of the enquiry. The objectives of these studies were the identification of the parameters and demonstration of shared consensus. Owing to the scope and nature of this chapter, three sets of statistical information from a total of 19 are discussed here.

Analysis of the collected data indicated that the third type of SPGs (i.e. site development briefs) is the most used document during the negotiation process of planning applications. Planners use these documents to describe the design requirements and to describe, when and where appropriate, the parameters involved. There is a varied frequency of usage that needs to be demonstrated to establish the suitability of the parameters. These were either regularly, often, or rarely described in the site development briefs as part of the so-called 'special design requirements'. Figure 16.1 shows the percentages of the parameters that are regularly and often used in the site development briefs. These parameters are considered as knowledge that would derive from the evaluation process, consequently providing the

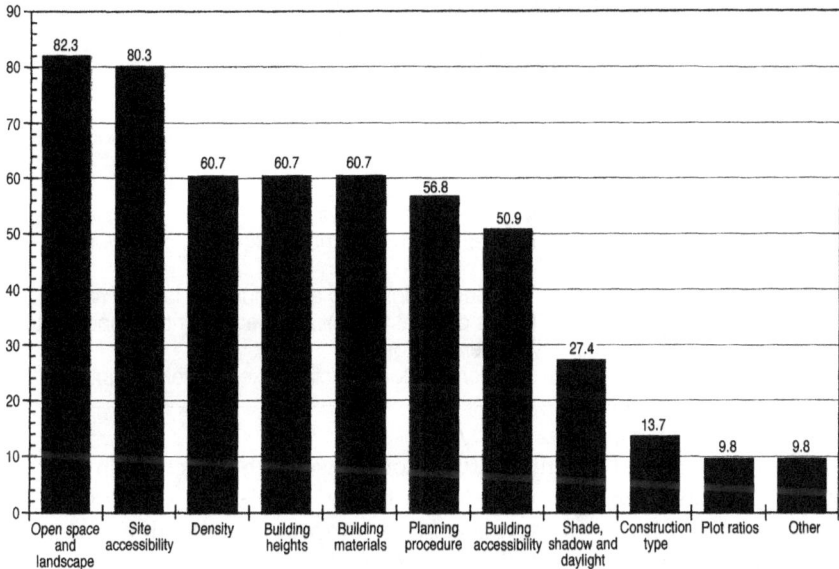

Fig. 16.1 Parameters used in site development briefs.

appropriate conceptual design support. Should these be computerized or automated, it would be possible to utilize them as tools for managing and monitoring the urban built environment.

It is also equally important to know how the planners describe or use them. There have been mixed opinions from the 32% of respondents (68% could not provide answers). Consequently, it was decided that measuring facilities need to be incorporated in the proposed system to assist potential users in calculating some of the parameters such as density and plot ratios (Table 16.2). These two parameters should be calculated in several ways depending upon the project type.

Planners and practising architects find it difficult to comprehend the concept of measuring open spaces. Simulating or representing the open space in a 3D-CAAD model could assist the designer or the decision-maker in visualizing the space. Besides that, if an open space could be represented by invisible shapes (i.e. cube) these could be calculated in conjunction with the surrounding environment (i.e. buildings). Hence, the quantification and calculation of an open space could be possible. For example, if a particular rule, indicated in the site development briefs, stresses that the open space should not exceed 40% of the site, it is deduced that two parameters could be known from a list of three: the site area, percentage of open space, or percentage of built areas. In this case, three objects could be defined in the model, each of which has its own attributes that could interact with others to determine the relationship.

Table 16.2 The design and local planning parameters

Attributes	Measurement and/or description
1. Open space	Square metres, volume
2. Site accessibility	Points of location (X,Y,Z), direction (north, south, etc.), degrees
3. Density	PPH, DPH, BPD, etc.
4. Building heights	Metres, floors, storeys
5. Building materials	Images (flags = method of search), alphanumeric description
6. Planning procedure	Text description, and alphanumeric tabular form
7. Building accessibility	Points of location (X,Y,Z), direction (north, south, etc.),
8. Plot ratios	X:Y, percentages
9. Project type	Residential, commercial, mixed development, etc.

Having a model of this nature could assist the decision-maker in visualizing as well as understanding the relationship between the components of the models. It is easy to comprehend the given relationship in the previous example. Nevertheless, when the size of the model increases, accommodating a large number of objects, it would prove to be difficult to manage such relationships without the aid of a CAAD system that provides interaction between objects and reports to its user.

Contemporary CAAD applications are not suitable for the suggested approach. They are a collection of tools to draft and edit 'dumb' objects suitable for design documentation and visualization only.

SPG AND PROJECT TYPES

From the collected results, it was evident that the project types influence the production of site development briefs and vary with the other documents. The planners were asked in the questionnaires to identify the production frequency (i.e. regularly, often and rarely) of site development briefs against a list of projects. Figure 16.2 indicates a summarized result of indicating the sum of the production frequency in one column and those LPAs that do not produce the SPG in another. The remainder of the percentages (i.e. 13%) are the LPAs that did not respond to the question. The LPAs pay attention to large-scale developments and those proposed within 'context-sensitive' areas (i.e. within conservation areas and the 'green belt'). For large-scale residential projects, the LPAs would consider production of a site development brief. More than 23% of the LPAs which responded produce design guides for small residential projects and more than 33% for large residential. About 60% of the respondents indicated that site development briefs are produced for large-scale

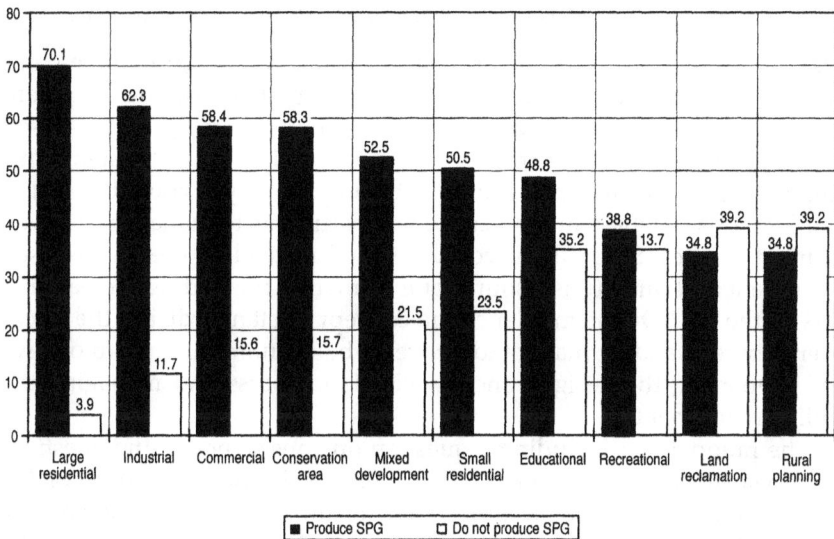

Fig. 16.2 LPAs that do and do not produce SPGs for certain types of project.

residential sites. More than 54% produced the same for commercial developments.

Consequently, it was possible to identify a different type of knowledge or to elaborate on the project type as an object attribute. Therefore, the project type is considered as a parameter and was included in Table 16.2. The recommended project types are those presented in Fig. 16.2, with the exception of recreational, reclamation and rural projects. The project type determines how the parameters or attributes should interact with each other. For example, the density of a residential development could be calculated in several ways, leading to different results. It is usually measured by the number of dwellings per hectare (DPH) or number of persons per hectare (PPH). Should the residential area be located in a conservation area, the calculated density following the previous two measures would be deceptive. In this case, the density should be calculated to reflect the number of inhabitants per dwelling. It is equally important to define the type of residential development, whether it consists of houses or a multi-storey block of flats, etc. This could be considered as another parameter. These considerations would give a clearer indication of the actual number of inhabitants proposed to occupy the residential development in the conservation area. Such knowledge is not accessible to the casual user and even some of the architects. Therefore, it would be advantageous to include it in the form of support.

CONSISTENCY IN THE CORE CONTENT OF SPG (STANDARDIZATION)

One of the significant results in the statistical analysis substantiates consistency in presenting the content and formats of the site development briefs. This supports the proposal for computerizing the paper-based document to a format suitable for incorporation in a CAAD system. This might become useful in two ways. First, and primarily, it could be used in the form of a database in the planning departments to manage the development of sites. Secondly, it could be used instead of the paper-based document and directly as a source of information for feeding the parameters to the CAAD system. Hence the concept of standardizing the document content and format could prove to be economical and innovative for supporting the design conceptualization process and managing the built environment.

The rationale for including a question on consistency in the questionnaire was to test the hypothesis that high consistency is desired for the presentation of the major sections of the documents. Some of the possible sections that could be standardized in the site development briefs are: the planning application process, referencing to the related policies, the graphical notations of site description and the parameters. Figure 16.3 indicates the various responses to the proposal.

METHODOLOGY FOR THE SUPPORT AND EVALUATION

The following section presents the methodological pattern for creating a 'product', which is in this case the 3D-CAAD model. The preceeding parts provide the essential considerations for utilizing the 'product' in the

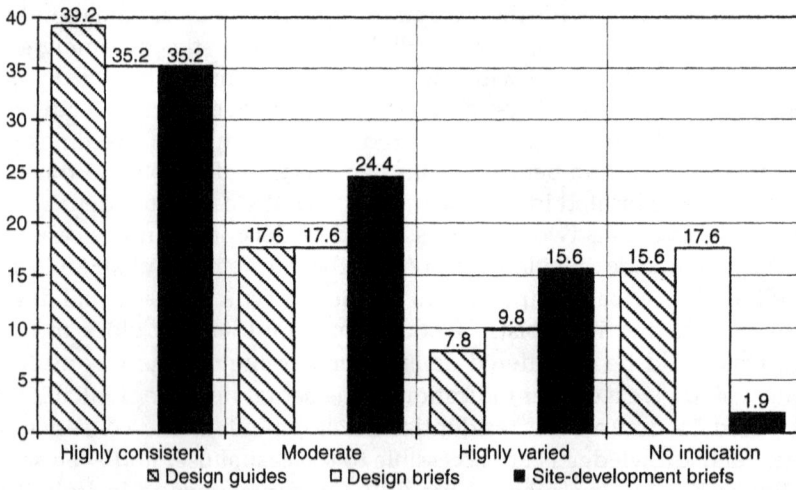

Fig. 16.3 Responses to the proposal for consistency in SPGs.

conceptual design development and evaluation process. In this sense the 'product' or the 'graphical model' has to be produced according to predefined criteria.

Sprague (1989) identified the three levels of technology in a decision support system (DSS). The first is the 'specific DSS', which is the application – hardware and software – that performs the actual work and allows the decision-maker to deal with a particular predicament. The second is the 'DSS generator', which is, as he describes it, the set of capabilities usually available separately in the information-technology market. For example, the generators could be a combination of a graphical display, commands, a set of task-oriented subroutines, report generation and the enquiry capability. The third is 'DSS tools' to facilitate the development of the 'specific DSS' or the 'DSS generator'. The 'DSS tools' are software and hardware which should constantly be under technological development and change to meet user demand.

Sprague (1989) defined the DDM paradigm as a technology for DSS, which must consist of three well balanced sets of capabilities: dialogue, data, and modelling. Sprague's definition of 'modelling' differs from that used in this chapter. His definition implies the structuring and formulation of a framework. In contrast, the term 'modelling' is used here to mean the three-dimensional models, always referred to as the 3D-CAAD models. However, these capabilities should: (i) be easy to use to facilitate interaction between the system and the user, (ii) be accessible to a wide variety of data, and (iii) provide analysis in several ways.

On the basis of the above and results of data collected from the questionnaires, interviews and the modelling exercises, two graphical prototypes were produced to elaborate on the concepts. These are presented in the following sections.

MODELLING SUPPORT SYSTEM SHELL

The Modelling Support System (MSS) Shell is a graphical prototype, represented in Fig. 16.4 as a screen image. The intention was not to create a fully functional application. Rather, the 'mock-up interface' was produced to illustrate the knowledge and some of the major components that are required for modelling support.

It was recommended, in the preceding analysis, that the expected users would be: the decision-makers, the novice and expert users of modelling applications. Therefore, the shell design should incorporate facilities and adopt terminology that are accessible to the average users.

The prime facilities for support are represented in three important features, which are located at the bottom of the MSS Shell. First, the command panel consists of a prompt and information panels to display file

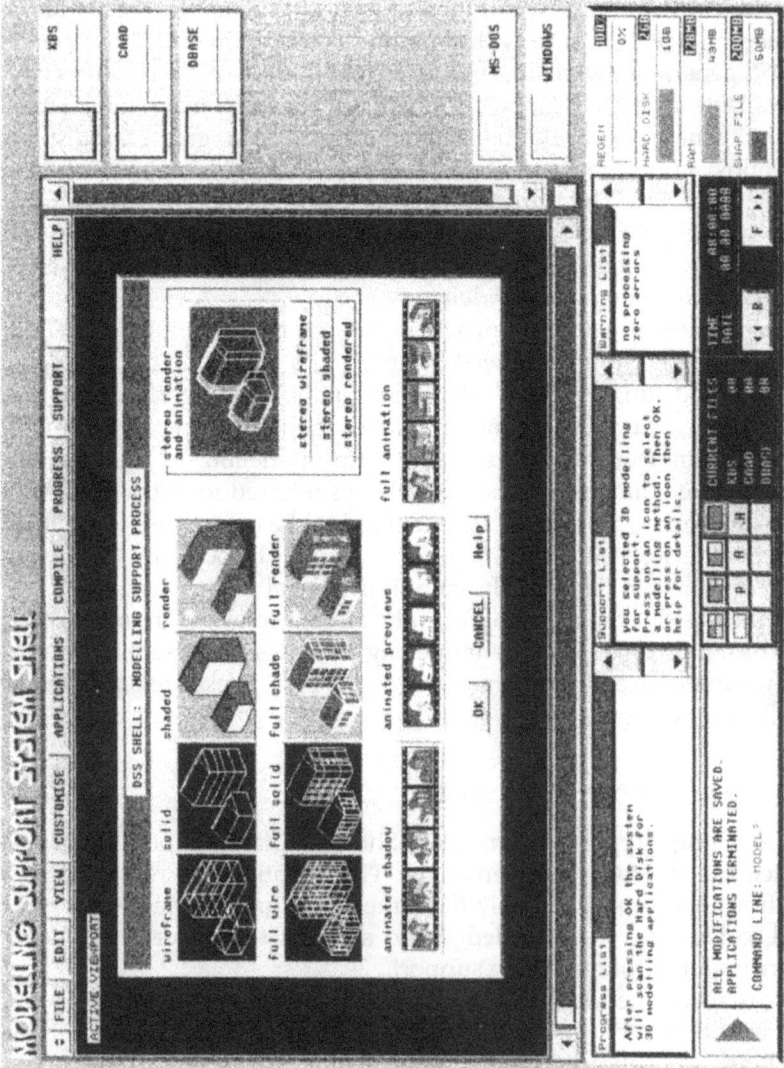

Fig. 16.4 A typical screen image of the MSS Shell.

information and date. It is possible to access the commands graphically through the menus; provisions for keyboard entry commands would also be beneficial. Secondly, at the bottom right is the configuration panel, which should provide on-line information about the hardware and software, all of which is displayed concurrently and interactively while modelling. This would assist the novice and expert users in determining the software capabilities in handling the requested information. Thirdly, the most important feature is the list panel, which consists of three dialogues:

1. Warning list (to store all previous error messages); this is to inform the users and provide a record of errors for evaluating progress.
2. Support list (the selected command); to inform the users with details relevant to last entered command.
3. Progress list (the consequent action); this should provide information about the operation proceeding as a result of the chosen command.

The simplest analogy that describes the role of the list panel is to provide information about the past, present and future actions. This method of operation will sustain a level of support that provides enough information for the casual user to operate the MSS Shell independently.

The MSS Shell should have a dual role: to inform the user before and during the process of modelling. It is an interface or a front-end for a number applications; a knowledge-based application to manipulate interactions between the modelling constraints (the specific); a database collection to edit and manage the processed information (generator); and the available set of modelling applications (tools). The research is concerned with the 'specific' and 'tools' by identifying the parameters and their relationship, and then defining an approach for adopting a methodological framework for modelling (the 3D-CAD modelling paradigm).

Here we can assume that a decision-maker wishes to be informed about modelling to make a managerial (i.e. strategic) decision; two actions could be structured. First, the decision-maker could provide the initial instruction in a question format to invoke a search function to activate the command or obtain help, if the command format is wrong. If the command is a 'model?', a dialogue box would appear to display all available modelling types. The list panel would concurrently display all relevant information about the selected command, as presented in the previous figure. Secondly, after the selection of a model type, another dialogue would appear requesting other 'modelling constraints' (i.e. the model form, size, initial time estimated to complete the model and the location of the drive(s) to carry out the search). The input and output could be represented as follows:

Enquiry type: Modelling support process
You have entered the following parameters:

Model Form:	Complex; contains various details
Model Type:	Full details; rendering required
Model Size:	Urban; 250,000 sq m
Time:	Two weeks
Drive(s) to search:	Local drives; C:, D: and H:
	Network drive; J: and K:

Results of the search...

Model Form:	Can be achieved
Model Type:	Can be achieved
Model Size:	Can be achieved
Time:	Can be completed according to deadlines
Users (available):	Three users on network available
Processor Speed:	120, 90 and 66 MHz; capable of handling the required details
Drive(s) searched:	Local and network search successful
RAM (available):	32, 16 and 16 MB; capable of handling the required details
Hard Disk (required):	Estimated space required 250 MB
	Available free space 550 MB on drive J
	Available free space 1.2 GB on drive K
Swap File (required):	Estimated; varies on used application
	Approximately 50 MB.
Modelling Applications (found and available):	Two applications were found; acad.exe for DOS and Windows, and 3ds.exe for DOS
Support results:	Modelling can be achieved according to selected parameters

Do you wish to reset the parameters? (Y/N):

The above method, in this case before modelling, is presented in a structured linear format to the decision-maker. The provision of such information could assist in planning the initial activities of the project. An expert user may not need to be informed before commencing the modelling task, but this could be vital during the process. However, this type of support is intended for determining the technical prerequisites before suggesting any commitments to a model that cannot be achieved due to some limitations.

The general framework of the MSS Shell could be described as an advanced application to clearly inform the decision-maker with the predetermined consequences of a particular action. It is essential to appreciate at this stage the importance of distinguishing between supporting the decision-makers and making decisions. For example, the user, either as an individual or as a group, consults the system with a particular action for advice. The system will prompt the user with all options outlining the relevant paths and their advantages and disadvantages. The user or in this case the decision-maker will consequently be better informed and responsible for making a decision based upon the system briefing.

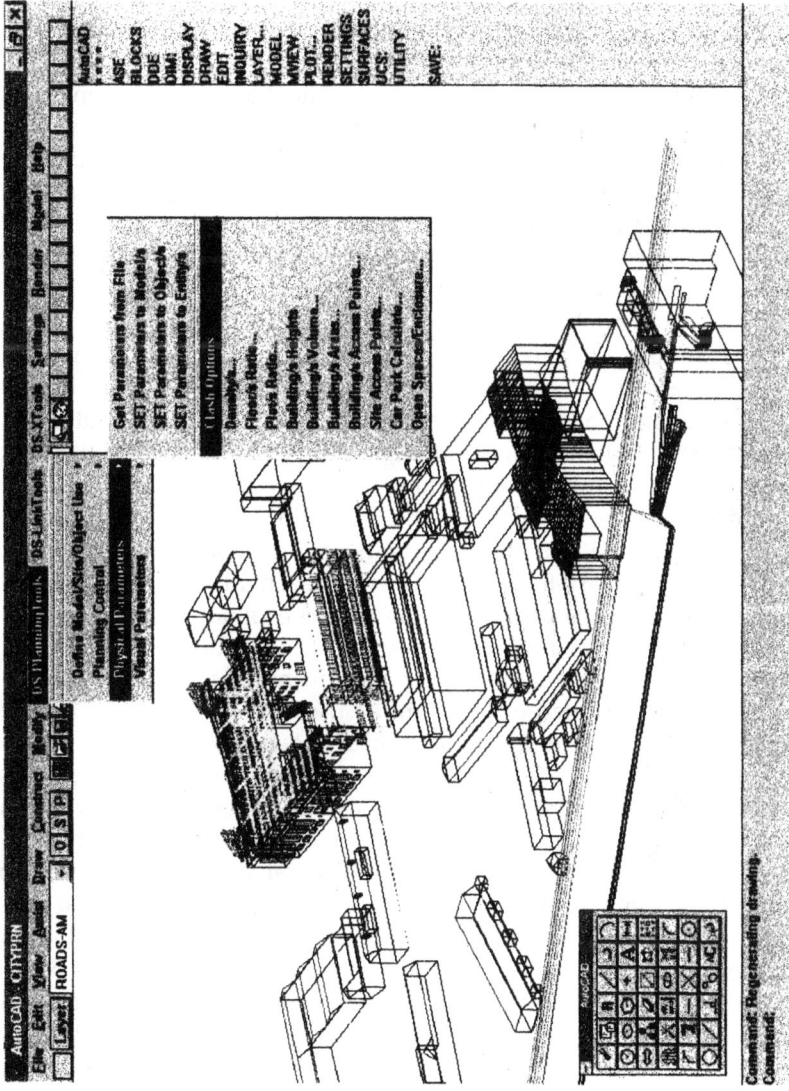

Fig. 16.5 A typical screen image of the DS-CAAD tool.

EVALUATION AND SUPPORT FROM THE LOCAL PLANNING ATTRIBUTES

The second prototype is called the Decision Support for Computer-Aided Architectural Design (DS-CAAD) tool (Fig. 16.5), which is for evaluating the conceptual design based upon the parameters (i.e. objects' attributes) from the local planning practice.

According to the classification of the three levels of capabilities, as described in Sprague (1989), the prototype is the third level (i.e. a DSS tool). The prototype was developed under the AutoCAD R12 environment. The editing strength of AutoCAD in two- and three-dimensional spaces combined with Windows GUI provided the required flexibility for manipulating the interface. All were implemented through the customization of menus, macros and AutoLisp routines. AutoCAD was selected due to its popularity among the construction industry professionals, and the availability of more than 360 third-party applications. The prototype accommodates AutoCAD functions alongside the three new sets: Planning, Link and Xtools. The Planning tool allows the user to select the parameters (i.e. attributes) and assign them to every entity. When the minimum and maximum values of some of the attributes (i.e. density, plot ratio, floor ratios, building heights, areas, etc.) are defined, the user can work around these values. There are three stages that need to be completed prior to obtaining the evaluation. First, the user should have a database file (in ASCII format) that contains the attributes. Secondly, it is necessary to validate or assign each attribute to its respective entities, an essential stage to ensure correct evaluation or feedback to the user. Thirdly, the user will be required to select options or criteria that evaluation will be based upon, either one attribute or all. It is assumed that, to make an informed evaluation, the user will be required to select the clash detection option: the interaction between all attributes.

In applying the evaluation process, it is possible to manipulate entities according to the design requirements. This worked appropriately when designing according to predefined area and volume of the relevant entities. It is essential to exchange the attributes' values with each other to achieve a reasonable result of evaluation. It proved to be difficult to construct them in an 'object' form that can maintain one or several attributes. Even when the entities were grouped as an AutoCAD 'block' it was possible to assign those attributes, but not store them for interaction with another 'object'. At times it seemed that the appropriate evaluation would never be achieved. Nevertheless, a lower level of evaluation could be maintained in the form of warning messages: whether the entity exceeded the permitted limit or not. This seemed to be a highly structured way of evaluation and unlikely to sustain interest.

Owing to the difficulty of constructing a group of entities that could simulate an independent 'object' with multiple attributes, it was decided to port the prototype to another system. Currently, major alterations are taking place to adopt a UNIX-based modelling application, Reflex Modeller. Its scripting language, Virtual Environment Language (VEL), allows the creation of fully interactive 'objects' in 3D. Initial tests show that, as in the appendix to this chapter, an 'object' of type residential project as a site type could be constructed and given any number of attributes. Qualitative attributes such as 'material' can also be assigned, on a separate layer, to allow textual and graphical visualizations. Other attributes such as number of people and number of houses could also be calculated interactively.

Despite the change of the platform and the modelling application, much of the prototype and the structure of the design and evaluation process would remain the same. The major change lies in redefining the role of the objects. There is a well-structured plan that would assist in developing the method of operations, described as follows.

1. *Attribute abstraction*: After the construction of the primary shapes to represent parts of the site development (i.e. various types of pitched roof houses), the data abstraction for each subsystem will be identified. This is, by far, expected to be the most demanding task in the design process and the selection of the object attributes that influence the entire evaluation process.
2. *Interaction*: The messages that objects send to each other would need to be identified. Here, the presentation of the messages and their clarity to the design developer is of great importance.
3. *Conformity*: It is a validation process to recheck that inheritance was appropriately defined as a result of the developed abstractions.

Adopting this approach to achieve evaluation seems promising by utilizing a fully interactive object-oriented environment. One of the unresolved problems is concurrent support while carrying out the actual design. The only support that could be achieved at this stage is when the users temporarily interrupt the design process and re-evaluate the recent input. Alternatively, there is, though, a costly solution that could be adopted to obtain concurrence in support, which is through system detection to the user's frequent input. When the system detects or finds a constant delay between the input intervals (either through the entered command or the cursor movements), the evaluation part of the tool could recheck and update the attributes and present them to the user.

CONCLUSION

There are two types of parameters that have been presented here, each of which is suitable for particular tasks. The first types are technically oriented and suitable for identifying the appropriate method of modelling to achieve the 'target' model. This is supported by the user's knowledge of the 3D-CAD modelling paradigm. Adopting this approach of support would seem to be beneficial to the decision-makers and the average CAD users, whereas expert users could benefit from support during the process of modelling. This is in addition to carrying out the actual design evaluation that relies on a different type of parameters. A number of local planning parameters were identified as attributes.

The completed tests indicated that currently the most suitable approach to achieve design evaluation while modelling is via the implementation of the object-oriented technology. The prime focus of this chapter is to demonstrate that there is a shared opinion and scope for computerizing or automating a particular part of the design and local planning process that could serve both the architects and planners. The parametrization of such a process is a demanding task and requires an understanding of the relationship between the parameters. There could be advantages in considering the computerization of the regulations found at the local planning level to assist during the design development and the generation of alternative proposals. This could be implemented in managing the urban built environment and the preparation of site development briefs.

APPENDIX

```
//global declarations for site type boundary defined as Residential
elements SITE
{
//saved
float       LENGTH              = 50000
float       DEPTH               = 3000
integer     DOPOINT             = 1
integer     DOSTRETCH           = 1
integer     XCOORDPT [100]
integer     YCOORDPT [100]
integer     ZCOORDPT [100]
integer     NUMPOINTS           = 0
string      MATERIALS           = 'grass'
integer     xworld              = 0
integer     yworld              = 0
integer     parameter           = 0
string      SITETYPE1           = 'Residential'
private
            void OnEdit ( )
            void OnSave ( )
views
```

```
                plan
                elevation
                view3d
dialog
                SITEDlg
}
Link SITEDlg
{
                DEPTH                   Tdepth
                SITETYPE1               RBsitetype
}
//here to load the position of houses and check related parameters
integer     layer = RewindLayer ('Housinglayer')
string      UID = ' '
integer     count = 0
integer     countpeople = 0
float       countarea = 0
while ((UID = Scanlayer (layer, current))! = 'Finished')
{
string name = NameGet (UID)
if (name = = 'House')
{
float xx = GetNodeXCOORD (UID)
float yy = GetNodeYCOORD (UID)
float zz = GetNodeZCOORD (UID)
integer num = GetValuel (UID, 'NUMBEROFPEOPLE', 0)
float area = GetValueF (UID, 'HOUSEAREA', 0)
count + +
countpeople + = num
cpuntarea + = area
}
}
if(count > SITEDENSITY)
{
string errorstring = 'The density is too high...recheck' + count
Error (errorstring)
count < < 'House Density' < < count/SITEDENSITY < < end1
}
}
```

BIBLIOGRAPHY

Beheshti, M.R. (1990) The prerequisites for building design in an information environment In *Delft Progress Report: Information and Decisions in Design,*

Planning and Management of the Built Environment (eds M.R. Beheshti, R.E.C.M. van der Heijden and D.J. Sweeny), 14 (2), pp. 78–89.

Benyon, D. (1992) Task analysis and system design: the discipline of data, *Interacting with Computers*, 4 (2), pp. 246–259.

Bjork, B.-C. (1992) A conceptual model of spaces, space boundaries and enclosing structures, *Automation in Construction*, 1, pp. 193–214.

Christiansson, P. (1991) Building a city advisor in 'Hypermedia' environment, *Environment and Planning B: Planning and Design*, 18 (1), pp. 39–50.

County Council of Essex (1973) *A Design Guide for Residential Areas*, County Council of Essex.

Guba, E.G. and Lincoln, Y.S. (1989) *Fourth Generation Evaluation*, Sage Publications.

Ismail, A.L.R.M. (1994) Strategic CAD modelling: the misconception. In *Proceedings of the 12th Conference in Education in Computer Aided Architectural Design ECAADE*, The Virtual Studio, Glasgow, September 7–10.

Ismail, A.L.R.M. (1995a) Singularity and pluralism in multimedia: a key theoretical approach to the model. In *Proceedings of the 13th Conference in Education in Computer Aided Architectural Design ECAADE*, Palermo, Italy, November 16–18.

Ismail, A.L.R.M. (1995b) Intelligent virtual knowledge for 3D-CAAD and urban modelling: misconceptions, counter-knowledge, and logic. In *Visualisation and Intelligent Design in Engineering and Architecture* (eds S. Hernandez and C.B. Brebbia), Computational Mechanics Publications, pp. 91–98.

Ismail, A.L.R.M. (1995c) Pragmatic visualisation: a detour from the Nth dimension to infinity. In *Visualisation and Intelligent Design in Engineering and Architecture* (eds S. Hernandez and C.B. Brebbia), Computational Mechanics Publications, pp. 99–106.

Ismail, A.L.R.M. and McCartney, K. (1993) A tool for conceptual design evaluation based on compliance with site-development briefs and related planning regulations. In *Proceedings of the 11th Conference in Education in Computer Aided Architectural Design ECAADE*, Eindhoven University of Technology, The Netherlands, September 10–13.

Shaviv, E. Kalay, Y.E. and Peleg, U.J. (1992) An integrated knowledge-based and procedural system for the design of energy conscious buildings, *Automation in Construction*, 1 (2), pp. 123–141.

Sprague, R.H. (1989) A framework for the development of decision support systems. In *Decision Support Systems – Putting Theory into Practice* (eds R.H. Sprague and J.H. Watson), Prentice-Hall International, USA, pp. 9–36.

van Nederveen, G.A. and Tolman, F.P. (1992) Modelling multiple views on buildings, *Automation in Construction*, 1, pp. 215–224.

Computer-mediated cooperative spatial planning

17

Thomas Gordon, Nikos Karacapilidis, Hans Voss and
Andreas Zauke

INTRODUCTION

Usually spatial planning problems involve a large number of decision-makers with different backgrounds, interests, authorities and interpretations of some of their issues. A cooperative process has to take place, which will reconcile the individual approaches and lead to solutions that satisfy all, or most, participants. The well-tried interaction of decision-makers with geographical information systems (GIS) has to be integrated with a framework for fair, rational and efficient decision-making procedures. This chapter gives an overview of a computer-mediated system for cooperative spatial planning. The decision-making support is provided by ZENO, a mediation system being implemented for the World-Wide Web.

ZENO allows an arbitrarily large number of interested parties in various locations to take part in a decision-making process extending over a long period of time. This will be a new kind of issue-based conferencing and group decision support system. Unlike conventional groupware systems, ZENO supports decision-making among individuals and groups, with often conflicting interests, distributed across organizations throughout the world. By sending their messages to a ZENO mediation server, an issue-based information system for the World-Wide Web will be constructed. Using any Web browser, users will be able to use hyperlinks to access a structured protocol of the discussion and to quickly find the corresponding issues, positions and arguments. Hypertext links between these kinds of elements and the original messages will allow quick and easy access to the full text of the cited messages. ZENO also provides

Decision Support Systems in Urban Planning. Edited by Harry Timmermans. Published in 1997 by E & F N Spon. ISBN 0 419 21050 4

various ways of searching and sorting messages, for example by author, date or issue. The system aims at providing intelligent assistance to human mediators, facilitators, arbitrators and other kinds of trusted third parties. The services to be provided include managing the dependences between arguments, claims, positions and issues and providing advice about procedural rules. It is not the role of a mediating system to rigidly enforce formal rules, or to help managers control or monitor the performance of employees (Jarke *et al.*, 1987). On the contrary, the role of trusted third parties, assisted by a ZENO mediation system, is to remain neutral and help assure that the interests and goals of all members of a group, regardless of status, are respected and appreciated. Special emphasis is also given to security, authenticity and privacy issues.

The system places issues, positions and arguments into a structure which is richer, more precise and more focused than mechanisms typical of news groups. Using the graphical interface over the Web, even inexperienced users can easily view the structure of the arguments presented so far, retrieve contributions submitted by other parties and add their own issues, arguments and positions. These contributions may include additional documents, such as links to other resources on the Web, images, movies and sound files. ZENO will be further developed as part of GeoMed (Geographical Mediation), which is a project financed by the European Commission within the Telematics Applications Programme. Using the World-Wide Web as its basic infrastructure, the project implements a distributed system providing open access to geographic information resources for public planning and political decision-making. Pilot applications in real urban and regional planning processes will guide the further evolution of ZENO's functionality. As part of a feasibility study for GeoMed, a model was created in cooperation with the City of Bonn to demonstrate ZENO's potential benefits as a mediator's assistant: the documents of a five-year regional planning project were modelled as ZENO messages.

The rest of this chapter proceeds as follows: the next section sketches the various phases of a cooperative spatial planning procedure and discusses the user requirements for computerized support. The third section describes the architecture of the proposed framework in more detail, and the fourth section illustrates a real application scenario concerning the allocation of a new technology park in the area of North Rhine–Westphalia, Germany. Finally, future and related work are discussed in the last section.

COMPUTER-MEDIATED COOPERATIVE SPATIAL PLANNING

Problems that need to be dealt with during cooperative spatial planning have been extensively discussed in Karacapilidis *et al.* (1995). As shown there, the first sub-goal in such a procedure is the interpretation of constraints provided by the participants in the discussion. In general, there are no widely accepted definitions for spatial constraints, and semantically different concepts are sometimes attached to the same linguistic terms (Frank, 1992; Papadias and Sellis, 1994). Thus, the several constraints imposed have to be translated into a unified model capable of expressing the various perspectives in a coherent manner. After the constraints are expressed in a unified model, there is the second problem, namely to devise tractable algorithms that efficiently detect inconsistencies in the imposed constraints. Such inconsistencies depend only on the nature of the constraints; their early detection helps to avoid unnecessary extensive access to stored data. In real applications that involve a large number of constraints imposed by numerous agents, the detection of inconsistencies requires sophisticated spatial inference mechanisms (Egenhofer and Sharma, 1993; Grigni *et al.*, 1995).

When some inconsistencies have been detected, the agents will have to revise their constraints, which is in essence a negotiation process. The nature of this process is highlighted in Golay (1995), which proposes that *distributed cognition* can be achieved only if one considers the participants in a spatial planning debate as *conversation-makers*, instead of classical decision-makers. This shifted role of participants would be a remedy to the lack of social and behavioural attributes in most current information systems. In other words, flexibility for representing human desire and purposefulness cannot be achieved by following highly normative models, but only by emphasizing the role of the human conversation-maker and letting computers do the processing tasks for which the human abilities are limited.

Having the above problems solved, efficient spatial access methods have to access large amounts of geographic data in order to retrieve the appropriate information (Egenhofer, 1994; Papadias and Sellis, 1995). The output of these procedures is then returned to the agents for evaluation and approval. Information may be stored in distributed repositories, which include heterogeneous GIS, databases and knowledge-based systems, designed in the past only for single-user workstations. Consequently, spatial data are mainly stored in proprietary formats and *interoperability* between systems should be achieved with appropriate converters. Specification of international standard formats plays a central role here. The above phases are illustrated in Fig. 17.1

As further discussed in Voss (1996), it is surely impossible and undesirable to completely automate the planning process described above. Too many organizations, administrations and individuals are involved, with diverse and conflicting interests and positions. Nevertheless, the use of information technology may assist planners and other people involved in the planning process in different ways. One important goal is to provide easy access to the current state of the planning process, at any time. This

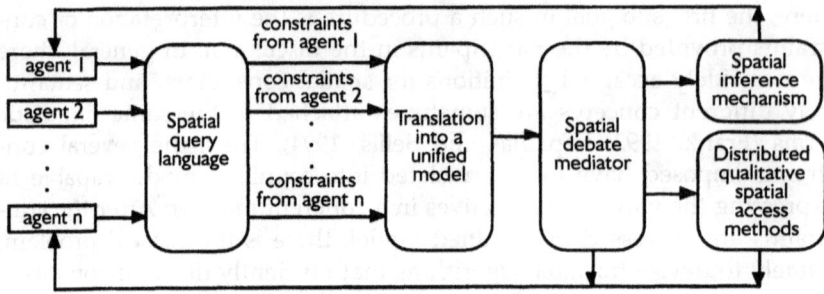

Fig. 17.1 Phases of collaborative spatial decision-making.

goal would be greatly facilitated if all relevant planning data and documents, including cartographic and thematic maps, decisions, minutes, evaluations, etc., were to be made available and maintained in electronic form, in a well-structured and organized way.

Another possibility would be to provide direct computer support for the argumentation, negotiation and mediation process. A computer network can be used as a medium for the planning process, in which documents are structured and indexed according to their role and function, using a model of argumentation.

Many years ago, Petri developed his theory of regulated and reasoned communication, mediated by information technology (Petri, 1962). Related ideas about an 'Issue-Based Information System' (IBIS) were developed in the early 1970s (Kunz and Rittel, 1970; Rittel, 1972; Rittel and Webber, 1973). IBIS was used in some pilot applications, but was not widely adopted due to limitations in the state of technology at the time. One reason was the restricted availability of computers and computer networks and their prohibitive expense. In addition, the lack of computing standards inhibited electronic communication in heterogeneous organizations and computing environments. Finally, the user interfaces available at the time were too difficult for most people to use.

For the development of the ZENO system, the above implied three major practical requirements: the system must be available on all prominent operating systems and hardware platforms; it must provide relatively inexpensive access to a broad public; and it must have a very intuitive and easy user interface. The Internet, and the World-Wide Web in particular, provides a nearly ideal foundation for meeting these requirements.

THE SYSTEM

The first version of ZENO provides basic issue-based information services to the World-Wide Web. By filling out a Web form, a group of users may set up a mediation system to discuss a set of related issues.

Receiving contributions from the users, the mediation system may create and install a set of Web pages, with appropriate hyperlinks to parts of the previous messages of the discussion (Fig. 17.2). A group may choose a human editor to be responsible for adding this information. In this case, users' messages will be automatically forwarded to the editor, who would add information and return the marked-up version to the mediation system. The only tools required to participate in a ZENO-mediated discussion are Internet access and a Web browser, such as Netscape or Mosaic.

Building on decision theory and a formal model of argumentation (Brewka and Gordon, 1994; Gordon, 1994; Karacapilidis *et al.*, 1995; Karacapilidis and Gordon, 1995), ZENO offers intelligent assistance to human mediators and other participants in the planning process by providing an issue-based discussion forum or conferencing system.

The messages sent to the ZENO system are structured and indexed according to the model of argumentation. Our argumentation model, based on IBIS, uses the concepts of issues, positions and arguments (Fig. 17.3) to organize the discourse in a manner which is richer and more precise than the simple *thread* mechanism typical of news groups. The argumentation structure provides a view on the messages which substantially facilitates the browsing and retrieval of relevant past contributions to the discussion. Furthermore, preferences and value judgements expressed in the messages can be modelled, using a reason maintenance procedure, so as to indicate which of the alternative solutions proposed meet selected proof standards or decision criteria. This feature turns ZENO from a mere information retrieval tool into a competitive arena for exciting debate. Users will be able to see easily whether their favoured positions are currently *winning* or *losing* the debate, helping them to focus their argumentation resources on the most controversial issues.

A future version of ZENO will make use of the roles of participants in the planning process, and models of procedural norms, to advise users about their rights and obligations in the proceedings. ZENO is not, however, intended to play the role of a policeman or judge. If a planned action would violate the norms of the proceedings, according to the model, ZENO's task is limited to advising users of this fact. The users remain free to decide for themselves just how rigidly they wish to follow the model. ZENO will also provide facilities for defining and monitoring electronic voting procedures.

The ZENO server is a piece of software written in Java, a new programming language from Sun Microsystems which is especially well-suited for Internet applications. Java is portable, enabling ZENO servers to eventually be installed using a variety of operating systems. The indices managed by ZENO are processed using conventional relational

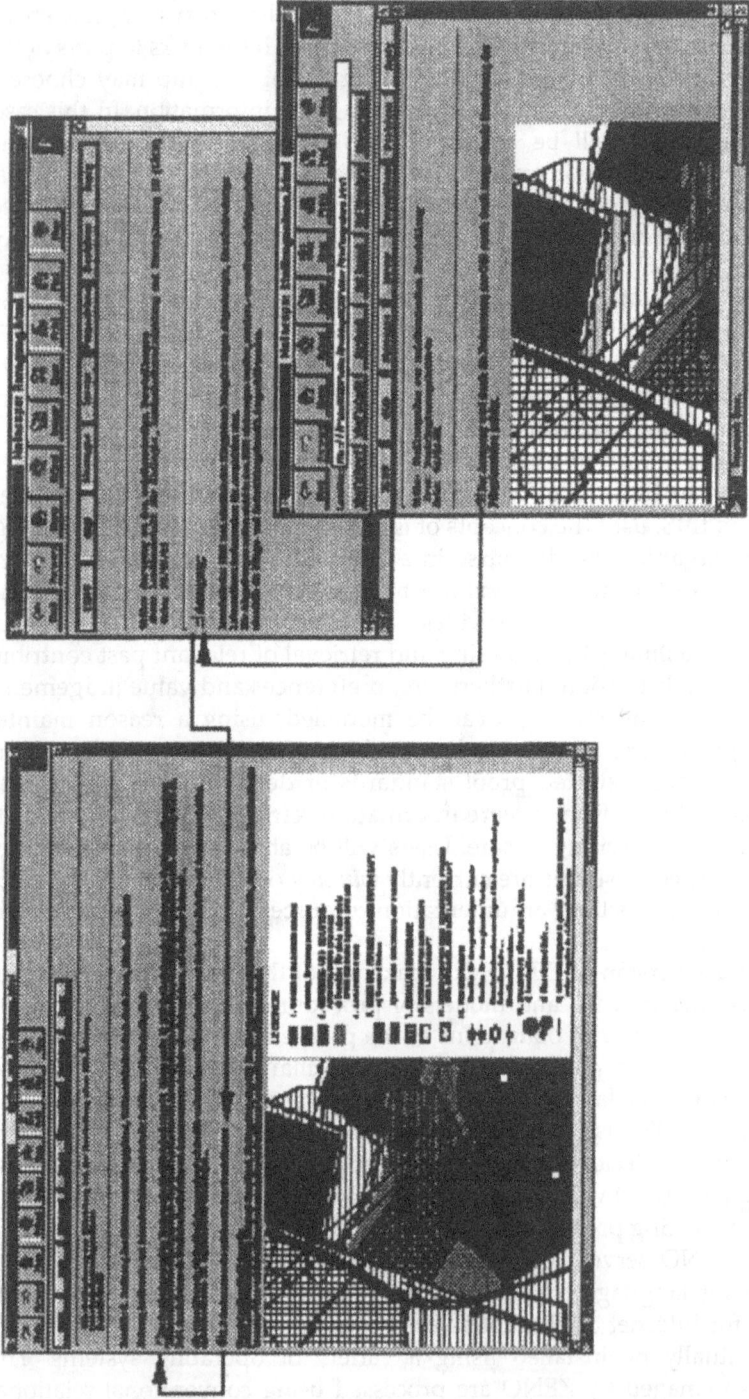

Fig. 17.2 Linking of documents on the World-Wide Web.

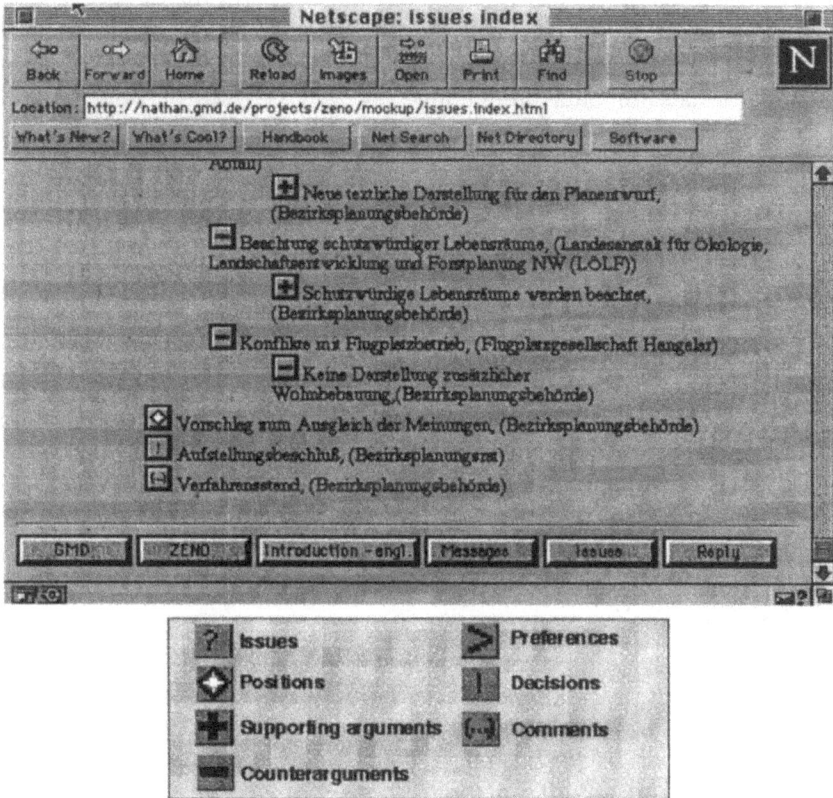

Fig. 17.3 The structure of discussion in ZENO.

database technology, allowing messages and the argumentation elements within messages (such as issues, positions and arguments) to be selected, filtered and sorted using standard SQL queries. Any database supporting SQL can be used with the ZENO server. The ZENO interface hides SQL technicalities from the user. The use of established database technology provides transaction control and improved security; user management and password protection can be implemented easily.

ZENO is being further developed in the GeoMed project. Urban and regional planning, environmental assessment procedures and Internet brokerage services for GIS data have been selected as pilot applications. Using the Web, the goal of GeoMed is to provide open access to geographical information resources, i.e. GIS data, and provide advanced support for public planning and political decision-making processes. Three major types of services are currently envisioned, namely information, documentation and mediation services.

- *Information services* will provide easy and cost-effective access to distributed, heterogeneous geographical databases. This includes facilities for finding relevant GIS data, converting proprietary GIS data to standard formats for data interchange, as well as ways of viewing and browsing GIS data from within Web browsers. Many of these functions will be implemented using custom GIS applets written in Java.
- *Documentation services* will provide a 'shared workspace' for storing and retrieving documents and messages related to particular geographical planning projects. This will be a convenient way for ordinary users to add information to the hyperspace of documents available on the network. GeoMed plans to apply the BSCW system developed at GMD (Bentley *et al.*, 1995).
- As discussed above, ZENO provides the basis for the *mediation services* being developed in GeoMed. Pilot applications in the area of urban and regional planning will guide the evolution of ZENO's functionality, as it complements the information and documentation services within GeoMed. The basic version of the integrated services will be available for pilot applications in the second quarter of 1997.

A CASE STUDY

The mediation support presented above is generic and can be used in any planning or decision-making context where conflicting interests, goals and alternative solutions prevail. In this section, we sketch the city and regional planning context, and we illustrate a real planning application.

Communal and regional planning processes are embedded in a network of many laws and regulations, at different levels of authority, which define or constrain details of content and procedure. Of course, and fortunately, some choices are left for individual negotiation. An eventual hearing of citizens, for example, is mandatory, but the specific embedding in the temporal sequence of events and activities can be chosen according to the demands of the specific application. Conflicting requirements of the affected parties are typical and often time-consuming to resolve. Decisions made early in a long planning process may need to be revised later, as further information becomes available or the world changes in unanticipated ways. For example, changing political values and priorities might indicate allowing industrial use of a district which had been reserved for residential use some 20 years ago. Once the general goals are clear and after some preliminary analysis and account of the situation, the central task of responsible planning parties is to organize and mediate the following analysis and discussion.

As part of a feasibility study for GeoMed, a model was created in cooperation with the City of Bonn to demonstrate ZENO's potential benefits as a mediator's assistant: the documents of a five-year regional planning project were modelled as ZENO messages. The neighbouring cities of Bonn and Sankt Augustin in North Rhine–Westphalia, Germany, were initially involved in this project. In 1991, they started planning a 'residential and technology park', located in the area between the two communities. The intentions of the two cities were in conflict with the zoning scheme of the applicable regional plan, which only allowed agricultural land use for the area in question. To permit housing, business and industrial land use of the area, the city of Bonn and the district administration for Sankt Augustin, the Rhein-Sieg-Kreis, applied for a revision of the regional plan to the regional authority in 1993.

In the subsequent proceedings more than 80 local, regional and state authorities and organizations were requested to send their suggestions and considerations about a draft plan revision to the regional planning agency. The results of this participation procedure were considered in a second draft plan. Based on that, a revised regional plan was approved by the responsible state agency in 1995. Detailed planning of building plots, local transportation, public facilities and infrastructure is currently in progress by the two cities. Figure 17.4 illustrates three maps of the area under consideration, which correspond to various stages of the planning procedure described above.

DISCUSSION

ZENO is especially suitable for planning procedures involving a large number of geographically distributed persons and groups. In a conventional planning process, participants exchange messages via paper mail and travel to take part in planning meetings. Using ZENO with wide-area electronic networks permits extensive savings of time and costs. But in addition to these short-term economic factors, ZENO contributes to the quality of the planning process and its results; the planning laws

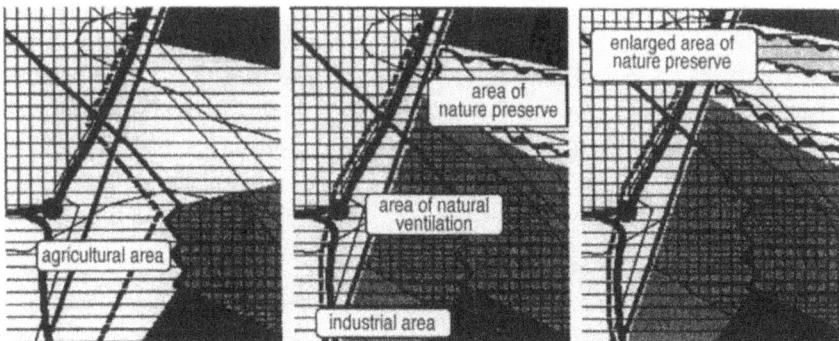

Fig. 17.4   Three stages of the planning procedure.

explicitly require the solicitation of an 'arrangement of opinions' when developing a state or regional plan. For this purpose, suggestions and considerations are currently sent by ordinary mail to the regional planning agency, where they are structured, aggregated and indexed. To prepare a planning meeting, a collection of the aggregated documents is sent back to every participant. Using ZENO, all arguments would be documented, structured and made accessible to the participants via the Web. By indexing messages according to their argument structure, it will be much easier to retrieve relevant documents, even many years later. German law requires 'public and private interests are to be duly weighed and fairly balanced' during urban planning. ZENO technology could substantially facilitate this process. A further significant challenge will be to get citizens actively involved in a ZENO-mediated planning process, in a larger-scale pilot application. ZENO can be used to open and democratize public policy-making and planning procedures, helping to improve the quality and acceptability of decisions.

Advanced systems should also support innovative representation mechanisms based on interactive maps and computer-supported cooperative work technology. Such tools should provide a means for the elicitation of the spatial decision-making process, enabling the agents to be aware of the evolution of the planning debate. It is widely argued that high visualization is the key for the efficient user participation in spatial planning procedures, especially in models of uncertainty (Goodchild *et al.*, 1992).

ACKNOWLEDGEMENTS

The authors would like to thank people from the Planning Department of the City of Bonn for their valuable information on the application area mentioned in this chapter. This work was partially funded by the European Commission (DG XIII, Information Engineering Program), under the GeoMed project. The GeoMed consortium consists of Intecs Sistemi (Italy), GMD (Germany), Intrasoft (Greece), Vrije Universiteit Brussel, TNO-FEL (The Netherlands), TNO-Bouw (The Netherlands), City of Bonn, City of Tilburg, Tuscany Region and the Technical Chamber of Greece.

REFERENCES

Bentley, R., T. Horstmann, K. Sikkel, and J. Trevor (1995) Supporting collaborative information sharing with the World-Wide Web: the BSCW shared workspace system, *Proceedings of the 4th International WWW Conference*, Boston, Mass., December 11–14, pp. 63–73.

Brewka, G. and T. Gordon (1994) How to buy a Porsche: an approach to defeasible decision making, *Working Notes of AAAI-94 Workshop on Computational Dialectics*, Seattle, Washington, July 31 – August 4, pp. 28–38.

Egenhofer, M. (1994) Spatial SQL: a query and presentation language, *IEEE Transactions on Knowledge and Data Engineering* 6(1), pp. 86–95.

Egenhofer, M. and J. Sharma (1993) Assessing the consistency of complete and incomplete topological information, *Geographical Systems* 1, pp. 47–68.

Frank, A.U. (1992) Qualitative spatial reasoning about distances and directions in geographic space, *Journal of Visual Languages and Computing* 3, pp. 343–371.

Golay, Fr. (1995) System design methodologies to support collaborative spatial decision-making, Position Paper, *First Specialist Meeting of NCGIA Initiative 17: Collaborative Spatial Decision-Making*, Santa Barbara, Cal. September 17–20.

Goodchild, M.F., G. Sun and S. Yang (1992) Development and test of an error model for categorical data, *International Journal of Geographic Information Systems* 6(2), pp. 87–104.

Gordon, T. (1994) The pleadings game: an exercise in computational dialectics, *Artificial Intelligence and Law* 2(4), pp. 239–292.

Grigni, M., D. Papadias and C. Papadimitriou (1995) Topological inference, *Proceedings of the 14th International Joint Conference on Artificial Intelligence (IJCAI-95)*, Montreal, Canada, August 20–25, pp. 901–906.

Jarke, M., M.T. Jelassi and M.F. Shakun (1987) MEDIATOR: towards a negotiation support system, *European Journal of Operational Research* 31, pp. 314–334.

Karacapilidis, N. and T. Gordon (1995) Dialectical planning, *Proceedings of IJCAI-95 Workshop on Intelligent Manufacturing Systems*, Montreal, Canada, August 20–25, pp. 239–250.

Karacapilidis, N., D. Papadias and M. Egenhofer (1995) Collaborative spatial decision-making with qualitative constraints, *Proceedings of the 3rd ACM International Workshop on Advances in Geographic Information Systems*, Baltimore, Maryland, December 1–2, pp. 53–59.

Kunz, W. and H.W.J. Rittel (1970) *Issues as Elements of Information Systems*, Working Paper 0131, Institut für Grundlagen der Planung, Universität Stuttgart.

Papadias, D. and T. Sellis (1994) Qualitative representation of spatial knowledge in two-dimensional space, *Very Large Data Bases Journal*, Special Issue on Spatial Databases, 3(4), pp. 479–516.

Papadias, D. and T. Sellis (1995) A pictorial query-by-example language, *Journal of Visual Languages and Computing*, Special Issue on Visual Query Systems 6(1), pp. 53–72.

Petri, C. (1962) Kommunikation mit Automaten, Ph.D. Thesis, University of Darmstadt, Germany.

Rittel, H.W.J. (1972) On the planning crisis: systems. Analysis of the 'first and second generations', *Bedriftsoekonomen* 8, pp. 390–396.

Rittel, H.W.J. and M.M. Webber (1973) Dilemmas in a general theory of planning, *Policy Sciences* 4, pp. 155–169.

Voss, H. (1996) Dimensions of KBS applications, *Proceedings of the 2nd Knowledge Engineering Forum*, Karlsruhe, Germany, February 29 – March 1.

Parking simulation using a geographical information system

18

Peter van der Waerden and Harry Timmermans

INTRODUCTION

Geographical information systems (GIS) are used in a variety of application contexts. In some fields such as geodesy there is already a long tradition in using GIS. In other fields of application, such as transportation, GIS is relatively new (Niemeier and Beard, 1993). Because of the complexity of many transportation issues, both within and across modes, a lot of information from different transportation departments is required to fully consider the various alternatives (Opiela, 1991). Opiela indicates that the capabilities of a GIS in the transportation field will permit the assimilation, integration and presentation of data collected and stored by each of the transportation divisions involved. To get insight into the possibilities of GIS for transportation '... there is a need to identify current applications of GIS concepts and technologies in the transportation field, to identify uses that may be possible with the development of advanced GIS concepts and technologies ...'. One such application may be the simulation of the parking behaviour of motorists.

Parking is an important aspect of urban transport planning and policy (Polak *et al.*, 1990). Parking measures can have significant direct and indirect effects on travel demand, transport system performance and wider economic and social goals. Examples of parking measures are changes in scale or composition of the parking stock, adjustments in tariff structures, stricter enforcement measures, and improvements in walking routes between parking lots and destinations. To get insight into the effects of such parking measures one needs to be able to establish the relationships, if any, between such policy measures and people's parking

Decision Support Systems in Urban Planning. Edited by Harry Timmermans. Published in 1997 by E & F N Spon. ISBN 0 419 21050 4

behaviour. Effects of parking measures can be studied at three levels (DHV, 1978): (i) effects on the parking system; (ii) effects within the more general transportation system; and (iii) effects on land use planning. A parking simulation model allows one to assess the effects of parking measures on all levels.

To conduct a parking simulation a variety of mostly spatially oriented data, data-handling and analysis techniques are required. A GIS can offer data-handling and analysis utilities for building and using simulation models. Bonsall (1991) already noted that 'GIS's and other databases are becoming a very valuable secondary source of contextual data for parking analysis'. Young and Taylor (1991) suggest that 'modern developments in GIS software have provided the basic communication net for connected models'.

The aim of this study is to develop a parking simulation using a geographical information system, with special attention to the tools that a GIS offers to conduct such a simulation. The study is the first phase of a larger study of the parking behaviour of visitors to inner cities. In this phase most attention will be paid to the way parking behaviour can be simulated in a GIS environment.

This chapter is organized as follows. First, the conceptual framework underlying the parking simulation model is described. This is followed by a section about the data and procedure requirements of the suggested parking simulation model. Then, the developed and applied computer program for the parking simulation is presented. Next, the parking simulation model is illustrated using hypothetical data and models in the GIS environment of TransCAD. The chapter ends with some remarks about the use of a GIS for parking simulation studies and about future research efforts.

A FRAMEWORK FOR PARKING SIMULATION

A variety of approaches concerning parking simulation are described in the literature. Examples include the simulation model of TNO used in The Hague (TNO, 1979), PARKSIM used in Amsterdam (Brohm and Reichelman, 1984), CLAMP (Bradley *et al.*, 1986; Polak *et al.*, 1990) and Young's parking model (Young and Taylor, 1991). Essential components of these parking simulation models are the generation of the number of cars arriving at a destination (trip generation), the choice of a parking lot and the determination of the parking duration. In some studies mode choice is also part of the simulation (e.g. Polak *et al.*, 1990). Trip generation can be based on origin–destination matrices per motive (TNO, 1979) or on arrival rates (Bradley *et al.*, 1986). Parking choice behaviour is mostly described by a parking choice model. These models describe either the choice between types of parking lots (Bradley *et al.*, 1986) or the choice between parking lots (TNO, 1979). None of these studies, except

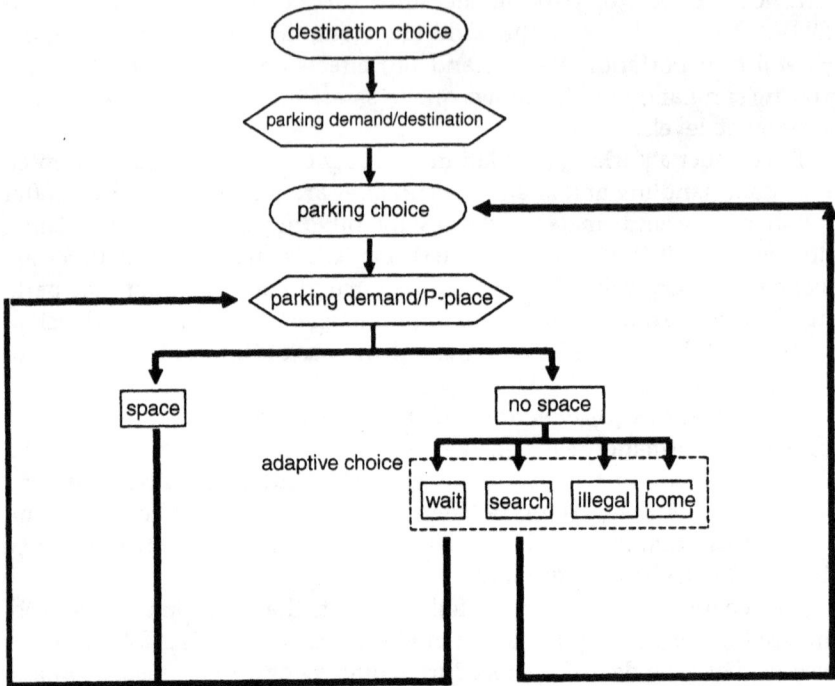

Fig. 18.1   Conceptual framework for parking simulation.

for the first one, considers the reaction of motorists when a parking lot is full. In the TNO model, the motorists have to choose a second parking lot when the first lot is full. In almost every simulation model the duration of parking is derived from an observed distribution.

The parking simulation model conducted in this study (Fig. 18.1) is largely based on the studies mentioned above. However, there are some essential differences. First, the simulation model is concerned with the choice of both destination and parking lot. The aim of the model is to get insight into the effects of parking measures on both choices. A second difference concerns an explicit consideration of adaptive parking choice behaviour. In contrast to the earlier studies, the reaction of motorists who find a full parking lot is categorized into three different adaptive choices: (i) wait until a parking space becomes available; (ii) go to another parking lot; and (iii) park illegally (van der Waerden et al., 1993). Finally, the simulation is conducted in a GIS environment with GIS databases, analysis and presentation utilities.

The proposed parking simulation model will be a dynamic model in that it should allow the prediction of changes in the parking system over the day. Thus, the first step in the parking simulation is the assessment of the demand for parking space per destination (destination choice) at various periods (time slices) of the day. Each motorist is given a series of characteristics (such as arrival and departure time, and origin zone), the values of which are derived from the relevant empirical distributions. The incoming motorists are assigned to a parking lot by a parking choice model. The demand for parking space for each time period consists of incoming motorists, motorists who have already found a parking space, and motorists who are waiting for a free space.

All or some of the motorists who want to park their car will find a free parking space. Those who cannot find a free space will reveal some kind of adaptive parking choice behaviour as explained above.

REQUIREMENTS FOR PARKING SIMULATION

To conduct a parking simulation as described in the previous section, a variety of data and procedures are required. For all the spatial entities distinguished, data must be available to estimate and evaluate the choice models and to evaluate the parking system. The following spatial entities should be distinguished for the suggested parking simulation:

- The motorists' origin zones
- Destination zones, with the supply for an activity (in the case of shopping: number of shops, price level, branches)
- Parking zones (for example, the number of parking spaces, parking costs)
- The road network (for example, road type, average speed, capacity)

Depending on planning goals and planning measures, different levels of detail can be discerned. In the case of shopping, data on destinations can be stored at three levels: (i) shops, with characteristics such as branch and price level; (ii) shopping centre, with number of shops and number of parking places; and (iii) shopping areas, with number and location of shopping centres. Parking-related data can also be stored at three levels: (i) parking space, with characteristics such as length and width; (ii) parking lot, with number of spaces and parking costs; and (iii) parking area, with number of parking lots and type of users.

Some of the required data is more or less independent of the parking system, such as number of shops in the shopping centres and parking costs on the parking lots. Other data is more system-dependent; the data is extracted from the system itself or from changes in the system. Examples are travel time between origin and destination zones, walking distance between parking lot and the shopping centre, and occupancy rate of parking lots. To get this kind of data, manipulation and analysis procedures are required. The following procedures will provide such data: network analysis routines to estimate travel distances, parking management procedures to calculate occupancy rates, turn-over rates and average parking durations. The simulation requires also possibilities to estimate and evaluate (choice) models, to generate random numbers and to fit distribution functions.

The kind of attribute that must be part of the databases is partly dependent on the specification of the choice models. The following choice models can be part of the simulation:

- *Destination choice model,* for example with the number of shops, the amount of floor space and the travel time by car between home and shopping centre as independent attributes.
- *Parking choice model,* for example with maximum parking duration and walking distance between parking lot and the middle of the centre as independent attributes.
- *Adaptive parking choice model,* for example with number of cars waiting, number of lots visited before and travel time to alternative parking lot.

The most appropriate models to describe choice behaviour are multinomial logit models. In this kind of choice model the probability of choosing an alternative depends on the characteristics of the alternative and of the other alternatives. The multinomial logit (MNL) model may be expressed as follows:

$$p_i = \frac{\exp(V_i)}{\sum \exp(V_{i'})}$$

where P_i is the probability that alternative i will be chosen, and V_i represents the utility associated with alternative i.

Different types of output are required for planning activities: occupancy rates, turn-over rates, average parking duration, average wait time, etc. The output can be presented in two different ways: spatially and non-spatially. Spatial presentation can occur on the level of parking lots or on the level of destinations or origins. In the case of non-spatial presentation, the emphasis shifts to the development over time, e.g. occupancy rate during the day.

A PROGRAM FOR PARKING SIMULATION

The parking simulation program used in this study is written in Fortran and contains input and output links to ASCII files and TransCAD table files. The simulation program consists of three major modules: data input, the simulation model and the output of results (Fig. 18.2).

The first module of the parking simulation program contains input routines for the required data. In this module the characteristics of the destination zones and the parking lots, and the distances between parking lots and destination zones, are collected for the simulation.

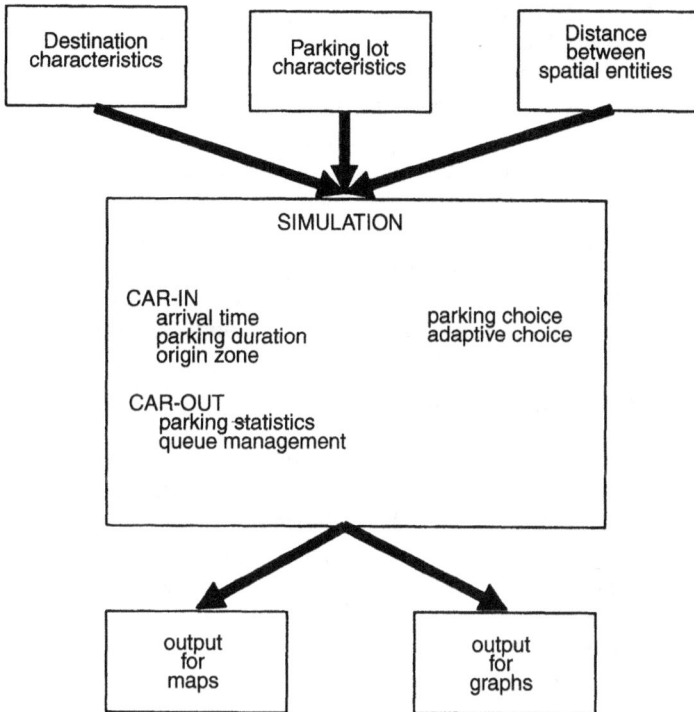

Fig. 18.2 Structure of the parking simulation program.

The simulation module, where all data is used, can be divided into two modules: a module where cars come in to the parking system ('car-in' module) and a module where cars leave the system ('car-out' module).

The *'car-in' module* is the module where, per time slice (1 min), cars enter the parking system with intervals that follow a negative exponential distribution with an average of 0.25 min. This distribution is the most appropriate because the intervals between the arrivals of the motorists are independent of each other. The time intervals are selected randomly from this distribution. As mentioned before, each car that enters the system gets a series of characteristics such as a randomly selected parking duration and an origin zone selected from a destination choice distribution. The parking lot where the motorist parks the car is determined with a parking choice model. Most cars that are coming into the system will find a free space. However, some motorists may be faced with a full parking lot. In this case the motorist has to decide what to do. This behaviour is described by a model of adaptive choice behaviour that was developed at an earlier stage (van der Waerden *et al.*, 1993). Those who are prepared to wait will enter a queue (with a first in–first out mechanism). Those who decide to go to an alternative parking lot will enter the system at a later time slice (travel time to alternative parking lot). In the case of all other decisions (park illegally and go home), the motorist leaves the parking system.

The *'car-out' module* is the module where, after a certain parking duration and sometimes a certain waiting or adaptive time, motorists leave the parking system. In this module the queue is checked for waiters. If there are still waiting motorists in the queue, the open space is occupied by a waiting motorist before the simulation model continues to the next time slice.

The final module of the program contains output routines for the presentation of results of the simulation. Spatial data are directed to the different databases, and non-spatial data are written to ASCII files.

PARKING SIMULATION IN A GIS

The parking simulation model was developed in the GIS environment of TransCAD (Caliper, 1990, 1992). In this section we will illustrate its potential use using hypothetical data and choice models. The illustration concerns a parking simulation in the context of shopping (Fig. 18.3). The hypothetical situation used in the simulation consists of the following entities: one destination zone (in the middle of the map), three parking lots in the surroundings of the destination, and seven origin zones. Most of the required attribute values of the entities can be prepared and stored

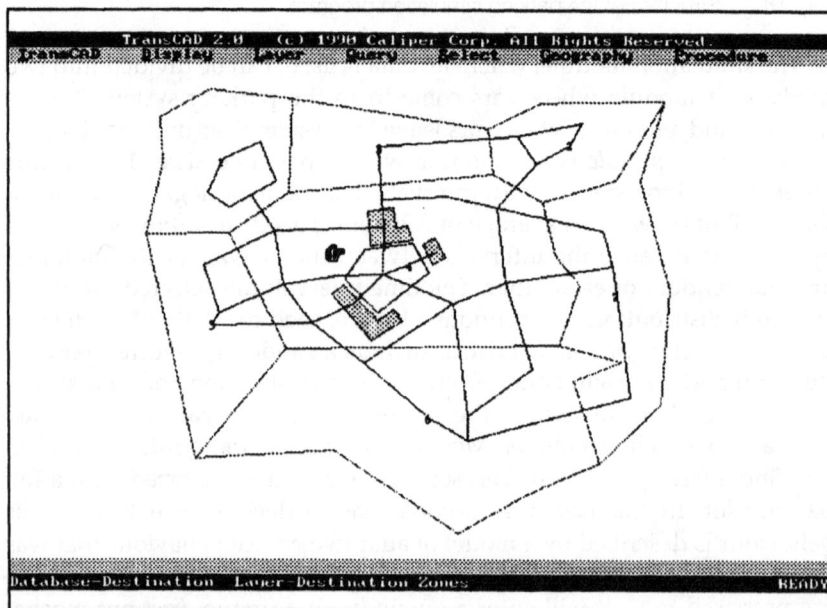

Fig. 18.3   A hypothetical situation for parking simulation.

directly in the database: for example, the amount of floor space and the number of parking lots per destination, and the number of spaces and distance to the shopping area per parking lot. The distance between origin and destination zones can be calculated with a shortest path routine. TransCAD offers possibilities to build a network based on a line database. The network can be built using the length of the network links, or the travel time. Dijkstra's shortest path routine (Dial *et al.*, 1979) can be used to calculate the shortest distances between parking lot and destination.

TransCAD does not yet offer possibilities to estimate and evaluate multinomial logit models which are required to model the different choice processes of the parking simulation model. There are no procedures for updating attribute values, for generating random numbers and for estimating distribution functions. TransCAD does have a toolbox, however, to develop an interface between the package and the external procedures. Hence, we developed these routines ourselves and linked those to TransCAD using the interface.

DATABASES

The following TransCAD databases store the required data. First, three area databases were built: (i) for the origin zones of the motorists (neighbourhoods), (ii) for the destination zones (shopping centres), with information on the supply of shops, and (iii) for the parking situation (parking lots) (Fig. 18.4). Next, a line database was built with the road network on both city level, for distances between origins and destinations, and destination level, for distances within a destination.

TABLE FILES

Distances between origin and destination zones, and between parking lots and shopping areas, can be stored in TransCAD table files. A table file is separated from a TransCAD database and contains one or more individual tables. TransCAD offers three types of table files: a database matrix, a database table and a simple table. A database matrix is a file that has database entities on both row and column dimensions, for example an origin–destination demand matrix with traffic zones on both row and column dimensions. A database table has database entities on the row dimension, but has columns that are not associated with any particular entity, for example a table with traffic production of origin zones for several years. Simple tables contain data that do not correspond to the entities in a database, for example a correlation matrix. All types of table files are binary files, and can be read by external procedures.

TransCAD PROCEDURE TOOLKIT

TransCAD offers a procedure toolkit with tools and utilities to develop and implement stand-alone DOS programs. The toolkit contains a variety

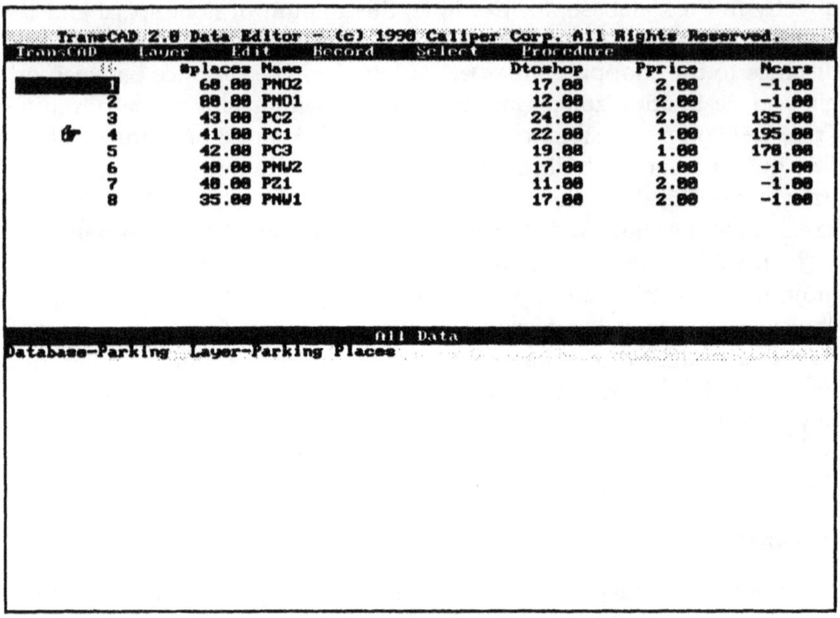

Fig. 18.4   Part of a TransCAD area database for parking lots.

of statements (command directives) that are processed by TransCAD before or after a procedure is executed. Command directives can be used to check the current settings in TransCAD, to pass information or parameters to a procedure, or to control processing of a solution file.

In the current application the following command directives are used. Each command directive is illustrated with a simple example. It should be noted, however, that the toolkit of TransCAD offers many more possibilities that are not described in this chapter. The command directive *Verify* is used to check the type of the current layer (e.g. Verify layer base2 warning 'Layer has to be the Parking Layer'). To identify the different table files that will be used by the simulation, the *Choose* command directive is called (e.g. Choose file table prompt 'Choose Parking Distance table...'). The attribute values of the relevant entities necessary for the evaluation of the choice models and the calculation of some statistics can be exported from the databases to an ASCII file with the command directive *Dump* (e.g. dump selected attributes to parkin.dat 8 'ID' '#places' 'Dtoshop' 'Pprice' 'Ncars' 'Pdur' 'Orate' 'Tover'). The external procedure is started with the command directive *Run* (e.g. run procedure 'psm01\\psim' using psm01\\parksim.bck). After running the simulation, some results are imported from an ASCII file into the databases with the command directive *Import* (e.g. import file parkres.asc).

THE EFFECTS OF PARKING POLICIES

As noted in the introduction to this chapter, the aim of the parking simulation model is to get insight into the effects of parking policies. To illustrate this, a parking policy is introduced for the hypothetical situation. We assume that the policy is to reduce the demand on parking lot 'PC2' by raising the parking costs of 'PC2' from NLG 1.00 to NLG 2.00 per hour. The parking simulation model calculates new parking statistics such as changes in average occupancy rates for the three parking lots (Fig. 18.5). In this hypothetical example, the average occupancy rate of parking lot 'PC2' decreases by 9.50%. The average occupancy rate of parking lot 'PC1' increases most (+ 3.14%). In Fig. 18.6, the occupancy rates during a part of the simulation period are presented for both before and after the increase of the parking costs of parking lot 'PC2'. The curves show that in some time slices the occupancy rate of the 'after' situation is less than the rate of the 'before' situation, and in other time slices it is inverted.

CONCLUSION

In this chapter the principles underlying the construction of a parking simulation model in a GIS are outlined. The chapter consists of two parts: a description of the conceptual framework underlying parking

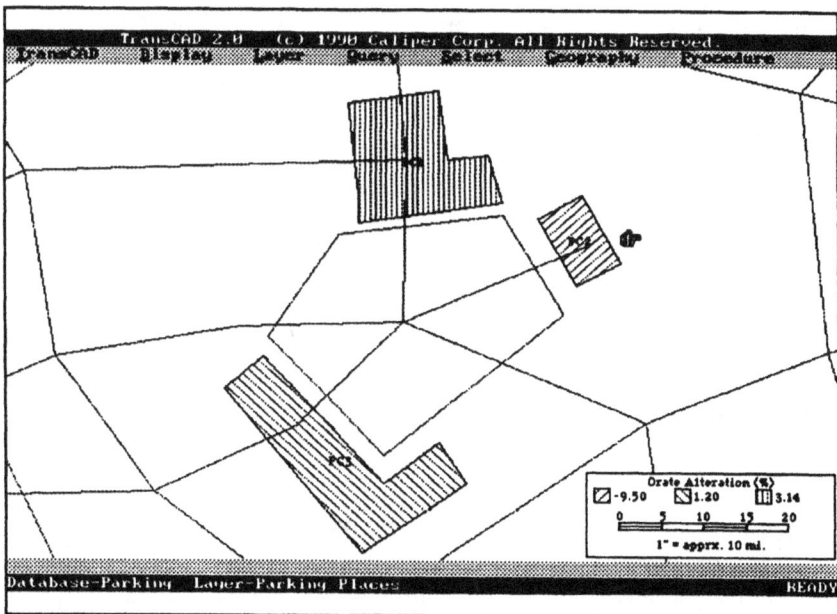

Fig. 18.5 Alteration of average occupancy rates after parking costs measure.

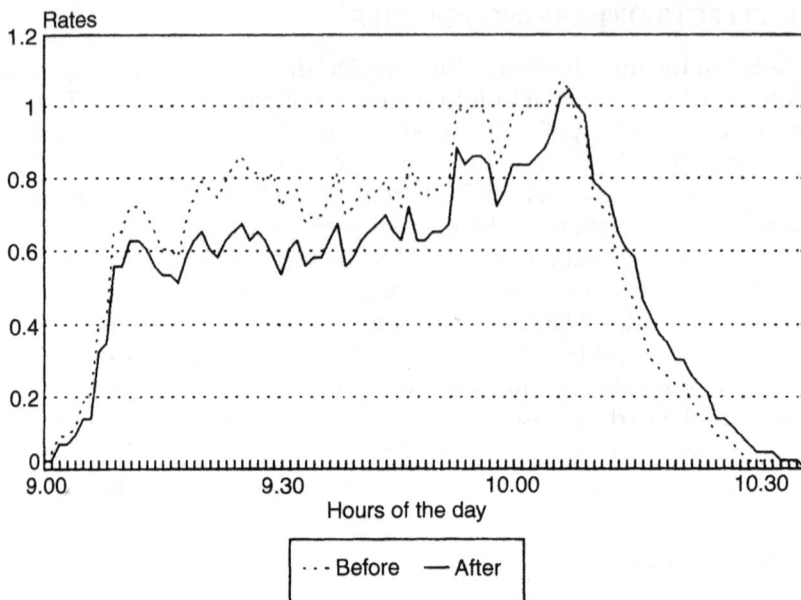

Fig. 18.6   Occupancy rates before and after parking costs measure.

simulation models, and a description of an implementation of the simulation model in the GIS environment of TransCAD. The simulation is
based on hypothetical distributions and choice models, and contains
just a few spatial entities. The results of the simulation consist of average occupancy rates, average parking duration and average turn-over
rates per parking lot.

The study shows that a GIS can offer some basic tools and utilities to
conduct a parking simulation study. Especially, the network routine
'shortest path' and the storage of characteristics of defined entities in several databases can be very useful. Other required procedures, such as
data fitting, random number generation and managing parking lots, are
not provided by TransCAD and hence need to be written separately and
linked to the GIS. Reading from and writing to TransCAD table files can
be done in the external program. Database information only can be read
from or written to an ASCII file, which can automatically be imported
and exported. Hence, this study suggests that a parking simulation
model can be developed within the TransCAD environment as long as
one is willing to write some additional routines.

Future research involves a variety of activities. First, the distributions
and choice models must be estimated using empirical data. To place
parking behaviour in the context of urban planning, the simulation
model has to contain links between the parking simulation model and,

for example, the use of the urban network or the performance of destinations. Also, alternative ways of trip generation can be useful in this respect. For example, trip generation at origin zones offers the possibility to admit mode choice in the simulation. The last phase of the research project contains the user interface, so the user can implement parking measures and study the effects.

REFERENCES

Bonsall, P.W. (1991) The Changing Face of Parking Related Data Collection and Analysis: The Role of New Technologies, *Transportation*, 18, 83–106.

Bradley, M. *et al.* (1986) Simulation Parking Policy with 'CLAMP'. Paper presented at *PTRC Summer Annual Meeting*.

Brohm, K.A. and Reichelman, F. (1984) Parking Simulation Models for the Innercity of Amsterdam (in Dutch). Paper presented at the *Colloquium Vervoersplanologisch Speurwerk*, The Netherlands.

Caliper (1990) *TransCAD Transportation Workstation Software*, Reference Manual 2.0, Caliper Corporation, Newton.

Caliper (1992) *TransCAD Transportation Workstation Software*, Manual Supplement Version 2.1, Caliper Corporation, Newton.

DHV (1978) *System Analysis of Parking* (in Dutch), Working Group Parking.

Dial, R.B. *et al.* (1979) A Computational Analysis of Alternative Algorithms and Techniques for Finding Shortest Path Trees, *Networks*, 9:3, 215–248.

Niemeier, D.A. and Beard, M.K. (1993) GIS and Transport Planning: A Case Study, *Computers Environment and Urban Systems*, 17, 31–43.

Opiela, K.S. (1991) *Implementation of Geographic Information Systems (GIS) in State DOTs*. A Digest (number 180) of the National Research Council of the Transportation Research Board.

Polak, J., Axhausen, K. and Errington, T. (1990) The Application of CLAMP to the Analysis of Parking Policy in Birmingham City Centre. Paper presented at the *PTRC Summer Annual Meeting*, Brighton.

TNO (1979) *A Simulation Model of the Parking System* (in Dutch), Institute IWIS-TNO, The Hague.

van der Waerden, P., Oppewal, H. and Timmermans, H. (1993) Adaptive Choice Behaviour of Motorists in Congested Shopping Centre Parking Lots, *Transportation*, 20, 395–408.

Young, W. and Taylor, M. (1991) A Parking Model Hierarchy, *Transportation*, 18, 37–58.

Index

For Product Safety Concerns and Information please contact our EU
representative GPSR@taylorandfrancis.com
Taylor & Francis Verlag GmbH, Kaufingerstraße 24, 80331 München, Germany

www.ingramcontent.com/pod-product-compliance
Lightning Source LLC
Chambersburg PA
CBHW070901080426
R18103400001B/R181034PG41932CBX00008B/15